D0643129

VINYL
COUNTDOWN

GRAHAM SHARPE

Oldcastle Books

First published in 2019 by Oldcastle Books
Harpenden, Herts, UK
www.oldcastlebooks.co.uk

© Graham Sharpe, 2019

The right of Graham Sharpe to be identified as the author of this work
has been asserted in accordance with the Copyright, Designs and
Patents Act 1988.

All rights reserved. No part of this book may be reproduced, stored in or
introduced into a retrieval system, or transmitted, in any form or by any means
(electronic, mechanical, photocopying, recording or otherwise) without the written
permission of the publishers.

Any person who does any unauthorised act in relation to this publication may be
liable to criminal prosecution and civil claims for damages.

A CIP catalogue record for this book is available from the British Library.

ISBN:
978-0-85730-314-1 (print)
978-0-85730-316-5 (ebook)

4 6 8 10 9 7 5

Typeset in 11.75pt Goudy Old Style
by Avocet Typeset, Bideford, Devon, EX39 2BP
Printed and bound by 4edge Ltd, Hockley, Essex, UK

To Julian & Helen, who run Second Scene and who not only made me welcome, tolerated my presence, answered my questions, and gave me discounts, but were happy not to demand to see in advance what I'd written about them. I thank them and really hope I've done them justice.

Redundancy after almost half a century spent working for the same company prompted Graham Sharpe to turn to his enduring first love to cushion the blow, sparking a unique autobiographical journey through his life via his ever-growing vinyl record collection; in the process forensically examining every aspect of record collecting; and launching him on an immersive, ongoing ambition – to visit every second-hand record shop in the land, perhaps, even, the world...

IN WHICH…

Foreword		11
Introduction		15
1.	I Count My Blessings	17
2.	I Reveal How This Book Was Born	25
3.	Jack White Denied Vinyl Was Dead	29
4.	Vinyl Escapes from the Grave	37
5.	I Fear a Nightmare Dream	41
6.	I'm Shaky All Over	46
7.	I'm a Record Lover	48
8.	I Ask How Much Mint Matters	53
9.	I'm Out of Condition	59
10.	I Tull You About Jethro	63
11.	I'm Stoned	67
12.	I Discover Psychedelia & Acid Rock… Man!	73
13.	I Celebrate My Anniversary Alone	80
14.	I Regret Selling My Vinyl Soul for Filthy Lucre	83
15.	I Feel Sutch Melancholy	89
16.	I Take on a Haunted Look	93
17.	I Express My Disdain for Record Store Day	104
18.	We Go Kiwi	111
19.	Oz Is Wizard	118
20.	I'm Hungary for Vinyl	120
21.	I Recall Concrete Memories of Local Gigs	126
22.	I Act Post Haste	131
23.	I Decide Fairs Are Fair	139
24.	I Punctuate Hendrix with Grammatical Grumbling	144
25.	Addicts, Compulsives and Hoarders Appear	150
26.	Mark My Words, I Consider Pathological Collecting	158
27.	I Try to Come Clean	164
28.	I Sniff Out Julian's Problem	170
29.	I Fail to Score	174

30. I Doubt a Bowie Blotch   181
31. The Show Mustn't Go On   185
32. I Wonder What Comes First – Disc or Gig?   189
33. I Back a Real Winner   192
34. I Bet on My Future Career   196
35. Music Is My First Love   204
36. I Snap – Amen to That!   208
37. I Reveal Vinyl Suicide Techniques   215
38. I Enjoy a Pierless Experience   219
39. I'm Love-Ing It!   222
40. I Stand Julian Up   227
41. I Ask: Could CDs Become the 'New' Vinyl?   234
42. I Pose a Question of Moral Judgement   240
43. I Compliment Compilations   244
44. I Channel the Hunt for Record Shops   249
45. I'm Listing to One Side   259
46. I Wonder How to Make Money by Selling Vinyl   263
47. I Contemplate Devastating Loss   275
48. A Loss Is Dealt With, By George!   280
49. I'm Floating an Idea...   283
50. I Come Across Fake News   287
51. I Get Bladdered   290
52. I'm Beatling Along   297
53. An Anorexic Mannequin Is Proudly Regarded   301
54. I Date Julian   303
55. A Friend's Pleas Don't Please Me   307
56. I Realise – I'm 'Record Guy'   312
57. Vinyl Peeves Appear   315
58. 'Mountain Boy' Is Reborn   318
59. I Remember Bruce Langsman   322
60. There Are Deaths in the Vinyl Family   331
61. I Fear Record Shop Rage   335
62. I Wonder Wat's Going On   340
63. I Sign Off   343
64. ... And Vinyly   347
Epilogue   350
Bibliography   351

FOREWORD

by Danny Kelly (music fan, former editor of
NME and Q, helpless vinyl junkie)

You hold in your hand a miracle. What other word can you use
to describe a book, published two decades into the twenty-first
century, about the myriad delights of vinyl records?

If, just ten years ago, you'd said that vinyl would now even
still exist - never mind be the subject of widespread conversation,
adoration and learned tomes - men armed with tranquiliser darts
would've lurked outside your house, questioning your cognitive
health.

All of which goes to show just what a long, strange trip the
whole world of vinyl has been on.

For four decades, from the invention of the Microgroove some
seventy years ago, to the coming of CDs, the plastic record (LP,
single, album, 45, disc, platter, long player, shellac, EP and 100
other variants) ruled the musical roost. Records sold in uncountable
numbers, became fetish objects; radiograms, stereograms,
Dansettes and stereo systems competed with televisions to be the
centre of household attention. Every home had records and the
means to play them.

Discs became identifiers, cultural name-tags. When I was at
school in the 1970s, the LP you carried under your arm - Deep
Purple, Curtis Mayfield, David Bowie, King Crimson or Nick
Drake - spoke of which tribe you belonged to, and broadcast a
loud message of how exactly you saw your teenage self.

Records were important. Records were loved.

Then, with bewildering suddenness, it seemed over. Compact
discs were the shiny harbingers of a new world of apparently
perfect sound, less cumbersome playback gear and, for those with
lots of music, fewer fears of catastrophic spinal damage.

Vinyl became old hat, a hissy, popping reminder of post-war

austerity, the three-day week and greasy-haired youths in bell-bottoms.

People threw whole collections into skips; charity shops were swamped with Leo Sayer, ELO and Paul Young; people like me who clung on to their precious plastic were mocked in the street by local urchins, dismissed as geeks and freaks. The reign of vinyl ended, consigned to the dustbin of memory and the creaking, dusty shelves of a few diehards.

But somehow – mysteriously, incredibly – it didn't quite die. Though record shops went bust and the gates of pressing plants were padlocked, records refused to completely depart the stage. Hip hop artists, recognising that the imperfect vinyl sound was human and warm, sampled it into their otherwise flawless digital robo-sounds. Advertising agencies used records and record players to convey an authenticity and tactility increasingly lacking from modern i-life. And music folk – fans and artists alike – began to ache for a connection with their beloved sounds that amounted to something more than a faceless file arriving in your download box. A whole technology that had been left behind was suddenly once again front and centre, gloriously ubiquitous, and hilariously hip.

I honestly can't think of a historical precedent.

The enduring, often opaque wonders of records, record labels, record players, record shops, record cases, record shelves and record collecting do need chronicling, explaining, enjoying and celebrating. And who better to do it than a man who certainly never made the schoolboy error of offloading his Tamla Motown A-labels on to the local branch of Oxfam?

I first met Graham Sharpe when he invited me to become a judge on the William Hill Sports Book of the Year, the important literary award he'd developed with his great friend, the late John Gaustad. At first, if I'm honest, I thought he was just a sharp(!)-dressed man who worked for a bookmaker. My illusions were quickly shattered. It turned out that, sure, Graham was a smiling advocate for horse racing and betting, but also harboured ocean-deep passion for football, Luton Town, great writing of every kind and a host of other enthusiasms that most definitely included the universes of records and record collecting.

By the time I discovered that he had bought at auction the leopard-skin-design jacket of the late Screaming Lord Sutch, I knew for certain that this was a man with whom I could do business.

In the intervening quarter of a century, Graham and I have become firm friends. In between a full-time job and a busy career as an author – I talk about writing books, he gets on and does it – he continued, and still does in semi-retirement, to buy, collect, treasure and talk about music on physical, grooved, formats. His understanding of the quirks and foibles of collectors – a mixture of possessiveness, weird gallery curation, completism, lonely late-night filing and hopeless addiction – means that I can talk to him about my own out-of-control hoarding without fear of being embarrassed or judged.

Indeed, when I recently revealed to him that I was wasting my life savings on renovating a vast old rustic cowhouse to shelter my sprawling array of vinyl (sub-categories include Poetry 45s, Unlistenable Modern Classical, and Advertising flexi-discs) he just beamed broadly. 'Can't wait to see it,' he said.

You hold in your hand a miracle. A book about a passion, and the hipsters, oddballs and old heads who share it, written by one of their number, albeit a ludicrously erudite one. I've no doubt that once read, it will take its place on those groaning shelves, proudly sandwiched between the gatefold sleeves, coloured vinyls, lead-heavy box sets and multiple copies of 'Forever Changes'.

It deserves to.

Summer 2019

INTRODUCTION

IN WHICH THE AUTHOR ADMITS TO VINYL ADDICTION AND EXPLAINS HOW IT HAS IMPACTED ON HIS LIFE

'Vinyl's making a comeback, isn't it?'

The man in the record section of the charity shop was making friendly conversation as he spotted me looking through the discs.

I looked up and regarded him, perhaps a little too sternly, before responding, perhaps a little too aggressively:

'It never went away.'

I believe that anyone who owns two or more records is self-evidently a record collector.

Whenever you add another one to however many you already have you are enhancing that collection.

I have thousands of the things, and despite the incomprehension of my Mum who, when asked to make my Christmas present an LP one year, replied, 'Why? You've got records already', I continue to add to the total regularly.

This book deals with every aspect of record collecting I could think of. How it's done, when it's done, where it's done, why it's done, who does it and how one goes about it.

Read this book – with its tales of countless hours spent in 100s of record shops worldwide, at record fairs, car boot sales, online and real-life auctions, romances consummated in vinyl, fruitless searches for elusive records, selling, buying, exchanging, coveting, losing, loving, hoarding, hating, finding, wanting, demanding records – and you may just begin to comprehend the emotions involved in a lifelong vinyl love affair.

If you used to be a collector but believe you aren't one now, think again. Get the record player out of the loft, gently caress the dust off the first disc to come to hand, and give it a spin.

You'll wonder why you ever stopped doing it. If you don't, you've lost forever what would once have been one of your simplest, but greatest, pleasures – playing favourite records.

If you, your grandparents, Mum, Dad, brother, sister, aunty, uncle, friends, or workmates have ever shown an interest in, and/ or collected, records, 33 and 45 rpm circular (usually, not always) vinyl discs, this book – my vinylography, although the publishing poohbahs wouldn't let me call it that! – should prove a real treat for you or them.

Records have a greater capacity than Doctor Who's Tardis for transporting you back in time. Even someone as 'woke' and on trend as the highly influential writer for *The Times* Caitlin Moran acknowledged as much when, in April 2019, she explained how records encapsulate 'everything you were before' and should therefore be revisited and revered, otherwise 'you're selling out the only person who has believed in you... : you.'

This book seeks to reawaken the often dormant desire which first promoted the gathering of records, and to confirm the belief of those who still indulge in it, that they happily belong to, and should celebrate the undervalued, misunderstood, significant group of music-obsessed vinylholics, who always want – need – to buy... just one more record.

IN WHICH... I COUNT MY BLESSINGS

When, aged eleven, I acquired my first single, American string-plucker Duane Eddy's 1962 Top 10 hit, '(Dance With The) Guitar Man', I had no thoughts whatsoever of creating a record collection.

But it wasn't that long before the single – which hangs above my desk even as I type these words – was joined by my first long player. Which, it turns out, despite my belief when I began writing this book, was NOT the Rolling Stones' debut, as I've been telling anyone interested for many years, but The Beatles' *Please, Please Me*.

Odd how time can turn the truth – or the version of it you have adopted – on its head.

I can now be so sure, because I went through all of my Stones and Beatles' LPs, and there on the back cover of my mono copy of 1963's *Please, Please Me* (seemingly a fourth pressing, according to the *Rare Record Price Guide* 2020, and thus worth £150 if only it were remotely close to being in mint condition), written in a combination of black felt tip, blue and red biro are the following markings:

G.S. (1) G Sharpe. 20 Borrowdale Avenue, Wealdstone, Middx. HARrow 0257.

The (1) was clearly superfluous. At this point I owned just this LP.

The Beatles' LP was soon joined by Number (2), the Rolling Stones' eponymous April 1964 debut. Mine is, I believe, the second pressing with the 4.06 minute 'Tell Me' and listing 'I Need You Baby'. (Which gets it a £200 rating, with the same caveat). It, too, boasts my initials – together with red biro 'real writing' signature, address and telephone number.

These two records demonstrate starkly the differences between The Beatles and the Stones in those days, when your street cred could depend on which of the two you were aligned with.

To refresh my memory, I decided to listen to, and look closely at, both albums, one after the other. I wouldn't have done that since 1964.

Please, Please Me was released on 22 March 1963. I'm not sure when I managed to get a copy but it won't have been long after release. I was 12 years old. The Stones' LP, *The Rolling Stones*, was not released until 16 April 1964.

The first obvious difference between the two is that The Beatles' album has its title on the front cover, the Stones' on the back. The Beatles are smiling at their prospective buyers, the Stones gazing stern-faced at their potential audience. The Beatles offered 14 tracks for the money, the Stones a dozen.

I want to mention at this point how vital covers are to LPs. The number of records I've bought on spec, purely as a result of deciding the cover photograph or image suggests the musical content will meet with my approval, is astonishing. Occasionally it can mislead you, although, when it does, it is usually because the record company wanted to 'suggest' that the contents would be something they actually never were.

A poor cover can ruin any chance the record contained within it ever had of reaching its true potential. Check out Harsh Reality's sought-after, £500-valued 1969 schlocky, gory, awash with fake blood *Heaven & Hell* cover. ('Blighted by one of the most inappropriate sleeve designs of its day' wrote John Reed in notes to a 2011 reissue.) It was designed by one Phil Duffy, but would have sold more with a better sleeve which didn't shout 'trying too hard', although (ironically) it would now be worth less.

But a great sleeve design can enhance an average record to the point where its impact exceeds its quality – witness Quintessence's 1970 eponymous £80 album cover's inspired, innovative, eye-catching central door-style opening. To my ears the music came nowhere near matching the cover's impact.

The music on The Beatles and Stones' records highlighted differences between the groups' images. The Beatles were far more approachable, with eight self-penned tracks, all pretty much love-based, very catchy and almost sing-along, definitely ultra-commercial. The other tracks included middle-of-the-road fare by Goffin-King, and Bacharach-David-Williams. 'Twist And Shout' was the grittiest track, which had recently been a hit for the Isley Brothers, while 'Anna (Go To Him)' was by bluesy soul singer Arthur Alexander – from whom the Stones would shortly afterwards borrow and improve 'You Better Move On'.

Paul and John shared lead vocal honours, but The Beatles showed a little group democracy by chucking 'Boys' to Ringo, and letting George lead the way on 'Do You Want to Know a Secret' a question markless song which Billy J Kramer would later take into the Top 10.

There was no question (and never has been) of Mick Jagger letting the rest of his group muscle in on his lead vocals, and he fronted 11 of the 12 tracks on the Stones' album; the other, 'Now I've Got a Witness (Like Uncle Phil and Uncle Gene)' was an instrumental on which Gene Pitney played piano. Uncle Phil was a reference to Phil Spector, who co-wrote 'Little by Little' with the writer(s) of 'Now I've Got a Witness' – Nanker Phelge. 'Nanker Phelge', with occasional minor variations, was a collective pseudonym used in their early years as a catch-all songwriting name for several group compositions.

Explained bass player, Bill Wyman in his 2002 book, *Rolling with the Stones*:

'When the Stones cut "Stoned" – or "Stones", according to early misprinted pressings – as the B-side to their second single, 1963's "I Wanna Be Your Man", Brian (Jones) suggested crediting it to Nanker/Phelge.'

The entire band would share writing royalties. 'Phelge' came from Edith Grove flatmate Jimmy Phelge, while a 'Nanker' was a revolting face that band members, Brian in particular, would pull. The 'sixth Stone', Ian Stewart, who played keyboards on four of the debut album tracks was also included. Only one track was credited to Jagger-Richard – 'Tell Me (You're Coming Back)'. At this stage Keith was still Richard, rather than Richards. None of the Stones' LP tracks was issued as a single.

This is a harder-edged album than *Please, Please Me*. There is far more R'n'B and blues than pop influence on the tracks. Andrew Loog Oldham's sleeve notes justly describe it as 'a raw, exciting basic approach' while, in his *Please, Please Me* sleeve notes, Tony Barrow oddly describes the music as 'wild, pungent, hard-hitting, uninhibited' – a description not entirely justified by the tracks on offer.

Very different albums, very different groups and images – but both appealed to most of the same audience as a whole, as they were both so vibrant, young, and refreshingly different. Most of those listening had never heard such music before. But even at this stage, the 'safer' option to side with was The Beatles. If you wanted 'edge' you lined up behind the Stones. Both groups were pinching styles from older soul and blues artistes, adopting, adapting, sometimes blatantly stealing, yet it was all new to the majority of my baby-boomer teenage generation.

Money was tight for me as a young, still-at-school teenager, whose weekly pocket money was about half a crown. My LP Number (3) was, slightly oddly, *Out Of Our Heads*, from 1965, by the Stones – their third LP – and not, by the look of it, a new copy. I clearly hadn't been able to afford a copy of their second outing; (4) was also second-hand, *Aftermath*, from 1966, the Stones again, while (5) was the 1965 *Hang On Sloopy* LP by US pop group, The McCoys, whose British fan club I would eventually end up co-organising.

Although I was clearly a Stones' man, I had to wait to acquire 1965's *Rolling Stones No 2* – it was my Number 26 LP. Their *Between the Buttons* from 1967 was my Number 7, and the same year's *Their Satanic Majesties Request* Number 9.

My 'new' records were coinciding with birthdays and Christmases, the second-hand ones indicating that I was now seeking out record shops selling such things. It was some while before I began to lose count of how many I had, but during the late 1960s that happened, as I began to store them all over my bedroom, in cupboards, on shelves and under the bed. It would be over 50 years before I could again say with certainty how many LPs were in my collection. I counted them specifically for this chapter.

This wasn't a straightforward undertaking.

In the front room there were two cupboards-worth, plus one bookcase shelf full of LPs, half a dozen shelves containing runs of between 50 and 100. Oh, along with the two sets of Beatles and Stones records standing on the floor. Then I moved into my study area in the hall to count how many albums there were on the middle shelf to the right of my laptop. After they'd been added up, I moved to the wardrobes in the main bedroom, where there are a couple of hundred. Then there is the 'library' room where my horse racing and gambling books live alongside quite a few albums – several hundred here, in fact. Up the steep, alternate step staircase to the top room – which now holds the largest segment of the record collection. These used to live in the room immediately below – number two son's bedroom which was, though, adversely affected when a leak enabled an ingress of water, responsible for the Great Cover Disaster of 2017.

As a result of this I now own more records with water-damaged covers than, frankly, I would have liked. Some of them very collectable items indeed. Amongst them, *Little Free Rock* (£175); Audience's *Friend's Friend* (£100); *May Blitz* (£400); *Quintessence* (£80); Bowie's *Hunky Dory* (£50); and *McDonald and Giles* (£150).

This should make me feel angry and upset every time I see them. But, just as when I look at the sun-damaged, football-wrecked, alcohol-bloated, overwork-battered bodies of my now ageing friends of many years standing, it only makes me fonder of them to think of what we have gone through together, and despite all of this managed somehow to remain standing, albeit unsteadily.

My insurance company did shell out to enable me to replace the damp discs – well, with reissues. They even sent the covers off to a specialist company who endeavoured to bring them back from their watery grave. A valiant, but largely ineffectual, exercise.

Fortunately, water does not have an adverse effect on vinyl, so the only obvious evidence of their ordeal is in the condition of the covers which have concertinaed up, but remain obviously what they are.

I have no desire to chuck them out and bring in equally ancient copies with different marks of longevity about which I know nothing, or to replace them with prettier, younger yet not quite the same 'reissues'. They are now uniquely 'storied' and I very much doubt that I would ever have parted with them anyway. Well, maybe Quintessence.

After five days of counting – a very frustrating undertaking as slippery plastic covers make it too easy to count three as two or vice versa – which wears down the will to live, and inflicts numerous small, but painful plastic- or paper-cuts, I completed the task.

I can tell you that as of 10.43am on Tuesday 27 June 2018, having earlier reached the 3000 mark by counting the Robert Cray Band's *Too Many Cooks*, I was the proud(ish) owner of 3239 LPs – give or take a few. The last one counted was The Herd's *Paradise Lost* (£70 if in good nick, which this one definitely isn't). Technically this belongs to my wife, but on the basis of what's mine is hers and what's hers is hers, I'm including it. That's probably 10 per cent more than I'd reckoned on, and a little down from the peak amount, given that I had recently been selling a few off, albeit also gathering more in, but please don't tell Sheila that...

Really, who NEEDS over 3200 LPs? No one, if I'm honest.

Probably closer to 3500 by the time you read this. After all, I brought back two dozen from my last trip to the Antipodes in 2019 alone. Then there was the June 2019 San Francisco haul... I can thoroughly recommend Haight Ashbury's Amoeba Records for its selection, its prices – and its bulldog clip system of enabling you to leave your bags at the counter.

It also contained many examples of my own vinyl catnip which explains why I persist in buying and listening to music from my formative years: records made in the late 1960s/early 1970s, by groups of similar age and thoughts to me, but which made no impact, weren't played, publicised and popularised at the time, but were written for people like me and sound as fresh and exciting as the day they were recorded. Rediscovered and reissued by specialist labels, they are what I seek out.

I could spend five hours daily playing a completely different set of nine LPs for an entire year. And at the end of that year I'd still have played every record I own just once.

Do I collect to impress people by telling them how many records I own? That is quite possible, but if so, it doesn't work. A look of uncomprehending pity is the default reaction should I admit this shaming statistic to someone. The next reaction, one word: 'Why?'

I do it largely to impress myself, for sure, but that's pretty pointless, isn't it? Am I going to tell myself I'm NOT impressed?

I do it because I want to do it.

I do it because I CAN do it and because when I first started wanting to accumulate records I couldn't really afford to do it without sacrificing some other, more essential purpose to which the money could be put.

I was thoughtful enough on my own and, soon, my wife's account, when I was contemplating buying a dozen LPs at the Sellanby second-hand shop during the 1970s and 1980s, always to choose the cheapest version they had available – that was my idea of compromising and saving money, thus allowing us to pay the mortgage. Which does at least indicate that I wasn't over-concerned with sell-on values.

I do believe collectors are divided into those who long for pristine, blemish-free, silent-background record reproduction and those who, like me, enjoy (indeed, possibly prefer) hearing the accumulated scratches earned during the long, active life of a second-hand disc bought frugally.

Having totted up the LPs, I was now wondering how many CDs I owned, so started to count them as well. I took a breather on reaching 1000. I counted double albums as one in the vinyl tot-up, likewise with the CDs. Box(ed)-sets I'll call just one.

The CD count did not take as long as the vinyl, mainly because I wasn't going to let it, so I may have slightly rushed. I'm confident the final total was, er, getting on for 2500. Ish. Thus, as well as playing nine different LPs every day for a year I could also play six different CDs without, etc...

I've also just realised that I left the 60-plus CDs by Free, Paul Rodgers, (Small) Faces, Bad Company, Bon Jovi, AC/DC, Humble

Pie, The Killers, etc designated as Sheila's, but which I bought for her, off the list. Because they're stashed on a shelf in the kitchen – not my territory.

Are these excessive quantities?

A Facebook post from collector, Mark Turner, asked members of the vinyl group to which we belong:

'How many records are enough?'

Before trying to answer this question, perhaps we should consider Rutherford Chang. The last time I checked, Rutherford Chang owned 2435 numbered copies of ONE RECORD alone – The Beatles' *White Album*. Not content with that, he is constantly seeking more. His collection has been displayed at KMAC Museum, Louisville, Kentucky. 'Each individual album is posted @webuywhitealbums. If you have a copy in any condition please let me know: rutherfordchang@gmail.com' he pleads.

Mark Turner's 'How many?' query prompted a deluge of responses, including mine: 'To many of us there is no such number.'

By and large responders agreed:

'When your wife/husband says "anymore and you sleep in the garden".'

'Just one more...'

'The Limit does not exist.'

'11,672.'

'One more than I already have.'

'The one you buy tomorrow will be enough.'

'When you can't remember how many you already have.'

'I'll let you know when I get there – 12,000 and counting.' (Designer Wayne Hemingway MBE recently boasted: 'I have more than 13,000 vinyl records.')

I empathise with all of these sentiments, but let me now tell you how and why I came up with the idea for this book...

IN WHICH... I REVEAL HOW THIS BOOK WAS BORN

Because I was born in 1950, and am therefore of a certain vintage, collecting music by downloading or streaming just does not appeal to me. I want something to own, to hold, to look at – even better, something to read – while I'm listening, to give me a certain connection with the artist(e)s who originally created it. I'm happy to pay to do so. To tread this path, I can either choose to hunt for records online, or visit the constantly fluctuating number of shops selling only second-hand music.

There are also increasing numbers of shops which stock only new vinyl, albeit often containing reissues of previously issued music, or vintage sounds not deemed worthy of issue at the time.

New shops are appearing regularly, many of them combining food and drink facilities with records for sale. Some established shops are closing, for various reasons, perhaps because the owner has not taken notice of the old but established adage, 'give them what they want and they will come', or because (s)he has chosen the wrong location.

After I was made redundant, I realised I needed something to occupy my time. The idea of managing to take a look at the many record shops I was aware of, but had never yet visited, due to time constraints, loomed large.

I pitched a feature idea to one of the magazines to which I have subscribed for years: *Record Collector*, launched in 1979, and now the UK's longest-running music magazine. I hoped they might not be able to resist a story about someone setting out to visit every one of the 90+ record shops in England selling second-hand vinyl which currently advertise in their mag. The article was duly commissioned and printed across two pages in October 2017.

I was pretty sure that it would immediately produce a barrage of complaints from readers that they had already visited all the shops and that my 'mad quest' as Ian McCann, then RC Editor had dubbed it, had been done before. It didn't. It appeared that, if I could indeed create and complete this journey of, sorry, discovery, I might even have a valid claim for an entry in the Guinness Book of World Records.

The feature was illustrated by a photograph of me standing outside Second Scene, my local record shop in Bushey, near Watford, run by Julian and Helen Smith, who have become friends over the past few years, and from whom you will be hearing in this book on a number of occasions.

There it was in print. I'd pledged to visit almost 100 record shops. That meant I would now actually have to set about doing it. Fortunately, I hadn't been rash enough to set a time-limit and had realised, too, that on its own, such an idea wouldn't sustain a full book, involving too many, too similar chapters. Instead, the idea was growing of combining multiple record shop stories with stories about every other aspect of record collecting.

I started to travel around the country – the world – somewhat randomly, ticking off shops as I went. I began to enjoy the experience of visiting new places, taking in the local record shops of Australia's Blue Mountains, Salisbury, Liverpool and Stockton on Tees; San Francisco, Oxford and Cambridge; Harrow and Hereford; Oslo, Guernsey and Jersey; New Zealand, Norf and Sarf London. Always returning to Second Scene to report on my progress.

I decided that, unless a conversation began naturally between us, I would not go out of my way to instigate verbal contact with record shop staff, other than Julian, as I wouldn't want them to clam up if I mentioned I was writing a book, or begin bigging themselves and/or their shops up to me.

It is amazing what you might hear if you just listen. Vinyl Revelations is located at 59 Cheapside, Luton, along with the message: 'We do not have a letterbox so please do not use this address for postal correspondence!'.

The almost inevitable middle-aged proprietor is telling a customer, 'I've been in the record business for twenty-four years. I've seen the ups and downs.'

The customer wanted to sell him two records: 'I'd like a tenner for each.'

'But I already have copies of both that I'm selling for four quid a throw.'

'Well, how about a tenner for the two?'

Fortunately, it didn't take long to find a publisher as keen on the book idea as I was, and as I travelled around, talking to knowledgeable, obsessive record collectors, phlegmatic record dealers, depressed record shop owners, optimistic online vinyl traders, I soon appreciated just how deeply ingrained the love of, and for, records and record shops has become over the years.

Virtually everyone to whom I mentioned the book idea was able to recite with very little prompting the names of the first record they had bought and the shop they had bought it from. Even though they may not have played or bought vinyl for many years they smiled at the memory of first hearing those amazing, new sounds on tinny, usually tiny, transistor radios. And at the way in which they then felt compelled to dash out to buy their own copies, enjoying the follow-up chat at school or work they created.

Reminded about that experience, most of them then said they still had that and many other discs stashed upstairs in the loft. They kept meaning to get them down to listen to them again on the vintage record player that was stored there as well. This had allowed them to stack up half a dozen singles which would, one by one, plop down satisfyingly on to the one which had just been played – albeit by that action they were leaving scratches and other marks which inevitably affected their sell-on value adversely.

But who then suspected there might ever be such a bonus for the far-seeing collector?

Back then, everyone owned, or had access to, a record player. Even the greatest sportsman to tread this planet – Muhammad Ali.

I met Ali's biographer, Jonathan Eig, when he came to London, having been shortlisted for the prestigious William Hill Sports Book of the Year award in 2017. He told me that he owns Ali's record player:

'I found a listing for Muhammad Ali's record player. The seller claimed to be the son of one of Ali's early lawyers. The opening bid was $250. No one had bid. Figured it wasn't really Ali's record player. I bid anyway. I was ready to send the money, but the seller emailed me and said he was bringing it to Chicago. Definitely has to be a scam, right? Figured I'll never get the record player. Then I got a call. He was in Chicago, and wanted to meet. He pulled up in a huge van. He was a big guy – 6′5″, 280lbs. He opened the trunk and showed me the record player. His name was Frank Sadlo. Frank knew Ali for years. He helped clean out the house after Ali's mother died. That's how he got the record player. Frank's dad was a white lawyer working in the poor black neighborhoods of Louisville in the 1940s and 1950s. He represented Cassius Clay, Sr. and wrote the first professional contract for Muhammad Ali.'

How cool is that, owning Ali's record player!? I do, at least, own a copy of his 1963 LP, *I Am the Greatest*.

The mechanics by which 1960s record players allowed discs to drop one by one could be altered to play the same record over and over, particularly when it was relevant to a recently terminated teenage love affair.

I recall listening to the Kinks' 'Tired of Waiting for You' sixteen times in succession, in frustration that my then girlfriend, Pauline, from a few doors down the road, appeared to be far more interested in taking the bus to Heathrow Airport in the hope of seeing the Walker Brothers fly in or out than in walking up the road to see me.

The Kinks had already become important to me. The life-changing, instant impact of hearing the opening bars of 'You Really Got Me' absolutely charging out of the one tinny speaker of our black and white telly in the summer of 1964! I can't remember whether the record was being played on *Juke Box Jury*, or the group was featured on *Ready, Steady, Go*, but I was left virtually paralysed as the record roared out – and into my heart forever. WHAT a sound. WHAT a riff. Whoever played it. I was thirteen and a half. Of course, I had to have that record, and rushed out to buy it at the first opportunity.

So influential to me were the Kinks that I would have laughed at the very idea of any group ever pretending to be them, and actually becoming successful by charging people to watch them not quite be the Kinks. But this phenomenon would emerge. I put it down to baby-boomers wanting to recapture their halcyon days...

IN WHICH... JACK WHITE DENIED VINYL WAS DEAD

Kevin Godley, of prolific vinyl hit-makers, 10cc, told *Mojo* magazine in January 2018, 'I have a soft spot for vinyl. It reminds me of when music was rare, significant and a work of art...'

He was born in 1945, five years before me, and like most of my contemporaries, grew up with records and music always close at hand and ear. This attitude towards records was the prevailing one for many years – Jack White of The White Stripes, born almost exactly 30 years after Godley, inherited it and defends it to this day, recalling how:

'I remember in 1999, and 2000, The White Stripes asking television hosts if they could hold up the vinyl record instead of the CD. And at that time they were like, "Why would we do that?" That's how dead vinyl was.'

Unlike today, of course, there were relatively few competing personal entertainment options in earlier days, and hit records would sell hundreds of thousands, or even millions, of copies. Most of those who bought, or were given these records were, as I was, entirely devoid of any musical talent whatever. I may have had a toot on a recorder as a kid but displayed zero ability and have genuinely never even strummed an electric guitar to this day, other than in an air-guitar way. Yet music has dominated much of my life. But then there are people obsessed by football, golf or horse racing who can't kick a ball straight or hole a putt from six inches and have never sat on a horse.

Initially, popular, or 'pop' records released in the late 1950s and early 1960s were likely to have been heard by eager, young, potential consumers on non-BBC, usually foreign, radio stations like Radio Luxembourg and American Forces Network.

Rock 'n' roll music was leading the way then. Guided by usually financially motivated managers and agents (okay, some things never change), Elvis Presley, Chuck Berry, Fats Domino, the Everly Brothers and many others first embraced, then pop-ified rock 'n' roll's harsher elements, which emanated from the States, with their roots in the blues.

Their influence quickly spread across the water, but was then somewhat emasculated in Britain when Cliff Richard, Marty Wilde, Billy Fury, Adam Faith, Tommy Steele et al began to move from their imitative, wannabe Yank teen-idol phases, towards a more middle-of-the-road, commercially attractive, yet blander, sound.

Then, though, The Beatles arrived to stop in their tracks the careers of those who had thought they had the mainstream music scene sewn up, and to spark the whole 1960s explosion of pop, psychedelia, rock music and so much more, leading on to prog(ressive) rock, punk, heavy metal and many other hybrid styles of music.

Soul and ska music also became important, particularly to those youngsters who loved to dance. Stax, Tamla Motown and Trojan became go-to labels for those attending and DJ-ing at discos.

In 1964, the massively influential commercial 'pirate' radio stations arrived – amongst them Radios Caroline, London, and Sutch. Music was avidly consumed by those of a certain age – mine – almost by osmosis, and a huge proportion of those so affected wanted to own that music for themselves, so that they could play it whenever they wanted, rather than having to wait for it to be played on the radio.

BBC Radio continued broadcasting what was described as 'light' music to an indifferent British audience, until 1967 when, under pressure from the 'pirates', it launched Radio One, but, as the name suggested, it was largely inoffensive, repetitive, chart-based bland fare, unlikely to appeal to the more musically adventurous.

Nearly everyone of my acquaintance in the mid-1960s soon owned, or had access to, a portable or transistor radio, a record player (often a 'radiogram') and/or a portable cassette recorder/ player.

Discs, as the presenters invariably called them, spun on the programmes hosted by popular disc jockeys, would enter the collective consciousness by being bought or recorded, then played almost continuously. Some programmes, usually going out late in the day or overnight, became a cult listen for those seeking to dig deeper into the sounds available. Leading the way in this respect was John Peel.

Ageing baby-boomers may today struggle to recall their own names as advancing years take their toll, but will almost invariably still be able to remember the first record bought for, or by, them. It would usually be a 45 rpm single. 'The 7″ single, as an entity is an absolutely powerful, possibly other-worldly object', guitarist Johnny Marr would perceptively observe.

Singles were really, more accurately, doubles, containing at least two songs – or tracks – one on either side. Although to my schoolfriend, John Maule, they really *were* singles. Every time he bought one from our local record shop, Carnes in Wealdstone, and brought it home, he'd take it out of its sleeve, play it, then throw it across the room to join the growing pile on the other side. Why? Because, as he told me at the time, 'There's never anything any good on the B-side.'

How wrong I felt he was – then, and particularly now – both in his dismissal of the 'other' side, and in his cavalier treatment of his vulnerable vinyl. I'm certainly not alone in believing that. In his introduction to his biography, *Bowie*, Paul Morley writes of how the first singles he bought were 'carefully chosen and cared for like nothing else in my life'.

My fellow baby-boomers also retain fond memories of the (often small, usually local and frequently independent) shops where they lost their vinyl virginity. Yes, there were places like Woolworths and Boots, as well as department stores, that sold them, but it was much more interesting to build a relationship with the local independent outlet and the person there who would generally be knowledgeable about forthcoming releases and records similar to the one(s) you were about to buy, but which you may never have heard of. They'd tell you what new discs would be appearing shortly and, if there was likely to be high demand, reserve you a copy.

Another of my friends and contemporaries, Martin Wilson, also challenged John's B-side disdain, when he told me: 'I invariably played the B-side first – I already knew what the A-side sounded like, but who knew what treasure might be lurking underneath when you flipped it over?'

John, later a '£10 Pom', and I met up for a reunion in New Zealand in 2018. I'd brought with me a late Christmas present for him, which he hastily unwrapped – duly discovering that I was returning to him several of the singles he'd given to me when he fled the country half a century earlier.

Those from better-off families or with well-paying Saturday jobs (something else which my generation experienced almost universally, but which now appears to be heading towards obsolescence) may have bought, or been given LPs. Even John Maule didn't hurl these pricey behemoths across the room. But he did manage to scratch them, if not in the way that club DJs later started to do, either. So, by the time he moved to the other side of the world allowing me to inherit most of his badly wounded records, few of them remained playable.

One of them that did, was the Small Faces' LP, *Ogdens' Nut Gone Flake*, the ground-breaking psychedelic record Steve Marriott, Ronnie Lane and company created with the help of the gloriously word-mangling comedian, Stanley Unwin. The latter's crazily hilarious interventions between tracks helped it become one of the iconic records of the period, thus ensuring that the value of a copy in decent condition soared consistently over the years. It also boasted a unique-at-the-time round cover.

For reasons best known to himself – surely he didn't fancy her?

– John had handed his little-played copy of this LP to my sister, Lesley, who resisted every attempt I made, once I learned that she had it, to acquire it from her. Eventually, and only as recently as 2017, I had to shell out a substantial, three-figure sum to do so. Sisterly love, huh...

This raises a question. When did records, initially regarded as disposable items with little intrinsic value, begin to acquire a serious financial worth, which would appreciate with time?

Once records became established as a teenage essential of the 1960s and 1970s, shrewd entrepreneurs spotted a gap in the market. They began to offer the opportunity for those with too many records, or ones which they had grown bored with, to part with them for a modest fee. Whereupon the profit-savvy purchaser could sell them on, a little more expensively, to buyers who did not already have, and wanted to acquire them, but without having to pay the full cost of a brand spanking new version. Thus did the second-hand record market first appear, and rapidly grow, helping committed but impecunious vinyl addicts remain active.

In the States, a gentleman called Jerry Osborne began producing guides to the values of popular records from 1976 onwards. A Facebook acquaintance told me that 'in 1978 I purchased a book titled *The Record Collector's Guide* by O'Sullivan & Woodside.' A year later, *Record Collector* magazine appeared.

Suddenly records had a calculable worth. This wasn't, though, why I was already collecting. I just loved LPs and singles, and the life-enhancing qualities of recorded music, and wanted as many of them as my meagre disposable income would permit.

Today, the collecting world is divided into those who collect for the love of music, and those who collect to profit from collecting, the latter group described by *Record Collector* editor, Paul Lester as 'Machiavellian high-end dealers for whom vinyl is a semi-abstract commodity much like stocks and shares.'

Most people's vinyl love affairs dwindled as real-life responsibilities took over from their party-central teenage years. I was amongst a select few, like-minded, stubborn vinylholics, who continued to acquire, purchase, cadge, borrow, review, and occasionally sell records, for nearly 60 years after Duane Eddy first came to my attention, persisting long after the novelty had worn off amongst most of my friends, most of whom stopped buying records completely once they embarked on permanent relationships.

Music dropped off their radar, probably until their children had grown up, at which point they slowly began to realise that some of the groups whose records they had liked and bought all those years ago were still around and touring. Perhaps they were coming to a local theatre, albeit with some new, some deceased and increasingly few original members – like the 'Herman's Hermits' I saw once, with no Herman (aka Peter Noone), and then again, even later, when only the original drummer remained, who still had the cheek to claim all the credit for the '30 million records we've sold'.

But as other groups packed it in, fell out with each other, retired and died off they created a gap in the market – soon filled by bands such as the Small Fakers, who replicate the original performances of Steve Marriott, Ronnie Lane, Kenney Jones and Ian McLagan; the Bootleg Beatles and Rollin' Stoned, who do likewise, resuscitating a heavenly John Lennon, George Harrison and Brian Jones along the way. Obviously, even though these guys quite probably play the original songs more enthusiastically than the ageing 'real thing' could do today, they make no claims to being anything other than a pastiche of the band itself.

What does that make a group like the Kast Off Kinks? They play all of the Kinks' great hits, and initially included two long-serving members of the band in their number, drummer Mick Avory and bassist John Dalton, while another former 'proper' Kink, the late Pete Quaife, used to turn up for occasional shows. But they had no one called Davies in the line-up. All the great songs were written by Ray Davies, and brother Dave contributed the slashing guitar riffs to those songs. The KOK clearly had almost no genuine claim to be the original 'group'.

The current Dr Feelgood, who legally own that name, and who all joined the band as it progressed, while the originals dropped out, or died, contain no original members whatsoever. (In passing, my sister recently told me she had bought tickets to see Dr Feelgood. I told her I was surprised as she was not a 'rock chick'. 'No,' she said. 'To be truthful, I thought I was booking for Dr Hook!') So are Dr F the real thing or imposters? Legally the former; morally, perhaps, the latter.

The Drifters, formed in 1953, and a wonderful original band, perhaps set the trend for groups to change over time, effectively becoming brands, with the music taking priority over the individuals in the group. The latest list of one-time members of the group shows 65 different names – including one familiar to baby-boomers – the late Doc Green!

If you delve far enough back into the 1960s there was a phase when anyone attending a gig by, for example, Fleetwood Mac, Moby Grape, The Zombies, might wonder why the band members did not look familiar. It was because rogue promoters were duping concert-goers by deliberately sending out ersatz, fake groups which, unlike today's tribute acts, were actually pretending to be the real thing.

A conscientious tribute band will have worked very hard to ensure that their sound is almost a precise match, note by note for the original version to which they are paying tribute. When *Sunday Express* editor, Martin Townsend went to see the Small Fakers in autumn 2017, he was so impressed that he declared their versions of the hits 'so good they made the hairs on the back of my neck stand up.' I've seen the Small Fakers several times and also rate them highly.

But in 2018 the Fakers marked the 50th anniversary of the band they celebrate, by playing their psychedelic masterpiece, *Ogdens' Nut Gone Flake*. My local venue, 'Tropic' in Ruislip, was packed, so much so that it was difficult to find somewhere to sit. The band announced that *Ogdens'* would take up the first section of their performance, and that they would then take a break, returning with a 'greatest hits' set. I was particularly looking forward to *Ogdens'*, and the audience pressed forward eagerly. Gradually, though, the crowd eased as people nipped to the bar, to the toilets, for a fag, realising they didn't recognise much of this material. As the group moved on to the LP's surreal second half, interspersed with (to me!) hilarious vocal interventions as contributed by the late, great

Stanley Unwin to the fore, the crowd thinned even more - many sat down to chat with friends. But when the hits began the crowd thickened, surged forward and danced with delight. I went home.

The truth is that people who support tribute bands tend to be those who might have bought the original band's Top 10 singles and 'greatest hits' records, but who rarely, if ever, delved into the material they produced outside of these iconic songs. Nothing wrong with that, of course, but probably depressing for the originals, let alone the tributes, when they feel the need to stretch out a little from their tried, trusted and adored golden oldies only to be firmly steered back to familiar, safe territory by the lack of audience appreciation.

To give additional support to the originators of great music worth paying tribute to, I must add that, much though I have enjoyed watching The Counterfeit Stones, Rollin' Stoned, The Bootleg Beatles, Like The Beatles, Small Fakers, AC/DC UK, Counterfeit Quo, Kast Off Kinks, Absolute Bowie, Roxy Magic, Fleetwood Bac, and the brilliantly named Creedence Clearwater Revival Revival, I have *never* bought a record by any of these acts.

Many of my contemporaries are astonished that anyone should have retained a love of the original music of their youth into their dotage. They are happy to recall and relive it on occasional nights out, but seem neither to notice nor care that it isn't as it was, because to them that's all it ever was - background sound accompaniment to their way of life at the time. But there are still surprisingly many early enthusiasts who have stayed the course and are proudly flying the vinyl banner. Facebook group, Vinyl Hoarders United boasted 24,865 members when I last checked. The site offers the 'opportunity to share pictures and information of your vinyl collections, ones you want to hunt down, or any interesting vinyl you think the rest of the members should know about.' Vinyl Records Forever, had attracted 13,449 members, Vinyl Records For Sale & Wanted had another 8,500. These are far from the only ones...

As for that Kevin Godley quote from the beginning of this chapter, it continued: '... though I no longer have a record deck.' D'oh!

IN WHICH... VINYL ESCAPES FROM THE GRAVE

Like some kind of vinyl vampire, the long player refused to die, no matter how many times popular opinion wrote it off and consigned it to the dustbin of history. Slowly but surely it clawed its way out of the graveyards created for it when firstly CDs, then downloads and streaming looked to have all but buried it under a torrent of seemingly fatal disdain and abuse.

Vinyl was uncool, unloved, unmourned. Yet, though backing away to the musical margins, vinyl's valiant rear-guard action not only halted its retreat, but fought off those who would condemn it to the past, and began to attract the attentions of contrarians, opinion-formers and hipsters cool enough to recognise its unique qualities and realise it still had much to offer.

Slowly, but inevitably, even big business began to notice the reactivation of the vinyl market. It must have done, surely, as while I was eating my breakfast recently, I looked at the box from which my wife was spooning her 'Dorset Cereals', made of trendy 'nutty granola'. There on the back was the legend: 'Life's not a dress rehearsal... So, go on, join a choir, make a bark rubbing... go record shopping.'

The Times' colour supplement magazine of 18 November 2017 featured in its 'Shop! 150 Christmas Gift Ideas' display, a full-page photograph of a Santa-and-his-sleigh toy figure and other items, all scattered on a turntable playing a 45 rpm single. Marks & Spencer featured the image of a vinyl record playing on a turntable as an important element of their Christmas 2018 TV advert. Not only that, McDonalds launched a 2019 TV advertising campaign promoting the addition of bacon to their Big Mac, with one of the scenes set in a busy second-hand record shop specialising in jazz. In May 2019 TV ads for a new Seat car featured what was clearly a second-hand record shop.

These and similar adverts and features are aimed not at me and my already hooked vinyl contemporaries, but at what they, and I, believe will become the new generation of vinyl fans, ensuring that records remain desirable objects for many years to come. Even we hardest of the hard proponents of second-hand vinyl will accept that there is a place not only for newly released reissues, but also for freshly released original records.

The only problem I can see with millennials embracing vinyl is its sheer cost. I have a very few newer acts in LP form - but I baulk at paying 20 plus quid for them - and I definitely won't pay that for new editions of old records, the costs of making which were covered many years back. Don't under-estimate the danger of greed once again putting vinyl's future at risk.

That said, some of the new vinyl covers are extraordinarily attractive objects, and really can outshine even pristine old albums - but don't have the built-in memories and effortless elegance of what we more mature types will always regard as the real deal.

Some vinyl has become so desirable and valuable over the past half a century that certain records must eventually become genuine antiques. Not, though, the LP featuring one of his own tracks that 'Little' Jimmy Osmond bought when appearing on TV's *Celebrity Antiques Road Trip*, selling on for a tiny profit.

I am fortunate to own a good few records, originally sent to me to review when I was a local newspaper hack, and which I liked enough to keep, but which sold in such tiny numbers that they have acquired considerable rarity value. Largely ignored then, almost no one got to hear how good they were, even in the heyday of pirate radio stations. I had convinced myself on occasion over the years that I should cash in on the current value of these records as, surely, it must be set to plummet as vinyl 'freaks' begin to age and ultimately disappear. So, I took the plunge and offered some for sale. I sold a much sought-after album by a totally obscure band for a little under £400. It would have cost under three quid to buy it on its original release date. I let several others go for significant sums, but soon began to regret this aberration.

Not because the sales cost me potential profit - they didn't really, because antiques, and record sell-on values are like shares – you can never really know for sure where the bottom or top range of their value is. Some long-standing valuable vinyls are, though, now beginning to shed, or not enhance, some of their financial potential as their current/prospective owners/purchasers die off.

My plan now is to hold on to most of my 1960s and early 1970s record rarities, so that I can not only enjoy the bragging rights of owning them, but also the memories they retain for me, regardless of value. It's different, of course, even for confirmed collectors if someone offers you serious money for a record you don't like. But then, why would most people have that record in the first place? The ones I didn't like when I was reviewing were the ones which ended up in one or other of my local second-hand dealers' shops.

My collecting of vinyl was definitely boosted by a man who inspired and promoted so many of the artists I grew to admire – John Peel. An article in the *Radio Times* many years ago was illustrated by a photograph of him in a room entirely surrounded by floor to ceiling shelves – all bulgingly full of LPs. I gazed at it, entranced, for some minutes, marvelling at what it would be like to own such a cornucopia of treasures and to be able to reach into it and discover at will something you'd be guaranteed to enjoy. From that moment, I set about emulating JP, albeit, inevitably, on a slightly lesser scale.

These days, of course, I no longer buy records I don't already know and like – at least, not without listening to at least some part of them first. Really? Who am I kidding? I do, as you will no doubt have already assumed, frequently buy records just on the basis of looking at the cover, reading the sleeve notes, or second-guessing what the tracks will sound like, based on their titles and writers, the label the record is on, the year it was made and maybe the name of a session musician or two that I recognise. So I certainly do buy records blind or, at least, deaf...

I could check them out on YouTube first to hear whether I will like them – but the reproduction on my laptop is tinny, and really that also takes away much of the anticipation of owning a record I didn't even know existed just a few minutes ago. Better to wait until you can play and hear it for the first time on your own. That way, no one else will get to hear should you have misjudged, and it actually sounds like a gang of squalling cats retreating from a bunch of barking dogs.

There is also the risk that if you ask to listen to the record in the shop where you've found it, the dealer will hear it and think, 'Hm. That sounds better than I remember, I think I'll keep it for myself.' That's genuinely happened to me before now. Either that, or someone else in the shop might offer more for it than you...

I have become acquainted with record shops of virtually every description – tiny, huge, filthy, spotless, floating, spooky, invisible, friendly, neutral, unwelcoming, expensive, reasonably priced, cheap, accessible, hidden away. One with a water well in it; one with water all around it. Others that also deal in fireplaces, boxing memorabilia, jewellery, menswear or offer wine-quaffing alongside the discs.

I have discovered many characters, most quite happy, proud even, to describe themselves as vinyl addicts, whose obsessions and compulsions can be compared with those hooked on the more usual drink, drugs, gambling and tobacco. Most of them are male, but there are a significant and, I suspect, growing number of female sufferers. These are the people for whom there is always another record that they absolutely need to own – to be able to take it from a shelf, hold it, look at it, listen to it, discuss it, love it.

I'd always believed my own vinyl compulsion began in late 1962, but when my mother died in 2017, my siblings gave me the task of going through her own record collection – a grand description of what was basically scores of badly looked-after Frank Sinatra, Johnny Mathis and Nat King Cole albums and singles, most of which we had bought her over the years as presents. As I did so I also came across several kids' records – 'Sparky's Magic Piano', 'Rumpelstiltskin', 'Three Little Pigs' and others – which had all formed part of the soundtrack to my infant years. I'm not even sure they were made of vinyl – it may have been shellac or some other substance – but they were recognisably records. And they were mine. So, I'd been groomed even earlier than I had always assumed – particularly as I would later buy almost equivalent records by Sparks, obscure 1960s rock band Rumpelstiltskin, and, er, 'Piggies' by The Beatles. Spooky, eh? Spooky Tooth, at least.

Today, now I am coming towards the end of my seventh decade, the addiction shows little sign of being cured, or even curbed. Not that I have ever tried to do either. Watching Mackenzie Crook's brilliant BBC2 show, *The Detectorists*, I realised I was watching people living in a parallel universe to the one we record collectors inhabit – people prepared to go out at all times of day and night, ignoring scepticism and downright abuse from friends, families and passers-by who 'don't get it' and trawl through difficult terrain and unpleasant conditions, hoping to discover buried treasure.

So, what will happen to my own buried treasure when I finally go? My wife, Sheila, who undoubtedly will outlast me, has the telephone number of Second Scene's Julian Smith, younger by some years than me, and she is under instructions to call him and let him come round and buy my collection, lock, stock and Blossom Toes (two albums worth at the moment around £800 each) barrel.

Allow me to introduce you to the couple who were, in my eyes, living the vinyl dream...

IN WHICH... I FEAR A NIGHTMARE DREAM

Confirmed compulsive collectors may imagine that running a second-hand record shop would be some kind of dream existence. Those actually doing it might disagree. When I visited Julian and Helen Smith at Second Scene in Bushey, near Watford, on Friday 29 September 2017, their body language and exhausted demeanour were suggesting they were seriously considering whether, after six years running the shop, they should close it and just trade records online. The business was going well financially, but appeared to be taking an unexpected toll on their personal well-being.

Julian, also a musician who plays drums with cult outfit Cranium Pie (and their associated Baking Research Station), changed direction from selling fireplaces to selling records, albeit from the same premises, which led to a few comical misunderstandings in the early days of the new business. But now his initial enthusiasm and enjoyment were being chipped away - mainly because of certain customers.

'My ideal customer would be a Russian who came in with loads of money just wanting to pay good prices to take records back to Russia to sell there. But many of the customers I get would despise someone like that. They consider themselves to be the true elite of record buyers - but they can come in, spend hours talking to - or more often at - me, and then walk out, having got in the way, caused more work for me by moving stuff around, listened to records they had no intention of buying and then cleared off, having spent nothing.'

Did he mean customers like me, I began wondering, a little anxiously?

His wife, Helen, was even more damning of some of their clients: 'I started off quite liking records but now I've grown to hate them, they're just square packages with discs in. Sometimes customers make me feel like just shutting the doors, locking them up and walking away.'

Perhaps it was just an iffy day. After all, when a lady came in, asking for a couple of singles with which to decorate the cake she was making, Helen handed her half a dozen and charged her nothing at all, after she explained the cake was being made in memory of someone who had recently died, aged just 45: 'It's very sad, really - his brother asked me if I'd do it.'

I suggested to the couple that maybe their problem was that they didn't take enough time off, away from their admittedly rather small shop in which claustrophobia might occasionally overwhelm them. Couldn't they make a little more time for themselves, instead of opening five days out of seven as they currently did? They would go on to implement that suggestion, closing Sunday, Monday and Thursday.

Or how about putting someone else in charge when they fancied taking time off?

'We did try that, and had a lovely girl looking after things, but one day I was out and a guy came in wanting to move a huge collection of records which he'd been asked to clear on behalf of a former DJ - literally thousands of singles, which he wasn't even looking to get money for. She took the ones he'd brought in, but didn't ask for any contact details. I reckon he may have had thousands more. OK, everyone makes mistakes and we all have to learn the hard way, but that probably cost me a fortune - I still have nightmares about it,' said the obviously still frustrated Julian.

I had an almost opposite experience once. I was taking the dreaded walk to a dental appointment, hoping against hope he would have been taken ill and the appointment would have to be postponed, when I noticed a container sitting on a wall I was about to pass. As I glanced down, I saw that it seemed to be full of LPs. Closer inspection showed that indeed it was. And there were two more, equally well endowed with vinyl. What were they doing there? Was someone moving house? Had they been left there for a purpose? There was no sign of anyone in the garden behind the wall on which the records were perched, and no removals van parked anywhere nearby. I looked around wondering whether there were hidden cameras anywhere, whether this was some kind of sting or set-up. Couldn't see anything.

Hm. I could hardly pick up an armload and lug them all the way to the surgery, really, and if I picked some up and took them back to my car, I'd be late for the appointment which, although fearing, I really needed. Common sense won out and off I went to see the gnasher mechanic. Returning about 40 minutes later, the records, like most of my teeth, were still in situ. There was still no one around. This time I did scoop up as many as I could hold - noticing from the covers that they were predominantly heavy- and death-metal style albums, most of whose band names I didn't recognise.

I put about 30 or 40 in my car and went home, telling my disbelieving wife where they came from. As she was accusing me of having bought them and not wanting her to know how much I'd spent, I offered to show her where they'd actually come from, and drove her back to Spencer Road. There were scores of records still sitting there. 'Now will you believe me?' I asked her.

Of course, I felt obliged to rescue the remaining records from this state of unappreciation and imminent decay once the rain started. I went back again the next day and got some more. To this day I have no idea what was going on there. But I managed to flog off many of the albums for a decent profit!

Back in Bushey, Julian was even beginning to rail against some of his regular customers, quickly adding, 'Not you. I like you, but there are plenty who come in here probably because they have nowhere better to go and spend an hour and a half in here without buying anything.'

A surreptitious glance at my phone revealed that I hadn't yet been in the shop for much longer than an hour, watching Julian run a stream of singles through his cleaning apparatus before putting them out for sale. But, no, I hadn't bought anything, even though I was casting covetous glances at the £50 Audience album, displayed beguilingly on the wall. I own a copy, but its cover was damaged in my personal 'Watergate' disaster. But, if I just purchased the cover of another copy and inserted my original copy into it, would I really then have a flawless copy? I didn't buy it. Now he'll definitely hate me too, I thought.

There are other reasons Julian and Helen may take against their customers. Some of them whiff a bit, some haggle too much over price, others don't like to haggle at all, but he wishes they would! And he certainly doesn't enjoy it when customers try to find out whether he has better records than they do and then complain about him when he almost invariably does.

I concluded that it was a bad day at the office and that the two had been imposing too much pressure on themselves and not paying enough attention to their own health.

They are a genuine, generous, friendly couple who created a thriving business from a standing start but who, like so many small-business operators in all kinds of different fields, may occasionally feel overworked and under-appreciated.

I wouldn't fancy doing it myself. I know that, because I could easily have sought to get involved when I heard that the Sounds Retro shop in Watford would soon be closing, and that the business was buyable for the right price. The idea of checking it out and considering a purchase did enter my head for a few fleeting moments. It didn't remain there for long. Poachers really shouldn't turn gamekeepers. Plus, Julian had told me that when *Record Collector* had run the story about my intention to visit all of the record shops, illustrating it with a photograph of me standing outside his shop, this had apparently enraged Sounds Retro-man for some odd reason, given that we did not know each other. I doubted he'd want to sell to me.

A couple of weeks later, a friend wanted to film a short interview with me about my experiences during a working life in the bookmaking game. It would become part of a series Simon Nott was creating to go on to the website of his employer, Star Sports Bookmakers. I'd be in good company, as amongst the most recent subjects were Mick Channon, international class footballer turned international class racehorse trainer; and successful jump horse trainer, David Pipe, son of a record-breaking father in the same line, Martin.

I was naturally flattered to be asked to join such illustrious company, and when he asked for an appropriate if quirky location, I suggested Julian's shop, hoping that Simon, who has a serious record collecting background to go with his bookmaking expertise, might be able to include Julian in the interview at some point and thus give him a little positive PR.

Julian was happy to let me use the shop on the day but told me that he was now 'on tablets' and had been advised that he might be better off not spending as much time there, as he currently did. He wasn't, though, quite sure how he could manage to do that and still run the business efficiently. He really was having doubts about the long-term viability of the shop. He talked again about the rigours of having to be pleasant to some customers who he felt were time-wasters.

I would soon hear very similar views from another record shop owner with whom I'd become quite pally. He was frustrated by the uneven spread of business he was experiencing since he'd started a couple of years earlier. He, like Julian, was dealing only with second-hand vinyl, no new stuff, no CDs: 'I think I may have to get a steady, reliable job. This is an unpredictable business. One week I can take almost nothing financially, the next someone can come in with a large collection and I can have a really good week. But with a young child to worry about bringing up we really need a reliable income.'

I knew running a record shop was unlikely to lead to instant riches, but had always believed job satisfaction would compensate. Now my clearly rose-coloured impression was being shown up as unrealistic and simplistic. I began to worry about the well-being of these good people and the viability of the businesses they were running, which had to support their families and lifestyles. It was time to change the subject...

IN WHICH... I'M SHAKY ALL OVER

I mentioned to Julian that I had just sold, on eBay, Shakin' Stevens' first single, 'Spirit of Woodstock', for £74. I'd been delighted to do so, even though I knew that some copies had gone for three figures. I'd initially been unaware that I even had the record, or that it had any serious value, so I'd marked it down as charity shop fodder until I started checking out my singles to help with my fledgling project to downsize my collection. It was an EMI promo copy which I'd been sent back in 1970 for review. It was produced by Dave Edmunds, who co-wrote the B-side, so there was an indication there that it might hold an interest for collectors.

But, as I then rhetorically demanded of Julian, why had I kept hold of this record for well over 40 years without ever having played it after the initial review spin? Given that I did not dislike Shaky, but had never been any kind of real fan? I would not turn his songs off if they came on the radio but would never go out of my way to seek out his music. It made me think of the popular TV shows which reveal the inside of hoarders' houses, piled high with all manner of rubbish and dirt. The show producers invariably send in professional cleaners to help the hoarders throw out as much as possible of the rubbish – but the hoarders are generally reluctant to part with as much as a used bus ticket. Was there a lesson here for me about my ever-increasing record collection?

The morning after this conversation I was reading *On Form* a book by former England cricket skipper, Mike Brearley. On page 332, I came across this paragraph:

'Inability to choose may also result from our refusal to give up a desired course of action. We can't let things go and then face the fact that we are likely to miss them and have to mourn them.'

This struck a chord with me immediately. It seemed to explain much of the reason that I have ended up with a collection of thousands of records, many of which I will never play again (indeed, some I have never played), yet every time I try to let some of them go, something persuades me that I may well 'need' them in the near future, even though deep down I know I will not. In some cases I seem to be able to overcome the objection to parting with them if there is sufficient financial reward as an incentive. Sometimes not even that motivates me to do so.

Take the example of a Rose Royce album, featuring a couple of their better-known tracks, and several more cuts, of which I couldn't even sing you the opening bar. But there it sat in the collection, since its 1977 release when I received it for review. I still remember how 'Wishing on A Star' goes and find it an enjoyable listen. But 'Ooh Boy'? 'Funk Factory'? 'You're My World Girl'? Nope. You could offer me fortunes and I couldn't recall a thing about any of them.

So how and why did I still own the record in 2019? Yes, it boasts a gatefold cover, and the great Norman Whitfield had a hand in writing six of the eight tracks. He has a wonderful Motown pedigree, having written and produced many terrific hits for various label artists, amongst them '(I Know) I'm Losing You', 'I Heard It Through the Grapevine', 'Cloud Nine', 'Ball of Confusion', and 'Just My Imagination'.

But did I have the Rose Royce hits on any other records or CDs. Yes. Check. Okay, any friends who might like to have the record? No. Check. Saleable on eBay or Amazon? Tried it a couple of times at very low price. No bites. So no real justification for keeping it on the premises. At last, into the 'Charity Shop Bag' it went.

Multiply this process by a few hundred and you'll see how difficult it has proved to make significant inroads into reducing my quantity of vinyl – and don't forget I am also still bringing in new examples. Recently I adopted a new scheme and created a bank account expressly to contain the money I received when selling records, so that at least I know how much I have made. What I haven't always done, though, is taken an equivalent amount of money *out* of that account every time I buy another record to bring *in* to the building.

Now I'll tell you how records were a vital part of my limited teenage romantic armoury...

IN WHICH... I'M A RECORD LOVER

1960s and 1970s singles are circular time capsules. Just placing them on to a turntable and swinging the stylus across and down transports me back to my formative years. While writing these words I heard the Beach Boys' single, 'Do It Again' being played on BBC Radio 4, selected by *Desert Island Discs* guest of the week, Tim Martin, chairman of the Wetherspoons' pub chain. Immediately I visualised myself on holiday at Butlins, Clacton in August 1968. It wasn't that hard. A photograph of that very scene sits on my desk, reminding me just how badly dressed I was back then, in the summer of the record's release. With my longish hair and scruffy sartorial style, I'd found myself something of a stylistic misfit. Not a mod, not a rocker albeit, even in those days, I was something of a mocker. Perhaps too often for my own good.

My short-haired, wannabe skin 'ed friend Paul, aka Chuff, and I had become friendly because of our shared love of football. We found ourselves teamed up with a rather intimidating bunch of genuine skinheads who, for some reason, had decided to befriend us. Possibly because we had somehow become pally with a pair of shatteringly attractive sisters. (Timid as ever, I'd ended up dating the younger one, Maureen, rather than the far more interesting, but louder, older one, Liz.)

I survived the week, but was never again able to hear The Nice's rousing version of 'America' without immediately thinking of bacon and eggs, as it was invariably being played at ear-shredding volume in the cavernous restaurant-cum-canteen each morning when we arrived there. The camp disco – no pun intended – favoured reggae music.

My fledgling romance soon faded. Not, though, before I had tracked down a copy of Paul Revere & The Raiders' difficult-to-find single, released in June 1968, 'Mo'reen' with its opening line, 'Oh, Mo'reen, girl you look so clean...' Which may have been not quite what I was hoping...

However, the romance was doomed, largely due to the distance we lived apart and my lack of a vehicle. I was firmly in North West London, where I've been ever since, and she was in Burton Latimer where they may still, as they did then, create Shredded Wheat and/or Weetabix. Not that it held her back for long, as she ended up a Page 3 model who at one time was shacked up with the maverick QPR footballer, Stan Bowles.

By this point I'd clearly decided to adopt the tactic of using vinyl records as emotional props and/or seduction methods. I recently found a cache of letters from 50 plus years ago, amongst which was one from Maureen:

'I'm listening to Pick of the Pops on the radio and every time a good record like "Hold Me Tight" or "On the Road Again" comes on I get up and dance (that would explain the uneven handwriting, then!). It's a shame "Rough Rider" isn't in the charts, but I'm going to try to buy it from somewhere.'

'Rough Rider' by The Four Gees was a terrific reggae single on the President label. Eddy Grant wrote this track, along with other members of The Equals, with whom the then blonde Eddy would ultimately hit the big time. (He was also deeply involved with the Pyramids, whose 'Train Tour to Rainbow City' was almost as popular with my crowd at this time.) It would later be covered by reggae great, Prince Buster, who tried to claim it as his own work.

Obviously, I couldn't have Maureen being unable to hear 'our song', so I dispatched a copy up to her. A postcard soon arrived:

'Dear Graham. This is just to say thanks very much for the record. It came Monday morning before I went school. I even had time to play it 5 times before I went.'

Maureen and Liz went home while we remained at Butlins for another week, during which I met Lynda from Harlow. She later wrote to me:

'I can't get that record anywhere, but I'll keep on trying as it reminds me of you.'

I promptly sent her a copy of 'Rough Rider' too. Not my fault it never made the charts, Eddy – I think I bought at least half a dozen copies. I must have come into some money around this time, as I was recently reminded by a female friend from those days that:

'You bought me a Jimi Hendricks (sic) LP... sorry, don't have it anymore.' Well, that last little dig backfired as I was able to point out to her that whichever of his early albums it was is now a three-figure record and she's managed to lose or give it away!

My relationship with Maureen continued until distance took its toll, but not before I'd written a short ghost story entitled 'A Rough Ride', immortalising that whole holiday, 'dedicated to, and inspired by Maureen'. I'll spare you the whole seven pages, but it does also namecheck 'Ride Your Donkey' by The Tennors; 'Lickin' Stick' by George Torrence; 'Beggin' by Timebox; and 'The Horse' by Cliff Nobles. Singles which I frequently dust off and leap around the room to, like the 17-year-old I was then. The story didn't have a happy ending.

I still own 100s of singles, a good proportion either now approaching or just having passed their half century, but still usually in better nick than their owner. Even those which I misguidedly took along in my luggage the first time I ever ventured to the Spanish Costas, when I traded up from Butlins.

Another friend, Brian Walker had become the proud owner of a briefcase record player, an ingenious piece of kit for the time, the design of which permitted a turntable and two removable speakers to be packed into a cunningly designed plastic briefcase. He didn't seem to have many discs, other than a few very listenable Tamla Motown singles, whereas I had plenty, but nothing to play them on whilst seated on a hot Spanish beach in Salou. So we'd agreed that he'd bring the equipment and I'd supply additional music.

The combination of sand, sun, sangria and soppy sods like us resulted in several subsequently very valuable records being melted, warped, sand-blasted and sicked-on for a fortnight, with unfortunate consequences, particularly for a now much sought-after early release called 'New Day' by a then obscure band with a girlie name – Thin Lizzy. That record is now rated at £300 by the *Rare Record Price Guide*. Mine is probably worth under 300 pence, if that, as whatever I use in an effort to clean it, it still sticks and jumps all over the place.

It was one of those then still usable discs we were playing (as loudly as it would let us) on Brian's machine when we held an impromptu party in our hotel room. I suspect we were playing one of our favourite reggae singles – 'Ride Your Pony', perhaps, or maybe 'Train Tour to Rainbow City' or even 'Phoenix City' by Roland Alphonso. This latter 1966 dance floor filler, with its irresistible rhythm, appeared on the Doctor Bird label, misspelled as 'Pheonix City' and was credited to Roland Al and the Soul Brothers. Or, and I still really like this one as well, it could have been 'Al Capone' by Prince Buster with its 'Don't call me Scarface' refrain. This used to embarrass me because the girl I'd fallen for at the time, who lived four doors down the road, Walker Brothers-mad Pauline, did actually sport a facial scar, above her lip, which

I thought just made her all the more sexy, but which, inevitably, allowed my mates to dub her (reggae 'joke'!) 'Scarface'.

Whatever we were playing, the racket had not gone down that well with those trying to relax in neighbouring hotel rooms. They complained to the manager who came up to find out what was happening. When he and a sidekick hammered on the door (I did later wonder why he hadn't brought a key), we did the obvious stupid thing and endeavoured quickly to 'hide' ourselves on the narrow balcony. We didn't take much finding, but the manager's face was still a picture when he threw open the sliding doors to be confronted by sixteen teenagers apparently chatting quietly and sipping, er, lemonade. Even if some of them were doing so whilst standing on tables and chairs. From such incidents would the TV series *Benidorm* and *The Inbetweeners* eventually be created...

Back home, by now, in September 1971, and having recently lost my teenager status, I received a letter from 'Bromborough, Wirral' where Janet, who I'd met in Salou, lived. We were just good friends - the letter ended 'Good night, God bless' - and there were no kisses - but she told me:

'I must say I like your choice of records. Brona and I are going to see Gene Pitney on Sunday. I think he is a first class artised (sic)'

You might wonder why I have even kept this, and the other, similar letters from half a century ago. But they, like the records, have a wonderful, powerful ability to time-travel me back to those influential, innocent days.

As writer Caroline Atkins put it in her marvellous recent book, *What a Hazard a Letter Is*:

'Read one sent to you 20 years ago, and it takes you straight back to a specific moment in your life. Read one that you wrote 20 years ago, and it's like a shortcut to your former self.'

I'm not sure anyone will ever regard emails and text messages, etc as being endowed with similar powers.

Records possess the amazing property of being able to hibernate for longer than a hedgehog, but still sound just as good, if not even better, than when you last played them when they reappear. The ones I took to Salou are the exceptions which prove that rule.

Sadly, none of them could now be described as being in mint condition...

IN WHICH... I ASK HOW MUCH MINT MATTERS

By now, you'll have realised I am deep in the grip of an addiction. You might even have the propensity to join me in it. You might already be deeply mired in it. But how are you supposed to know? A true record collector stumbles into collecting. It happens almost subliminally over a period of time.

You may set off initially to purchase a particular record you've remembered, heard on the radio, online or on TV, or which you've read about, been told about, or has been recommended to you. You visit a shop you think may have the record for sale. But while you're there purchasing what you came for, you look around to see what else they have in stock. You see a record you *think* you might like, but you are not convinced you should buy it. But you put it to one side, just in case. Then you come across one you *know* you'd like, so you put that to one side as well. What's this? Another record that you don't *know* you'd like, but you have already decided, perhaps because of the cover, maybe because of the name, or a member of the group, that you *want*. So you add that to the growing pile you are beginning to create. Then, the clincher – you see another record you don't only think you'd like, but know you would, and already want it so much that you actually *need* to own it just so that when and if you next decide you have to hear it, it is going to be there for you even if that day may not be coming for weeks, months, years, even decades down the line.

Now you're hooked. Now you're a record collector, and now I'd like to discuss a question/conundrum which seems to divide opinion amongst us vinylatelists. There is a great deal of pride and exhibitionism connected with the second-hand record industry. There are whole websites devoted to people boasting about the valuable records they have. I did manage to retain some of the more desirable items which came my way as a record reviewer, and which are now so valuable that I barely dare to play them for fear of affecting their value. Not that I am ever going to sell them.

I will admit to buying CD versions of some records so that I can keep the equivalent LPs in decent nick, but I must admit that I don't really 'get' what seems to be one of the key features of record collecting for some today. Who buys 'mint' vintage records and why? And how or why have those albums stayed mint for all these years?

The matter came to a head for me when I visited a London shop selling second-hand records alongside film and literary memorabilia, and the proprietor proudly showed me a 'mint' copy of an album by a very obscure group called The Paisleys. So obscure that their one album was only ever issued in tiny quantities. I collect 'psychedelia' for want of a better catch-all term for what I like, but although the cover looked to be sending out all the psychedelic signals I could pick up, I had never heard of The Paisleys. He told me that it was from a small, privately released limited edition, and was for sale for £650. I was intrigued. I wasn't going to buy it at that price, despite him telling me how good the record was, but I wondered why it should be so expensive. After giving a couple of unconvincing reasons why, he told me that really, he reckoned it was because the record had changed hands regularly between dealers, all enjoying the kudos of owning something almost no one else has.

Thus, over each successive transaction, which each purchaser had almost certainly made with an eye on future profit rather than enjoying the sounds contained in the grooves, the value grew substantially every time it changed hands, to its present, ludicrous level. I am convinced he won't be able to sell it at that price. But that, if he does, it will soon reappear on the market at about 800 quid.

I went away and listened to some of the record on YouTube. Yes, it was my type of thing, albeit not the best I'd ever heard, but pretty good of its kind, with plenty of Beatles-influenced material. I sent off for a CD copy at just under a tenner. I played it when it arrived and maybe a total of five or six times since, which would mean it would have cost me some £80+ a listen had I bought the mint vinyl - which I'd probably be unwilling to play lest I should inadvertently damage or scratch it.

There was another option. I eventually found at a record fair, and bought for a mere tenner, a brand-new copy of the 2015 Sundazed reissue of the LP at a time when I could find just one original copy offered for sale on Discogs, in 'Very Good+' condition from a seller from the 'Russian Federation', at £436.78. I was passing the shop in question again, some six months after my previous visit, and The Paisleys were still there on a top shelf, accompanied by equally overpriced copies of Art's *Supernatural Fairy Tales*, a Downliners Sect LP and some Chocolate Watchband and 13th Floor Elevators for company. All of which I recognised from my previous trip.

I have never collected as an investment. I've collected in an effort to own as much of the kind of music I have always liked - particularly the stuff which was obviously being made alongside the successful artistes of the mid to late 1960s and early 1970s, but which, like The Paisleys, achieved very little exposure at that time.

Seal is without doubt a fine singer. 'Kiss from a Rose' is a remarkable track, and I own a couple of examples of his work. So, Seal records are not a problem for me, but 'sealed' is definitely a problematic area of record collecting.

An online message from Giorgio Guffanti, a member of a Facebook group of very keen and knowledgeable collectors to which I belong, sparked some serious thinking about sealed records:

'Open in this moment for a spin for the first time in almost 50 years. Did I (make) a wrong choice?'

Giorgio - whose first language, as you may notice, is Italian not English - was posting that he had just taken a previously sealed disc from the cover in which it had been concealed and therefore unseen for half a century or more, and was now about to remove its virginity by playing it.

The record, an LP by The Tea Company entitled *Come and Have Some Tea with the Tea Company*, was released in 1968. I was not instantly familiar with the title but, according to a website I consulted, this was a psychedelic band and album.

Almost immediately someone else in the group observed of the sealing breach:

'Some dumb collectors get furious, haha.' Then added, 'Let it live!'

Giorgio appeared to agree – and to be unrepentant:

'As you know I'm not a dealer. Just a music lover. If I don't have it, a sealed copy (the only one I have) is a bad choice. Listening in this moment for the first time in my life 😂. For some records I want to let the surprise side intact.'

Bravo for him, I thought. As did Arv:

'Records are meant to be played. I got a sealed Moving Sidewalks. I opened and played it. I don't regret it for one moment.'

Giorgio pointed out, though:

'But (sealed) is always a good investment.'

Another member of the group, Stephen B M Braitman offered an alternative take:

'I'm against older sealed albums because one can never predict the actual condition of the disc inside.'

I did then ask Giorgio whether he himself had owned the album for 50 years and was only now playing it, or whether he had just acquired it. He said he'd bought it in the previous week at a Milan record fair, and added in his charming broken English:

'I was attempted to left it sealed. But I never heard this record in my life in any format. So left it sealed sounds like a stupid choice ☻. Don't care about loss of collectable value.'

Watching and contributing to this debate I found myself automatically on the side of those wishing to play rather than preserve the record. But I felt something of a fraud when I began to check what sealed records of my own I might have lying around. I have castigated 'mintys' for as long as I can remember but, once I began looking through my collection with a view to trimming at the edges, I began to discover that I too had mint copies, and needed to find out why. Why had I never played albums by, for starters, Chaka Khan, Cheap Trick, Deep Purple, Dion, Jay Ferguson, P J Proby, Eddie Rabbitt, Rough Diamond, Joe Tex, Wishbone Ash – and a double psych collection, *Insane Times*? Nor even the reissued new copy of The Paisleys' LP.

These were all *sealed* records and therefore one assumes them to be mint – not necessarily the case, of course, as they could have been resealed after use. But even if that were the case I wouldn't know – as I have never unsealed them myself.

The price tag of 50p probably explains how I came to own a record with one of the longest titles I've ever come across – *Deep Purple and the Royal Philharmonic Orchestra, conducted by Malcolm Arnold, in live concert at the Royal Albert Hall: Concerto for Group and Orchestra, composed by Jon Lord.*

Crikey, apart from the odd single or two I have never been a Purple aficionado, (remind me to tell you about the time I falsified a Top Ten chart in the *Weekly Post* in order to convince a fellow hack that the bet we'd struck about Purple's 'Strange Kind of Woman' hitting Number one had been won by me) and as for Lord, God rest his soul, I'd rank him alongside Keith Emerson in the pantheon of show-offy keyboard tinklers, whose ability to swoosh and thump the keys for hours without a break is a skill in which I have zilch interest...

So, even if the price did induce me to purchase, it can only have been in the expectation of being able to shift the record on for a profit or in hope/expectation of my tastes changing gradually as I grew older, more mature, and more sensible – none of which happened, as you may already have deduced.

It came out in 1970 and I still have it. A quick perusal of a website which calculates today's values compared with earlier years, suggests that today a 1970 £1 would be worth £15.67, which would mean that, in order even to claim a 'profit' from the Purple record, I'd have to sell it for more than £7.83. I've tried. Quite hard. No one wants it on Amazon, eBay, or amongst my circle of friends. Not for today's £7.83, or even a 1970 50 pence piece. So, should I rip the sealing off and have a listen? What if I *really* like it? I'll get more than £7.83's worth of self-punishment over how much pleasure I have foregone for nearly 50 years by depriving myself of hearing it. How would I live with myself after that humiliation?

There is, bizarrely and a little troublingly, something about a sealed record which deters me from actually opening it up and deflowering it. Whether this is a telling psychological flaw of mine, I'm not sure. Why buy the thing in the first place if I had no intention of listening to it? If I'm now never going to listen to it, why not just flog it off for whatever pittance it might command? Somehow, I can do neither, and there it remains... a permanent accusation that I just cannot make up my mind.

I can try to justify it any way I want, but how can I explain why I splashed out a three-figure sum to buy the Pretty Things' box set, *Bouquets From A Cloudy Sky*, when it was released in 2015? This despite the fact that I already owned most of the contents of the box, and had bought many of the component parts over the years. Today, the box set is long sold out of its limited edition, but there are still copies up for sale, albeit starting at about twice what it cost originally. I spotted one this morning offered for £1030.32 which, I strongly suspect, will not sell.

Yet I am neither tempted to try to sell my copy, nor can I bring myself to open it up. Not even to remove the cellophane wrapping. Not even when I know that each copy contains an artwork by lead singer Phil May – and one of them the original of that artwork. As far as I know I could have that original. I have not seen any reports of who does. But even if I knew it hadn't been won and that there were only a few unopened copies out there, I'm pretty sure I *still* wouldn't open mine to find out. Why is that? You tell me. To quote Badfinger, 'Maybe tomorrow', I'll be able to explain why.

But first...

IN WHICH... I'M OUT OF CONDITION

I joined a Facebook group which invites people to post pictures of records they own or have recently acquired and to ask others in the group whether what they have is really a first edition, or just (for example) a Bulgarian bootleg rip-off version. I have never posted any photographs of my own records there – I suspect a lot of those displayed are there just to enable the owner to show off a little – but I have occasionally raised the odd point here or there. It is called Show Me Your Record Label... Is it the first issue? and, astoundingly, it has over 3200 members. That's only a few dozen short of the number of LPs I own.

I have admitted to buying CD versions of some of my treasures so that I can keep the LPs in decent nick... but this gets to the heart of another of the key questions about 'mint' records. Who, back in the 1960s, bought a copy of every Beatles and Stones record which came out, to play and listen to – and then bought another one just to look at? And why would they do such a thing? Who suspected back then that records would ever have any value beyond what they had just cost you in the record shop?

I get that some people worked in the record industry and would have been given records. And that some journalists were fortunate enough, like me, to have been sent loads of discs in an effort to persuade them to tell their readers all about them and how good they were. But to do that they'd have had to play them in the first place, at which point they would no longer be 'mint'. As for the ones that they didn't want, or couldn't be bothered, to play, well, how likely is it that they would just stash them away in the hope that they might grow to like them in the future or that they would suddenly become valuable? After all, records have always taken up a good amount of space if owned in any quantity and stored properly.

If mint records are inexplicable, then mistreated ones are surely innocent victims in need of protection. I was finally pushed over the edge to take verbal action when I came across a stall at a car boot sale offering for sale a variety of records with one significant feature in common – they were all in diabolical condition, with damaged, ripped, bestickered, written-on covers. A quick look inside at the actual vinyl content of these sleeves revealed gouges galore, scuffs aplenty, scratches in abundance and unspecified spills and stains.

'You do realise,' I told the unsuspecting stallholder, 'that if these records were children you would be held to account by the NSPCC and probably prosecuted for the cruelty which has clearly been done to them...'

He looked at me open-mouthed as though I had taken leave of my senses:

'If you don't want 'em, mate, you don't have to buy 'em.'

I've often thought that there should be a group devoted to the protection of records. They bring so much pleasure to people that it is impossible to understand how so many owners treat them so disrespectfully and inflict such awful indignities and hurt to these innocent victims. Children have an organisation dedicated to their protection. So do pets. Where is the Society for the Preservation of Ill-treated Vinyl, or SPIV, when you need it?

I'm pretty sure that *Record Collector* reader and correspondent Craig Fleming from Lancashire would become a founder member of SPIV, to judge by his reaction when, as a student back in the early 1970s, he witnessed an act so depraved and casually perpetrated in a record shop, that he was reduced to shocked silence.

He watched as a customer ahead of him handed over the

record she was about to buy to the assistant, who removed the inner sleeve and record to put them into a paper bag, then took the cover, and made a fold down the side of it before squeezing that into the bag, too. Presumably stunned at this wanton act of destruction, the customer 'just paid and left'.

Craig passed over his own chosen record – the LP *Arena* by the band Marsupilami– assuming that what had just happened was some kind of bizarre one-off. But, no, in front of his widening eyes, he saw history repeating itself as she again removed the inner sleeve and disc, 'and slid it inside a paper bag'. As though caught in a dream and powerless to stop what he knew was about to happen Craig managed to croak out a question as 'she gripped the textured cardboard cover'. His demand of 'What are you doing?' stopped her in her tracks and 'she replied that the bags were not big enough, so she would have to fold the cover to get it inside'. Snapping out of his temporary paralysis, Craig told her in no uncertain terms that 'I was not having my cover damaged and would manage without a bag'. This did the trick, and he was able to wrest the cover back and depart with it and the internal contents undamaged... just as well, given that today original copies of that album can sell for £200 or more!

She was out shopping recently while I was delving through discs, when I came across Sheila's copy of the Small Faces' second LP. It was covered in carefully cut strips of Sellotape. Sellotape which was no longer clear, but now stained a tobacco-like brown with age. It took me a couple of hours to remove the strips, one by one and place them carefully in a carrier bag.

When she came home, I handed her the bag, into which she looked, before glaring at me and snarling:

'What's this?'

'Sellotape. It's yours.'

'What do you mean, mine? It's rubbish.'

'Yes, it is YOUR rubbish. You're the one who wrapped her Small Faces' record in it, probably forty-odd years ago. Why would you do that?'

She had no idea. The record was still playable and we had a listening that evening. Good record, still decent sound – yours for two hundred quid!

Telling this story to Julian in Second Scene, he pondered, then told me: 'I think I remember seeing an article in the NME many years ago suggesting that covering records in Sellotape would protect their covers. Perhaps that's why she did it.'

Once the Sellotape fetish was over, Sheila's tastes matured a little and she became, and remains, in thrall to Paul Rodgers in all of his guises from Free to Bad Company to The Firm to The Law, to his solo career – probably, though, to be honest, drawing a veil over what we both agreed was his somewhat dubious role of Queen front man.

I was delighted to be able to get her a face-to-face meeting with her hero before a 2017 Bad Company gig at the 02. Paul was friendly, if a little awkward, Simon relaxed and friendly, while Mick Ralphs seemed well enough, but suffered a stroke not long after.

However, not all collectors even *want* their records in pristine condition. What are we to make of recording artist and self-publisher of comic-book *Fuff*, Jeffrey Lewis who says of his record collecting strategy: 'I don't buy records that cost more than $15.' Yet he specialises in 1960s psych which normally goes for way more than that and which, if it is selling for $15 or under, is likely to be in less than mint condition. *Much* less than mint condition.

But that's what Jeffrey relishes. 'I don't care about condition. If it's noisy with surface scuffs, crackle and pops that's almost preferable to me; it gives the listening experience more personal character.' He has even 'fantasised' about creating a digital app designed to add 'layers of vinyl surface-scuff noise to digital album files.' He positively thrives on smelly record covers – 'Rot, mould, that particular smell of a sleeve that has been kicked around for decades... that's really something.'

You've got to believe he really gets off on an olfactory trip whilst listening to his rank records, as he says of finding three West Coast Pop Art Experimental Band albums after many years of patient hunting and tracking down for the right price: 'I spent some time just sniffing the records before even daring to listen to them. I can buy a $100 album for $100 any time, but so what? The $10 album, that's the "priceless" one – that's the copy Donald Trump can't afford.'

I was so intrigued by Jeffrey's unusual views on the superiority of cheap and scuzzy over expensive and well-groomed that I bought a couple of examples of his own music. Taking a lead from him, I got them as cheaply as possible: 'A Turn in the Dream-Songs' and 'It's the Ones Who've Cracked That the Light Shines Through' for a smidgeon over six quid the two.

Someone else who buys terrible condition records as a matter of course is one of Julian's Second Scene customers, as I discovered when he told me when I picked up a particular record: 'That's unplayable, don't bother.'

'I'd quite like just to own the cover.'

'I'd have to charge you a fiver though, as one of my regulars gives me that much for any records I deem unsellable – and then uses them to make artworks which he sells off for serious money.'

More on this guy later, but now, I wanna 'tull' you a story...

IN WHICH... I TULL YOU ABOUT JETHRO

Inspired by the article I wrote for *Record Collector*, I officially launched my 'previously unvisited record shop' odyssey on Friday 11 August 2017 with a visit to Hitchin in Hertfordshire, where Gatefold Record Lounge (cunning tagline – 'Welcome to the Fold') opened in 2016. It is one of a recently appearing breed of shops which double up as cafe-cum-record emporia.

This one offered a smallish, but perfectly priced, second-hand section from which it came down to a choice between handing over a fiver for either Jethro Tull's *Songs from the Wood* or Wishbone Ash's *Number the Brave*. I could have bought both, but decided to opt for the Ash album, not one with which I was familiar, but I have consistently enjoyed every Wishbone Ash track I have come across – even since they split into two different groups (which one is regarded as the 'tribute' act, I wonder?). I was fairly sure I'd play and enjoy it frequently. I was right.

Whereas I reckoned I'd probably have played the Tull once. (I won't waste too much time reminding you that the group's initial 1968 single, 'Sunshine Day', on the MGM label misidentified them as Jethro Toe and is thus valued at up to £500 for an excellent/mint condition copy.) I would then have consigned it to obscurity, given its bucolic cover, which suggested a somewhat niche style of music contained within it.

Over the years, Ian Anderson has, of course, enjoyed jumping and hopping about, both on stage and in a musical manner, and mention of his group gives me licence to regale readers with my favourite Tull story, involving a trip with my best mate Graham Brown to see them play at the Alban Arena in St Albans in, I'd say, the earlyish 2000s. We were sitting close to a couple, the female half of which seemed a little aggravated with her male companion while the opening act played. When the support finished and people popped out for a beer or ice cream before the arrival onstage of Tull, this couple did not seem to be getting on any better.

'When does he come on?' she hissed at him. 'I'm bored – that last act was rubbish.'

'Soon. It won't be long,' her companion reassured her.

She must really be an Anderson addict, I thought. Further complaints and moans followed as the auditorium filled up, the lights went down and the audience settled down... on to the stage walked the great man, together with his Tull cohorts.

'Who the bloody hell are that lot?' demanded the female half of the couple. 'That's not bloody Jethro.'

They jumped to their feet, pushed their way along the row they'd been sitting in and stormed out – presumably to find out how they'd been conned into buying tickets for a cod-pieced rocker, rather than the Cornish comic with a similar name.

Back in Hitchin, whose regular market stalls can offer rich pickings at penury prices for attentive vinyl diggers, I went looking for a supposed CD shop in the town, but couldn't find it, so detoured to a local charity shop, emerging triumphantly with two 50p greatest hits CDs by, respectively, Eddy Grant, and Alice Cooper. Uxbridge hosted a record fair the next day. I nipped over and came away with a Mark Knopfler double CD and two LPs – an obscure 'various artists' set of US garage tracks, and a Bam Caruso 12″ single featuring different bands on each side. What I didn't buy and am still a trifle perplexed to understand why, was the sheet music to The Hollies' 'King Midas in Reverse', a big psych favourite of mine, penned by Graham Nash. It seems this was the beginning of the end for him in the band when it didn't crack the Top 10 and Nash sensed the other group members were not quite on the same page as him regarding the musical direction they should be taking.

I had been aware for some time of the well-regarded Casbah record shop in Greenwich, which left its local market location to become a shop in 2009, but I had yet to get around to going over there. A Docklands Light Railway train deposited me a couple of hundred yards from the shop. Anticipation turned to disappointment. I was the only customer, but the youngish male and female staff members seemed more concerned with chatting, rather than greeting what they obviously took to be a hopelessly out-of-his-depth potential customer. Indeed, having taken a good look at me, they'd obviously weighed up their scruffy, 60-something, white customer as a fan of rap music – and, had I been such, they were providing an appropriate musical accompaniment while I busied myself looking through their limited stock of 1960s and 1970s rock.

I have noticed that a record shop staff member assessing the likely tastes of its customers and playing music aimed at them appears to be a relatively rare phenomenon. However, top marks to the LP Cafe in Watford which, when I arrived recently, immediately slapped on Quicksilver Messenger Service's mega guitar soloing album, *Happy Trails*. Mind you, as I do already have two copies of that LP, I almost let them down by leaving empty handed, but spied a reissued Sam Gopal LP + bonus 7″ for £15.

The Casbah's shelves of second-hand records seemed to be stocked somewhat half-heartedly and thinly. Maybe someone had been in the day before and purchased the bulk of them, although

I doubt that. They had some more interesting reissue albums and one, *Enclosed* by the Detroit band Magic, caught my eye, but at a tenner more than the equivalent CD I wasn't persuaded that it represented a worthwhile investment. I did later grab a cheaper copy of this enjoyable 1969 guitar-driven LP which was reissued in 1998, later than anticipated after bass player/vocalist Nick King was tragically killed in a car crash. Must have caught the Casbah on a bad day, I dare say, or they me.

A brilliant example of just how to engage with a customer unfolded in front of me in a shop with a rather different attitude to customers.

'I haven't seen this record for years,' said the lady of a certain vintage, walking up to the counter of the Eel Pie Records shop in Kingston, Surrey. 'How much is it?'

The record she was clutching was a copy of the 10cc single, 'I'm Not in Love.'

'All the singles in that box are a pound each,' said the assistant. 'But I'll tell you what – today's special offer – sing it to me, and you can have it for nothing.'

She looked at him, evidently a little flustered. 'Er, I'm not sure I know all the words. I'm not a very good singer – here's the pound. Thanks. Goodbye.'

She fled, clutching the single tightly, but I am willing to wager she would be engaging with friends and telling them this story. In her version of it she quite possibly warbles a note-perfect version of the song!

Boogaloo Broadway record shop is in Dawes Road, Fulham – except that, when I turned up there on Friday 17 August 2017, it looked as though it was an ex-record shop, a deceased disc-den. Shutters were down, and there was no sign of life when I peered through the gaps to see into the shop interior. Despite the typed notice in the window, saying 'open on Friday, noon-6pm', it was already past 1pm and it was blatantly un-open. There was a phone number displayed, so I rang it. No reply.

Oh well, to paraphrase the *Auf Wiedersehen, Pet* theme tune – nobody said it was gonna be easy.

IN WHICH... I'M STONED

I made an early start to get to a Luton Town home match, diverting en route to Black Circle Records in nearby Leighton Buzzard. A very pleasant shop, offering a good selection of new and second-hand stock, but little or no psychedelia, my own preference, on show. The friendly young lady behind the counter addressed customers as 'mate' and had to deal with persistent enquiries as to where owner, David Kosky, might be. It seemed, though, that he didn't usually turn up on a Saturday.

A man and his wife were browsing. Well, *he* was browsing, while she, apparently good-humouredly, asked the counter lady, 'Can I bring his bed down?' as he showed few signs of wanting to move on. There was a bargain-priced CD box edition with book(let), of the latest Rolling Stones' album, *Blue & Lonesome* which sees the band tackling some of the basic blues numbers with which they first began their career. It was new, but priced at 20 quid, quite a markdown on the original price, although it seemed to me when I checked, that the basic version of the record, which I'd already bought on LP at half of the box price, contained exactly the same tracks, if not the associated, inessential fripperies.

Just who actually buys these 'deluxe' versions of albums, either new or reissued/remastered/restored/revised, baffles me. If they are bought for their content then the purchaser is shelling out an awful lot for maybe a couple of extra, afterthought 'bonus' tracks, an often hastily compiled, if good-looking, book(let) and a few pictures or posters. If bought in the hope that these 'limited edition' (they seldom tell you just *how* limited) copies will soar in value, then I fear they will have a very long wait. Just maybe their great-grandchildren will be able to sell them for a measly profit during the 2060 series of *Flog It*. That's assuming there is still television...

I'd quite enjoyed listening to that Stones' *Blue & Lonesome* album, although there was such a contrast between the listenable, but ever so slightly routine renderings of the tracks, and the semi-bootleg style releases I'd also recently acquired. These contained live versions of very similar material from early 1960s, usually BBC radio broadcasts, which vibrantly captured the early enthusiasm and vigour of the optimistic, youthful Jagger, Jones, Richard, Stewart, Watts, and Wyman. Yes, the band are now far more professional, but inevitably some of the optimistic swagger with which they played then, charging past the odd bum note, overwhelming it with the bravado and sheer *joie de vivre* of youth is missing.

The contrast between the two demonstrates why I now prefer, and enjoy watching and listening to, tribute bands like the Counterfeit Stones or the Rollin' Stoned, who play the Stones' back catalogue with the energy they used to display themselves back when they were *still* the Stones and not leaving themselves open to allegations of being just a pale imitation of their own imitators. The 'real' band has the authenticity, and seeing and hearing them play is something of a rite of passage for many generations. But the original shock and awe of seeing and experiencing their performance are gone, replaced by the tick-box duty of watching living legends move about and the anticipated kudos of being able to say, 'I've seen the Stones. They've still got it.' And yes, they have. But the 'it' they now have isn't the same 'it' that 'it' used to be. Is it?

I was fortunate enough to see the Stones in their pomp – albeit on perhaps the saddest day for the group – at their legendary concert in Hyde Park in which they released butterflies galore to mark the death three days previously of estranged founder Brian Jones, who drowned in a swimming pool in early July 1969. Despite various conspiracy theories which have been, er, floated, there has been no 'evidence' produced compelling enough to suggest it was anything other than an unfortunate tragedy caused by the influence of drink and/or drugs, with the official inquest ruling 'misadventure'.

In late May 2018, I sat in an almost full Alban Arena in St Albans, to see, and hear, at close quarters, the Counterfeit Stones, delivering a satisfying two hours of Stones' music to an appreciative audience which hadn't paid much more than 20 quid a head to be there at a time when the 'real thing' were also touring. Even 'Nick Dagger' commented in a jokey aside how much better a deal we were getting than those opting to pay through the nose for being able to say they were there to see the 'real' Stones in a cavernous arena where they might as well be watching a DVD of the band in action projected on to giant screens around the venue. Some of us don't believe that even if they had been at the Jagger-Richards-Watts show that they'd have been watching a true version of the Rolling Stones. They wouldn't have seen Brian Jones, or Bill Wyman. No Ian Stewart.

Don't get me wrong. I love the Stones and have bought every album, and all the early 1960s and 1970s singles they have issued, as well as many they haven't. I even have a couple of Ronnie Wood prints hanging in my hall looking askance at me as I write these critical words. There's a 'Mick' of his, with Charlie hitting the skins behind him, and a wonderful, contemplative, strumming 'Keef'. But I don't have a Ronnie 'Ronnie' as I genuinely cannot regard the former Face/Jeff Beck Group member as a bona fide Stone. Any more than Mick Taylor before him.

Seeing the version of the group any court of law would almost certainly uphold as being the proper band, Craig Brown, columnist for the *Daily Mail*, wrote of his trip to watch them play in late 2018, under the heading 'Seeing The Stones? Take Binoculars!'

'"Premium" tickets which might get you within viewing range cost £282.45 including booking fee,' he declared, adding: 'Most of the audience doesn't watch the concert, but a live film of the concert. In fact, it could as easily be a film of a concert that took place last year.'

Without the screens, Craig, from his viewpoint (the cheapest seats cost 'just under £100') 'had no way of telling whether the little chap at the front was Mick Jagger rather than, say Kylie Minogue or, indeed, Jacob Rees-Mogg.' Although Mick's voice was still in fine form, 'it was not their fault that the acoustics of the London Stadium are hopeless.' He concluded that, 'I could have had the same experience for free by sitting in a field watching the Stones on TV through binoculars held the wrong way round.'

If there were ever two greater gestures of contempt towards those who hoisted their careers skywards and kept them there, one was surely the actions of the Stones in 'celebrating' the free concert in Hyde Park after the death of Brian Jones, by charging a small fortune to attend the band's concert there, on 6 July 2013, ostensibly part of their '50 and Counting' tour to mark the group's 50 years of existence.

Then there was the issuing of a 2012 TRIPLE CD greatest hits-style compilation with 48 tracks which virtually all loyal fans would already own, but also including on it *two* tracks unavailable elsewhere. No wonder it was called *Grrr!* – they, or their commercial people, must have known that would be the reaction. The BBC online review by Sean Egan of the record, noted:

'The stupid title and stupider cover artwork of *Grrr!* seem to suggest that enthusiasm was in short supply as the Stones' camp approached yet another permutation of their greatest hits.'

He adds that 'all they can muster in the way of new material to mark the milestone of their half-centenary is 'Doom and Gloom' and 'One More Shot', a brace of tracks that – in the typical modern Stones style – are just riff, slogan and biscuit-tin drums.'

These two tracks could have been released as a bargain price, or even free, thank you to long-suffering, completist followers. Some small recognition of the loyalty of their now elderly core support would not have gone amiss.

You may conclude that I have a down on the Rolling Stones. But perhaps those we love the most we give the hardest time.

It is hard now to recapture the way in which the arrival and impact of The Beatles had such a seismic effect on me and so many other early teenagers. This amazing group seemed to have arrived from out of nowhere, and began to reinvent the entire world of music, simultaneously energising and exercising the media from newspapers to radio to TV to movies.

Almost everyone of a certain age and mindset took to them immediately and gave them virtually unconditional love. They brought with them to our previously monochrome world sunlight and bright colours. But then, a few months later, the Rolling Stones turned up. If The Beatles were the flamboyant technicolour photograph, the Stones were the scruffy, dark negative. Many of us who had already welcomed The Beatles with open arms and minds began to have second thoughts. Perhaps these polar opposites were the truer reflection of the era we were living in. The rivalry between the bands began to feature in the media coverage and, for me, the decision had to be made virtually on my 13th birthday.

By November 1963 The Beatles were exploding into the public consciousness. They already boasted three massive hits: 'Please, Please Me', 'From Me to You' and 'She Loves You' dominated the charts, following on from their initial chart success, 'Love Me Do'. You could even argue they'd already peaked, as 'She Loves You' would be their biggest selling UK hit of all. Meanwhile, although their untidy image had started to aggravate parents everywhere, the more rebellious kids were championing the Stones over The Beatles. Initially, it seemed a one-sided contest as the first Rolling Stones' single, 'Come On', peaked at Number 21. Now came the first real point at which a choice had to be made. Like an owner throwing a hungry canine the contents of a tin of supermarket own-brand dogmeat, so The Beatles unexpectedly handed over an unwanted song, 'I Wanna Be Your Man' for the Stones to record. They did so, and the resulting single became their first Top 20 entry, reaching Number 12.

Here was a focal point. Yes, The Beatles wrote the song. Their own version, though, was given to Ringo. It was regarded as a run-of-the-mill song which the drummer sang, as a filler track on the *With The Beatles* LP. He may have been joking but John Lennon told the writer David Sheff in a 1980 interview in New York, which was one of the last, if not *the* last, he ever gave: 'It was a throwaway. The only two versions of the song were Ringo and the Rolling Stones. That shows how much importance we put on it: We weren't going to give them anything *great*, right?'

The choice, which was pretty much going to decide which side you were on for the duration of the contest between them, now had to be confronted. Did you prefer the version by The Beatles or the Stones? For me, the Stones' was clearly the better, catchier, more aggressively played treatment, and remains one of my favourite singles of all time. But did the fact that The Beatles wrote the song trump the fact that the Stones performed it better?

Some reports suggest that watching The Beatles creating 'I Wanna Be Your Man' in the studio encouraged the Stones to write their own songs, while the other explanation for them doing so has always been that Andrew Loog Oldham sent Mick and Keith into a room and told them not to come out without a song – which, so legend has it, was the genesis of 'As Tears Go By'. The Stones wouldn't have a Jagger/Richards-written hit single until March 1965 when 'The Last Time' opened the self-penned singles' floodgates. Once that happened there was no holding them.

The establishment and the authorities had begun to pick on them for various reasons. This was the time when William Rees-Mogg, editor of *The Times*, used a quote from Alexander Pope's *Epistle to Dr Arbuthnot* ('Who breaks a butterfly upon a wheel?') as the heading for a supportive editorial on 1 July 1967 about the 'Redlands' court case, when Mick and Keith appeared before magistrates charged with drug offences, resulting in prison sentences. All of this just cemented their place in my affections and although 'We Love You' in August 1967 was their least successful single for some time, I absolutely loved it, particularly its strikingly flower-power B-side, 'Dandelion', the name Keith gave to his daughter.

You will probably not be very surprised to know that the psychy *Their Satanic Majesties Request* is my favourite Stones' LP. How weird it is that, with thirteen weeks in the charts, reaching a highest Number 3, according to the book *Guinness British Hit Singles & Albums*, this album outdid the follow-up, the much more critically-lauded *Beggars Banquet*, which was also a Number 3 but only spent twelve weeks in the charts.

When that dismal disco period of the dirge-like 'Miss You' and its album *Some Girls* arrived around June 1978, three years after Ronnie Wood replaced Mick Taylor, I decided it was time to pay just lip service loyalty to the band. Despite the short-term recovery of 'Start Me Up' in August 1981, they have never since threatened to come anywhere near former glories. Bill Wyman's official departure at the end of 1992 was further proof that an era was over, although the remaining trio would never accept it.

In February 2015 Wyman put the band's roots and history into perspective with his comments after a plaque commemorating the chance meeting between Mick and Keith was unveiled at Dartford station, reading:

'Mick Jagger and Keith Richards met on platform 2 on 17 October 1961 and went on to form The Rolling Stones.'

Wyman made a warranted public complaint, pointing out on BBC Radio 5 Live:

'Mick Jagger and Keith Richards didn't create the Rolling Stones – they were part of The Rolling Stones like all of us. Brian Jones wanted to form a blues band and he enlisted each member one by one. He gave the name The Rolling Stones, he chose the music and he was the leader.'

But if the Stones and Beatles were amongst my first musical loves they only dabbled, albeit very influentially for a while, in the style which would remain for me, the greatest rock music genre of them all...

IN WHICH... I DISCOVER PSYCHEDELIA & ACID ROCK... MAN!

I'll always have a soft spot for him, but I rapidly moved on from Duane Eddy's twangy geetar sounds once Ray Davies had kickstarted my love of rather noisier, discordant guitars. Not that far on, to be honest... screechy, sweet-sounding, very loud guitaring still does it for me, if not for the other, long-suffering members of my household. Number One son, Steeven, does value heavy metal guitars, and has spent much of his teenage and adult years following Metallica around the world. Number Two (in age only!), Paul, is a Green Day loyalist.

Although my own social life as a teenager involved playing football most evenings of the week and, more competitively, in Sunday league teams, as I worked on Saturdays, there was plenty of room for music. As well as my football mates, there was another group of acquaintances who were more concerned with growing their hair even longer than was fashionable and, so it was whispered, smoking cigarettes containing substances other than tobacco. This seemed to render them incapable of conversing sensibly about any subject other than music – and about how marvellous groups were of which I had never then heard, and which usually hailed from the States.

One night two or three of them – Steve Searle, Dick 'Strick' (he worked in Stricklands record shop), Ian French, perhaps – invited me round to the home of one of them in Herga Road in Wealdstone. ('Wanna hear some sounds, man?') I've no idea why they did so, as, being a year or two older than me, they were entitled to ignore me or, had they been of a tougher variety, to beat me up whenever they fancied. They did no such thing. When I turned up at the house, they all seemed to be lying around, smoking, drinking and listening. There were no in-charge adults to be spotted anywhere. The smoking – even the sweet-smelling variety – and drinking did not remotely appeal to me... but the listening, wow, that did. I didn't know what or who I was listening *to*, but the sounds, particularly those wrung out of guitars, were like nothing I'd heard, even from the Stones and The Beatles. I was hooked.

This change of musical emphasis, whilst psychedelia was swirling unchecked on to the airwaves, was to blame for one of the most embarrassing moments of my life. The 1967 'summer of love' saw even we suburban grammar school kids feeling we had something in common with groovy hippies, and one of the easier ways of demonstrating that was through clothes. I acquired a loud, paisley-style kaftan-type shirt, teamed it with low-slung, possibly white, hipsters, held up by a wide, white leather belt, set off by some kind of moccasin-like sub-trainer style footwear, worn with a wonderful brown velvet jacket and a very small, ahem, bell, around my neck. Yes, yes, OK. Guilty. Hands held up, etc.

This, I recall, was the 'gear' I was wearing to chill out in down by

Poulter's chip shop in trendy downtown Wealdstone one evening, where a few friends were sitting about, listening to a pirate station on a transistor radio and just discussing, probably, football, girls, and music. We were rudely interrupted by 'The Man', otherwise known as a couple of the local 'bobbies' or 'fuzz' in the vernacular of the day. They clearly had little to do and weren't in sympathy with our musical tastes. They stopped for a friendly chat, inviting us to 'Fuck off out of it.' For sure we weren't 'out of it' in any serious sense but when we didn't immediately leap to our feet and clear off, one of the cops leaned over to tell me that he meant what he said and if I didn't leg it asap he'd 'stuff that fucking bell down your fucking mouth, son.' Police brutality, man! But, objective achieved. The bell was immediately retired from active duty.

Poulter's chip shop was run by John and Alan of that ilk. I lived next door to Mrs Poulter, matriarch of the fish 'n' chip family, whose grandson Paul was a schoolmate of mine and a demon bowler on a cricket pitch. We used to spend time at his gran's listening to music, and around this time he invited me in to listen to two LPs he'd just acquired. They were *Evolution* by The Hollies, whose psychedelic cover and Graham Nash-driven contents delighted me, and sunshine pop trailblazers The Turtles' album, *Happy Together*, whose irresistibly catchy choruses and harmonies immediately made a huge impression. As I left, probably for 'my tea', Paul nonchalantly told me, 'You can have those records if you want.' I needed no second bidding. Still own them, still play them, still think they're wonderful.

Back in Herga Road, I'd later discover that I was hearing groups (I'm sure they were always described as groups rather than bands back then) like Quicksilver Messenger Service, Big Brother & The Holding Company, Jefferson Airplane, Country Joe, Spirit, Captain Beefheart, Hendrix, etc, and, boy, did I like... no, I *loved* the sounds they made. Acid rock or (the American version of) psychedelic music was what it was called and it rapidly became the love of my musical life. It was a short-lived phenomenon in terms of mainstream appeal, but has gone on to become probably the most collectable, most valuable genre of rock music. Even now I am still discovering more of it which was created from 1966 to the early 1970s, much of which either sold painfully few copies, or never secured a release at the time.

I'm not the only one not entirely clear about what is, or isn't, psychedelic. Look through the 'Psych' section of a number of different record shops and you'll see for yourself how tricky it is to decide. There are many nominations for the 'first psychedelic record' honour. You could write an entire book about the subject. Some people have. Perhaps one of the best attempts at the subject is *Record Collector 100 Greatest Psychedelic Records*, from 2005, which came down in favour of The Beatles' 'Rain', B-side to 'Paperback Writer', released in June 1966. 'Rain... is the first fully-formed English psychedelic creation', declared the publication.

I wouldn't necessarily dispute that. I loved 'Rain' as soon as I first heard it but I will always refer anyone who is genuinely interested in a definition of psychedelic music to 'Strawberry Fields Forever', released in Feb 1967. That, to me, typifies the genre, with its eerie atmosphere, unexpected rhythms and sounds, mysterious lyrics and genuinely original tune. The backwards section, chiming guitars and pure 'difference' made it special from the first hearing – and, for me, each subsequent one.

The ordinary – such as finding a flaw in one's footwear (consult Traffic's 'Hole in My Shoe') – becoming extraordinary was a common theme in Brit-psych. 'My White Bicycle' (Tomorrow); 'I Can Hear the Grass Grow' (The Move); 'Itchycoo Park' (Small Faces); and 'Apples and Oranges' (Pink Floyd) are all of this type. There was also what became known as the 'Toytown' element to it, which music writer Paul Morley described well in his 2016 biography, *Bowie*. Seeing its arrival as 'a fascination with traditional symbols of British national identity' he feels there was a 'desire to reframe the influences of a post-war childhood in the mind-bending new context of psychedelia.' 'What', went on Morley, 'if the Goons, Alice in Wonderland, C S Lewis, Charles Dickens coexisted with experimental pop music?'

This kind of psych clearly 'speaks' very clearly to my generation, which was brought up on these books and similar radio and TV programmes during our formative years and relates sympathetically to it when prompted by lyrics referring to them and others of similar ilk, written by group members cut from the same cloth. This view of psych is the specific focus of the triple CD compilation, released in 2016 by Grapefruit Records, featuring 80 'British psychedelic sounds of 1967'. Well, 79 really. Quite how 'Support Us' by The QPR Supporters justifies inclusion is beyond me.

The title of the collection is *Let's Go Down and Blow Our Minds*, an inspired choice, which is not only part of the opening line to the opening track of the box set, the single 'Toyland' by The Alan Bown!, but also completely captures the atmosphere of the music therein. That song, by band members Tony Catchpole and Jess Roden, who would also turn up in the under-estimated Bronco, remains 'a classic slice of childhood-inspired English psych-pop whimsy' as the box set's accompanying booklet written by David Wells put it.

As, indeed, does Past & Present's 5-CD, 82-track romp from 2010, *Chocolate Soup For Diabetics* which mines similar fertile ground, and another triple CD delight from Grapefruit in 2017, celebrating 'The British Psychedelic Sounds of 1968' under the heading *Looking At The Pictures In The Sky*. I'd suggest that only those there at the time could have come up with these evocative memory-jogging headline names, such as *We Can Fly*, the catch-all title of another terrific set of psych's forgotten voices and sounds well worth any aficionado's investigation

In late 1967, along came the latest Moody Blues' LP, *Days of Future Passed*, which saw psych, still in its infancy to a large extent, begin to morph into yet another segment, 'progressive music' and/ or 'prog rock'.

American psychedelia/acid rock was fundamentally similar, but at the same time very different. 'Get Me to the World on Time', demanded the Electric Prunes in May 1967, having already explained in November 1966 that, 'I Had Too Much to Dream Last Night'. But Jefferson Airplane's 'White Rabbit' was inspired by a prime piece of British literary psychedelic heritage. 'White Rabbit' was one of vocalist extraordinaire Grace Slick's earliest songs, written during either late 1965 or early 1966 and released in 1967. It uses imagery found in the fantasy works of Lewis Carroll, author of *Alice's Adventures in Wonderland*, first published in 1865, including changing size after taking pills or drinking an unknown liquid.

Slick claimed the composition – reportedly written after a 'trip' – was supposed to be a slap in the face to parents who read their children such novels and then wondered why their children later used drugs. Characters Slick referenced include Alice herself, the White Rabbit, the Dormouse, and the hookah-smoking caterpillar. There is an element of acid of another type in Rob Chapman's excellent book, *Psychedelia and Other Colours* which covers the full gamut of the genre's derivation and progression. A review in a Bibliophile catalogue observed of the music – that it had 'its roots in fairy tales, myths and fairgrounds, the music hall, the dead of Flanders' fields, the Festival of Britain', and that it feeds into 'that peculiarly British strand of surrealism that culminated in the Magical Mystery Tour'.

I'd say the first really psychedelic US offering came courtesy of the Byrds' literally electrifying 'Eight Miles High', released in March 1966. It left those listening wondering whether the official explanation that it described the latter stages of a flight by the band from the US to London was entirely accurate, or whether another kind of trip was the true inspiration.

Other American bands are often tagged with the psych label – but maybe acid-rock, a brasher, more aggressive, more political animal, is a more accurate term to use for their style, while garage-rock is something else again, often lumped in with psych/acid but rougher and readier than those two. Although ten or more years earlier than punk, perhaps it has more in common with the aggressive, confrontational aspects of that mid-1970s explosion.

That some of the US bands were also inspired by the Brit fairy tale genre is clear from the fact that in 2013, when the much-respected Charly Records compiled a double disc of music called *The Great Lost Southern Popsike Trip*, they subtitled it 'Alice in Wonderland and other Rainy Day Girls', largely on the back of the fact that the opening track was The Berkeley Kites' 'Alice in Wonderland'. Sam Szczepanski, the author of the accompanying booklet, dubbed this 'pure toy town pop' with its nursery rhyme references and 'whimsical' flute.

A - THE, maybe - major link between British/American psych/acid rock - apart from the obvious influence on both of illegal and illicit substances - is the one person who could, and did, straddle both and more besides - when, in March 1967, he unleashed 'Purple Haze' on the unsuspecting world - yes, of course, Jimi Hendrix.

I love and embrace all of these genres, but when forced to side with one, it is the British psych style which does it for me just a little more. Perhaps this is because of the impressionable age I was when this music made its presence felt, not only on disc, but also in a number of influential movies. They may look old fashioned and out of time if watched today, but they really hit the spot at the time *and* boasted brilliant soundtrack albums.

Here We Go Round the Mulberry Bush was a rite of passage film with a Spencer Davis/Traffic soundtrack, notably the title track - but it also featured a wonderful Andy Ellison solo effort, 'Been A Long Time'. Then there was the politically edgy kitchen-sink cum-swinging-London mix of *Up the Junction*, the film version of Nell Dunn's novel, which involved members of Manfred Mann, notably the evolving writing talent of Mike Hugg, particularly in evidence on the title track. Add to these two films the Sidney Poitier/Lulu vehicle, *To Sir, With Love*, and the Lovin' Spoonful soundtrack 'You're A Big Boy Now' and music was sucking me into its grasp wherever I looked and listened. Bizarrely, old-school comic Norman Wisdom also got in on the act in his movie *What's Good for the Goose* which featured a great soundtrack by the Pretty Things.

All of this helps to explain the answers to questions often posed to me. 'Why do you almost exclusively collect and listen to music from 50-plus years ago? Don't you realise there's been great music appearing regularly since then and there is still much that is terrific being made now?' Of course I do - I'm as avid a viewer of Jools Holland's TV show as the next person. But the point is that the music I loved first was that being written by my contemporaries, and by and large aimed at people just like me. Yes, much of it has become over-familiar over the past few decades, but the real joy for me now is unearthing the stuff that was also being made back then but which did not capture the airwaves, did not make the charts, was not picked up by major labels. That too was being made for the likes of me by the likes of me and to discover it now, still sounding fresh and contemporary to the part of my brain which never wanted to 'move on' to other areas, is just an amazing delight.

I'm no longer 17 in looks, but a large part of me remembers precisely what it was like being that influential and impressionable age, and how I felt about life and the world, and to rediscover the way in which others were experiencing just those emotions and feelings is the next best thing to boarding a time machine and returning to those long-gone days.

IN WHICH... I CELEBRATE MY ANNIVERSARY ALONE

On 31 August 2017, as a 43rd wedding anniversary treat to myself (my long-suffering wife Sheila's treat was that she would be free of my presence for several hours), I girded my loins and did something I'd never previously done. I went to Deptford, to visit the unfortunately initialled Vinyl Deptford which doubles as a cafe and second-hand record shop.

The place, down a little side street, had a nice, relaxed atmosphere with music talk going on amongst the coffee drinkers, and a charming lady in charge of the pastry-making at the counter, who handed responsibility for totting up my £51 of records to a colleague because, she said, he was better at maths than she is. I pointed out that although I have always been pretty useful at basic maths, I have no pastry skills whatsoever, and, in the greater scheme of things, hers is by far the more practical ability.

The chap – the owner, Ronnie Morrow, I believe – whom I paid for the records responded to my haggling by rejecting my effort to beat him down to 40 quid for the albums, but he accepted 44. Since I'd found for just £9, and in very decent shape, what I regard as a three-figure LP, *Eyes of the Beacon Street Union*, to accompany the band's second outing which I'd bought in Chesham recently, I was very pleased with my morning's work. I also came away with a Blues Magoos' *Psychedelic Lollipop* record. Although I already owned a copy of this, I didn't have the essential cover in which to dress it. So, of course, I now have two records to share one cover. I also bought a Fanny album for some strange reason, as I *do* already have both cover and record; a Gypsy LP, and another by a band I'd always ummed and ahhed about but never previously purchased – CCS, (aka Collective Consciousness Society) featuring the late Alexis Korner, one of the most influential figures of the 1960s British blues boom.

Ronnie is as much a vinyl veteran as the records he sells. And he has a great philosophy: 'I prefer music which is obscure because I love the chaos. The dynamic, the energy that somehow made a DJ go, "Oh, that's rubbish" and put it to the side. Years later, people listen to it and go, "Oh my god, where did you get that record from?" "I just found it in a record shop" – I love the reasons why that happens.'

A couple of days later, I jumped on an H12 bus to visit South Harrow's Music Archaeology shop. I had quickly become a fan of this bijou unit in the Market, close to the site of the extinct, but legendary Sellanby second-hand shop. Partly because virtually no one else seemed to know it was even there, giving me the opportunity of grabbing some decent goodies without having to beat off rival grabbers. When I arrived, owner Chris was talking to an acquaintance who was not only clearly into music, but also gardening – so much so that he was off to a show that very afternoon:

'Entering anything?' Chris asked him.

'Was going to put my tomatoes in... but I had to eat them the other day.'

Departing from Chris's, with Audience and Brunning Sunflower Band LPs, I realised the local tube station was on the Piccadilly Line, by which means I could nip up to Fulham to check out whether the recently shuttered Boogaloo On Broadway had become an ex-record shop, or was still in the game.

It was and I was soon browsing the large selection of vinyl, although I could only get up any enthusiasm for a Greg Kihn LP at just £2.99. Then I spotted racks of CDs on the other side of the shop and headed over for a squint. There was plenty of tempting material – almost all of it selling for an extremely reasonable £3 or £4 a go. I soon grabbed a compilation by legendary heavy/psych band Andromeda; a relatively new Lindsey Buckingham set; an Atomic Rooster double CD and a Tony Joe White.

Wandering over to hand over my thirteen quid, I tapped my foot impatiently as the chap in front took his time settling his bill. When he finally did so and turned to leave, I realised it was Dave Carroll, an old pal and team-mate from the days when we both played football for local side, Hatch End – he in midfield, me up front. We spent the rest of the afternoon reminiscing, not least about the time he volunteered to entertain the assembled masses on the piano, during a somewhat drunken football tour. He entertained us, all right, not with his flashing fingers and dashing digits, but with the way in which he removed the pint balanced on the piano cover by lifting the cover straight up, thus depositing the amber fluid on the carpet. Dave told me he was a regular in this shop – 'they always order anything I want for me' – and explained that the reason it was shut on my earlier visit was because the proprietor had been taken ill and rushed to hospital that very morning – but had happily survived.

Next morning I was at the Bushey (Hertfordshire) Record Fair browsing a stall when I overheard the following conversation:

'I've got 60,000 CDs, but I haven't even looked at 40,000 of them,' declared the Tottenham Hotspurs-supporting stallholder.

'Oh,' said his Watford-supporting customer, 'What's going to happen to them when you're gone? I suppose the wife will get them?'

'No. They'll be burned with me. Like a funeral pyre.'

'All that burning plastic, that won't be very environmentally-friendly.'

'I won't care. I'll be dead.'

I liked the cut of his jib, so I bought five of his 60,000 collection – by Rush, Denny King, Bob Smith, Beggars Banquet and Country Joe & The Fish. They cost 15 quid the lot, and cut down a little on future pollution.

I feel you may now have an idea of the type of stiff upper lip, all-round good egg kind of chap I am, so I can take you into my confidence about the greatest self-inflicted mistake of my vinyl life...

IN WHICH... I REGRET SELLING MY VINYL SOUL FOR FILTHY LUCRE

Over the years I have acquired some now-valuable records which, when they were released, were unheralded, and easily obtained for little money, but have now been accorded cult status, and thus become sought after. A few years ago I decided the time was right to let a few of these records go. They were fetching what I thought were inflated values and, like shares and antiques, there had to be the possibility that they may begin to *lose* value as the generation which coveted and might still want such gems began to die out or decide they had enough records. So I sold some. Amongst those to depart were LPs by Aardvark (now £325), Bakerloo (£300), Fire's *The Magic Shoemaker* (£600), Five Day Week Straw People (£150), Paper Bubble (£200), Someone's Band (£600), and Titus Groan (£350). I got about 800 quid for them – all, not each!

Even so there are only two records of which I genuinely regret depriving myself. Of the two, I am slightly less distraught by my decision to make £500 quid by handing over Kaleidoscope's justifiably legendary *Faintly Blowing*. This record by the British band of that name, not the US group from the late 1960s, was released on the Fontana label in 1969. This now commands between £400 and £1000 depending, according to the *Rare Record Price Guide 2020*, on whether the copy comes with or without 'watermark on beginning of each side'. What, would you imagine, bestows the extra 600 quid on the value? Tricky, eh? Actually, it is the ones without watermarks which are worth more. Who knew? What I *do* know is that I sold my copy for £500, in 2006. So, depending on whether that had the watermarks or not, I either received a ton more than it is now worth, or £500 less. And I have not the slightest idea which one it was...

Once I sold *Faintly Blowing* and began regretting it, I quickly collected virtually every note recorded by Kaleidoscope at the time they were together, and much of the material recorded individually by them since. Parting company with the record alerted me fully to the talents of the band, and that may well not have happened had I held on to it. I'd have been doing so purely for the monetary value, regarding it as some kind of vinyl ISA savings account.

By far my favourite of the pair that I let go (admittedly for a pretty hefty sum) was Arcadium's *Breathe Awhile* – a psych-prog or prog-psych record I took to immediately, from the first time I played and reviewed it in 1969. Why the title *Breathe Awhile?* That question appears to be answered by the wonderfully 'prog' quote from one David Groome, printed on the back cover:

'The inheritance of future sinners and the writings of future revelations will be our final downfall. We can all worship the devil if we please but while there is still time just let us breathe awhile.'

The LP was released on the tiny Middle Earth label which produced only five records in total, and it was sent to me, along with its stablemate LP, *Power of the Picts* by Writing on the Wall. Or was it *Writing on the Wall* by Power of the Picts? I'm still not quite sure to this day. I sold that one, too, for a substantial amount (now valued at £400) but, in the case of this album, buying a 'replacement' CD proved adequate compensation.

The Arcadium record, though, remains intriguing and frustrating for me, to this day. A brilliant thing which stood out immediately I removed it from the packaging in which it arrived on my desk at the *Weekly Post*. The striking cover design is by

Michael McInnerny. I later discovered that Pete Townshend credits him with helping to shape the final sound of the *Tommy* album through his art for its cover. For *Breathe Awhile* Michael came up with a painting of three naked women and two cloud-adorned silhouettes of naked women, which, of course, had little to do with my obsession with the record. On the back there are three photographs of the band by Michael H Evans. In the top one they all wear gas masks; in the second their faces are bandaged, and in the third they are smilingly showing off their shaggy hairstyles.

I managed to contact Michael McInnerny, who responded with some first-hand information:

'The artwork was created specifically for the (Arcadium) album. The commission would have come directly from Dave Howson after he set up Middle Earth Records with Paul Waldman.

Arcadium was released in June 1969, a month after the release of *Tommy* by The Who. I mention this because I can only assume the shallow spatial illusion featured in the Arcadium artwork (created after I had designed the *Tommy* cover) was heavily influenced by the shallow sky illusion of *Tommy*. I can only assume the cover image attempts to present an environmental message. A loss of innocence in the Anthropocene with a world in stress.'

I can't imagine that the record sold more than a few hundred copies when it was issued. It received very little airplay that I can recall, and certainly didn't trouble the charts. A non-album single came out around the same time, but the quintet never followed up the LP. Although Greek ex-pat, vocalist and guitarist Miguel Sergides - inevitably known as Big Mig - wrote all the tracks, lead guitarist Bob Ellwood, whose brother Alan played keyboards, seems to have been the only member to make any subsequent impact following Arcadium's disintegration. He turned up in the Kingdom Come group, fronted by Arthur Brown - he of the flaming headset, and 'Fire' hit. The very obscurity of the group and scarceness of the original issue would have acted as an inbuilt collectability factor almost immediately, particularly as, according to the usually reliable chronicler of such matters, Vernon Joynson, in his 2014 masterwork *The Tapestry of Delights*, 'due to mediocre vinyl there are practically no copies to be found nowadays in truly excellent condition.'

Few others were as bowled over by Arcadium as I was. 'Somehow lacks impact' sniffed *Melody Maker*. 'Spirited performances don't make up for bad vocals', harrumphed *New Musical Express*, while *Disc* damned it with faint praise as 'not particularly outstanding... in parts monotonous.' Despite my own rave review in the *Weekly Post*, it flopped, doomed to disappear almost as soon as it had surfaced... only to live on and increase steadily in value over the next 50 years as other more vaunted records became blighted by their familiarity.

Record collectors, as has become ever more obvious, hold great store by rarity and one-upmanship. 'What? You've never heard of Arcadium or their one LP? Good Lord, old chap, you don't know what you're missing. You won't hear it on the radio, and there are very few copies of the original record to be had, but take my word for it that it is essential listening. Of course I have a copy. Perhaps I can put it on a cassette for you if I get chance.'

I really did, and still do, love the record. I sold *Breathe Awhile* for £380 in 2006. It can now go for a grand. A ridiculous profit, though, for a record which cost me nothing. It went to George Dragic, of New South Wales, Australia to whom I had already sold off some lesser items. George sent me a note after he bought the record: 'I have been after this LP for so long, so you can imagine how happy I was when you confirmed I can have it.' Hm. And you can probably imagine how bloody happy I am now that I sold it! Payment appeared in my bank account on 13 March 2006.

I have regretted that decision to this day, and when I started writing this book, I wrote to George, from whom I had never since heard, at his Aussie address, to ask him what had become of the record. Had he sold it on? Had he kept it and looked at it but not played it, for fear of affecting the value? Or was he happily playing a record he loved without any thought of its value?

George emailed me a few weeks later. This is his precise wording and spelling:

'I was pleasantly surprised to find your message last night. I also have to apologies to you not getting in touch earlier since i got your letter while ago but misplaced it and only come across few days ago stuck in between pages of Record Collector magazine. I still own all of the records i have purchase from you and i will never sell any of them. i don't play them as much as i used to in fact most of my playing time is in the car listening CD's or CD'Rs or at home u-tube or diskog I still regularly buy LP's from all over the world and occasionally trade with few dealers i know from the old days. Good like with you book sounds very interesting. Are you still selling some of your collection and do you have anything at the moment? Please let me know.

All the best from now.

George'

I was very pleased to hear he still owns *Breathe Awhile*. And somehow reassured to learn that although the record had gone halfway around the world it hadn't then been passed on like an unwanted pet and subjected to different homes which might not have appreciated it as much as both George and I did. He may not have enough time to devote to his hobby, but George is still thinking like a collector. Note how he closes by asking whether I had any other records I'd sell him!

It was fascinating to read about how George, originally, I think, from Serbia, got into record collecting, which appears to have been via a blade! He told me, again using his own spelling and wording:

'Don't actually remember what was firs LP I have bought but remember trading nice knife for double LP by Grand Funk "Live" US pressing all scratched but living in Belgrade in communist country did not have much choice. People use to travel and bring records from western Europe so I was able to get few gems at the time (Late '70's/'80's). Moving to Australia in '85 was another chapter in my collecting but never got serious till I come across first price guide and all those books about psych/prog '60's/'70's music and obscure bands like Arcadium itself (OZ pressing exist). Another moment was when I took box full of LP's to local record fair and got cleaned out in 5 minutes by dealers before door even open for the punters. Everyone was dumping record collection at the beginning of '90's but now vinyl is bigger then ever and with ever rising prices for primo collectables market is stronger then ever.

PS if you in Birmingham make sure you visit Psychotron records and say hello to Pete. Used to trade with him heavily and even got DARK and 1st COMPLEX from him 20 years ago.'

Pete at Psychotron subsequently told me he remembered George, adding that he was 'rather busy with a 5000 LP collection I just bought.

I shan't be repeating this tracking-down process for any of the other records I ill-advisedly sold. Hearing from George that he too has benefited by association with Arcadium represents closure for me and I have now almost come to terms with, and can just about live with, that fateful decision. The £380 George sent me is still in one of my bank accounts. I never did anything specific with it. I do still play the CD of the record. I even bought myself a new reissue of it, so that at least I have the cover to look at when listening, and even though it has suffered one of those fashionable remasterings, it is still a great piece of work – and the new issue also included a bonus single, on which there is a previously unissued demo of the album track, 'Poor Lady'.

I have even seen – and been sorely tempted by – genuine original copies of the LP offered for sale. But I know full well, if I bought another original copy, I still would not feel that I had my own record back. The only one which would really allow me to breathe awhile, and conclude that I was properly reunited with the record would be the one I sold in the first place to George. Nothing else can replace it in my heart of hearts. So, if, somehow, George, you ever happen to read this book and still have the record – I am willing to pay you £1000 to reclaim it.

Now, a change in atmosphere as I introduce you to the most influential second-hand record shop I ever frequented, where I bought not only Kaleidoscope's 'Faintly Blowing', but hundreds of lesser LPs...

IN WHICH... I FEEL SUTCH MELANCHOLY

'For me, a spotty teenager of 14 or 15, with a couple of quid from my car-washing crumpled in my jeans' pocket, the smell of both old and new records was the aroma of sheer pleasure and feverish expectation.' So wrote Martin Townsend, the editor of the *Sunday Express*, on 20 January 2013 in an article in which he reminisced about his favourite haunts as a youngster:

'Record shops... I can still see them, I can still hear them and I can definitely still smell them... the heady perfume of newly minted album releases, lovingly enfolded in sleeves printed almost always courtesy of Garrod & Lofthouse. In the second-hand record shops (Sellanby in Harrow and Eastcote, Beanos in Croydon, Reckless in Soho) it was the unique, musky whiff of rack upon rack of ageing cardboard, sometimes crushed into a shop the size of a corner grocer.'

I'm a little older than Martin, but any mention of 'Sellanby, (Discs & Tapes Bought & Sold)' which lasted until about 2008, sends me immediately back to the early days of my vinyl addiction. Most of my unwanted records ended up being sold to them (you will have noticed the 'sell and buy' pun) usually at their branch in Northolt Road, South Harrow.

Although their father had begun the Sellanby empire in the early 1960s when he opened under the local railway arches, buying and selling both records and books, the two sons, Dave and Pete Smith ran the larger shop. They were both a little older than me, and they employed a string of part-time staff, some of whom were an attraction for shoppers in their own right. When you took a record or two in to sell they were invariably disdainful of its condition and bona fides and estimated that they could just about manage to squeeze out a tiny amount of cash, usually at least 50 per cent less than you had hoped to get by even the most negative calculation. They would allow a slightly larger amount against purchases if you opted to recycle your allowance back into the business.

One of the brothers had a slight stammer, which worsened just at the point that he was making you an offer... 'I can give you f-f-f-f-f...

'A fiver?'

.........ifty pence.'

You reluctantly accepted the offer on the basis that you couldn't be arsed to take the objects away with you, and then gave them back everything they'd just given you by buying a couple of over-priced LPs which caught your eye. One of these would later prove to have a scratch on the very track which had persuaded you to buy it in the first place; the other you'd realise you didn't much like after all. When you returned to the shop next time you found all the things they'd bought from you last time up for sale for four or five times the amount you'd got. But it was a life lesson, and you didn't fall for it after the third or fourth time... and, to be honest, there were bargains galore to be had if you were selective with your purchases.

They also opened a satellite branch in Eastcote, under the tender stewardship of Symon Munford, the brothers' long-serving accomplice, and a knowledgeable and friendly man – until haggling time arrived, at which point he turned into a prototype Alan Sugar.

The original, spacious shop, was dominated by second-hand records initially. (I don't think the expressions 'pre-owned' or 'pre-loved' existed then, and I rather wish they didn't now.) Some space was given over to cassettes, but the vinyl capacity began to dwindle as CDs rose to prominence, while videotapes, and then DVDs appeared as well.

They sold comparatively few new albums – those that they did were usually affordably priced 'cut-outs' or deletions which came generally from the States – many of which I still have.

It was in Sellanby that I first felt a very real frisson of concern and guilt that I was regularly spending too much money on records. Even though I'd take some in to part-exchange I'd regularly walk out with half a dozen more, and it was not uncommon that I'd leave with two or three of their stylish yellow and black bags, bulging with, on one occasion, fifteen LPs. Those feelings are not unknown to me these days, but fortunately my wallet is better able to sustain the assault, even if I have to resort to sleight of hand or distraction tactics to smuggle them into the house.

I did eventually get to know the brothers well enough to chat to them on my visits. When I came to write my biography of the late David 'Screaming Lord' Sutch, rock'n'roller-turned-'politician', who lived literally just around the corner from Sellanby, they both stressed that whenever he came into the shop his main concern was to buy one of his own records if they had any in the place. Sutch was a compulsive hoarder.

David was publicity mad and whenever I was short of a story with press deadline looming a call to him would invariably produce a yarn with which to fill the gap. One afternoon in 1969 my phone in the *Weekly Post* office rang;

'Graham! Dave here. Grab a photographer and get down here. My house is on fire. It'll make a great picture story...'

'OK, David, but by the time we get there it'll be out.'

'It won't.'

'How come?'

'I haven't phoned the fire brigade yet – I've got a bucket of water here. I'll call them when you arrive and get the photos of me pouring water over the flames.'

We scrambled to Sudbury, and screeched to a halt outside his house, where smoke was emerging from the upper storey, anxious-looking neighbours were milling around outside, pointing upwards, and Sutch was standing with one foot on the ladder he had leaned up against the wall, holding the bucket of water.

'Right, let's get the photo then I'll ring the fire brigade.'

We got the photo. He got his publicity, and the house survived.

Sadly, David hanged himself in 1999 in his house just a couple of hundred yards from Sellanby. I'd stayed in touch with him –

in fact, had been in Wales with him two days earlier as he gave his final show, before taking his own life. The idea of writing his biography came to me on the day which turned out, although I didn't know it at the time, to be his birthday – 10 November in 2002. Someone I'd never met or spoken to pulled up in a car when I went looking for his grave – told me to get in her car, and took me straight to him.

When his pal, respected rock musician Alan Clayson, wrote and recorded a tribute song to David, 'The Last Show on Earth', I drove to his grave to play him the song on my car's CD player. I opened the car doors to allow the track to ring round the deserted graveyard. As it played, a single large, black bird flew on to a branch of the tallest tree overlooking David's burial place. It began chattering animatedly, until the song finished. The track died away... but immediately started up again... then again. No CD had ever done that before in my player. It kept repeating as I drove home and eventually I had to turn it off manually.

I made it my business to acquire as much of David's recorded output as I could. I still have the records, the first of which, 'Till The Following Night' came out on the HMV label in 1961. Its follow-up, 'Jack the Ripper', which would become his best-known and most controversial offering, appeared on Decca in 1963. Even 50 plus years ago that was a terribly poor taste song, and over the years performing it live resulted in all kinds of controversies, which David thoroughly enjoyed. Amazingly, Jack White played and recorded a version of the track on a White Stripes' album. He sent me a written tribute to Sutch for use on the cover of my book – and I arranged in return for him to receive one of Sutch's stage coffins.

In 1964, Sutch had launched his own pirate radio station, Radio Sutch, initially from a boat, the trawler, *Cornucopia*, and then from a disused Second World War anti-aircraft fort, Shivering Sands, in the Thames Estuary. The station jingle was 'For a little bit of Heaven tune to 197' and the first record to ring across the airwaves was, inevitably, 'Jack the Ripper'. As one of the station's DJs, Sutch would regularly play his own back catalogue and, in the dead of night, amuse himself by reading out horror stories, as well as *Fanny Hill* and *Lady Chatterley's Lover*.

David never enjoyed a conventional hit record, but his *Lord Sutch and Heavy Friends* album on the Atlantic label, released in 1970, despite being once named the worst album of all time, did actually become his only genuine chart LP, squeezing into all three versions of the US Top 100. It has seldom been unavailable since and can be found on all manner of different labels under a myriad different titles. The record features not only Sutch, but also his 'Heavy Friends' who include Jimmy Page, John Bonham, Jeff Beck, Noel Redding, and Nicky Hopkins. Page was credited with writing all or part of five tracks, although he would subsequently deny it, claiming he had been 'duped' as to what the album would be like. Any serious fan of rock music, Sutch, and/or Page should find a copy and make up their own mind. To my mind, David's best record was a 1966 single which has a touch of early psych about it, released on CBS and called 'The Cheat'. I recommend it.

When David died I acquired some of his personal possessions and amongst them was a cassette of never-released tracks, which I hope may still see the light of day, with the assistance of John Beecher at Rollercoaster Records, who has promised to include some of them on a future retrospective – and long overdue – Sutch compilation. Sutch was a fan of schlock horror records and similar Hammer Horror movies but even he never experienced a haunted record shop...

IN WHICH... I TAKE ON A HAUNTED LOOK

On Tuesday 21 November 2017, I heard my first ever ghost story about a record shop. I've always been fascinated by the paranormal. I even subscribe to *Fortean Times* magazine, which concerns itself purely with unusual and incredible events.

I was in Julian and Helen's Second Scene which I've already

mentioned. But what I haven't mentioned is that the building is haunted. I was standing in the upstairs room where the events occurred, having been invited to look at the massive store of albums Julian kept there. From neatly filed multiple copies of 'middle-of-the-road' discs by the likes of Perry Como and such crooners, to massed bundles of Beatles' *White Albums*, almost certainly filed in descending order of cover number, from classical desirables to jazz rarities. The wall-to-wall shelving was clearly just a few singles away from buckling under the strain of the huge weight.

Record shops, by their very nature, are full of the ghosts of deceased artist(e)s responsible for the music contained in the album grooves. They are reborn every time someone picks up, plays or discusses one of their records. They are all around you as you go through the shelves and racks. Julian was bemoaning the gradual diminution of available incoming stock, equating the downturn with the fact that there were now, he believed, 'over one million records being offered for sale at any time on eBay alone.' He was taking comfort that he had already reaped the harvest of recent years and thus had sufficient stocks of ever in-demand 'classics' from the likes of Zeppelin, Stones, Queen, Bowie and The Beatles, that he had once thought might be tricky to shift, but which now seemed to be the purchases of choice of youngsters introducing themselves to vinyl delights.

He'd invited me up to look at an item he had acquired – an original 1960s green dartboard bearing the name and image of The Beatles – together, importantly, as they completed the set, with a number of matching green darts which, he told me, had impressed London's respected Bonhams auction house to the tune of four figures when he'd sought a valuation.

'They said they'd occasionally seen the boards before – but never with the original darts. I could sell them tomorrow for a small fortune, but I quite enjoy impressing Beatles' collectors who think they've seen everything there is, when I show them this set. One woman who came in looking for Beatles LPs was so excited that she insisted on having her photograph taken with them!'

As we chatted on, I mentioned to Julian that I had put some of my records, books and other memorabilia into a forthcoming auction and delved into my pocket to show him the catalogue, only to bring out by mistake my latest copy of the earlier mentioned *Fortean Times*. When Julian saw the magazine, he pointed to it and told me: 'This place was the subject of a letter in that magazine some years ago – and what happened took place right where you're standing now.'

I shifted slightly and looked around.

'It happened when we were actually living upstairs above the shop. This was our living room, packed with records of course, and over there (pointing to a room whose door in the corner of the room was ajar) was our bedroom. I was in here, rather like today, showing off records to a friend, when there was a really loud, prolonged noise out of nowhere, which neither of us could account for. It definitely wasn't traffic noise – we are bang on a busy road here, so we hear that all the time – and it wasn't an aeroplane flying overhead. You recognise these sounds – it was neither. But it was *so* loud that it stopped us in our tracks, and I can only explain it by saying it was as though time had stood still – eventually, as things returned to normal, we looked at each other and could only ask, "What was that all about?"'

This hadn't been the first such incident for Julian, though. 'Helen and I were in bed one night when we both saw a green glow in one corner of the room where we had no light or lamp. There was nowhere it could be coming from. It spooked the pair of us. We just dived under the covers and didn't come out until morning.' There were more incidents, and Julian remembered that the previous occupant of the house had vacated the premises at very short notice, leaving behind personal possessions including a ouija board and other ephemera associated with contacting the dead.

Incredibly enough, I was soon to hear about another haunted record shop, which seems to exhibit virtually every ghostly trope in a horror author's armoury. Angela Collings started selling records 'or as we now seem to have to call it "vinyl"' over 30 years ago:

'I did a car boot sale to raise funds as a poor student and sold my Clash, Buzzcocks, Pistols collection. Something I instantly regretted. When I was later starting as an antique dealer I remembered how well records had sold and had a box at the front of the stall. Gradually they took over and I became a record/CD dealer. I quickly graduated to owning two shops in Nuneaton called Entertainment Exchange with 80,000 records in stock.

'We held the, er, record of being the only record store ever to have an armed robbery. They raided the tills and safe, but also stole from the wall an American Beatles Christmas fan club LP. I often wonder if it was done just for that.

'Record collectors are a strange bunch. I had the man who came in every day to sniff the vinyl. He never bought anything – he was addicted to the smell of new vinyl. The man who had been looking for a certain single for years. When I found it for him, he cried and said: 'What am I going to do now?' There was the man who came in once a week to play "The Ripper" by Judas Priest – and then left. And the Japanese record dealer who assumed my male manager owned the shop – I always made him tea and brought him his McDonald's – and let him think it.'

Angela now had two stores in Nuneaton:

'For nearly 20 years we were trading there as Entertainment Exchange, which myself and partner Dawn opened in 1994, and became the biggest music/gaming/film collectors' store in the West Midlands. They were housed in two buildings next door to each other. 60 Queens Road focused on the video games and movies, whilst 62 was the music and vinyl store. I've been incredibly lucky, I always seem to turn up good collections. The shop was dripping with rarities.'

But it contained some rarities not even the most dedicated collector wanted to discover. Here's Angela's haunting story:

'Both buildings were historic and atmospheric. 62, the music store, was mainly my responsibility. Some of the things I experienced here may seem to be the stuff of the movies or nightmares. Dawn and I made a success of Number 60, and expanded into 62 to turn it into a two-floor music store. We were due to open on a Monday so the Sunday before I spent upstairs in the shop pricing vinyl and laying out displays. Dawn dropped me off, locking me in, and promising to pick me up in four hours. I set to getting my store ready. The vinyl was mainly based on the second floor. I had boxes of new stuff I wanted to price. Off I went up the stairs with the company of a radio tuned to the chart show.

'I became engrossed in pricing. Suddenly, totally caught up in putting LPs in racks, I saw something in the corner of my eye near the old office. I caught the image of a small, dumpy woman dressed in black with dark hair up in a bun. I turned my head straight to the store room door and the image vanished. Absolutely shocked, I had seen something I could not explain and I had to stay locked in that building for another three hours in a state of suspended panic. The only thing that kept me sane was the radio. I refused to look up towards the store room again. When I heard Dawn knocking I switched the radio off and *ran* downstairs.

'I knew I would have to keep this to myself. We employed a lot of young staff, who I was worried could be quite impressionable. I did not want to tell Dawn because I knew she was more disturbed by anything supernatural than I was. I started to notice other weird things occurring – very mild at first. I would put items down and within minutes of turning back to pick them up they would not be in the same place. I noticed a smell in the mornings when I would open up, like old-fashioned pipe tobacco mixed with furniture polish. It would dissipate quickly but then sometimes appear again.

'Out of the corner of my eye I would occasionally catch the shape of somebody or something, turn my head quickly and there would be nobody, nothing there. This got to be extremely annoying and frequent. About three months after my first experience on that scary Sunday, I was travelling home in the car with Dawn when she suddenly asked me:

'"Have you ever experienced anything odd in the music shop?"
'"What do you mean by odd?"
'"Creepy, unexplained, ghostly?"
'There was no point in lying any more: "Tell me what you saw first before I say anything."

'Dawn told me that when painting the floorboards of the shop upstairs before it opened, she had seen in the very same place as I had, an image of a woman matching the same description as I had seen. I was both shocked and relieved. This verified what I had seen. I told her of my experience and from that point we swore to share anything that happened with each other, but not with the staff.

'One Friday night I was the last person out of the shop and made sure I had tidied a CD rack before I exited. I was first to enter the shop on Saturday morning – the rack was now half empty with the CDs thrown around the shop.

'Bit by bit the staff started to take me into their confidence and tell me about the things they had experienced. Many had encountered the figure in their peripheral vision, also noises were occurring upstairs. We heard footsteps on the upper floor after the shop was closed and lots of noise coming from the store room area.

'"Robert" came to work for me (I have changed his name) eventually staying for nearly 15 years and becoming the overall manager of both stores. It was now widely discussed by staff that there was something extremely strange going on at 62 Queens Road. Robert would have no truck with this. He laughed when anybody mentioned an odd happening, proclaiming himself an atheist and non-believer in anything that did not have a rational explanation. That did not last long.

'It started with Robert feeling somebody who was invisible push past him on one side of his body and then the other. Then he started to get the shape in his peripheral vision. It seemed to focus on him until one day Robert came down the stairs himself as white as a ghost. He told me he had seen an apparition of a male at the end of the upstairs floor that seemed to shimmer then disappear.

'The strange events increased almost at a daily rate. We had a top alarm system installed but it was continually going off at night and we had to drive back to the shop. Each time the panel would indicate that something upstairs had triggered the alarm. The most dramatic of these false alarms was on a New Year's Eve. I had not had a drop to drink. I started to join in the countdown to the New Year on the TV. At three seconds to midnight the home telephone rang: "Hello, Miss Collings, this is Warwickshire Police the alarm has gone off at your premises." We drove to the store. There was no reason for the alarm to have been triggered. It was something upstairs that had caused it. We received a warning letter from the police that our alarm was going to be unmonitored if this continued.

'Once I was working late with three other staff members, when we heard the sound of heavy running footsteps coming from upstairs. It sounded like about five or six people. We all froze. Rapidly running out of courage, I sent my staff up those stairs first. There was nobody there.

'I was the first up the stairs one morning on to the record floor and there on the record player was a 1970s photograph of a young girl's first Holy Communion. She had a bouquet of roses clutched to her that looked almost blood-like. 62 Queens Road was at one time a photography shop. We discovered the female figure that Dawn and I had both seen fitted the description of the lady who managed the shop for many years. What of the male figure Robert had seen? One morning I mounted the stairs up to the top floor. There in front of me, five years after Robert's experience, was the figure of a late-middle-aged man. This shimmering image disappeared before my eyes. I went downstairs, told Robert and we both laughed about it.

'Staff would continually come to me with stories. Some nearly 20 years after they left. I had a lot of very cool young people work in the shop. Teresa changed her hair on a daily basis. One day a pink Mohican, then a green skinhead. She told me one day that she had been eating her lunch in the staff kitchen when suddenly a man approached and stared right at her, very close up, looking in particular at her hair. Then he vanished. Not long after, Teresa left.

'A photographer for the local paper, a guy in his late fifties, once asked me, "Have you ever experienced anything strange in 62?" He told me he had learnt his craft at 62 when it was a photography shop and even then it had been haunted. Staff had refused to work after 6pm as they felt something was trying to get them out of the shop. He thought the answer lay in the archives of the *Nuneaton Tribune*. The shop was bombed in World War Two. Where the upstairs extension now was, there had been a shelter which received a direct hit and been obliterated.

'I got used to the weird stuff over time. We never once tried to publicise it. Having a ghost was not going to increase our sales. As downloads became king, our business changed. Mail order and eBay became far more important. This eventually meant that upstairs at Queens Road became a mail order floor. I was upstairs on the computers, listing. This could mean being locked in the shop until ten at night, making sure all the addresses were printed and all loose ends tied up. Often the metal shutters would be pulled down at the front and back for safety. Now, as I sat at the computer, the peripheral vision shapes escalated. The activity seemed to increase, the atmosphere seemed as thick as fog. I was looking for a particular address, and felt as if everything around me was shimmering. I had the feeling I could actually slip or disappear into another world or time-zone the air felt so thick. Dawn later told me she had experienced the same feeling upstairs. One night I was sitting working and playing an audio book set in the war. A siren sounded. The minute that siren sounded the atmosphere around me changed. I could hear in my ears, indistinguishable but very clear, whispering and the whispers became louder. I was terrified. I picked up my mobile and called Dawn: "Hurry up... just come and get me."

'I am not sure how I managed to tolerate a lot of what happened, other than we had to earn a certain amount of money so I just got my head down and carried on. 62 was on a lease. We finally handed the lease and the property back to the landlord. Things didn't end there. We were still based next door and could see who occupied 62. The first tenants did not last long after telling us they found the shop incredibly creepy. The next tenants put a manager in the store. Adi was working and staying until late at night.

'One day I asked him how he was. "Have you ever experienced anything strange in the shop?" I asked him. Suddenly, in what I can only describe as like something out of *The Stepford Wives* he turned to me and said. "There are six of them, they talk to me. Please don't tell anyone, please. Do you miss them? You can see them again if you want. You can talk to them again."

'"No thank you," I answered.

'I was shocked. After half an hour I went to my car. Adi ran out to me looking very disturbed. "Please do not tell anybody about what I have told you. They are really angry, Angela, they do not actually like you."

'I had never told Adi my name.'

Having left Number 62 behind, Angela, now thankfully ghost-free, concentrates on local markets, trading as Turntable Records:

'Since I've been back in the markets after selling my shop, and being in a new relationship back down south I've had some lovely stuff, including a 2000 LP blues collection. Which the man so wanted out of the house he put it all in the drive and left me with it in 90 degree heat. I was like a demon trying to get it out of the sun! I love being a record dealer. It's like being on a permanent treasure hunt. Being a woman has its benefits. You gain a lot of trust when people are selling which I always repay by being fair.'

Not quite in the same ballpark as these shop hauntings, but spooky enough, was the occasion when, during the sudden explosion of rock group interest in the occult, I gave a positive review to the first Black Widow album, *Sacrifice* in 1970. This was the year in which Black Sabbath and The Ghost both issued debut discs with 'spooky' covers. I was on good terms with a couple of guys who had started up the Farx Club in the basement of a pub in Southall.

They put on a Black Widow gig. Their LP included such toe-tapping ditties as 'Come to the Sabbat', 'Attack of the Demon' and title track, 'Sacrifice'. This was a time when 'Carry On' and 'Hammer Horror' films were popular, as were Dennis Wheatley's black-magic themed books. I figured this was a gig not to be missed. I even invited along my girlfriend, Sheila. It was only a small room, and it could get pretty packed, with the obvious result that the temperature would soar.

Come the night, and Black Widow were in full flow. The joint was rocking, the heat was rising. 'I conjure thee, appear, I raise thee mighty demon,' roared vocalist Kip Trevor as they performed 'In Ancient Days'. 'Read the tales and spells that turned the whole world upside down – the Four of the Apocalypse on horseback ever wait,' he warned wailingly in 'The Way to Power'.

We'd taken up a front-of-stage position. The crowd was pushing forward, better to see the action, as the band called out to the dark side, playing 'Come to the Sabbat'. Trevor threw himself wholeheartedly into character as guitars, keyboards, drums and brass pounded out the beat... 'Who dares to help me raise the one, whose very name near stills my heart? ASTAROTH!... join me in my search for power, we'll be as one within the hour... Come, come, come to the Sabbat. Come to the Sabbat... SATAN'S THERE!'

There we were, in a hot, sweaty press of bodies clustering as close to the stage action as possible, preparing to witness a human sacrifice... at which moment Sheila decided to faint clean away, and slump to the floor as dramatically as the victim of Satan, just inches away from her. As Sheila slowly crumpled to the ground – there was barely room to stand on your own two feet, let alone collapse – I realised she'd have to be dragged up, lifted as high as possible, and passed back over the shoulders and heads of the assembled multitude, otherwise there might be a real-life fatality stretched out on the stage.

In those days when micro-mini dresses were Sheila's favourite mode of attire, this involved a slight loss of dignity, but she was eventually helped to safety, revived in the cold night air, and survived to tell the tale – unlike the band victim, who was duly dispatched to the arms of the anti-Christ.

It may have been the title, *When You're Dead*, which caused me to give a record I was sent to review back in 1970 a little more attention than most of the run-of-the-mill releases by unknown bands. It was by The Ghost, on the obscure Gemini label LP, featuring a striking front cover image, showing the five-strong group superimposed, wraith-like, over and around an imposing gravestone in a misty atmosphere. Every track of the record, declares Carl Denker, writer of the sleeve notes 'is immersed in ghosts'. This is a terrific record, with or without ghosts. It is very good rock, flirting with prog and psych, but with the standout element the soaring voice of Shirley Kent. I gave their debut single 'When You're Dead' such a rave review in my column of 10 June 1970 that the record company used it as a press release to promote the forthcoming album.

When it comes to the ultimate ghostly records, Jason Leach should have the final word. John Hobson met musician and music producer Jason at a pub in Scarborough in 2007, several years after his mother's death. They discussed taking recordings John had of his mum, Madge's voice and somehow combining them and her ashes into a unique vinyl record, as a memento of her life. Jason turned this initially macabre idea into actuality, and thus, from death, his company And Vinyly was born (contact address: theundertaker@andvinyly.com). His first male subject was a French man, whose wife commissioned the job. Leach's service steadily grew as his discs containing ashes and voice recordings of the deceased, began to attract attention.

Dead easy?

I don't believe any of the record shops involved in Record Store Day are haunted... other than by those enticed to buy specially created 'collectors' items' which rarely turn out to be other than cynical cash-ins.

IN WHICH... I EXPRESS MY DISDAIN FOR RECORD STORE DAY

Count the ways in which I am completely indifferent, if not occasionally hostile, to Record Store Day...

For starters, why isn't it called 'Record Shop Day' in the UK? That's how such establishments are generally described here. BBC 6 Music presenter Stuart Maconie agrees. Writing about the event, he declared, 'Record Shop Day, as I insist we over here should call it.'

This is how a record shop of my acquaintance in Essex endeavoured to enthuse potential shoppers on Friday 12 April 2019 – the day before that year's Record Store Day took place:

'All releases are first come first served

You can buy as many different releases as you like, but only one of each

We'll be taking a list of the first 10 in the queue and bagging it up ready for 8am opening

10 people will be allowed in at a time until the queue dies down

There will likely be queues, so please be respectful of others

We open at 8am and will be closing at 6pm

We don't have loads of staff, so bear with us, especially in the first few hours, we're doing our best

Enjoy yourself, this is supposed to be fun!'

'Fun!'? Seriously? I can't think of anything less likely to encourage me to visit that shop on that particular day. It is as though record collecting is being turned into a sport, with rules to ensure that everyone behaves properly, does what they are told, when they are told and how they are told.

Alerted by spurious 'special offers', 'limited edition releases', 'expanded versions', 'remastered rereleases radically reimagined' and other heavily advertised and promoted pointless purchases, once-a-year vinyl enthusiasts, and those buying to sell, are drawn like dust to a stylus into a shop they haven't visited for 364 days since the last time they pitched up. There they are told by the frustrated and harassed guy behind the counter that, 'they only let us have one of them; the others didn't arrive as promised, but we do have a limited white vinyl ten-inch of Gary Glitter's *Greatest Hits* which is bound to increase in value, er... when he finally gets his official pardon.'

Declares the event's official website:

'Record Store Day was conceived in 2007 at a gathering of independent record store owners and employees as a way to celebrate and spread the word about the unique culture surrounding nearly 1400 independently owned record stores in the US and thousands of similar stores internationally. Today there are Record Store Day participating stores on every continent except Antarctica.'

What does RSD have against Antarctica? And how do I make sure I am there on the relevant Saturday in April?

The official website has more:

'This is a day for the people who make up the world of the record store – the staff, the customers, and the artists – to come together and celebrate the unique culture of a record store and the special role these independently owned stores play in their communities.'

Ah, I see. Nothing whatsoever to do with rampant commercialism, or corporate greed, then. The site is then unable to resist mentioning:

'Special vinyl and CD releases and various promotional products are made exclusively for the day. Festivities include performances, cook-outs, body painting, meet & greets with artists, parades, DJs spinning records, and on and on.'

I don't know about you, but these are the very things which I have always wanted to be absent from record shops.

I ran some of my doubts past the very helpful Megan Page, who handles media queries for RSD. She confirmed that the whole promotion began as 'Store' rather than 'Shop' and that is how it will remain.

'The aim of the Day is to encourage new people through the doors into record stores, usually young people who have never experienced them before. It is a really good way of recruiting new enthusiasts. The Day is partly about encouraging the new generation of record buyers, partly about reminding those already connected to vinyl.'

Megan accepted that the emphasis of the day is much more about 'celebrating, and keeping new music going', and aimed towards shops stocking the latest releases rather than those specialising in the second-hand market.

This is fine by me, as, ultimately, nearly all new vinyl will eventually become second-hand vinyl, and new vinyl buyers are the keepers/collectors of the future

When I discussed the 2019 RSD with my old pal Graham Jones, author of the excellent *Last Shop Standing*, and its recent follow-up *The Vinyl Revival*, I disagreed with his suggestion that 'within a week of RSD only around 2 per cent (of RSD "special issues") will be listed to sell. Pity these greedy flippers spoil it for true music fans.'

I responded: 'Two per cent? Where's that stat from? Suspect it is rather higher than that. And to judge from most record shop stocks during the rest of year, another significant percentage doesn't get sold at all – at least until it is drastically reduced!'

Graham told me that his stat had come from RSD, but added: 'You can do as much as you can to try and stop it but you will still get greedy sods denying true fans. Certainly a lot of RSD vinyl devalues quite quickly. I try to concentrate on promoting the shops and the Day as opposed to the product.'

John McCready of Manchester's Kingbee Records tweeted his take on RSD 2019:

'You won't find 50 quid mauve vinyl Bananarama box sets at Kingbee records as they don't do RSD. Every day is record store day at the best shop in the world. Maybe when you've finished fighting over Police 45s you could bob in and see what some of us do 365 days a year!'

To which I could only add 'Hear, hear'...

For RSD 2018, *The Guardian* took it upon itself to treat its readers to an article about the paper's 'record store crawls' around four UK cities. Off they went, to London, Bristol, Manchester and Glasgow. In London they chose Low Company in Hackney, but, 'not only is it not participating in RSD, it had considered not even opening on the day as it's the business's first birthday the day before and they'll all be hungover.' At Rye Wax in Peckham *The Guardian* talked to 'owner Tom', and learned, 'they're bypassing RSD releases and instead cutting their own single-copy dubplates.' Whatever they may be.

In Bristol's Idle Hands, *The Guardian* spoke to Chris Farrell, discovering that, 'RSD doesn't make much of a difference to the shop in terms of sales' and can also adversely affect the arrival of new stock 'in the weeks leading up to it' because 'all the pressing plants are booked up with limited edition novelty items such as translucent green vinyl Doctor Who soundtracks.' Glasgow's Rubadub told *The Guardian* they don't take part in RSD, and local label owner-cum-DJ, Dan Lurinsky, who works there, confides, 'I think most people feel it's all got a bit commercial.'

Another London shop mentioned in the article is Rat Records in Camberwell, on whose website, the following appeared:

'RSD has outlived its purpose, and the fact it has been hijacked by labels keen to get max dollar for Bee Gees B-sides and the new "Star Wars" soundtrack is so well known the music press are mostly too bored to talk about it.'

And that was written back in 2016.

I admit I do take advantage of/exploit RSD – by the simple expedient of ignoring every gimmick/special/limited record they produce – for the best part of a year, then making a point of visiting shops which I know support and promote RSD to check out which of those specials they are now flogging off at a vastly reduced price.

BBC 5 Live's morning programme, with Chris Warburton reporting on 2018 RSD and the queues outside shops in Letchworth and Hackney, saw the presenter musing:

'There seems to be a feeling that it (RSD) has been taken over by punters looking to make a quick buck.'

He was talking about how big a percentage of queuers were doing so to buy a record, whose seal would quite possibly never be broken and would very quickly find itself for sale at a mark-up. In this respect it would be no different from the instant and hugely marked-up relisting of tickets for big gigs and events, of course. But I suspect that only a small percentage of RSD 'rarities' appeal enough for buyers to want to pay through the nose for them, and those scalpers speculating on buying to make a future profit may have to wait a considerable time to do so.

An intriguing and welcome passing comment came from a *Guardian* interviewee from Manchester, 37-year-old Henrietta Smith-Rolla:

'I think record shops have got kinder. There's been a change in how women are looked at and observed. There's no surprise when a woman walks in to buy a Detroit techno record. I would get nervous going into shops when I was younger, but things have become more welcoming.'

On Record Store Day 2018, I headed for Sound of the Suburbs in Ruislip Manor. I didn't take to this shop that easily when it first opened but it is on my way to Wealdstone FC's ground, a semi-pro team in the National League I support, and I now show my face there frequently. I found the gent in charge being happily hassled by a couple of acquaintances enjoying ska music and attempting to sell him some sounds of their own. Someone else came in and enquired about RSD. 'I'm not involved with that. I have nothing to do with it and it doesn't make any difference to me,' he explained.

Initially I found his stock wasn't changing that often and if I was going to buy something it would be one of the reasonably priced and nicely different selection of CDs. Thus it was again today – although I must admit he finally seems to have found a source of interesting new vinyl reissues of 1960s and early 1970s obscurities, just the type of stuff to appeal to me. But I note he is pricing them at the top end of where they should be, so flip through the CDs, and come across a double set from a group I've been looking to buy into for a while. The CD is entitled AMMO – the group members are Chris Arnold (A), David Martin (M), and Geoff Morrow (MO). They also recorded from the mid-1960s to the early 1970s as Butterscotch, Moonlighters and Sky & Company – all to good, tuneful effect. Here were 40 tracks for a fiver in the shape of a promo copy of a double CD and booklet combo, including their best-known track, 'Don't You Know'. And you *would* know it if you heard it, I'm sure. I also selected a ridiculously cheap, sealed double CD of 59 tracks of Rolling Stones' early live material, *The Complete British Radio Broadcasts 1963-65*, taken from such programmes as *Saturday Club, The Joe Loss Pop Show, Top Gear* and *Big Beat* for just seven quid. It beats their recent *Blue & Lonesome* into a proverbial cocked nut-cover.

Over the next few days we visit Brighton, and in Vinyl Revolution I am welcomed by a female member of staff who asks 'Is this your first visit to the shop?' I tell her no, and she asks whether I'd been to a shop for Record Store Day.

'I might have done had it been Record *Shop* Day – who calls a record shop a record store in this country?'

She laughs and says, 'Well, yes, it is an American invention – but we had a great day. They were queuing outside at 3am.'

'Are you sure it wasn't a few stragglers coming out of clubs, looking for somewhere to sit?'

'No, they were all there for what they wanted and most of them were able to get that. There was a lovely moment when a guy bought the last Bowie Live LP we had. The woman behind him was almost in tears as she'd wanted one to give her husband for his birthday. When he heard that the guy just turned round and handed it to her – didn't even want paying. It was a lovely gesture.'

Even cynical old me can't argue against that!

'Then there were the four- and six-year-old sisters with their dad. The four-year-old "bought" the White Room's record after seeing them playing here on RSD – so that's the next generation of record lovers coming through.'

OK, I was now weakening somewhat and admitting that perhaps RSD had a little something to recommend it after all. So I did the gentlemanly thing and bought a record for a tenner – one I'd wondered about for a while – Naz Nomad and the Nightmares' 1984 LP – a purple vinyl copy. Naz etc was a cover for members of The Damned, including Messrs Vanian and Scabies, and the record something of a tribute by them to the early days of psychedelia.

Perhaps the marketing and PR for RSD does have an effect and stimulate general interest and sales. Steve Burniston, of Glasgow's Love Music shop told *Record Collector* in May 2019 that 'without the annual sales boost from RSD we would struggle to keep the doors open.' A few weeks after RSD I buy something in a record shop and am given my purchase in a white, plastic Record Store Day UK bag. It is adorned with the names of the official sponsors of the Day: Rega, the turntable manufacturers, and Sound Performance, who specialise in 'CD and DVD replication' and 'vinyl manufacturing'. Fair enough, I understand why they'd want to support RSD. But the other two official sponsors listed on the bag are Fred Perry – whose clothes, I accept, are identified with musical culture– and Friels vintage cider.

I wrote to both of these companies, asking why they became involved with RSD UK, sending my request via their official website 'contact' sections. It took a month to receive a reply from Dominique Fenn, a 'Brand Reporter' at Fred Perry:

'Sorry it's taken so long to get back to you!

We're really proud to support Record Store Day which we've done for a couple of years.

We share the same spirit of independence, and of course music is core to the Fred Perry brand with many of our customers being musicians and vinyl collectors! We've also profiled independent record shop owners (on the company website) to give them a platform too.'

Dominique also offered to feature this book on the FP website. Friels never replied.

IN WHICH... WE GO KIWI

My son and his family live in a small but historic New Zealand town called Petone, just outside of the capital, Wellington. It is where horses were first raced in this beautiful land, on the beach, which still looks much as it would have done back in the day, as, wisely, virtually no commercialism of the seafront is permitted. In several visits to Petone's Lo Cost second-hand record shop, which increasingly stocks new ones as well, I have acquired – admittedly after lengthy, dogged delving as this is not the best laid out of shops I've been in – such hidden gems as Mother Earth's *Living With The Animals* from 1968 (£25 in *Rare Record Price Guide*); Plainsong's *In Search of Amelia Earhart* (1972, £25); and Asylum Choir II from 1969, which features one of my offbeat favourites, Leon Russell.

During my 2019 visit I found LPs by Keith Christmas, whose work I knew, as well as The Motions, a Dutch group of the late 1960s, and Jake Jones, a group which I didn't know at all. The three came to a total of 80 dollars (a dollar was worth about 56 pence at the time) so I decided to try for a discount.

'Well, I'm already offering cheap prices, said the shop owner, who, minutes earlier had been slumbering in a chair despite the reggae music blaring out, as I entered his premises.

'But I've come 12,000 miles to get here – and travelling that far *isn't* cheap.'

'I suppose I could give you 10 off – 70 for the three.'

I gave him what I hoped was a steely gaze: '65?'

'Go on, then.' He almost smiled. 'So, you're on a visit – do you want a bag for them?'

'Thanks.' I handed him a 100 dollar note.

'Hey, you've got plenty of money... '

He *did* smile when he said that, but added:

'Had a guy in recently who bought a few records, so I asked if he wanted a bag as it was raining outside and he had to reach his car without getting the records wet. He accepted, and nipped off in the rain. Once he'd gone, another customer – in his 40s, I'd say – came over to the counter, glared at me and said, almost spitting it out, "It's people like you with your plastic bags who have fucked the world", then walked straight out of the door.'

'Should have told him you protect the environment by making sure thousands of vinyl records aren't just dumped into landfill.'

Wonderland is another New Zealand establishment, with erratic opening hours – and even more erratic in-store behaviour. Probably – no, definitely – the most untidy and disorganised shop I've ever come across. It is not that far from Petone, in the suburb of Wainuiomata, but it is always a gamble whether the eccentric chap who runs it – apparently the brother of the only marginally eccentric Lo-Cost owner – has bothered to open that day. The first clues to its modus operandi can be gathered from its website, which quirkily declares that it has 'been in the business of selling records since 1994... built up a large range of titles by a vast array of artists as diverse as Barbara (sic) Streisand; Elvis; Metalica (sic); Nina & Fredick (sic) and Joan Sutherland.' Elsewhere on the site 'Gerry and the Placemakers' get a mention.

Even if you've found the shop open – I have an under 50 per cent record of doing so – got in, made your way around the toppling, towering, scattered, dumped, piled-up heaps of thousands of records, tapes, CDs, DVDs, left higgledy-piggledy all over the shop, with no apparent rhyme nor reason to what is where, finding something is tricky, and buying it extremely difficult, frequently impossible. Requests to the friendly enough gent behind the desk, who is quite hefty and of advancing years – what some might refer to these days as a 'large unit' – usually elicits the confident confirmation that, 'Yes, we've got that'. A gentle hint that more information might be necessary to manage to find the record in question, however, produces scant encouragement vis-a-vis specific directions to its location.

On my first visit to the shop, back in 2014, I tried to buy OK Ken? by Chicken Shack. There was no price on it. When I asked how much it was, back came vague murmurings along the lines of 'I'm not really sure I want to sell it, but if I did, I'm not sure you'd want to pay that much.' 'Try me' produced nothing more concrete than 'It's a great record.' When I persisted, again enquiring as to the price, I was gently told I probably wouldn't be able to afford it. I suggested that perhaps I could – if only he would tell me what the asking price was. 'Well, I don't know, maybe 80 bucks.'

'Maybe?'

'Yes, why don't you look around to see what else you might like?'

'But I like this one.'

'Really, the records in the shop are here so that I can sell them online.'

I rather thought this must be a unique experience. After all, why run a shop and not even try to sell the records? He did eventually, reluctantly, let me buy a Chicken Shack LP – not the OK Ken? I wanted but a lesser, later title which featured just Stan Webb from the early line-up, and which, to be honest I shouldn't have bothered with.

In 2019 my first trip out to the shop proved fruitless. Shut. My son rang one afternoon to ask whether the shop would open at all that day. He was told it would be open until 9pm as the owner was in the shop cataloguing titles for the website. A little sceptical, three of us drove out to the shop at about 7.30pm.

'I stayed open for you three guys from England,' he greeted us.

Little had changed. All enquiries about buying records were countered with: 'That's about 40 bucks, that one's about 80 bucks', seemingly the only two prices he bothered to use – the equivalent at the time of around about £22.50 or £45. Most were shabby, scuffed, creased copies. He was, though, enjoying our company. Welcoming and chatty. We talked about the likes of Frank Zappa, Edgar Broughton, Human Instinct and many more. 'I'm really enjoying listening to you knowledgeable Brits,' he told us.

He recounted an odd personal encounter with Jimmy Page. 'He was once about 6ft 2ins tall,' he claimed, adding that the Led Zep axeman had since mysteriously shrunk by several inches as the result of a back problem. He may have been right. A check on Google brought up the stat that Page is 5ft 11ins tall but didn't reveal whether, and, if so, how, he had recently lost three inches.

The shop had been open for some years, the owner told us. 'I primarily trade online so don't need to price up the records in-store. For one thing, putting prices on the covers can damage them.' I wondered how you'd notice in most instances. During this visit I was not remotely surprised to note that the copy of OK Ken? I'd tried to buy on the previous visit, was still present and correct – in a box, on the floor, with no price on it. I didn't bother asking whether he'd be willing to part with it now. We left him at about 9pm, still animatedly chatting to us. He had allowed us to buy only a 20 dollar DVD of Megadeth, which my son's heavy metal pal, Simon, purchased. We shook hands and he waved us off happily. Once back home I endeavoured to buy something via his website, one of the most difficult to navigate I've ever come across. I failed dismally. So, that's Wonderland – difficult to get to, difficult to look around, difficult to buy from, but a great experience!

Part of the enjoyment of the whole experience of acquiring records for many of us has been and always will be the physical effort involved in getting to the place where you are going to carry out that transaction. However, my 'I've come 12,000 miles' schtick failed dismally in Mint Music in the Wellington suburb of Upper Hutt, which I visited to buy a Forever More LP, Yours, that I'd spotted on their website for a tempting 16 Kiwi bucks. The chap behind the counter just stared at me with an unchanging, unimpressed countenance:

'I've sold it.'

'So why is it still up on your website?'

No response. Just a come-on, I reckoned.

Instead, I bought a 1973 Scaffold LP, *Fresh Liver*, (£20), for 16 dollars. Well, it did have Zoot Money, Neil Innes and Pete Halsall on it. The Forever More LP was still being advertised on his website when I left the country after a couple of weeks. On a later trip I bought two LPs here and asked for a bag to put them in: 'Unfortunately, I don't have a bag... of that size.' Er, what OTHER size would you need in a record shop?

I didn't get off on the right foot with *Death Ray Records* in Newtown, a Wellington suburb. It's not a huge shop, apparently always teetering on the verge of bankruptcy, and it was probably ill-advised of me to try for a discount on my first visit. However, we made up on subsequent jaunts. A place with a vibrant atmosphere, enough new cutting-edge material to suit my eldest son, and enough elderly stuff to keep me quiet for a while. I bought competitively priced vinyl reissues of obscure US and Kiwi bands from here. During my 2019 visit I noticed the probably unique message on the door: 'Shop closes most midweek days between 2.55 – 3.10pm for school pick-up. Sorry for messing you around.' I'd arrived at 2.52pm, so I had three minutes of browsing before being slung out.

'But I've come 12,000 miles.'

'Sorry, bro.'

I couldn't hold a grudge, and returned a week later. This time I was able to browse contentedly until I found four records to buy. When I took them to the counter, 'Boss Dude' as I later discovered he was known, told me that he didn't supply bags for purchases. His website elaborates: 'Do the right thing, please bring your own bag – help save the world. Reduce and reuse.' Fine sentiments, which don't quite explain why he put each of my records in a new plastic cover before handing them to me. Well, which of us is entirely consistent in our beliefs?

However, spotting that I'd bought a reissue of a 1971 self-titled Kiwi psych album by Space Farm, described as 'one of the rarest psychedelic blues LPs from NZ', Boss Dude told me:

'Originals of this are hugely expensive, I found one once and paid a *lot* of money for it. But when I looked closely there was a small, round hole in the front cover which had not only gone through the cover but also right through the vinyl itself, affecting at least one of the tracks on each side. I complained to the seller, but it was a case of buyer beware – a tough lesson to learn.'

I enjoyed my time in this wonderfully right-on shop, in whose window I saw as I departed, another message:

'If Death Ray is closed during the opening times below, go to the shop Facebook page – Boss Dude posts up any shit regarding closure.'

In Napier, an atmospheric, art-deco NZ seaside town, lives Just For The Record, a joint vinyl/audio equipment shop with an excellent stock, not that many of them at bargain prices, though. I have bought plenty from here, despite the well-meaning, if a little pushy, boss.

Another Kiwi vinyl memory occurred in Martinborough – where we visited a little touristy gift shop and got talking with the owner who, it transpired, used to live in the same town in the UK as my wife and I. Further chat revealed that he too was something of a record collector – and a musician as well. A guitarist. We began talking favourite albums and the Zombies' 1968 LP masterpiece *Odessey and Oracle* was mentioned. 'I have a claim to fame as a result of that record,' he told me. 'I knew Chris White from the band and one day I loaned him my guitar while he was writing tracks for *Odessey*. Not only did he write the song 'Friends Of Mine' on that guitar, but he included in it the names of various pairs of married friends of his – and my wife and I were duly immortalised as a result.' Inevitably, the sting in his tale was that he and his wife are no longer together.

New Zealand's capital, Wellington, boasts a couple of splendid record shops, in one of the city's best known thoroughfares, Cuba Street. I was browsing through Slow Boat's huge stock, which covers virtually every area of vinyl and CD, ancient and modern, when I heard what sounded very much like a familiar voice, singing an unfamiliar song. It was Tony Joe White. I own almost all of his recorded output. This was his 2016 album, *Rain Crow*, which had somehow escaped my notice up to that point, so I snapped up the CD version in the absence of a vinyl one, to take home as a musical souvenir.

One of the quirkiest record shops I've been fortunate enough to frequent, the tiny Vanishing Point, just up the road from Slow Boat, had lived up to its name and, sadly, disappeared, leaving me thinking back to its friendly, if somewhat battered, proprietor and his small but always interestingly eccentric stock of offbeat records. I'd found Edwards Hand's second LP from 1970, *Stranded*, there, which was produced by George Martin and boasted cover art – a black and white drawing of a US sheriff's rotund stomach – by Klaus Voorman, designer of the cover of The Beatles' album *Revolver*.

Back in the UK I decided to listen to the Tony Joe White CD to bring back a few memories of killing time in Slow Boat. Unfortunately, when I opened the CD's sealed cover there was no CD inside. I was not best pleased. Couldn't really pop back to complain, could I? But modern technology does have its occasional benefits, so I emailed the shop, and was thoroughly impressed to receive a message back very quickly: 'What a coincidence – we've just discovered that we have a CD of Tony Joe White's new album – but with no cover!' They posted the CD to me, despite the postage probably costing more than the CD did originally.

I've also since bought original Yardbirds and Barry Ryan LPs there, and a slew of CDs featuring great Kiwi bands from the 1960s, but pride of place for me of the purchases I've made here goes to the oddly named Dutch band, Cuby + Blizzards' 1969 little-known blues-rock classic, *Appleknockers Flophouse*. Sample lyric:

'Appleknockers flophouse that's where we live in
Such a good place for you and for me
If you come to our Appleknockers flophouse
You don't know what you're bound to see'

Slow Boat, which I understand is a favourite haunt of Martin Freeman and Noel Gallagher when they're in town, is not the only record shop in Cuba Street. A few doors down is Rough Peel where I found a bargain price, good quality original 1973 Derek & The Dominos *In Concert* double album, as well as a pretty poor quality bootleg featuring the Stones and The Who.

Just over the 'ditch' from New Zealand is an odd island where most of the inhabitants cluster nervously around the edge of the place, seldom venturing towards the middle. The locals call it Oz...

IN WHICH... OZ IS WIZARD

Down under in Australia I've visited record shops in Perth, its Swan River neighbour Fremantle (some wonderful ones there), Sydney, Melbourne, Brisbane, and, most recently, the Blue Mountains, where LPs also abound in various antique shops, jostling for space with the usual old furniture, vintage clothes and pieces of pottery. Here, I found two terrific authentic examples of the record shop. In Katoomba lives the Velvet Fog shop whose name reminded me immediately of the late 1960s British psych band of similar title (although it had an extra 't' and 'g') which once boasted Black Sabbath's Tony Iommi in its ranks. Wondering about that, I quizzed shop guv'nor, Paul, and he told me:

'The first location of the shop looked straight out over the mountains, and the late summer skies were often a dripping purple curtain of clouds – hence the appropriateness of the name. I was aware of the UK band. I actually owned the album – but unbeknownst to me at that time, they had added the extra 't' and 'g' to their name so that they were not confused with (or in danger of being sued by) the great jazz singer Mel Torme – who was commonly referred to as "The Velvet Fog".'

Now, *that* is the type of charming and fascinating story which illustrates why I love record collecting so much. I was also fortunate enough to see that exact kind of weather phenomenon there.

This excellently stocked place had so much of the music I love at such reasonable prices that I had at one time a dozen or more records in front of me, only for my better half to remind me that I'd already acquired stacks of the things elsewhere on our trip and that we really only had the space to take a few more home. So it was back into the racks for the likes of Writing on the Wall, Dana Gillespie, Bakerloo and others while I opted to purchase Bram Stoker, Beggars Opera, Wild Turkey and - a real find, this - Circus Maximus.

I took my haul over to the counter and wondered whether a discount might be out of the question.

'Ah, yeah, mate, I'll do ya ten per cent'.

He looked at my choices, a look of mock horror on his face:

'Jeez, you've chosen all good'uns.'

He then told me that his colleague in the shop was a great aficionado of Aussie 1960s psych, of which they had a load stashed away that he'd be happy to show me when he came back in a few days' time, but by that time (damn it!) I would be heading back to Heathrow. I departed, so impressed by my purchases that I had to return ten minutes later to find my glasses, which I'd left perched on one of the racks.

The next shop was in nearby Blackheath, and called Hat Hill Gallery which doubles up as an art gallery. I was with my childhood pal John Maule whom I've been trying to encourage - unsuccessfully - to revert to the vinyl he used to love and own. As we walked up to the shop he stopped in his tracks and pointed - I was sure I spotted the glimmer of a tear in his eye - at the sparkling copy of Cream's *Disraeli Gears* in the window.

When we entered the premises the counter lady was carefully placing a record on the instore sound system - and out boomed the opening strains of the Moody Blues' LP, *Seventh Sojourn* and, blow me down (under), John was singing along. 'I used to have this, no idea what happened to it,' he breathed. I thought this might be the opportunity to draw him back into the tempting clutches of his former vinyl mistress. Sadly, he has hardened over the years and now appears immune to her attractions. But I wasn't, and soon noticed a display cabinet, whose top row boasted five LPs, one of which I immediately decided I was going to buy, two of which I already owned and two of which I had no interest in. I tried a small social experiment by telling my wife that I intended to buy one of these five records and inviting her to use all her knowledge of my tastes and likes to guess which one it would be. She got it spot on... at the fifth attempt.

It was The Monkees' *Head* which had been on my wish list for some while but which I hadn't previously found attractively enough priced. I thought that would be it and that my work in the shop was done. Until I noticed amongst a desirable but very pricey display of box sets all getting on for 200 Aussie dollars, a four-LP package of Kate Bush live tracks from her 2014 tour in a very fetching blue box, including a colour booklet. It was still sealed and clearly had been mispriced, with a sticker quoting 55 dollars – barely 30 quid at the going exchange rate. Clearly the price should have been *155* dollars. Well, I thought, if I take it to the counter, they will quickly confirm what the price should be and I'll put it back and we'll be off to find a cafe for refreshments.

'No, it *is* 55 dollars,' said the lady.

'I'll have it.' And I did.

Oh, and as we headed for elevenses, I realised I'd left my glasses behind again. I've done this in many countries...

IN WHICH... I'M HUNGARY FOR VINYL

Staying at a swanky hotel in Budapest in 2015, the plan was to experience one of Hungary's most important race meetings of the year, but I was equally interested in seeing some of the capital's most important record shops. No guide book seemed to have much to say about such an important part of the local cultural scene. So, how to find out? Plucking up my courage I decided to ask one of the impeccably attired, stuffy-looking reception staff whether they could help.

I sidled up to one of the elderly gents manning the desk, currently writing in a ledger. He looked me up and down, and asked slowly, emphasising the second word he spoke somewhat doubtfully, I felt:

'Yes... sir?'

'This may sound a little odd, but I was wondering whether you might be able to advise me as to the whereabouts of any vinyl record shops in the city? Please. Sorry.'

More looking me up and down. Probably thinking I'd wanted to ask about brothels but had lost my nerve.

'No, sir. I do not have any idea where such establishments may be located...'

'Oh, I'm sorry for bothering you.' I began to slink away, shamefaced, embarrassed for asking such a question.

'... but, sir, my colleague here is a very keen record collector himself and I am sure he will be only too happy to assist you when he finishes his telephone call.'

Never judge a book - or hotel concierge - by its cover. Sure enough, the colleague was only too pleased to show off his knowledge, quickly picking up a map and marking off several locations for me.

Needing no further invitation, I strode off into the 90+ degree (Fahrenheit. I don't do Centigrade) heat of the afternoon to look for the three shops highlighted on my map.

I soon found one of them - there it was, just past a bar that opened on to the pavement where a man was sitting who, as I passed, raised his hat, looked at the one I was wearing, and greeted me with:

'Hello, Mr Sherlock Holmes!'

Baffling. I was wearing a trilby.

Nonetheless, I managed to investigate what turned out to be a very well-stocked shop, with rows of shelves neatly laid out, albeit as you might expect, mainly containing foreign issues of records. It was called, I believe, Laci Bacsi Lemezboltja and I was surprised not to meet any Watford supporters inside – the interior was so very yellow. I found a Jackie Lomax album to add to my increasing collection of same, and it set me back the best part of 20 euros. Annoyingly, I resisted snapping up a Chris Farlowe record which I didn't recognise, and which seemed a little on the pricey side. I would later identify it as the scarce *From Here to Mama Rosa*, made with The Hill, which goes for £60 in top condition.

When, next, we arrived in Berlin, with little to do other than sup a local beer I was very pleased when one of the girls on the trip with us came over with a tourist map which she had marked with an 'X'. 'I've found a record shop for you to visit, Graham, while we take Sheila on a Rhine boat trip', said Julie, handing me a marked map. It took me 90 minutes to find the shop, whose window was packed with desirable discs, and a note explaining:

'Closed for refurbishment. Reopening in two months.'

I'd probably vote for Norway – well, Oslo, anyway – as the best European (Scandanavian?) venue I've so far discovered for ever-eager record collectors to slake their vinyl thirst. Slaking other kinds can be somewhat pricey here. However, records were far from exorbitant and both myself and my recent convert to vinylism, Mike H, were enthusiastic about our trek around the shops before and after we went to the races, where we watched the Norwegian Derby which was won for the first time by a horse ridden by a female jockey. Unusually, I backed the winner, meaning I had a few more pennies to spend on vinyl, including a record I'd been intending to acquire for some while – the 1977 debut solo album from former Moody Blues stalwart, John Lodge, entitled *Natural Avenue*. This is not a difficult LP to find, but my star discovery in Oslo's inviting Rakk & Ralls (you can probably guess what it means) was a copy of Jimmy Campbell's *Half Baked*, a very scarce, fully brilliant, gatefold Vertigo album from 1970. 150 of your English pounds, says RRPG, but here for just 15 krone.

In Spain's beautiful northern coastal resort, San Sebastian, I stumbled across a record shop with a window display suggesting that I had passed away and been immediately reborn in vinyl heaven. Obscurities galore from the 1960s - but the shop was never open during the entire time we were there. Other foreign locations to yield great booty include the French town of Nantes, where I picked up a top collection by reggae greats, the Pioneers, and the obscure, eerie acid-folk album, *Dreaming With Alice* by Mark Fry. In Rennes, we passed a record shop, from the interior of which some evidently 1960s psych rock was pouring. As I stopped and began to cross the threshold, I was warned in no uncertain terms by those with whom I was travelling that I had 30 seconds inside at most before they continued to explore the unfamiliar local streets. I just had time to use my much-neglected A-level French to find out that the record was by a group called Hunger, but I had to wait until we returned home to track down a copy of this 1968 stunner. Other European cities in which I have found excellent vinyl outlets include Zurich, Warsaw, Stockholm, Paris, Madrid, Lisbon, Amsterdam - although I have yet to frequent Red Light Records in the latter location which, I learn from website the vinylfactory.com is 'run out of a former prostitution window.'

I didn't find any specific record shops in Pasadena, USA - or stores as they would have it, there - but in one of the larger shopping malls was an antiques/collectables store which had within it a vinyl section. I browsed through it, finding three LPs which were to my taste - one by Moby Grape, another by the Lemon Pipers and one by... sensitive rock fans had better look away now... Tiny Tim. It *was* hot there that day. The dealer adamantly refused to offer even the smallest discount for buying all three, but as I wanted some souvenirs to take home, I paid the full whack.

Back in our hotel room after enjoying an evening drink or two, we settled down for a peaceful night's sleep prior to visiting Santa Anita racecourse the next morning. That didn't happen and we had to change rooms in a hurry, escorted by a member of staff, after upsetting the couple next door by complaining about the drilling coming from their room after midnight. I'd gone to investigate the noise, only to be chased back to our room by a man waving a gun about and shouting that he'd be quite happy to use it. On me. I called Reception, who sent someone to move us, and to remove the neighbours. At least I had the presence of mind to grab my records when we relocated.

On my one visit to New York I was not overly impressed by the record shops, although I must point out I was taking Sheila there for a special birthday trip. She was keener that we should look around Macy's handbags (she *was* impressed) than go searching for vinyl. I did find a record stall in a Chelsea area market, where I bought the Grateful Dead-connected Kingfish LP.

When we were in Princeton, the university town not that far from the Big Apple, we were in a charming coffee shop when one of our group of horse racing enthusiasts was asked about his impressions of Princeton. He declaimed loudly enough for everyone in the place to hear, 'I think this is the one place I've been to in America that I could envisage living in – if it wasn't for the Yanks!' At this point I thought I'd slip away before the violence started, as I had noticed a nearby premises called the Princeton Record Exchange (prex.com) which looked promising. I walked in and found myself in a veritable vinyl heaven and CD sensation. I'd genuinely never seen so much music assembled in one place, and at such affordable prices. Only restricted by how much I could carry back on the plane, I charged in and started buying – The Polyphonic Spree, Blues Traveler (five of their albums), a couple of Jeff Healeys, a Stevie Nicks, a George Thorogood – and these are just the ones which came to hand when I took a quick look around my collection for items still branded with a 'Princeton' sticker. None of them cost me more than $2.99!

In San Francisco during 2019 I again tried the 'ask the guy at reception' technique and again struck vinyl when he told me: 'Amoeba' on Haight Street used to be a bowling alley – it's huge, with a huge selection.' The shop claims 'the best crate-digging in the world' and I wouldn't argue too much. Yardbirds box set, Creation double LP, Blues Project, Marvin Gardens, Schwartz-Fox Blues Crusade... I could have stayed for hours but it wasn't allowed.

I treasure all of these foreign record adventures, but ZZ Top's 'Gimme All Your Lovin'' always reminds me of my most surreal record-related experience in another land. I was in Moscow in the early 1980s, just as Mikhail Gorbachev was endeavouring to reform his country, as part of a group of British newspaper 'hacks' travelling under the umbrella of the National Union of Journalists.

When we journeyed from Moscow to Leningrad, as it was then still known, we had a dream-like night on the train, drinking strong tea from the mobile samovar which made its way up and down the corridors on a regular basis, swigging slightly stronger liquids from bottles bought for just that purpose, and listening to the KGB man, who told us he'd been deployed to keep an eye on us to ensure we weren't seeking to undermine the Soviet Union, and played us spot-on renditions of Beatle tunes on his saxophone.

Earlier we had found ourselves in a couple of cabs speeding through a capital city which appeared almost deserted apart from more queues for who knew what essentials of life. We were disgorged into a hotel reception area and escorted down to a night club as disreputable and tacky as any to be found in either London or New York. There extravagantly dressed, evidently privileged male locals were quaffing champagne and puffing on huge cigars with rather younger, scantily clad female companions in close attendance. We looked out of place in our jeans and jumpers and were concerned that we would not have enough roubles to pay what were likely to be the exorbitant prices of drinks. Still, we ordered rounds of beers, having asked the waiter how much they would cost and how we could pay.

'Sir, we accept American Express and all major credit cards...'

Relieved, but not a little astonished, we walked into the discotheque area of the club, to hear the pounding sound system pumping out ZZ Top's very Western rock music. 'Gimme All Your Lovin'' seemed more appropriate in these surroundings than ever before. I looked at the guy who had organised the trip and raised my glass:

'A toast to Perestroika... Cheers!'

In July 2018 a good friend of mine took a trip to the Balkans

– then sent me a photograph of 'the record shop in Ljubljana for your collection.'

It appeared to be called Spin Vinyl and, along the canopy overhanging the shop front was what I took to be the shop slogan:

'rock 'n' roll ploscarna'.

I was intrigued by the photo and demanded more info:

'Didn't go in, no idea what it means. Looked like there was a lot of vinyl inside.'

Sometimes you just have to accept that not everyone shares your passions! Like the Harrow Commune audience...

IN WHICH... I RECALL CONCRETE MEMORIES OF LOCAL GIGS

I have a vague memory of seeing a couple of pop package shows at Harrow's Granada Cinema in the mid-1960s, but the first groups I saw close up were probably the local bands Smoke (not the 'My Friend Jack' chaps) and Axe. I was mates with one or two of the performers. This was at the Harrow Commune in Rayners Lane, which was also where my fledgling rock career began and ended on the same night, with a debut by Concrete Mosaic that was also the farewell performance.

Mosaic was launched by my great chum Martin Wilson – once with Captain Beefheart and His Magic Band – when there was a delay in proceedings at the Commune. Possibly energised by the vibe in the room and the substances wafting through the air, he decided to provide some entertainment of his own by creating music from anything which came conveniently to hand. Inviting me to join him we banged spoons, battered crockery, thumped furniture, and sang an improvised melody unhindered by anything as conventional as instruments. Martin, a traditional blues-man at heart, and master of the mouth-harp, hypnotically chanted his own original lyric as I harmonised:

'Blood spurts freely in seven different shades of red...'

I'll momentarily spare you the rest of the lyrics. We were given a standing ovation – there were no seats, as I remember – and we decided we'd never be able to match our debut, so we immediately announced our retirement. But there was a reunion of sorts when Martin, who worked in the darkroom of the newspaper where I was a rookie reporter, invited young snapper Phil to make us a trio. We posed at a photo shoot and were featured in the paper as *the* local band to watch. We began talking vaguely about taking time out to get our heads together in the country before starting work on our first album. We're still working on it.

To the point that I recently persuaded Martin to rewrite the next lines of our greatest hit, 'Blood Spurts'. In order to concentrate properly on the exercise he retired to the smallest room in his house, emerging some while later with a piece of paper in his hand, on which was written:

'BLOOD SPURTS FREELY INTO SEVEN DIFFERENT
    SHADES OF RED...
CASCADING DOWN THE FACE OF LIFE AS THE
    HEAVENS PART,
THE INNER SANITY OF YOUR MIND BEGINS TO
    STRAIN
TILL AT LAST IT EXPLODES AND EVAPORATES IN THE
    NEW DAWN.'

Martin's wife, Jackie, sent me the lyrics, along with her own exclusive review of them:

'WHAT A LOAD OF SHITE!'

By the way, Martin's stint with Captain Beefheart's band lasted some ten minutes. Martin had arrived at a local venue, Harrow's Tithe Barn, where the good, if very odd, Captain was to promote his latest LP, *Safe as Milk*. As he queued to gain entry the group arrived. Making their way in, long-haired, muso-looking Martin was quizzed by the venue owner: 'Are you with the band, man?' Martin told him he was. 'I then spent an awkward few minutes with the Captain, and, if I remember correctly, Magic Band members Ry Cooder and Winged Eel Fingerling, even accompanying the Captain, not on my mouth organ, but to the gents where we occupied adjacent stalls. I have little accurate recall of our subsequent conversation, but no contract to join the band was forthcoming.'

All of this was happening around the point at which I realised that I preferred hearing other people making music, and accepted that I had no ability whatsoever in that field other than being able to operate a record player.

These were days, though, when it was easier both to afford and get tickets for bands, particularly if you were working for the local paper and could offer publicity in return for free entry. Using this cunning plan I became pally with the guys running the Farx Club (they also ran another Farx in Potters Bar) in a small pub basement in Southall and there I saw many bands playing the type of music I love to this day:

*Audience, who just should not have appealed to me, because of their jazzy tinge and sax content, but their meaty, involving songs won me over.

*Blossom Toes, and their genuine, quirky psychedelia which turned dark on 'Peace Loving Man'.

*The Groundhogs, with Tony (T.S.) McPhee, so dedicated a blues enthusiast that producer Mike Vernon persuaded him to add the initials to his name to emphasise his affinity with authentic American blues-men. They weren't his own initials, but stood for Tough Shit. However, in 1970 the Groundhogs suddenly embraced piledriving heavy rock on their classic LP, *Thank Christ for the Bomb*.

*High Tide – so loud I remember the building shaking, and who had thrillingly included an amplified, screeching violin in their line-up on debut album *Sea Shanties*. Only in November

1979 would I again experience so thunderous a threat to the wellbeing of my eardrums – when Sheila and I sat innocently in our Hammersmith Odeon front row seats waiting for AC/DC to entertain us. The charismatic but doomed Bon Scott and the Young boys almost literally blew us out of our seats. After two or three numbers the audio assault sent us scurrying back several rows, looking for another couple to change places with. As a result, we can still just about hear today. I doubt that the other pair can.

One of the most sought-after singles from the psychedelic era is 'Boy Meets Girl' by Paper Blitz Tissue from 1967, currently worth £500. I saw the band play live, back in what must have been late 1967 or early 1968. I cannot remember whether it was at the Starlite or the King's Head – probably the former. I remember an impressive light-show.

The Starlite not only showcased top names like Cream, Pink Floyd, Jeff Beck, the Moody Blues, Small Faces, but also lesser lights I'd love to have seen but for the demands of homework during 1966 and 1967 – such groups as Open Mind, Human Instinct, Fleur de Lys, The Gods, Syn...

Despite being a rock and psych lover from very early on, I also learned to love reggae and disco as a form of self-preservation, if only, initially, to avoid getting my head kicked in. In November 1969, I was thinking that might be a real possibility. I'd been a little less than complimentary in my record review column – not to reggae, ska and rock steady, but to the skinheads who had adopted it. This resulted in a letter I received at work a couple of days after the '13-11-69' dateline neatly written at the top of a lined sheet of paper containing the following message:

'Mr Sharpe (note the absence of the traditional 'Dear' when writing to someone with whom you are not personally acquainted),

On reading your "Record Rendezvous" in this week's Post I object strongly to your idea to combat reggae music. Nine out of ever (sic) ten people between the ages of 15-19 have cropped hair.

It's people like yourself with your long blonde curls (last five words underlined in red, despite the fact that never in my life have I had such hair) that should be demolished, and that music, oh what's it

called! O! Yes progressive (*more underlining in red*), should find a
dark corner and seat (*sic*) on it.
Yours
Skinhead.
PS (*all of the rest of the letter was underlined in red*)

LOOK OUT FOR A MARK ONE GUIDED PROGRESSIVE
DESTROYER MISSILE. HA! HA! AND GROW UP!'

The evidence of my affection for this music is there to this day,
hidden within plain sight, in my singles' record collection. There,
amongst the bulk of rock and psych, are lurking a good few ska
and rock steady discs which proved to be lifesavers. You'd also
spot unforgettable and very popular soul tracks by Eddie Floyd,
Otis Redding, Sam & Dave, Wilson Pickett; lesser known floor
fillers by Cliff Nobles And Co ('The Horse'), Peggy Scott & Jo
Benson ('Lover's Holiday') and Rex Garvin & The Mighty Cravers
('Sock It To 'Em, JB'); plus, of course, maximum Motown. These
are records you couldn't persuade me to part with for substantial
financial amounts; they are too much an integral part of me and
my past. I didn't boast about owning these records then. They
didn't earn me any Brownie points amongst the psych cognoscenti
and blues-rock boys, but they helped keep me alive when quizzed
by the local hardnuts who could seem friendly one minute, before
appearing behind you waving a bottle at your head if they'd
decided you'd somehow offended their code of honour.

The most important discotheque to us was the King's Head
Hotel, on historic Harrow-on-the-Hill, home of the world famous
Harrow School, which educated and sent out into the world both
Winston Churchill and John McCririck, neither of whom, to my
knowledge, was ever spotted at the 'King's' disco, attached to the
side of that hostelry. The pub claimed to date back to the 1500s,
and Henry VIII was said to have been either a visitor or even
the owner. Churchill, no disco dancer, was, though, rumoured to
have been a regular in the infamous 'men only' bar.

Apart from buying so many of the records which DJ Bruce
would spin to get his regulars dancing, I also have a flashback to

the disco nights of the late 1960s and early 1970s at the King's every time I hear Steam's early 1970 Top Ten hit, 'Na Na Hey Hey Kiss Him Goodbye'. This was playing loudly in my friend Dave Furlong's car, in which I was a back seat passenger, as he endeavoured to park it close to DJ Bruce's rather sportier pride and joy, a high-performance Sunbeam Tiger, only to miscalculate and drive backwards into the front of this valuable vehicle.

This incident acquired a certain amount of notoriety when I wrote about it in my record review column in the local paper...

IN WHICH... I ACT POST HASTE

I wrote a world-exclusive, front-page story for the *Post*'s issue of 30 July 1969, Wembley edition, reporting that the local Starlite Ballroom, a venue which staged gigs by many of the top bands of the 1960s was about to reopen, after trouble and violence had broken out at discos staged there. I also reported that Steve Marriott had expressed a desire to debut his new band Humble Pie there: 'We certainly don't want to do an Albert Hall concert. I'd like to open up at the Starlite, to play to about 200 people.' Now you can't say that wasn't a scoop...

By now I was writing a weekly column, sometimes known as the Graham Sharpe Page, and also as Record Rendezvous. This began to help increase the size of my record collection – and, probably, my ego, too, as my dreadful, pudding-basined haircut from the photo on my earlier column, Let's Go, had been dumped in favour of a slightly less ludicrous head and shoulders image.

The new column would certainly also enhance the future value of the record collection. In December 1968, the Pretty Things' *SF Sorrow*, worth up to £700 these days, was released, and given a 'very interesting' welcome from yours truly. My best single of the week that fortnight before Christmas went to Donovan's 'Atlantis', although when writing this chapter I had to refresh my memory of that now obscure offering.

Back in the office with the New Year just a week behind us, I was idly musing on how we were going to find some decent stories to fill our quota, when Gina, our switchboard operative, put a call through to me: 'Hello, my name is Elton John. Well, that isn't my real name, it's Reg Dwight... anyway, I'm from Pinner, I've got a new record out, and Tony Blackburn has made it his Record of the Week on Radio One. I thought you might like to write about me.' Unable to resist joshing with someone who was clearly another of the no-hope pop wannabes from our patch, I quipped, 'Never mind, I suppose your career *might* survive the curse of Blackburn.'

Amongst our other local hopefuls were The Sweet, whose main man, the late Brian Connolly would soon ring to tell me, 'Our next single is going to be a big hit, you might want to cover the story.' 'How can you be so sure?' I asked naively. 'Our manager has just been out buying hundreds of copies from the shops which make chart returns,' he told me confidently and indiscreetly. I would also pop down to reception for a chat with hit-making Edison Lighthouse who, it transpired were all almost seven feet tall. So, I'd thought, anyway, until looking down to see they were all wearing five-inch Cuban heels and platform soles.

But back to Reg.

'The new single is called "Lady Samantha". I wrote it with my flat-mate Bernie. Perhaps you'd like to write about us.'

On this particular day I certainly wouldn't. I had quite enough to do as it was. We all had to contribute to the mounds of stories needed to fill the shared pages of the paper as well as inventing, sorry, sourcing those which would end up on the three 'change' pages dedicated specifically to each individual area.

'Hold on, I'll see if anyone's free,' I told Reg John or whatever his name was, whose patience was probably running short by now.

'Got some local bloke called Elton Dwight or some such, on the phone who says Tony Blackburn likes his new record. Anyone want to interview him?' I called out.

Most reporters didn't even look up, but carried on hammering their typewriters, talking on the phone, smoking, imbibing copious amounts of supposedly euphoria-inducing cough mixture, or flicking paper pellets at each other. The Editor twirled down the office, distractedly puffing on his pen.

'All right, Sharpe, I'll take it. Switch the call over to me.' Bill Kellow, Chief Reporter, sitting unconcernedly in his chair by the wall, put down his steel ruler, used for designing the layout of pages, and sword-fencing against other reporters, rubbed his jet-black moustache, and picked up the phone.

'Hello, Mr Reg, Bill Kellow here, how can I help?'

Over the years that followed I have regaled scores, if not hundreds, of friends and relatives with this anecdote, claiming that the *Post* was the first paper ever to write about Elton and that I had enabled that to happen. Yet I was always unable to provide specific proof. When I began writing this book I wondered how to find irrefutable evidence. I vaguely remembered that there had been an Elton John album which came with a pull-out containing a number of early articles written about him and Bernie Taupin before their careers had taken off. I soon discovered that the record in question was *Captain Fantastic & The Brown Dirt Cowboy*, released on the DJM label in 1975, in a gatefold cover, together with a 16-page colour song lyric booklet, *plus* another 16-page booklet, titled 'Scraps', containing early snippets and articles.

I found a copy for sale on eBay, which boasted that it came with all the extras issued alongside the record, and my bid of £15 was successful. There, on page five of its booklet was a story and photograph headed: LEAPING FOR JOY – AND NO WONDER. The photograph showed Messrs John and Taupin, clad in what appear to be coats made out of carpets, performing star-jumps in their garden. The accompanying caption declares 'Elton John and Bernie Tautin (*sic*) take time out to face *Post* photographer Peter Wilson.' The fact that we managed to spell Bernie's surname incorrectly is in itself evidence that this story did indeed come from the *Post*, where we invariably included literals (mistakes) approximately every couple of dozen words. Over on page 6 was Kellow's write-up, alongside an extract from Elton's diary, showing under the date of 17 January 1969, '"Lady Samantha" released', with further literals emphasising the fact that it was our story. 'Pop singer Elton John (alias Reg Bright (*sic*) of Northwood Hills, is carving himself a place in show business,' burbles Bill, informing readers that Elton, 21, 'composed "Lady Samantha" and was assisted with the lyrics by Bernie Tautin (*sic*).' Yup, there it is. A classic *Post* story – informative, ahead of the game and packed with inaccuracies!

In the same edition of the *Post* in which I broke the Starlite story opening this chapter, I was also 'shocked' by a track on the latest Sly and the Family Stone LP, *Stand*, called 'Don't Call Me N*****, Whitey'. (Not asterixed on the record). A few weeks later, I reviewed the new Bakerloo album, now selling for £300, as 'competent with a lot to please and a lot of promise'. Another new group getting a debut LP review from me was *Yes*, which I voted 'promising with plenty of contrasts and plenty of good ideas'. I still own this, with RRPG pricing it at £175. Number 1 in this particular week was the Zager & Evans' oddity, 'In the Year 2525'. I still have their first and only LP, *2525*, too. Now not worth even £25.25.

Under the headline 'Shiver me turntable "The Drunken Sailor" was never like this', I enthused about *Sea Shanties*, the LP by High Tide, the group 'that make Led Zep sound like the Sandpipers' – perhaps, I thought, 'the heaviest sound in the world... like an erupting volcano... a whistling hurricane'. This astonishing sonic sensation now has a £200 value. I'm also pleased to note that *Abbey Road* had a rave review. And the Farx Club was about to welcome gigs by Blossom Toes, Graham Bond, Savoy Brown and Roy Harper. Oh for a time machine!

Looking through old columns reminds me of what remains a truism to this day. Reviewing records is not easy. How do you keep coming up with something different to say without repeating yourself? And when an extraordinary record comes along how can you ensure you do it verbal justice? In October 1970, I had to deal with Fleetwood Mac's new single, 'Oh Well Parts One and Two'. You'll know the track, both sides of it, probably. How would you describe it? 'Immensely powerful. Racy, exciting guitar work interspersed with pauses for atmospheric vocal' wasn't that bad an effort for Part One, you will hopefully agree. There was also an

Andromeda LP. 'They thud solidly' was probably not an inspired reaction, but why in Heaven's name didn't I keep the record which now goes for a grand? I also had The Stooges' debut Elektra album (now a mere £250 worth) to give the once over. I should probably not draw too much attention to my verdict of 'frenetic shouting; only average heavy rock'.

Perhaps my favourite headline over any column I've ever written appeared on 14 January 1970 in Record Rendezvous:

'WIFE BEATING, CLANDESTINE LOVE, MURDER AND OTHER GOODIES!'

That entire headline referred to one track on the favourably reviewed Fairport Convention LP, Liege and Lief (£150) and that track was - still is - the eight-minute-long 'Matty Groves'. Listen to it, if you don't believe me...

The edition of 29 April 1970 (my wife-to-be's 16th birthday!) saw me reviewing a single by a new band offering 'an averagely heavy rock noise' - The Iron Maiden, four boys from Basildon. 'Throbbing beat, lengthy guitar, lasting for six minutes, but I like that name,' I wrote. I was right - great name but it would take a different group to make it the name of a successful band! And that one wasn't from Basildon but the single, still sitting on one of my shelves, sells for around £45 now. A few weeks later on 12 August 1970, I gave Alan Price my coveted 'Star Album' of the week award for The World of Alan Price which sold for a penny under a quid. (It's probably now worth less than that, allowing for inflation.) 'Phenomenal value,' I raved. It wasn't more than a few months earlier that I'd also handed him Single of the Week for his under-rated 'The Trimdon Grange Explosion'.

A few years later I paid slightly more than 19/11d to be abused by Mr Price. Not that that was the object of the exercise when tickets were purchased to see him play with his band, including the always excellent Zoot Money, at the Harrow Arts Centre, a local venue holding some 500 when packed. It was far from packed on this particular evening, and Mr Price was far from happy about that. So he set about berating those of us in the small audience -

who *had*, remember, made the effort and paid the money to see and hear him – about those of our neighbours who had found more interesting things to do, and how he'd have much preferred to be doing something else had he realised how few of us would deem his appearance worthy of our time, money and due devotion. Price didn't shut up moaning – to the extent that I had a quick word with Zoot Money, who had the grace to look apologetic about the headliner's curmudgeonly attitude, then wrote to his promoter to complain about his attitude. Didn't get even 19/11d back in response, but I've since had the last laugh. I've never been to see him again and never bought another one of his records.

By April 1971, with a new regime in charge, my *Post* column had become Sounds Good and I'm pleased to say I was ranting that 'I really cannot understand the prejudice that exists against reggae. This form of musical snobbery is utterly beyond me. Trendies dismiss it because it is so direct, danceable and enjoyable.' Being a journalist had always been my ambition and to achieve it before reaching the age of eighteen was very satisfying. In those days local newspapers were far more influential than they are today and, as a representative of the local media, even as ramshackle and unconventional an element of it as the *Post*, you had a certain amount of clout. People were slightly wary of you as they knew you could make or ruin a reputation.

I learned the profession literally on the job, attending college once a week to gain proficiency in matters of law, local government and shorthand. These were the best three years of my life, not that I was aware of that at the time. They set me up for what would follow – they also saw me confirmed as a hopeless vinyl addict. Cruelly, vinyl hastened my departure from this dream job.

Newish *Post* editor, Dina Machalepis, was an Elvis Presley fan. She asked me whether, after I'd reviewed the imminently-to-appear new album by 'The King', I would let her have it. Of course, I said I would. I was never an Elvis fan. She went off on holiday, anticipating that she'd have the new LP when she returned. But for some reason the record company, RCA, never sent it. Either that, or the postie or a colleague nicked it while it was on, or before it reached, my desk. On her return, Dina was not happy.

She accused me of keeping the record, which I'd never received. What started as an 'oh yes it did, oh no it didn't' row descended into a slanging match. I was reported to the MD, known as AJ, who called me into his office.

'Miss M tells me you called her a ******* ****. I think you should apologise to her immediately.'

He'd never liked me. I knew that, because when I'd started the record review column in the paper I'd taken to adding alongside my own thoughts, the opinions of 'my friend Martin', who worked in the paper's darkroom. AJ had demanded that I ceased using this phrase, lest people should think we were homosexual. Almost 50 years on from that incident, Martin – now a father to Ollie, who, I'm delighted to report, loves his vinyl – still identifies as heterosexual.

But back to 1971, and here was AJ insisting I should grovel and say sorry, despite being in the right:

'If you think that, you're a bigger ******* **** than she is.'

'I think you should leave immediately.'

I did, but had the satisfaction of winning a subsequent tribunal hearing and, despite having to repeat the words ******* **** to the elderly ladies ruling on the case, I was reinstated. But I never returned to the office.

Instead, I entered my wilderness year. I endured a few weeks on the dole before my Dad got fed up with supporting me and declared I must work for him on the building site where he was foreman. That was tough, and it was another record which finally forced me back on the straight and narrow. I was working on a site where 'we' were building a new warehouse. I was the labourer, in a stylish, over-large donkey-jacket, mixing cement, lifting every breeze-block and brick and, the only remotely enjoyable part of the job, zipping around the site in my mini forklift truck. Like on all building sites there was a transistor radio blaring out the hits of the day, and as it poured down yet again during January 1972, it seemed to me that the song 'Storm in a Teacup', the last Top 10 hit The Fortunes would enjoy, was played once an hour, if not more. I kept hearing its lyrics:

One drop of rain
On your window-pane
Doesn't mean to say
There's a thunderstorm comin',
The rain may pour
For an hour or more,
But it doesn't matter...

It did to me. I was bloody well fed up with both the rain and the cold, and when I spotted an advertisement in the local press for a boardman to work in a betting shop, I immediately thought, 'There's my way out of this incessant rain.' The 'boardman', no longer necessary in modern-day betting shops, was the person, almost invariably a man, who would, in ancient days, chalk up on a board the names of the runners and sometimes also the riders for each race taking place that day, later adding alongside the name the relevant odds as the race approached. After the race he would write up the result. As the world progressed, chalk was replaced by felt tip pens, blackboards by white boards, pure bleach for rubbing things off the board, by some equally skin-stripping liquid.

I sailed through the interview for the job:

'What does 2/1 mean?'

'For every pound you stake you will get back £2 if your selection wins, and you'll also get your original pound back.'

'Correct, when can you start?'

The man who gave me the job was Harry Lovett. He did love it – and so, I soon realised, did I. The donkey jacket was handed back to Dad, and I was now gainfully employed by the company with which I would spend over 45 years: William Hill. Although Record Rendezvous and my career as a reporter were no more, I managed to find a new niche for reviews and my Sounds International column was soon giving the lowdown on up-coming disco fare and dance floor movers to readers of *Sun News*, a weekly

English-language paper for exiled Brits on the Spanish Costas, as the 1970s boogied their way towards the 1980s.

IN WHICH... I DECIDE FAIRS ARE FAIR

Record fairs take place all over the country. I've always had mixed feelings about them. You'd imagine you are unlikely to find any great bargains at a record fair. The people who have records they believe are worth selling will almost certainly have done their homework to ensure they know precisely what those records are worth. Why would you go to a fair prepared to let people take advantage of your lack of knowledge?

On the other hand, if you can be bothered to go to a record fair to make money you must understand that you can only do that by persuading people to buy your wares. To do so, you need to have items attractive to potential purchasers. You probably will not be taking your personal favourites to be sold, so you won't have an excessive musical loyalty to your stock which will just be there to make you money. You also need to be able to recognise the point at which a price becomes a deterrent, and the point at which you've pitched it too low and your hand is likely to be wrenched from its wrist in the rush to buy. The 'sweet spot' between these extremes is where the seller must be prepared to deal, and as a buyer you need to recognise the advantage a fair offers, of probably a large number of desirable items in the same place at the same time, which is not usually a feature of an individual record shop.

Fairs will feature multiple dealers. They will be checking out each other's stock to ensure they don't miss an opportunity to acquire stuff they themselves would like to own. They may have the same records as other dealers but be desperate to sell, so be prepared to bargain. With so many dealers present, there is bound to be one or more offering examples of the genres which appeal to you. Not everyone can know everything about every different style of music. Maybe you will be able to delve through the goods on offer and find something worthwhile. You'll almost certainly come away with a story or two about what happened while you were there. Something you saw which amused you, or which you heard that didn't seem to make sense. Even if you don't buy anything, your day will be improved by looking at and hearing old records, likewise old collectors and vendors.

Vendors like the two I heard chatting to each other at the fair in Bushey, Hertfordshire.

'I usually do well at Canterbury. There's always a good turnout there.'

'Canterbury? Where *is* that – in London?'

'No, it's not in London, it's in Kent.'

'Oh yeah, I know it well.'

I'm smiling inside but splash out £3 on a Buddy Guy CD from the chap who knows Canterbury well enough not to know where it is.

Then I spot someone selling 'Prog/Psych CDs' and quickly pull out nine of them which I don't have, but would like and which would total £48 at the marked prices.

'Would you do these for £40?'

The stallholder looks doubtful. He mentally tots up the total price, looks unsure, then agrees to £40. I hand over four tenners, saying:

'I printed these off this morning.'

'That's OK. You do know you've given me six of them, don't you?'

We part on friendly terms.

Bargaining can be the difficult part of buying. But always bargain.

I have got myself on to the online mailing lists of a number of record shops, and they often send me a rundown of their latest wares. Occasionally they are trumpeting a 'sale' – which usually is shorthand for 'We haven't been able to shift these items at the outrageously over-the-top prices we've tried to con people into paying, so we've finally decided to pitch them at a more realistic level'. One list came in for a mint six-LP set of all the albums recorded by The Turtles, a group I particularly like. It claimed to be at 'half price' and it was, indeed, half the price they had previously asked. I watched, but like a patient angler, didn't immediately strike for fear of losing both bait and fish. Regular reruns of the sale items were sent, with the six-set still there each time. When it came in again on 'Black Friday', price unchanged, I checked whether anyone else might be selling it at a better price. I couldn't find one. The main drawback was the post and packing price, so I emailed the retailer, asking whether they'd waive that if I bought the set. They did. I bought it, although I felt I could probably have pushed a little harder to save a little more. My happiness was not quite so obvious when, even before my package arrived, the shop ran another promotion – offering *no* post & packing charges...

Back at the fair, I spot a man with a 'Beatles Box' priced at '£30 or an offer'. The box turns out to contain eight cassette tapes. I'm not sure how desirable they are these days. A quick search on my mobile reveals the same set online for a cheapest £43. Hm. 'An offer' – should I suggest £25 to the vendor, now talking to a neighbouring seller?

He's telling him, 'No one has even looked at these cassettes. No worry, though, I'll sell 'em online if no one's interested.'

The other guy says that he has seen a man whom he recognises as being a rival record fair organiser 'wandering around looking for vinyl'.

'What's he look like?'

'Tall and quiet.'

'Yeah, I know him – he looked at some of my stuff once, I had a load of Beatles' *White Albums*. Have you heard of them?'

'Yes, everyone has. The lower the number on them, the more valuable they are...'

'You see, the lower the number on them, the more valuable they are, and I had some low numbers, so I told him, "make me an offer".'

'And did he?'

'Yes. He said "30 quid".'

'What did you do?'

'Told him to add a nought.'

'Did he buy any?'

'No.'

'Did anyone else?'

'No, but I'll sell 'em online, I'm not going to give 'em away.'

I decided not to make him an offer for the Beatle cassettes. I figured he'd only suggest 300 quid...

'Excuse me, but is that Elvis Presley or Sophia Loren?'

An unexpected question, but it was being asked of one of the 20 or so record dealers pushing his wares inside Guildford's historic Guildhall, under its splendid 1683 clock, at the May 2018 record fair there. It was being asked by the male half of a relatively youthful mixed couple trawling the records, whose female half had just emerged from her delvings, with a Francoise Hardy LP and was flourishing it triumphantly.

'I've been looking for one of these for ages...'

The record dealer was torn between taking the money for the Francoise Hardy record and wondering precisely what the Elvis/Sophia query was all about.

'That album cover up there. I was wondering whether it was Elvis or Sophia on the cover.'

'No idea, it isn't mine... '

The couple wandered off, at the point I emerged from deep study of a box of CDs, clutching a Traffic live, an Arzachel and a Grail – the latter produced by Rod Stewart, no less. All three of them were new issues. It was likely to set me back three figures if I waited for vinyl versions of the latter two, even though the Traffic LP, described by one reviewer as 'variable quality Grey Market CD', can be had for 15 quid. The cheapest original vinyl Arzachel I could find on Discogs was £131.87 + pp from Spain, described as being in 'good' condition for the disc itself with a 'very good' sleeve, although the buyer bizarrely added: 'BETTER THAN DESCRIPTION!!!!' The 1969 Evolution label version of this record gets a £1000 rating in RRPG. Reissue vinyl copies can be had for £30. The Grail album, not even mentioned in RRPG, is going to cost you online at least £25 for a reissue version, and over £300 for an 'original'. So my outlay of £20 for all three CDs seemed a decent investment.

I'd now spotted a Francoise Hardy CD, so when I saw the Francoise Hardy album lady again at a nearby stall I decided to ask her whether she might have overlooked it. Except that it wasn't her after all, and the person it was looked at me as though I was some kind of lunatic-cum-stalker, stammered, 'I've no idea who Francoise Hardy is' and moved rapidly away.

I'd come to Guildford with a friend, Mike H, who had just put me to shame by producing a comprehensive list on paper of all the records he owns, designed to cut down those annoying double, or treble, purchases. We'd noticed the word 'collectors' was a topical one in Guildford. The record fairs, which attract hundreds of browsers, are organised by Ben Darnton, whose own local record shop in Tunsgate is called Ben's Collectors Records (no apostrophe), about which a regular noted accurately: 'moving around will be a little tricky unless you are super slim'. This shop is not to be confused with the Collectors Record Centre (no apostrophe) which is a couple of roads away at 89 Woodbridge Road. This is where Ben started to work in 1984, and where he clearly twigged that some form of the words 'Collector/s' and/or 'Record/s' might work when he came to run a shop of his own. It remains unclear whether Ben's shop ever had any relationship whatsoever with a shop not far away in Old London Road, Kingston upon Thames, called Collectors Record Shop (no apostrophe). I have been to that one and must say it had a more laid-back feel than Ben's emporium. But in late 2018 it morphed into Shaks' Stax of Wax.

I'd have liked to meet Ben in person, but when we ventured into his shop – as welcoming, atmospheric and reasonably priced as we'd been given to understand it would be – we were surprised to learn that Ben had left town for a few days. His shop is almost literally stacked to the eaves with records and CDs. There is a basic logic to the way in which the records are shelved and positioned, but you are still likely to find yourself kneeling on the floor to get to the boxes containing 'folk and country'. I had asked the guys in charge whether they had any folk, which resulted in a conversation between the two of them. Both, for some reason, were sporting leather satchels of the type used back in the day by your friendly local milkman or bus conductor, although I did not observe either actually putting any cash into them:

'Do we have a Folk section?'
    'Pretty sure we used to have.'
    'Where is it now?'
    'No idea.'

All of which suggested that there isn't a great demand for Folk music in Guildford – but Mike H, who specialises in this genre, did find a few records to buy. I contented myself with a Todd Rundgren and a Freakbeat compilation CD, all the time enjoying the very relaxed vibe, and also trying to spot more than the odd square inch of unused space – even the ceiling is covered in record-related publications.

When we first arrived at Guildford Station, Mike H and I made for the Collectors Record Centre (no apostrophe) sporting a sign in the window, 'Abandon hope all ye who enter here', displayed under a plastic skull and crossbones. Neither of us found anything to buy here but we did enjoy overhearing a snippet of conversation between owner and customer:

'Who's the least collectable artist on the planet?'
    'Probably Black Lace.'

Having pointed out apostrophic oddities, I now enjoy a spell of complaining ...

IN WHICH... I PUNCTUATE HENDRIX WITH GRAMMATICAL GRUMBLING

The Jimi Hendrix single, 'Purple Haze', used the spelling 'Foxey Lady', on the B-side of its US release, rather than 'Foxy'. It was claimed this represented the accepted American way of spelling the word, which I don't necessarily believe. More importantly, though – why was Hendrix's debut LP, *Are You Experienced*, denied its question mark? What in tarnation happened there? In 2017, the website Morrison Hotel addressed this question whilst writing about the record's 50th anniversary, and declared:

Hendrix originally wrote the title '*ARE YOU EXPERIENCED?*', ending with a question mark. Hendrix said that the title was meant as a question and an invitation to become experienced through hearing his music. However, the printer missed this and left out the question mark.

Maybe. Sounds unlikely, though – Jimi must have seen proofs of the cover before it was released and would have had the opportunity to correct it.

During the writing of this book, I discovered another problem someone had with 'Are You Experienced' which struck me as a little out of the ordinary. In November 2017, US record hunter Gary Piazza told online how:

'I found this (Jimi Hendrix record) at a yard sale a few weeks ago. I asked the lady if she had records and she pointed to a shelf in the garage, which had collapsed and there was water damage and mold (sic) everywhere. I was trying to look at the records but they were all stuck together because the paper had glued to each other. It was terrible, good titles too, Beatles, Stones, Zeppelin. Then I saw a box that was near the shelf, I looked inside and saw more records that were not molded, but did smell. The jacket's (sic) cardboard (sic) were wonky and bent out of shape from being stored in the moisture in the garage all those years. I gasped when I saw Jimi Hendrix's 1st in mono, record was really scratched but it plays fine. I need to get rid of the mold smell. Any of you reading THIS want to leave suggestions in the comments (vinegar? To kill any mold spores?) I'll do my best to air this thing out and retrain the cardboard.'

'Retrain' the cardboard?! Good luck with that, I'd say, if my experience with the odd water-damaged record is anything to go by.

I was in Stoke Newington in early February 2018, after a pal, Graham B – a big Hendrix fan with some very early copies of his albums stashed up in his loft which he refuses to get out, even though I've told him what they may be worth – called me to say he'd walked past this shop and thought it might be of interest to me. I arrived at Lucky 7 quite early in the morning, passing the time of day with the pleasant, young female assistant, who was playing a series of tracks evidently from different LPs. The latest one caught my ear. Good guitar playing going on there.

'Who's this?' I asked her.

'Jimi Hendrix'.

'Right. I don't recognise it. Which album?'

She showed me. I was none the wiser. Hendrix on the Pickwick label? It was an American record.

'How much?' I asked.

She made a phone call.

'The owner will be in shortly. He says he'll talk to you about it.'

He came in shortly after. We shook hands.

'Afraid I can't sell you that Hendrix record. It is actually one of my own – I've had it some time – since I was seven, in fact. I know every mark and scratch on it, and they all mean something to me, but I'll certainly see if I can order you another copy. I could get it for you for about twelve quid.'

By the look of him that would mean he'd got it at least 30 years ago, if not longer. I thanked him, but pointed out that as I'd made a special trip that morning just to check out the shop, I wouldn't be in this neck of the woods again for some while.

Once home I began to search online for the Hendrix record. Initially I thought I'd cracked it when I found a copy offered at a fiver. Checking what the postage would be I also enquired about the condition of the cover, only to be told there wasn't one. Delving a little further into murky cyberspace depths I was able to listen to a couple more of the tracks and then began to find threads discussing the record, some even doubting whether it was indeed Hendrix playing on it.

'The cover does not mention Hendrix anywhere,' claimed one poster, and another was adamant that it was someone else entirely. On the Discogs website, a French correspondent called fmhotte had recently posted: 'I have a copy of these recordings from France 1982, it's called: Super Hendrix on Musidisc #30 CO 1354. Most of these song are 100 per cent Fake Hendrix songs, he doesn't even play anything on them, there (sic) from an Hermon Hitson solo album that never came out and Hitson plays all the guitar and voice and Hendrix is maybe a little on Go shoes.' Further online probing produced the suggestion that: '"Free Spirit" is a 1966 song by blues session player Hermon Hitson (Philadelphia, 1943) which was mistakenly released as the title track of two albums of bootleg Jimi Hendrix recordings.'

I was, of course, aware, that Hendrix was rarely without guitar in hand during his short life and that an absolute deluge of albums have appeared in the years since he died, all claiming to be 'recently discovered' or 'previously unknown' recordings, some from before he burst into the public consciousness, when he made a living by being a backing musician. It all raised in my mind a similar question to the one often posed in the art world when the painter of a specific work is unclear. If it can be proved to have been by Picasso or someone of similar stature it becomes worth millions; if not, the value slumps to maybe a couple of hundred quid. All about provenance. But why? It is the same painting/ music, whoever created it.

So, would you have persisted in wanting to buy the 'Hendrix' album, given the furore around its authenticity? I found a copy with a 'very good' cover which, with postage added, would cost me £15.83. Seemed reasonable, so I made the purchase and anticipated the record's arrival, even though I could no longer remember what the track heard in the shop had sounded like. A few days later, my postie trundled down the drive with a parcel 'all the way from Portugal'. It was very well wrapped but once free of packaging one of the slurs aimed at the record – that it does not mention the name Hendrix – appears to be borne out. Nowhere to be seen – on the front cover. But, take the disc out of its sleeve and there sits a rainbow-coloured 'P' for Pickwick logo, not far from which, in silver type, appears the single word 'Jimi', followed by two words: 'JIMI HENDRIX'. I accept that this is not sufficient evidence to end the controversy over the contents, which will almost certainly never be categorically resolved one way or t'other, but as another illustration of the potential pitfalls of record ownership, I am more than happy to own a copy.

It is safe to say that even 'Are You Experienced' would almost certainly not have been the first to fall foul of the punctuation police.

And what about bands with an entire career behind them which are still operating without what one might have thought would be essential parts of their names? Who are they? The Guess Who... and The Who. Discussing the query quandary with Julian in Second Scene he came up with a blindingly simple reason for it, which I'd quite overlooked: '? and the Mysterians must have used them all up when "96 Tears" was big.'

Also, wonderful though my purple vinyl reissue copy of the 1972 LP by one of the few groups of that generation from Jersey, The Parlour Band (or, as the fantastic gatefold cover has it, 'the parlour band') is, I cannot work out why they would decide to call it this: *Is a Friend?* Is a friend *what*, for heaven's sake? What does that question mark signify?

Another example of an interesting use of punctuation was the decision by minor league mid-1960s band the Alan Bown Set to change their name, on their 1968 MGM single 'Story Book', to The Alan Bown! Yes, their new name included an exclamation mark. At one point Ultravox inexplicably appended an exclamation mark to their name, while there is some controversy over whether Leicester prog group, Pesky Gee who would morph into Black Widow, ever used an exclamation mark in their actual name, although that's what their 1969 LP was called. Images of the now £200 disc suggest that they didn't. But the 2020 *Rare Record Price Guide* and other respected reference books include the '!' in the group's entry.

Don't get me started on other such matters like the missing apostrophe in the title of the Rolling Stones' classic album, *Beggars Banquet*. I don't mind whether the apostrophe should have come before or after the 's', but can think of no good reason why it is entirely absent. When I first discovered the late 1960s 'group', Edwards Hand, I feared that here was another example of apostrophe aberration – until a little research revealed that the group was actually a duo – Rod Edwards and Roger Hand – so none was necessary.

You might expect that having survived and remained popular for 40 years, a band might know whether its name should contain an apostrophe, or not. And, for sure, whether that name should have a hyphen. Their website goes under the name gogos.com. Their Wikipedia page is headed The Go-Go's. The picture sleeve single of 'Head Over Heels' uses their name as part of the design of the picture sleeve: GOGOS. The record itself says underneath the title of the A-side, GO GO's. On the girls' website is a quote: 'The Go-Go's music really makes us dance.' If that quote is grammatically correct, then surely the band's name is The Go-Go?

Punctuation problems are one thing, spelling mistakes another. It is difficult to understand how Desmond Dekker must have felt when the first copies of his 1969 'greatest hits' album, released by his label, the much-admired Trojan Records, arrived with him, and at the shops selling it. There, proudly and prominently displayed on the front cover in large capital letters: 'THIS IS DESMOND DEKKAR'.

I suppose if you are going to misspell a word writ large on an album cover you're better off doing it with a title that most people may not even notice is wrong, which is the only saving grace for whoever okayed the proofs of the cover of an initially ignored but latterly almost deified record. *Odessey And Oracle* by The Zombies was released in 1968 to a torrent of indifference and disdain. The recently disbanded group were thus reassured that splitting up, which they'd done even before the record appeared, had been the right decision. According to Wikipedia, 'The misspelling of "odyssey" in the title was the result of a mistake by the designer of the LP cover, Terry Quirk. The band tried to cover this up at the time by claiming the misspelling was intentional.' By February 1969, 'Time of the Season', the single from the album, had hit the US charts, peaking at Number 3 and stimulating interest in the LP, which has never since waned, leading to its regular presence in prestigious lists of the best albums of all time. I was there at both the 40th and 50th anniversary concerts by the surviving original members of the band, celebrating the record, at the Shepherds Bush Empire and London Palladium respectively.

Shepherds Bush? Shouldn't that name have an apostrophe...?

IN WHICH... ADDICTS, COMPULSIVES AND HOARDERS APPEAR

In April 2018, I paid a visit to one of the record shops where the proprietor is now used to seeing me. I arrived shortly before an overweight chap a few years older than me who wheezes in, and asks to sit down - collapse into a chair, more like! He stays for a while, chatting to the owner, then departs with a couple of bags of records.

When the man has gone, the owner tells me:

'He's a hoarder. Lives on his own - you could probably tell from his appearance and odour. His house is crammed full of records, boxes of them, shelves of them, rooms, garages full of them. I've been there and seen very rare stuff just lying around, on the floor, or stacked up together. An original Fontana Kaleidoscope album, for example, just left on the floor; a Parlophone Beatles' black/gold label "Please, Please Me" chucked down on a chair, others worth three figures each strewn around. There's probably enough classic stuff just lying around to pay off his mortgage - if, that is, he even has one! You can barely get through his door or into the rooms. He also has a number of lock-ups which are packed to the rafters with records. He buys them from all over the place, not only from me. He'll pay the full "book" price even when the covers are tatty. I sometimes feel uneasy about the amount he buys from me. He is definitely a hoarder. I think the records are a protective, defensive shield for him, perhaps against family members he's had problems with. I've no idea what will happen to them when he dies, but I'm not the only person in the business who knows him, what the value of his records must be, and who lives close enough to him to join a race to be the first to get there when he goes.'

The owner also offers what seems like irrefutable proof that the man is more than a keen collector, but that he has a serious medical problem: 'He does not own a record player.'

I would not remotely put myself into the same league of hoarding as this man who clearly suffers, in my opinion, from a mental aberration of some kind which, if it didn't reveal itself via the hoarding, would almost certainly find another outlet.

When I was made redundant in 2017 it meant that after a lengthy period of forced separation, I was able to pick up where I'd left off with my long-suffering mistress. My wife had known about my illicit relationship, carried out clandestinely whenever she was out of the house and I had the place to myself, but she had tolerated it, knowing that, without what it brought me, I'd probably start looking for another outlet for my passions. In fact, there was indeed already another suitor – but, unknown to her, this one had by now begun to lose the grip on me which had once left me powerless to resist.

Sheila gave me an ultimatum. 'I don't mind you not getting another job, but if you're going to be around getting under my feet all the time, you are going to have to make compromises. You'll have to downsize.' The words struck a chill into my very soul. They meant I would have to cut down drastically on my commitment to what had been two of the major loves of my life – vinyl records and books. Both had been essential to my peace of mind over the years although I had used them terribly, without ever really being able to give them the love and affection to which they were entitled. I would expect them always to look their best and to be there for me when I needed the soothing balm of their presence. Now the time had come to re-examine our relationship.

The books, if I'm brutally honest, had been exploited by me, in return for little more than a commitment not to do them any harm. I used them mainly for research purposes, to help ensure that as much material as existed about the subject of the many books I wrote about horse racing and/or gambling, was available to help me create more volumes on a similar theme. Within a few weeks, though, I'd steeled myself and discarded hundreds of them. Many of them found a new home in local charity shops; others were sold via Amazon and/or eBay. Mrs Sharpe was very happy with this progress, but she was anxious that it should be mirrored on the vinyl front.

This turned out to be a much more difficult process. My record collection long ago became something of a comfort blanket for me. Whenever the world has been giving me a hard time I always know I can retreat into the welcoming, uncritical embrace of my vinyl. Surely it ought to be a straightforward process of elimination to discard records acquired for review purposes which I didn't like. Those which I bought 10, 20, 30, even 40 years ago for a bargain price yet still remain sealed and unopened. Why buy them in the first place if I didn't really want them? Could I seriously start learning to love them if I hadn't been bothered to do so for so long? Doubtful. Perhaps they were records I bought for the sake of buying records. The times when, like a junkie, an alcoholic, a compulsive gambler, I just needed a fix and it didn't really matter what it was. Champagne quality wasn't essential, cheap cider would do; a bet on the 2.45 at Sedgefield would serve the purpose equally as well as a wager on the Derby or Melbourne Cup. What about the ones I know to have a resale value which I never play and feel no affection for? Surely they can be dumped, or at least given to a friend, sold to a record dealer or on an auction site?

The overriding problem seems to be that I resent parting with anything which might possibly have a resale value. This is clearly a lingering hangover from childhood when both of my parents brought me up to understand and respect the value of money. The waste-not, want-not philosophy of most of those who had lived through the war was something they were desperate to instil within their children, not wanting them ever to go without, but not wanting them to underestimate what money could do for them.

Which might go some way to explaining why I found it so difficult to part with a reissue LP of the soundtrack to Cliff Richard's movie *Summer Holiday*. Like most people of my age, I saw the film when it came out, and enjoyed it well enough, but have never listened to the soundtrack since acquiring it for review more than 30 years ago. I offered Cliff up for sale to the world via eBay for £9.99. No joy. I reduced him to £6.99. A few looked, but no one bid. £4.99. Still no offers. Finally, I accepted that there was no great desire for this item at any price likely to produce any sort of profit worth the hassle of selling and sending it. With some regrets I eventually managed to slip it into the charity shop bag when my mind was occupied by other thoughts!

What is behind this hoarding tendency and virtual fear of parting with any records that mean virtually nothing to me? I found someone to ask questions of this nature. I was intrigued to learn that Lynsey McMillan, of Mo'Fidelity Records in Montrose, Angus, Scotland, has a unique qualification:

'I am a trained counsellor and split my time between my private therapy practice and our record shop. I love how these two seemingly different roles contrast and complement each other beautifully.'

I contacted Lynsey to get her perspective on issues facing record collectors and record shop owners, and began by asking: 'How would you counsel someone who admits to a compulsive, but probably just about manageable addiction to buy ever more records?'

'This is tricky to answer as I would be unlikely to take on a client who bought a lot of records, since it would be highly likely they would be a regular customer of the shop. My counselling practice and our shop are in the same town, and counsellors have to take care to avoid dual relationships. If a customer approached me for counselling I would refer them to a fellow therapist. I will answer more generally on the subject of compulsive buying/collecting. I specialise in eating disorders and specifically with compulsive over-eating, and the priority is to take care of the underlying issues that cause the compulsive behaviour, typically issues with trauma, loss, self-esteem, depression, anxiety, relationships, trust and (dis) connection.

'The goal is often to increase that person's ability to find other strategies to cope with life and in particular to develop more trusting relationships with others, so that food can resume its normal place in the person's life and be a pleasure, but not the be all and end all. I imagine there are some parallels with record buying, in that most people buy and enjoy their records, but that it doesn't take the place of other ways of coping with life - that there's a certain balance they are happy with.

'For record buying to be a genuine problem the person and those around them must be negatively affected, financially, emotionally, relationally, etc. The aim then might be to genuinely connect with their music collection, to curate, play, enjoy and share it whilst also taking strides to put in some limits and boundaries to mitigate the negatives.

'You can have too much of any good thing. Like food, I don't think you can "quit" music but you can learn to savour and slow down. Personally, I think that buying online encourages over-consumption more than visiting a record shop. Our ethos in the shop is all about mindful consumption, and our place in the community is that of a hub where people can get together and connect with the music, with us and each other. The customers who I'd say buy too many records are buying the majority online and visiting us only occasionally.'

Could you see Lynsey ever warning a potential customer that he or she should perhaps step back from collecting?

'My partner does flag this up with the occasional regular, and has been known to tell customers, "You already have this record in blue vinyl, you don't need it in red", or whatever. A potential customer, no, because we wouldn't know them or their habits to be able to comment.'

'And what', I asked, 'made you want to become a record shop owner?'

'My fiancé and I opened the shop some two years ago. He runs it most of the time, I'm very busy with my work and I help on weekends and my less busy days. I know a good amount but he's the true expert. We opened the shop when Neil was made redundant and we had the opportunity to take a risk.'

'Would you say females are under-represented amongst record collectors and/or record shop staff? If so, can you offer any indication why that should be the case?'

'Yes, the majority of our customers are older males, 40 plus, but we have a lot of couples who shop together and some younger female customers. I don't know exactly why – I was raking in record shops from the age of around 14, but my own buying tailed off as my life responsibilities increased and there was the switch in those days to CDs. I think the music industry in general is male-dominated, some genres of music more so than others. In general, I think men and women have been culturally conditioned to spend money differently. Women maybe spend more on clothes, cosmetics, appearances and on their children and homes. From a feminist perspective we might say that some women could be happier and more empowered if they spent more time in record shops than worrying about shoes and handbags!'

I'm relieved that it was Lynsey who made that final point – I wouldn't have dared!

However, returning to the hoarding and compulsive aspects of record collecting, I still had to answer the question: Am I a vinyl addict? Since my teenage years, I have consistently spent more time than is healthy, and frequently more cash than I could really afford, in record shops, listening to and purchasing music in its recorded form. At no time have I ever been warned that my behaviour is, or was, unacceptable and/or told that I have a problem which may require some kind of medical attention or treatment. No record shop assistant or owner has ever quizzed me as to whether I should really be buying that much vinyl, or whether what I am about to spend is within my affordable budget. I do not advocate that they should do so. But why is this? People who feel powerless to resist the blandishments of alcohol, cosmetic surgery, costly cars, drugs, gambling, luxury holidays, tobacco, works of art, are usually roundly criticised for wasting their money and frequently accused of being in the grip of a medical condition. They may even be advised to seek medical assistance in an effort to help prevent them becoming addicted. No such concern appears to exist when it comes to people for whom only a fix of new records will do when the longing looms.

Selling vinyl in establishments offering tea, coffee and other soft drinks is now by no means unusual. Thus far there have been relatively few set-ups which team alcohol with vinyl shopping, and even fewer which use high-end wine to entice customers along for a quaff, and then encourage them to mix pampering their palate with the opportunity to listen to seductive sounds of vinyl as they sip, and perhaps to buy what they are hearing.

Winyl is the first of its type that I've come across and it also achieved the feat of introducing me to a place of which I had never previously heard – Manningtree in Essex. One customer posted online: 'What a great store. A superb selection of pre-loved and new vinyl at very reasonable prices with the added bonus of being able to sip a cheeky red whilst browsing the racks.' Another confessed to being 'half-cut' when departing, but didn't reveal whether they were packing vinyl as they left. Another enthusiastic reviewer commented, 'What a great place! Such a lovely couple, who really know their stuff! Great to try some different wines, and listen to some records, before purchasing your favourites to take home!'

One member of that 'couple', Steve, told me how the shop had come about:

'I was in music retailing for 20 years and saw the rise and fall of vinyl. I always kept (most of) mine and with the revival I could finally make a business stack up. Plus I love wine, so thought I would create a space where people can have a glass whilst browsing and playing vinyl. We are licensed for on and off sales and have just introduced a small selection of beers. We have had a couple of events so far, a book signing and a vinyl "singles" club. As far as I know we are unique in the UK. There are plenty of record shops doing beer or coffee but not wine, especially vegan and organic wine.'

Steve even offered me a signing session for this book: 'Be very happy to host a signing, although last time got messy and was a bit of a lock in!'

He has also combined his products:

'I have traded old for new and even traded some vinyl for a bottle of wine, it's like bartertown.'

Returning now to Second Scene, where I often go to appease the 'must score some new old records' desire, boss Julian appeared to be developing something of a (probably unnecessary) conscience about customers who, he felt, might be spending too much.

'I had a guy who came in and chose a good few records, which came to about 500 quid. I thought he might have had a drink or two, so I said to him, "Are you sure you really want these records, they're quite expensive? Perhaps you should leave them here, go home and think about it and come and get them tomorrow if you still want them." Well, he did come back the next day and buy them. But then when he came in on the next couple of occasions he had started to look a little less well turned out each time, eventually even looking a little tramp-ish. Then he just sort of vanished.'

Julian's conscience was certainly pricked. But I pointed out that, in my opinion, other people's motivations shouldn't be his responsibility. Why should he risk losing perfectly legitimate business by trying to persuade people *not* to buy his wares even when they insisted they were perfectly able to afford the money they were spending and that they were in a proper state of mind to do so? He hadn't dragged them into his shop against their will when all was said and done. How is he to know how much disposable income they may or may not have? Why is it even his responsibility to do so? I would regard it as an invasion of my privacy if anyone tried that approach with me!

Now let's hear more on this subject, particularly the 'testimony' from someone who is outspoken about his own kind of vinyl dependency...

IN WHICH... MARK MY WORDS,
I CONSIDER PATHOLOGICAL
COLLECTING

In his extraordinary documentary film *Vinyl*, about record collecting, released in 2000, Alan Zweig profiled, amongst others, an extreme example of collecting pathology. This was a social recluse who refused to leave his record-lined apartment, where each time he used the bathroom it took him several minutes to relocate the records in front of the bathroom door. A Canadian filmmaker, Zweig investigated the world of record collecting in an effort to get to the bottom of his own obsession. In the film, Zweig sought to talk to people who collect records not in order to discuss music, but rather to discuss what drives someone to collect records in the first place.

Lurking in front of, behind, and sometimes almost within his camera, Zweig spends a large portion of the film in stylised self-filmed 'confessions', where he expounds on his life in relation to record collecting, feeling it has prevented him from fulfilling his dreams of starting a family. He talks to collectors, predominantly but far from exclusively male ones, including a car wash employee who claims to have over one million records and to have memorised the track listing of every K-Tel collection; a government employee who refuses to organise his collection because he doesn't want people to come over to visit; and a man who threw out his large record collection rather than sell or give it away because he didn't want anyone else to own it. I particularly enjoyed the gentleman who decided to sell off his massive record collection, using the money to buy himself a horse, 'which I ride four or five times a week.' Even I can see how these are extreme vinyl behaviours, and not remotely normal, or even acceptable.

Brazilian tycoon, Zero Freitas started collecting records in

1965, when he bought 'Canto Para a Juventude' by Roberto Carlos. By March 2015, he owned six million 'and counting' reported a story in *The Guardian*, which described it as 'the biggest record collection on the planet.' Freitas was creating a five-storey building in which to contain, lend and exhibit them. In a February 2016 interview with him by Anton Spice on 'The Vinyl Factory Limited' website, the writer suggested:

'What Thomas Carlyle once wrote about books applies to vinyl perhaps with even greater force: "in books lies the soul of the whole past time, the articulate audible voice of the past when the body and material substance of it has altogether vanished like a dream". Having listened to Zero Freitas, this motto could just as easily apply to his vinyl library project.'

The question of when record collecting tips over into extreme behavioural abnormality is a difficult one to answer. Mark Griffiths is, in his own words, a 'music obsessive' and an 'avid' record collector. He is also a chartered psychologist and Director of the International Gaming Research Unit at Nottingham Trent University's Psychology Division. Mark and I became aware of each other when I worked for William Hill. Neither knew the other was a serious record collector until August 2018, when I came across an internet piece he'd written about his voracious vinylising and compulsive compact discing. I contacted Mark and he was happy for me to quote from his work:

'When' wrote Mark, 'I get into a particular band or artist I try to track down every song that artist has ever done. I have to own every recording, including unofficially released recordings via bootlegs and fan websites.'

He referenced one of my own favourite groups:

'I had liked The Move since my early teenage years. Over the years, albums I had on cassette and vinyl were replaced by CDs. The Move's *Greatest Hits* was one of the few to slip through the cracks. The buying of the CD was an impulse purchase following a *You might like…* recommendation from Amazon. The album was *Magnetic Waves of Sound*, featuring all their singles. I bought it because it contained all the 10 tracks that were on my Pickwick label cassette, but also had an accompanying DVD of many rare TV performances. I played it repeatedly for the next few days. Within a few days, my thirst for The Move was unquenchable. I ordered all four of their back-catalogue studio LPs – *Move* (1968), *Shazam* and *Looking On* (both 1970), and *Message from the Country* (1971). All four had been re-released with extra discs' worth of unreleased material. I decided that I had to have every track they've ever recorded, irrespective of whether I like the songs or not. This is one of the worst things about being an avid collector. I simply have to have every note – good or bad – recorded by the band. I found out that The Move had released two live albums, so I ordered those.

'A 2008 4-disc box set, The Move Anthology, 1966-72 had lots of tracks and alternate versions of songs that weren't available anywhere else. I found a second-hand set for just over £30. Bargain!

'In about three weeks I completed my collection of everything The Move had legally produced.

'I then went onto YouTube and found rare live performances which I converted into MP3s to make my own rare bootleg LP collection of The Move live. That still didn't satisfy my thirst.

'Much of the reading I did about The Move focused on the 1970-1972 period (when Jeff Lynne joined) where there were two bands in operation simultaneously – The Move and the embryonic Electric Light Orchestra. I never realised in my early teens that Jeff Lynne was in later line-ups of The Move. Given that the Electric Light Orchestra were actually The Move in all but name at the beginning of the 1970s, I also ended up buying a 2-CD collection, *The Harvest Years*, featuring the first two Electric Light Orchestra albums, plus outtakes and B-sides. ELO's first hit single "10538 Overture", was originally recorded as a Move B-side. The Move's last Top 10 single, "California Man", crossed over with ELO's first in the British charts – and the two groups had identical core line-ups of Wood, Lynne and Bev Bevan. I found out that Jeff and Roy had been friends in Birmingham. Roy asked Jeff to join The Move in 1969 but Jeff felt he could get somewhere with his own band, The Idle Race, one of the first to perform a cover version of a song by The Move – "Here We Go Round the Lemon Tree". This led me to buying a copy of the complete (2-CD) recorded works of everything The Idle Race ever commercially released, for just £5.

'There were various tracks that Roy wrote during his tenure with The Move and ELO (Mark 1) that ended up on his subsequent solo LPs, most notably *Boulders*. I bought this as part of a £10 Roy Wood 5-CD boxset also featuring LPs by his next band, Wizzard, as well as ELO's first, and The Move's final LPs. I then bought a Roy Wood and Wizzard 'greatest hits' CD. I've been buying up the rest of ELO's album back catalogue. For some three decades, ELO were one of my guilty pleasures. I now have all the albums they recorded in the 1970s as well as the recent platinum-selling *Alone in the Universe*. All for less than £20 in total. Bargain! Whether I will end up being an ELO completist remains to be seen. A lot of their post-1980 output is not something I can honestly say I like. One of the worst things about being a completist is buying music that you don't like just to complete your collection.'

I also develop 'crushes' on particular bands and/or artist(e)s, but mine rarely go much beyond deciding I will seek to gather a collection by them, although not necessarily instantly. However, I do admit to buying six Beach Boys' albums recently on the strength of a single *Record Collector* feature on the group's lesser known back catalogue. I have, at time of writing some months later, yet to get round to listening to those records and CDs. But that doesn't matter. They're there for me to do so when I feel like it. Knowing that is as good as listening. Adds Mark in an explanation of this mutual quirk: 'Tracking down an obscure release is as much fun as the listening of the record or CD ("thrill of the chase"). Almost every record I have bought over the last decade is in mint condition and un-played, as many now come with a code to download the record bought as a set of MP3s.' The difference here for me is that I don't 'do' MP3s, and have no interest in them.

Recalling his descent into this desirable delirium which consumes so many of us, Mark explains:

'Every week, all of the money earned from my Saturday job would go on buying records. When I got to Bradford University to study psychology, my love of music and record buying increased. I became a journalist for the student magazine. Within months I was in control of the arts and entertainment coverage. The perks of my (non-paid) job were that (a) I got to go to every gig at Bradford University for free, (b) I was sent free records to review. During this time (1984-1987) my favourite artists were The Smiths, Depeche Mode and, my guilty pleasure, Adam Ant. I devoured everything they released. As a Depeche Mode fan, collecting every track became harder and more expensive, as they were arguably pioneers of the remix. During 1987-1990, my record buying subsided through financial necessity. I was doing my Ph.D. I simply didn't have the money to buy records the way I had before. This was the only period in my life that I didn't really buy music magazines; I thought, if I didn't know what was being released, I couldn't feel bad about not buying it.

'In 1990, I landed my first proper job as a lecturer in psychology at Plymouth University. For the first time in my life I had a healthy disposable income. My first purchase was a huge record and CD player. I could listen to my favourite bands at the same time as preparing lectures or writing research papers – something I still do. When CD singles became popular in the 1990s, I became a voracious buyer of music again. Bands would release a single across multiple formats with each format containing tracks exclusive to the record, CD and/or cassette. Artists like Oasis and Morrisey would release singles in three or four formats (7" vinyl, 10"/12" vinyl, CD single, and cassette single) and I would buy all formats. The music industry has realised there were huge amounts of money to be made from bands' back catalogues. I will happily buy a classic album again as long as it has an extra disc or two of demo versions, rarities, obscure B-sides, that will help me extend and/or complete collections.'

But Mark makes a very important point: 'I love music. However, I am not addicted. My obsessive love of music adds to my life rather than detracts from it – and on that criterion alone I will happily be a music collector until the day that I die.'

Here's a tick-box list of symptoms, claiming to indicate whether or not an individual is veering towards compulsive collecting addiction, from an article by Hale Dwoskin, CEO and director of training of *Sedona Training Associates*:

- You look for/buy/trade collectibles for hours on end, and the time you spend doing this is increasing
- You think about collectibles constantly, even when you're not collecting
- You have missed important meetings/events because of collecting
- It's difficult for you to not buy more collectibles, even for just a few days
- You try to sneak more collectibles into your home
- You have tried, unsuccessfully, to stop collecting
- Your family or friends have asked you to cut back on collecting
- Your personal interests have changed because of your collecting
- You have lost a personal or professional relationship because of collecting

OK, let's see. First one? Yes. Second? No, not constantly. Third, no (well, not business ones, possibly private/family ones). Fourth, um, I suppose that's probably right. Fifth, no, I brazenly bring them in – okay, being honest, yes. Sixth, no, never tried, never wanted to. Seventh, not in as many words but possibly in disapproving looks. Eighth, no. Ninth, no. I'll let you decide whether I've passed or failed the 'compulsive' test. Dwoskin adds: 'Collecting is a unique passion that can give you a sense of purpose and promote self-discovery. But what may seem to you like a passion may actually be more of an obsession or addiction.'

Another viewpoint was expressed by science writer, Sharon Begley, in her book, *Just Can't Stop: An Investigation of Compulsion*: 'Compulsion comes from a need so desperate, burning and tortured it makes us feel like a vessel filling with steam, saturating us with a hot urgency that demands relief.' I think most serious vinylists will relate to that description which could equally apply to a number of other, potentially more physically damaging personal requirements. Mark Griffiths believes, 'that it is theoretically possible to be addicted to collecting' but 'the number of genuine "collecting addicts" is likely to be very low.'

Perhaps my own collecting shows that I am just searching for excuses to explain my desire to continue the contrarian attitude I love to display in so many other areas of my life, and to demonstrate my determination also to collect records to wind up as many people as possible by so doing.

But once you do it you discover just how much time and effort you have to devote to keeping the damned things in usable condition...

IN WHICH... I TRY TO COME CLEAN

In a well-known record shop in London's West End, buying a newly issued Johnny Winter & Muddy Waters' live album, I noticed on the counter, with a glowing recommendation note from the shop, a bottle of liquid record cleaner. It cost a tenner, but I was running out of a similar product at home, so I grabbed the bottle, adding its cost to the record. I didn't pay much attention to the label until I was ready to use it. The introductory info on the container lifts the spirits: 'Our solution has been specially blended to make sure your vinyl is cleaned to the highest standard.' That's rather what you might think you're entitled to expect by the very nature of the product.

I read on: 'Integral ingredients... purified chemicals... best results in cleanliness... no residue remains on your record.' All stuff I'm happy to know. Hang on, though, I have noticed two symbols on the label, with the word 'Warning!' printed between them. One is a large exclamation mark, the other what appears to be a conflagration or blaze of some kind. So, I look towards the written blurb to the left of the symbols. 'HAZARDOUS INGREDIENTS' I read, '...propan 2-ol, isopropyl alcohol, isopropanol.' No idea what they are. Next line: 'Flammable liquid and vapour.' Good job I don't smoke. 'Causes serious irritation.' What does? This line arrives without obviously applying directly to the one above or the one below, which warns: 'May cause drowsiness or dizziness.'

Thus, it is no great surprise when the next piece of advice offered is: 'Keep out of reach of children.' The instructions keep on coming:

'Keep away from heat, hot surfaces, sparks, open flames and other ignition sources.'

'No smoking.'

'Avoid breathing fumes, vapours, mist, spray.'

'Wash hands thoroughly after handling.'

Advice now in case I spray it into my eyes: 'Rinse cautiously with water for several minutes... Continue RINSING.'

'Keep container tightly closed.'

I'm beginning to feel it is dangerous even having this product in my house. How can I get rid of it? Like this: 'Dispose of contents/container to hazardous or special waste collection point, in accordance with local, regional, national and/or international regulation.'

I'm now too nervous to risk squirting any of this noxious liquid on to any of my vinyl in case it explodes, poisons the atmosphere or asphyxiates me. Donning a pair of plastic gloves I empty the contents of the bottle into an empty tin, formerly full of peeled tomatoes. Then I head outside to a road several blocks away from my own, and pour the stuff down the drain. All the time, I'm worrying, what if I'd woken in a daze one day, showered and sprayed some of this substance all over my body, mistaking it for deodorant? I'd have probably turned myself into a walking hazardous object requiring disposal by some of the operatives called in to deal with the Salisbury Novichok contamination. Looks like it will be back to the tea-towel and water method. Although they don't individually cost a great deal, experimenting with different styles of record cleaner soon proves an expensive indulgence. Maybe foregoing all the liquids, anti-static carbon fibre brushes, stylus brushes, record-cleaning arms, wipes, cloths and sprays, but putting the amount they would cost towards buying a record cleaning machine of some kind is the answer?

It would put a dent in the price of owning an Allsop's Orbitrac, for sure. The sales blurb for this invention tells us that:

Allsop's Orbitrac 3 Vinyl Record Cleaning System is an all-in-one wet cleaning system with a rotating assembly that makes it quick and easy to clean your vinyl records and remove dirt, dust, debris, and fingerprints. The exclusive Orbitrac rotating design uses anti-static cleaning pads that follow the grooves of your vinyl for an extremely consistent and effective clean that won't scratch your records. The advanced liquid cleaning solution was specifically developed for vinyl records and ensures safe cleaning. The Orbitrac reviving brush extends the life of cleaning cartridges and removes debris in-between cleanings. The Orbitrac provides superior cleaning in less than 30 seconds and removes pops, clicks and other sounds caused by dirt or debris.

How much do you think you'd need to splash out to own one of these machines? The generous folk at Amazon were offering one for £59.99 when I checked in March 2019. Free delivery, too.

If you think that that is a little pricey then you're unlikely to be in the market for an Audio Desk Systeme Vinyl Cleaner Pro Machine for £2525. How does it work, what does it do? We're told: 'The Audio Desk Systeme Vinyl Pro Cleaner is an LP cleaning machine that incorporates an ultrasonic cleaning cycle in addition to a more conventional mechanical cleaning via bi-directional rotating microfiber cleaning drums, and the result is the cleanest LPs ever. The ultrasonic Vinyl Cleaner bursts millions of microscopic bubbles off the surface of the record all the way to the bottom of the groove, where no fiber (sic) is fine enough to reach.' Any the wiser? Hm. Send me two... on second thoughts, maybe the chances of finding a reasonably priced, easy to use, efficient record cleaner are about the same as finding that other no-show, the Loch Ness Monster. Right on cue, here is the Nessie VinylMaster Record Cleaning Machine, £1832.99 in June 2019 – 'a high-end record-cleaning machine that was developed on the basis of experience gained in many thousands (of) record cleaning cycles. Records cleaned with Nessie Vinylmaster® extend the service life of your pick-up system and guarantee unspoilt vinyl sound!' Monster value, no doubt.

These products seem to be at the extreme end of the price spectrum for such equipment. Those people I have spoken to who need such machines for professional purposes often favour products from the Okki Nokki stable whose benefits are claimed to be:

- Built-in safety features prevent fluid being sucked into the vacuum motor and the turntable motor overheating
- Cool running turntable motor allows for hours of use, no need for noisy fans
- Forward and reverse motor for 'scrubbing' action
- Virtually waterproof plastic / aluminium body gives increased stability
- Added soundproofing – the quietest of all comparable machines in its class

The 'OKKI NOKKI RCM Record Cleaning Machine Black' is going to set you back around £435.

However, this 'Moth Record Cleaning machine' Mark II was £599 when I checked:

- The Moth Record Cleaning machine is a wet cleaning/ Vacuum removal device with powered turntable and drainable internal reservoir. Fluid is applied by hand to a rotating record, scrubbed, and drawn off by a high efficiency vacuum system into a drainable reservoir.
- The MKII Moth Record Cleaning machine is based upon the well proven and accepted record cleaner that has been available from Moth for a number of years
- The MKII version allows for bi-directional operation of the turntable in both the fluid application 'Wash' cycle and in the vacuum 'Drying' phase
- The vacuum tube has been modified to offer a more efficient vacuum system

I genuinely don't even understand the blurb, let alone anything else about these industrial-style pieces of equipment. They strike me as so bizarre that I must check with the local Heath Robinson Museum, to find out whether or not the eccentric inventor ever devised a record cleaning contraption.

All of this palaver rather makes the whole idea of listening to music seem like a job of work rather than a relaxing exercise in auditory pleasure. BUT, if you can't afford, or fear the consequences of using, any of these new-fangled contraptions and cleaners, fear not. I am given to understand that all you really need to clean your records efficiently is... a wet goat! Well, the 'Tonar Wet Goat Record Brush'. This product will cost you a mere £15 or so, and of the 36 people who have taken the trouble to review it on Amazon when I look, 86 per cent give it a five star out of five rating.

'Why have I waited so long to find this genius concept?' asks Grant Howard. 'The only thing I can say is spin the goat!' raves Mark the Brewer. Krystal Kev enthuses: 'I have tried everything, apart from an automated cleaning machine, to clean crackling vinyl, this beats everything else by a mile, so much so I am not understanding why it is not the go to (*see what he did there?!*) method for all audiophiles.'

Some cleaning methods do not rely on machines, as I discovered when coming across a YouTube feature, hosted by a short-haired millennial discussing 'Washing a Dirty LP Record Using Soap and Water', which had 494,000 viewers. And, stick with me, here is the big one. The video about 'Vinyl Record Cleaning With PVA Glue'. I kid you not. I just had to watch this video, which should have carried a warning for nervous vinyl viewers that they might find its contents disturbing. The chap presenting giggled nervously as he took a crackly Beatles' album he seemed to have bought specifically for the experiment and began squirting a gloopy, gluey substance all over it in one long spiral, before smoothing it down with a credit card. He then uttered the immortal phrase, 'Here's one I made earlier.' He put it aside and said he'd be back in a day or so. When he reappears on the video it is to tell us that it took rather longer than a day for the substance to dry sufficiently on to the surface of the record. He dons gloves (on the risible reasoning that by doing so he won't damage the other side of the record), scrapes up a corner of the covering, then peels it back carefully and slowly. 'Let's put it on', he says, 'to see if it has made any difference at all.' He carefully places the record back on the turntable, gently lifts the stylus up, then down on to the surface of the record... which crackles, pops and snaps before, during and after playing 'The Fool On The Hill'.

My hopes of a proper solution were revitalised by the next YouTube video I consulted, which was entitled 'What to Do About Scratches on a Vinyl Record' in which presenter Barry Thornton, a man who appears to have some knowledge of the vinyl world, spends several minutes leading up to these brutally accurate words of vinyl wisdom: 'There's nothing you can do. In effect, you're screwed.'

But once we've (failed to) clean our records... how many times should one play the things? Who knew there was controversy about this in the collecting world? It appears that there is, judging by a segment I found on a YouTube channel called Vinyl TV, hosted by 'Craig', a long-white-haired fellow, in which he spends some 18 minutes discussing the question: 'How many times can I play my records?' As virtually all of us will know, the answer to this pointless query depends on any number of factors, ranging from the condition of every part of your playing equipment to the state of the record itself. Towards the end of his answer, and I paraphrase, Craig points out: 'There are new records which sound really bad and old ones which sound brilliant.' He also offers another solution to those concerned that their vinyl may wear out: 'If you're that worried, buy two copies.' Maybe there are people who genuinely believe that records have an in-built maximum number of plays.

I was impressed, however, by a couple of comments which appeared on the site, by passing observers, like Sixdogbob: 'The actual answer is, given proper care, 437 plays. After that, you just have to throw the record away. This has been proven by thorough scientific study, and by sacrificing many Abba records for the cause of knowledge.' Tuten Vanman came up with an even greater, probably definitive answer: 'Just play the damn things on any player. I do. So I don't care about so called immaculate condition. If I buy a beautiful looking cake I still eat it. I bought the records for me not you, so how I don't look after them is my business. Stop being so pedantic.'

How, though, might one tackle smelly records...?

IN WHICH... I SNIFF OUT JULIAN'S PROBLEM

It was not quite the welcome I'd anticipated when paying one of my regular visits to Second Scene in late spring, 2018. I'd not popped in to see Julian for a while. He and Helen were busy sorting, cleaning and pricing a batch of singles which had recently come in, and Julian was puzzled by an aroma which appeared to him to be wafting off a number of the discs he was handling. He thrust one at me for an opinion.

I admitted that there was certainly some kind of faint tang being given off, but that I rather felt it was being overwhelmed by the more obvious niff of stale baccy. Playing along, I told him: 'I'm getting notes of late flowering body odour, fragrantly blending with essence of wet plimsoll and damp pet.' But Julian appeared to be serious. He was convinced that the smell he had been noticing was emanating mainly from records on the Fontana label. 'Then you'd better check that it hasn't spread to your Pretty Things and Kaleidoscopes,' I warned. Julian elaborated on his theory that the older records became, the more likely that some kind of chemical reaction could be taking place within the very grooves of the discs. 'Who knows what went into the making of records back in the day?' he wondered.

Now Julian picked up a single which had clearly made him forget about his olfactory observations and start thinking about a potential significant profit. 'I haven't seen one of these before,' he said, showing me a 1969 DJM label single by Elton John. 'Trouble is it doesn't look in very good condition – otherwise it would be worth a good three-figure return.' I could trust Julian on his valuation – after all, he is a Watford supporter, like the artist in question. The record was Elton's third single, 'It's Me That You Need', which Julian played and to which we listened respectfully as befits the value of the record, which was very good indeed, particularly Caleb Quaye's guitar – which also had a very significant input to the B-side, 'Just Like Strange Rain'. The record would have been worth twice as much had it come in a picture sleeve, and although I wasn't about to hand over a ton for it, I did check out which album I might find it on. I duly ordered a 1995 reissue copy of Elton's debut LP, *Empty Sky*, which didn't contain the two sides of that single when originally released in 1969, but acquired both when reissued.

Julian was now showing me an apparently mint copy of a Peter Sellers' EP, part of the collection he was cleaning up. After we both agreed that (a) Peter Sellers is rapidly being forgotten, and (b) that we rather felt Bruce Springsteen is a somewhat over-rated performer, he played me a doo-wop version of 'Dancing In The Dark'. By now I'd found a record I fancied – a compilation of the group Earth & Fire, whose name I'd recently come across on a review copy of a single by them on the Penny Farthing label. I'd liked it, but not enough to resist an offer to sell it. Very successful in their native Netherlands, Belgium and Germany in the early 1970s, they never cracked the British or US market with their prog-cum-psych rock style. I put the record on and it wasn't long before both Julian and I were simultaneously uttering the names 'Jefferson Airplane and Grace Slick'. Once again – he always forgets he's said it to me before – Julian said: 'How do you always find records I've put out for sale that I'd probably like to keep?' 'Too late, she's coming home with me,' I answered.

This day was one when I wasn't feeling the pull of many records. We did listen to a recently issued live MC5 album, recorded originally in 1968, but agreed the sound was off-puttingly muddy, and gave up after a couple of tracks. Al Stewart is one of those artists I always enjoy listening to when his music comes on, but will only rarely choose actively to play. I spotted his *Past, Present and Future* sitting there in very good condition for a mere six quid, and looked at the list of guitarists playing on it: Tim Renwick, Isaac Guillory, B J Cole, with Rick Wakeman and Dave Swarbrick also appearing amongst the collaborators.

Shortly after, Stewart came to play locally – charging £90 for two tickets. I bought two different 'Original Album' 5-CD sets by him for £21 the pair instead.

By now the afternoon was moving into evening, I'd had a cup of coffee, courtesy of Helen (I only drink tea by choice, but if someone offers you coffee it is only polite to accept). Julian had finished sorting out his singles, so I figured it was time to make my excuses with the two records I'd picked. Then I noticed a copy of *Second Winter*, one of the few Johnny Winter albums of which I did not have a copy, largely because when it was first released, back in 1969 my dislike of his brother Edgar's less rocky style put me off. I do now – and it has become the only three-sided double album I, or most other collectors possess. Julian was his usual generous self, totting up the three records to a total of £31 then giving me a much-appreciated discount... of a quid.

My next trip was to a shop somewhere I hadn't been since my days as a footballing superstar – in certain circles. My big break into journalism had come when, shortly after leaving school, I went for an interview at the *Weekly Post*. The editor, John Hyam, was quickly bored by the cuttings from the school mag which I'd hoped might impress him and win me the reporter's job for which I had applied. Chewing a pen, and swinging back in his chair he put his hands behind his neck and snapped:

'I don't suppose you play football?'

'Er, yes, I play for a local team, Wealdstone Athletic on Sundays. I'm a right winger.'

'Hm. Would you be prepared to go to Lewisham each week to play for the team I run there on Saturdays? You'd get a lift.'

'Suppose so.'

'OK, you've got the job. Be here next Monday morning at 9am to start work. The football starts next Saturday.'

I ended up top scorer for his team, The Tab. But it took 50 years before I returned to Lewisham, this time in April 2018, to visit the imaginatively named local record shop Records. Before finding the shop I recognised the local clock-tower from past days, but nothing else whatsoever. I'd seen two online reviews of Records. One claimed, 'Many records are in appalling/unplayable conditions. It seems like prices were put on them decades ago and nothing has been changed since... he doesn't take cards so bring bundles of cash!' Another said, 'Only had time for a short visit. Found 4 albums I'd been searching for on eBay for a decent price – on eBay £40/50 – here, £22.'

Very different observations but both, as I would shortly discover, contained kernels of accuracy. You would struggle to call the premises spotless and the criticism of the condition of records also rang true. I searched through mountains of very poorly laid out shelves and containers for the best part of an hour, only latterly looking up, to see copies of decades-old *Men Only* magazines dangling down over my head. The absence of plastic covers for most of the records strewn here, there and almost everywhere was partly responsible for the less than pristine condition of many of them. But some of those which *were*, were housed in dusty, dirty covers. The closest I came to a purchase was a Don Nix LP in just-about acceptable condition, priced at £9.50.

Others did purchase, though. When I arrived, the elderly Catweazle-lookalike running the place was chatting to a guy who was trying to sell him a range of soul singles which, insisted the seller, 'people will easily pay a tenner for'. Catweazle seemed unconvinced, but did good-humouredly agree to take one or two from him to play to potential buyers. Good PR for his shop, at least. Not long after, in walked a gent who may well have been a DJ as he was going through handfuls of singles, playing short snaps of them very quickly, some of them jumping or sticking as he did so. He found a few he wanted. Catweazle totted up the price. 'Oh, and I'll let you have this one for two quid,' he said. 'No,' insisted the DJ. 'It's marked at £2.50, so that's what I'll pay for it.' Honour between buyer and seller. Impressive. Restores one's faith in human nature. I left, feeling vaguely unclean, but morally cleansed. On the way out I glanced at the notice on the window: 'Many rare albums in every category of modern music.' Well, I didn't believe that one. But there was another one: 'DANGER – don't lean on the glass.' I definitely did believe that one.

Having bought nothing in Lewisham I soon realised I'd started a losing streak...

IN WHICH... I FAIL TO SCORE

If a striker fails to fire and goes a few games without a goal, (s)he gets out on the training pitch and puts in more training. If a jockey undergoes a spell of several race meetings without a winner, (s)he shouts out the agent and demands that (s)he finds him/her some better mounts. If a cricketer is out for a sequence of ducks, (s)he's off to the nets for more preparation. But what can a record collector do when a run of record shop trips results in no purchases? It happened to me during a period from late May to early June in 2018. I appreciate that could mean all of two days, but it was somewhat longer, and it felt like an unprecedented drought of 1976 proportions at the time.

I realised it had kicked in after I decided to catch a tube train out to Amersham to take a look at The Record Shop, which had certainly been smartened up a little since I'd last been there. It now had some eye-catching framed music press front pages on display in the window. This was a clever and topical touch given that recent weeks had seen the demise of the print version of the *NME (New Musical Express)* which, along with *Melody Maker* and *Sounds*, was one of the major influences on the musical thinking of so many of my contemporaries during the 1960s and 1970s.

I walked in on a posh couple buying musical equipment for their daughter, another string to this shop's bow. I always like to look through their selection of vinyl rarities – which included this time an original May Blitz LP for 200 quid. Fortunately, I have one. They always stock very decently priced CDs, but nothing leapt out at me that day. I went all through their rock LP sections to no avail, but was entertained by the posh gent discussing the smooth jazz album which the shop owner had put on 'to make sure it plays through okay before I put it out for sale'. Very relaxing, really not my style. But posh gent said: 'This is great. I'd love to buy it, but I don't have a record player. Never thought I'd want one again. But now I hear this I think I'll have a word with the chap who is currently kitting out my music room and tell him to add a deck and speakers.' Different world for some, what?

I pondered a reduced box set of seven reissued Fleur de Lys singles, down from £79.99 to £50, but that still struck me as plenty to pay for tracks I already own, wonderful though they are. I even looked through the selection of new issue albums and, bizarrely, found a copy of the Nuggets' compilation I'd bought from them for £12.50 not long ago, now offered for £24.99. There was an interesting section with 'two for £12' albums which were otherwise £8 each – a decent sales technique, although the selection was mainly records which I'd expect most seasoned collectors to own already. I couldn't bring myself to shell out for anything on offer.

Next morning, a Saturday, with no football to worry about because the season was over, off I set for the record fair in Uxbridge where I generally alight on something to buy. Not this time. I was, though, entertained by a conversation between an elderly couple and some of the dealers. The oldies were asking whether their collection of country music would be of any appeal. A selection of lovely non-sequiturs followed:

'Have you got any early Dolly?'... 'No, we've tried her but she's not our style. We've got Steve Earle, though.'

'Merle Haggard?'... 'Well, The Dillards, we've got some of them.'... 'There's a name I haven't heard for many years.'

I was thinking, 'I have – I know just where that Dillards album I've been trying to get rid of for years is'.

If only I could suddenly have produced it out of thin air to impress this potential audience. I came out of my reverie to hear one of the dealers entering tricky terrain verbally. Responding to a couple of country names which the couple had chucked in his direction, he said, 'I think the gypsies – can I call them that? Well, the travellers, is that okay? Anyway, they like them...'

I was now distracted by an Earth & Fire LP in a very dusty – no, be honest, it was disgustingly dirty – plastic cover. I checked the condition of the record – as thoroughly as it is ever possible to do in the type of environment offered by gloomily lit shops, and record fairs, which tend to be held in elderly council halls, where atmospheric contaminations galore have accumulated during many years of staging random events, classes and displays. It is difficult to form any sort of opinion in such circumstances, other than that the reality will probably be worse than it appears in situ, once you get it home for a proper look. I played the only trump card the would-be buyer holds over the seller – the 'Fine, I won't buy it, then' one, and put the record back, tried unsuccessfully to wipe the dust and dirt from my hands, and moved on.

Flipping through some CDs under a 'Progressive' heading, I dallied over one by a group called Cyrkle, which looked like my sort of thing. There was precious little information on the cover but a surreptitious online search on my mobile revealed them to be 'garage rock' rather than 'psychedelic', and this copy to be at best 'unauthorised' – a polite term for 'bootleg'. I did feel that a fraction under a tenner for a Cyrkle CD whose contents might disappoint was not justified, so I didn't buy. However, my curiosity is now piqued and I will almost certainly react by buying the blooming thing next time I see it.

When I visited the newly established Twickenham Record Fair, I soon realised that I still didn't have my buying head on. There was a good range of stalls and I was getting stuck into the

'£12 each, five for £50' box belonging to a chatty chap I've become familiar with, previously buying from him at Spitalfields and Guildford.

He had a wide range of sealed copies of mainly live recordings by 1960s bands, many of them of interest to me. I thought that a quintet consisting of a Jeff Beck, Insect Trust, Iron Butterfly, Spencer Davis, and Ultimate Spinach might be worth half a ton. Then I thought again. Most of the Beck tracks are on the *Truth* studio LP I own; Spencer Davis were live in Finland and how motivated would they have been to do the business out there?; the Iron Butterfly album didn't even have an 'In-A-Gadda-Da-Vida' live version; I've lived for years without ever hearing Insect Trust, who I'd always been told were too jazzy for my taste (turned out that was right); and I recently bought a studio Ultimate Spinach record, which I'd only listened to once since.

Then my phone vibrated. It was younger brother, Barry, about some family business. I told him where I was and he mentioned a mutual artist we both like – GT Moore and the Reggae Guitars. G T was one of the first white artists to champion reggae music, even before the Specials, UB40 and Madness et al widened the appeal of reggae, ska and bluebeat. He'd previously been a member of acoustic folk-'rock' band, Heron. When our discussion was over I turned back to the stall and decided suddenly that I didn't really fancy shelling out 50 quid for quite a lot of music I was already very familiar with and didn't actually need alternative versions of, plus another lot I wasn't at all familiar with and didn't much want.

I wandered around the rest of the fair, flicking here, pondering there and mulling elsewhere. There was a lively, encouragingly young throng, male and female, around the large dance music section, alien to me but an important part of the vinyl scene. I heard a father telling his seven- or eight-year-old daughter, 'You like The Beatles, don't you?' He showed her an LP. 'This is how we used to listen to The Beatles.' She looked baffled. Probably thinking he meant that the cover somehow made the music.

I left the hall and nipped in to Eel Pie Records, in nearby traffic-free Church Street where, not only had the shop organised the record fair I'd just visited, but there was also an eco-friendly street food cum shabby-chic-cum-trendy-stuff street market going on. The shop doubles up as a cafe and there was an easy vibe about the place with several coffee-quaffers chilling as record hunters foraged. Two older examples of the latter were conversing about a current dispute between a man of their own generation, Jimmy Page and his next-door neighbour whose name neither of them could recall. 'That pop star bloke, what's his name?' one asked the other. 'Oh the feller from the That group, isn't it?' Yes, the 'feller' from the Take That group. 'Robbie Williams', I reminded them, receiving a grateful acknowledgement.

They cover most of the bases here but £36 for a brand new *The Who at Fillmore East* reissue album, and £32 for a double LP of the recent *Rolling Stones at the BBC* set? Okay, these may have been expanded editions of the basic albums, and admittedly this was in well-off Twickenham, but that's surely a 'try-on', even for rugby fans.

As is normal, my latest fallow vinyl spell finally ended with a glut when I paid a visit to London's Spitalfields Fair – and almost instantly on arrival found five buyable items. Spitalfields has a genuinely buzzy atmosphere, with the record stalls surrounded by shops, bars and food kiosks. There are scores of grizzled veterans from either side of the vinyl trading process and no shortage of new recruits. Some have already become familiar faces, others bring with them an air of mystery. What are they offering, where will they slot in the cost league?

One guy who turns up sporadically sells still-sealed CDs by named and obscure artists for a mere 50p. I was amazed at how many copies of the Pretty Things' *Balboa Island* he had on offer. They're one of my all-time favourite bands and I paid probably 11 or 12 quid when that album came out. I'm concerned that there were way too many pressed up, judging by the level of remainder copies presumably offloaded by the record company. Other more than respectable names like Cockney Rejects, Arthur Brown and even Hendrix (a double CD) were included in the ten-bob section, while for a mere two quid I found a relatively recent Robin Trower CD. You're unlikely ever to undercut this fellow – elsewhere I saw the same CDs offered at £10 or more on different stalls.

There's always entertaining gossip to be heard at Spitalfields: 'Paul Rodgers rang me on my birthday, to say...' 'Don't tell me: Happy Birthday?' The trader, who had been watching me as I pondered buying the live 1970 concert album by Mr Rodgers' group, Free, was telling me about his friendship with him, while he also kept one eye on other potential purchasers. He spotted one who was just reaching out his arm to go through his box of reissued obscurities and collectables. But, even as he addressed his selling pitch to the man reaching out his arm, we both saw the potential customer withdraw that arm rapidly, as though he had been stung by a wasp, or realised he was about to touch something toxic and potentially fatal. With a small jump backwards, the man recoiled. 'I don't have anything to do with...' he hesitated very slightly, before spitting the word out, '...*new* records!' And then he was gone. 'No pleasing some folk,' observed the trader.

Personally, I am very pleased to see the recent introduction of new versions of old, often unobtainable rarities from the late 1960s and 1970s. Even if I was prepared to pay the money demanded for original copies of these LPs, I'm not sure I'd want, or could afford, to do so for any more than a handful. But these sometimes bootlegged, sometimes genuine, legal reissues, available for a tenner upwards, do provide the opportunity to own vinyl versions of records which might otherwise take a lifetime's searching to source and a month or more's wages to own. Or to take a chance on undiscovered music one might never have otherwise been tempted to taste. Many have been available on CD for some while and, in many instances, that is not only acceptable because it allows one finally to own the music in a physical format but also because it often provides additional 'bonus' tracks. These, of course, are almost always disappointing and of iffy quality, but they do at least bestow some bragging rights to the owners.

I recently discovered the work of the early 1970s heavy band Agnes Strange and was able to acquire most of their lively, riffy, recorded output for under 20 quid. Yet, here at Old Spitalfields, was a reissued version of just one of their LPs for 25 quid. I'll leave you to decide whether the physical attraction of the shiny but limited content vinyl format warrants a significant price premium over the more convenient but less desirable CD version which, like any new car, immediately sheds a large percentage of its value the moment you take possession of it. Whereas with vinyl even the new reissues seem to hold most of their value in a resale situation and could even rise when the limited-edition releases have all been sold.

I stopped to take a look at another stall and heard a not entirely serious contretemps unfolding:

'Why do you have a section for "male singers" and a section for "female singers",' demanded a middle-aged man 'but nothing at all for LGBTQ singers?' He glared at the seller, who began to stutter a little as he sought for an explanation. Whereupon his provoker burst into laughter, just as a man came up and asked, 'Will you be here at the next fair?' When told that he would, he admitted, 'I've seen some records I want – but I've bought so many recently I don't know what I have, so I thought I'd note the ones I want and then check whether I've already got them and come back if not.' 'You can buy them now and bring them back if it turns out you already have them,' he was told.

I moved on to the next stall and, glancing at the selection of LP covers hanging behind him, I spotted a copy of Chicken Shack's OK Ken? album from 1969, which had long been on my 'want list'. The Rare Record Price Guide 2020 rates a top quality example at £100 in its stereo incarnation. This one had an £80 sticker on it. The would-be vendor saw me eyeing up the display.

'One caught your eye?'

'Yes, OK Ken?'

'Yeah, good copy that. Got 80 quid on it. Could do it for 60.' He began to scrabble around in a box for the disc itself. 'In great nick, barely a mark on it,' he enthused, and showed it to me.

'This mark here, across track one and edging into track two, that's barely a mark, is it?' I enquired with a smile, already knowing how difficult it is to identify significant flaws on an LP even in bright daylight. It didn't look terrible, though, to be fair, and it is 50 years old. Few of us look the same 50 years on from any particular birthday.

'Well, we can discuss the price if you're interested. Is the price frightening you? We could do 50.'

'No, I'm not frightened, but I think I'll carry on browsing to see what else is around,' I told him.

It really is a good idea if you are conflicted about a purchase to take time out and walk away. If your mind keeps telling you to go back for another look, you'll probably end up buying it, but just by walking away you may encourage the seller to trim the price. But if you walk off and find yourself looking at other possible purchases without giving another thought to what you walked away from – then you evidently can live without it and didn't really want it enough to shell out.

I do have an *OK Ken?* CD, so do I require a vinyl version? Let's put it this way, three days before I typed this, I was in Second Scene where I paid 40 quid for an original vinyl copy of the Steamhammer LP, *Mark II* which I already owned on CD. You tell *me* why I did it. Except that when I played it I knew I'd done the right thing.

As I did when I went to Kent...

IN WHICH... I DOUBT A BOWIE BLOTCH

I'd decided to take a trip to indulge in whatever delights would be revealed at the Bionic Promotions' Record & CD Fair in Orpington, Kent, taking place there in early July 2018. Even I was unable to avoid locating the fair, held in the Crofton Halls, next to the railway station. They charged a quid a head to get in, and as I handed mine over there was a chap coming in the other direction who demanded of the lady collecting the cash: 'Suppose I've got to pay a quid to get out, too?!' She smiled good-naturedly. He didn't.

This does raise the question of whether potential purchasers should be charged to come in and spend money with dealers. I wasn't that bothered, but reckon that, over the course of a year, the total cost of entering record fairs could set one back by the amount of a couple of decent LP purchases.

This fair boasted of being 'South London's Biggest Event'. This is debatable, but, yes, it's probably 'South London's Biggest Record Fair'. I'd estimate it had around 30 dealers, including the one from whom I ended up buying a Blues Project double CD and a John Grant album. The latter is someone who is a bit modern for me but every time I've seen or heard him performing, I've enjoyed him.

Walking into the main hall, I passed a fellow who appeared to have for sale virtually every Bowie record variation there is, but no customers. Nor did he have any when I went past on the way out an hour later. Whether he found time to look around the hall, I don't know, but thumbing through a selection of 'rare records' on one stallholder's table, I noticed a copy of Bowie's *The Man Who Sold the World* LP, released in the US in 1970 and 1971 in the UK. The US release, a copy of which I do have, came in a cartoon-like cover drawing by Bowie's friend, Michael J Weller, himself a former inmate, featuring a cowboy in front of the Cane Hill mental asylum. British copies showed an androgynous Bowie wearing a dress, but even that only helped propel the record into the mid-twenties in the album chart, while in America it didn't even crack the Top 100.

The copy I was eyeing at the record fair was the 'cartoon cover'. It includes a blank speech bubble in which, reportedly, the phrase 'Roll up your sleeves and show us your arms', a pun on record players, guns, and drug use, would have been inserted if Weller had had his way. It seemed in fair enough condition apart from a dark blotch on the middle section of the front cover, yet it was priced at £250, whereas I'd checked the value of mine recently and knew that Discogs listed decent copies at around £50. As I turned it over to look at the back of the cover, the dealer excitedly reached over and pointed to the front cover blotch, telling me: 'Look, it's a signed copy.'

He didn't produce any proof that this was a signature rather than the blotch I'd taken it for, and apparently he expected me to take his word for it. Not that I have any reason to believe he was anything other than an honourable man. I humoured him with a weak smile, slotted it back into its box and continued flicking. A few seconds later the dealer leaned over towards me again, and said, 'Sorry, can I just...?' He picked the record out again before calling over a woman nearby and asking her: 'Have you seen this?' She was handed the record and told, 'Look, Bowie's signature'. I thought she might faint from excitement. Almost cuddling the cover, she uttered thrilled exclamations along the lines of 'Oh, he must have actually held it...' but became a little calmer once she noticed the price.

'Would you take £25 down, the rest at 25 quid a year?' she asked optimistically and probably not entirely seriously.

'Get the old man to buy it for you as a birthday present,' the dealer suggested.

'It's not till November.'

'That's not long,' both the dealer and his female companion responded together. The date was July 1.

The record went back into the box. I'm pretty sure the Bowie expert by the entrance would have seen the 'signed' record and rejected it. I mean, even if he hadn't, wouldn't you, if you were the one selling it, have taken it over to show the specialist guy and asked him for an opinion of its veracity?

The dealer also had a copy of Miller Anderson's solo album *Bright City* which was apparently 'mint'; I already have a non-mint copy for which I paid 25 quid. But this 'mint' one had, I am positive, a £20 tag on it. I didn't look that closely at it, but wished I had when I later checked RRPG and saw it rated at £175. Hm, I told myself that I must have mis-seen a £200 tag as a £20 one.

When you go to a record fair you have the advantage of seeing a huge amount of stock, but what you are seeing will almost certainly have been examined by other dealers, and any errors in pricing might well have been taken advantage of before the public is even invited in. In a record shop it is far more likely that you'll find a true bargain, given that most owners and dealers want/need to enjoy a healthy turnover so have to sell, but specialise in specific areas and won't know everything about every genre. At a fair, it is probable that there is more than one expert in attendance for every area of the business, which virtually eliminates the chances of hidden bargains lurking. Back home, I looked at website 'The Signature Library' (thesignaturelibrary.com) which had available an example of *The Man Who Sold the World* cartoon cover signed by Bowie, but with firm photographic provenance, available for $2000. Not sure their signature matched the fair one. In most cases, buying a signed album relies on a leap of faith, unless there is photographic or written evidence of some kind.

Further on in the fair, the chap from whom I made both of my purchases was talking to a dealer on his day off, who was out buying for his own collection and asked, 'I wonder how long this latest vinyl revival will last? It used to be two-thirds CDs to a third vinyl, but now it is almost 50-50 – that's clearly helped out by the new and reissue LPs, don't you think?' 'Maybe,' the stallholder replied, 'but I still wouldn't want to be running a vinyl-only shop. I couldn't make that work. Can't see myself doing this much longer – I've done me back in lifting this lot in and out of the van. Think I'll end up working at Asda before long.'

My first visit to 'Chester's Luton Record Fair' – which boasts of being 'the country's longest running specialist Record Fair, now in its 38th year' – was an enjoyable experience. I came away with some very attractively priced goodies, not least a brand new copy of Mark Knopfler's 2015 double LP, *Tracker* for a tenner, a £4 copy of the Allman Brothers' *Live at Fillmore East* double, a £2 New York Dolls and Melissa Etheridge CDs. I also realised that the 'Chester' in the fair's name referred to the late Johnny 'Chester' Dowling, who wrote four books replete with memories of his life in the 1950s and 1960s – 'the cafes with jukeboxes, black and white TV, British motorcycles, X-rated films and the back row of the cinema'. They cost £25 each – volume 1, *The Story of My Life*, has sold out but the other three are all available – and come with a free CD.

There was a healthy turnout with a decent percentage of females in the hall, while the number of sellers, and would-be purchasers, of rock 'n' roll records (speciality of the house, I take it) was higher than anywhere else I've been, with singles definitely outnumbering albums as browser targets. With a number of vendors bringing record players with them and a jukebox blasting out rockin' riffs, I was again made aware of how strongly much of this type of music can shape up against all competition. However, I know so little about the genre that I don't feel able even to begin to get into what I know would be an enjoyable detour away from my more usual stamping ground. I must also commend the dress sense of so many of those there for this type of music – they certainly put myself and most other untidy crate-diggers to shame with their sartorial sense and dapper duds. Kudos to them, not a regular feature of fairs of my acquaintance.

It is very rare to visit record fairs only to discover that they are not taking place – but that's not always the case with rock band gigs...

IN WHICH... THE SHOW MUSTN'T GO ON

Dave Mason was the sole (*sorry*) writer of 'Hole In My Shoe', Traffic's follow-up hit to 'Paper Sun', and its 'out-there' psychedelic feel was again combined with nursery-rhyme-style lyrics, mixed with weird musical input. Mason's involvement with these two Top 10 records singled him out to me as someone to follow wherever his musical meanderings took him, which is how I came to acquire the majority of his oeuvre. This made it a certainty that when he came to my neck of the woods to play a gig with his own band a couple of years ago, I was going to be there. I was so keen not only to be there but to get a prime viewing spot for this seated concert that I was actually the first person to book front row seats in the balcony, the best viewing spot offered in the Alban Arena. My booking was made months before the scheduled date of the show, and I marked it boldly on the calendar.

A few weeks later, I was contacted by the Alban Arena, telling me that it had been decided 'by the band's people' that the balcony area should not be made available for the show and that everyone attending should be in the stalls. 'Come on,' said I to the minion deputed with the task of passing on this information, 'It seems to me that the only reason for a band to make such a request would be that the concert is selling so poorly that the sparseness of the audience will be all too obvious if all parts of the auditorium are available.' The minion did not confirm that this was the case but neither did she deny it. From that point on, I had a lurking feeling of dread about whether there would even be a concert, and a day or two before the scheduled gig I rang the venue to confirm the 'doors open' time, only to be told, 'I'm afraid the concert is off. Dave Mason is unwell.'

I was shocked. Sympathetic, of course, had he been struck down by illness. But, call me a cynical hack, to me this sounded extremely suspicious. My journalistic instinct was sharpened to the point at which I decided to make the local media aware of my belief that this concert might have been called off as much for disappointing ticket sales as any health issues. The media got to work, doing not much more than believing me, and sticking a story online outlining the cancellation and one fan's idea of why it was not taking place! Not many hours after the story was published, I received a phone call from someone claiming to be Dave Mason (I believe it *was* him) who assured me that there was indeed illness in the camp, and that was the actual reason for having to scrap the show. It isn't every day one of your musical heroes gives you a bell, and apologises personally for not being able to fulfil a commitment. But those legendary days of 'the show must go on' have clearly departed.

'We'll be playing in London in the not too distant future,' the voice that was probably Dave Mason's said, 'so...' He's going to give me complimentary tickets to make up for the disappointment, that's nice of him, I thought... 'so, if you come along, have a word with our merchandise guy and he'll sort something out for you.' Great, pay up again for another gig in central London, inevitably more expensive than this one, and if you're lucky and believed by the merchandise bod, we might chuck you an oversized, badly printed t-shirt or some other bit of tat.

This wasn't my first experience of a high-profile no-show. My then girlfriend Sheila and I were anticipating a good night when we turned up at the Farx Club in Southall to see Status Quo in the very early 1970s. I'd very much enjoyed their big hit, 'Pictures of Matchstick Men', in early 1968, and I was one of the few equally keen on its under-achieving follow-up, 'Black Veils of Melancholy', back in the day when the received wisdom was that 'if a record is a hit, the follow-up should sound almost exactly like it.' Tamla Motown were amongst those following this invariably inaccurate advice, which usually resulted merely in big hits being followed by sound-alike, but lesser, imitations.

'Matchstick' made Number 7; 'Melancholy' didn't even crack the Top 50. Quo quickly changed tack and by August of the same year were back in the Top 10 with 'Ice in the Sun'. They under-performed during 1969 as 'Are You Growing Tired of My Love' (no question mark) misfired at Number 46 and had to wait until May 1970 for 'Down the Dustpipe' to restore them to the Top 20. By now, the band had made the decision to dump commercialism for what they wanted to play and were establishing a live following for their three-chord, heads-down boogie rock-blues trademark sound.

I think we turned up to see them around the time of 'In My Chair' which would just miss out on the Top 20 in late 1970, but the style they had now adopted appealed big time, so there we were, sitting in front of the curtained stage, shortly before scheduled kick-off time. We'd said 'good evening' to the guys who ran the place, with whom I'd become pally through my association with the local paper. We were so busy having a drink and a chat that we hadn't realised how few people were coming through the doors. There were maybe a couple of dozen of us sitting around when a head popped through the curtain, looked quickly around at the sparse audience and rapidly disappeared back behind what was beginning to look literally like a black veil of melancholy covering the stage. More minutes passed. Then another Quo peeped through the curtain and actually took to the stage. It was – and this must be true as it is my now wife Sheila, who has a razor-sharp memory, recalling – bassist Alan Lancaster. But he was the only member of the band to appear, and, after stuttering out some kind of barely believable excuse for the band not appearing – outbreak of rabies, Rossi abducted by aliens or some such nonsense – he skulked back behind the cover of the curtain and that was the end of the non-gig.

Dave Mason and Quo disappointed me by not performing, but I am also concerned when a band does appear – and then expects me to become a choreographed part of their show. I detest, hate and resent audience participation:

'Let's hear you all sing along with the band on this one...'

Why? I am paying to see and hear *you* entertain *me*, not vice versa. If I were as good a performer as you, there's a chance it would be you paying to see me in action, but I'm not so why are you expecting me to get up and embarrass myself by croaking out a few words of one of your songs?

I also hate:

*People leaping up out of their seats to dance as soon as the concert starts, thus ensuring that those unfortunate enough to be sitting behind them either have an entirely blocked view or have to get up themselves, thus spoiling things for the people behind them... Also, just because you were too tight to shell out for a decent ticket, why do you feel you can rush down to the front of the stage and ensure a lesser experience for me?

*People who attend concerts to watch them through the tiny perspective of their mobile phone, recording tinny versions of the live amplified sound, rather than experiencing the full three-dimension actuality of what is going on. And those who keep taking flash photos during the gig.

*People in smaller venues who apparently come along prepared to pay the entry fee in order to sit or stand, drink to excess and talk/shout through the performance – particularly the ballads and quieter songs while we're trying to listen to the act and not hear about your holiday, your aches and pains and your bloody new car.

*Lengthy breaks in performance – so that ostensibly the act

can go off and recuperate after putting all their energy into their first half exertions. Rubbish. It is just so that the venue can sell overpriced drinks and flog glossy but insubstantial programmes. Get on with it, play through – blimey, the majority of people work for hours before getting a lunch-break and you've had all day to relax and prepare, so just play through, without an interval – we'll appreciate you more for doing so, be more well disposed towards buying a CD, and enjoying a drink *after* the show all the more – *and* get home half an hour earlier!

Let me ask you this – how often is your buying of a record by an artiste for the first time influenced by seeing them perform live?

IN WHICH... I WONDER WHAT COMES FIRST – DISC OR GIG?

What comes first for you – buying a record because you have seen a live performance, or seeing a live performance because you own a record by the act in question? Seeing an impressive live performance by someone I hadn't expected much from will often spark me into action, rushing out to acquire as much as possible of their lifetime's work. My local live music venue of choice is connected to one of my two favourite football clubs. The Tropic is a smallish, about 200-capacity hall at the ground where Wealdstone FC, the non-league club whose old boys include international skippers Stuart Pearce and Vinnie Jones, play their matches. It tends to attract mostly tribute acts, but to their credit, the organisers do like to find original acts to put before a smaller, but usually more discerning crowd. I saw Thunderclap Newman here – yes, the real one – and the Glitter Band – without *him*– and an ailing T S McPhee.

This is where I have discovered bands who have never reached the level of popularity which their talents suggest they deserve. For example, Never The Bride, fronted by boisterous singer Nikki Lamborn, of whom Roger Daltrey, no less, is a big fan, and keyboardist/guitarist/singer Catherine 'Been' Feeney, who co-write the music. With fine back-up musicians, their sound incorporates classic rock, blues, and soul and the girls certainly know how to whip up a crowd, often with the aid of additional member, Jack Daniels! Their songs can be very powerful and having seen them half a dozen times I own about that number of their records.

The first time we saw rock-blues guitarist, Larry Miller at Tropic, we agreed that you could pay ten times what it cost to see his show and still not see talent of this quality. Sadly, Larry, a big Rory Gallagher fan, suffered a stroke, and at time of writing has yet to return to action. The records of his I have bought are a constant reminder of both his dynamism and the personal tragedy that has befallen him. I really hope that the title of his LP, *Unfinished Business*, proves accurate. American Willie Nile is pally with Springsteen and has played with the E Street Band, but when he made his Tropic debut you could count the crowd on your toes and fingers. Didn't matter to him, he and his band played as though they were at nearby Wembley Stadium. Since then he has been back several times and now you need to book early to see him. Willie is not blessed with great height but the energy he throws into his performances – and we have seen him when he has been wracked with illness but carried on regardless – plus his individual charisma and talent, always win over his audiences.

Having bought four of another chap's LPs back in the 1970s I'd never seen him live, so when I noticed that he was playing locally in 2018, I was quick to acquire tickets. That's not enough of a clue to name him, but if I tell you that he is best known for his work with the likes of Neil Young, the groups Grin and Crazy Horse and that he has had two hip replacements as a result of his love of playing the guitar whilst back-flipping on a trampoline... maybe you'd identify Nils Lofgren. The show was a two-man, virtuoso performance by Nils and sidekick Greg Varlotta, who also played keyboards, used his tap-dancing skills to drum and played mariachi-style trumpet. Without an interval, the pair produced

an absolute masterclass in how to play an audience as skilfully as
their instruments.

The only tiny criticism I could have of one of the best live
shows I've witnessed was the slightly over-enthusiastic efforts to
promote 'the last 30 or 40' copies of Nils' massive *Face the Music*
box set CD collection, consisting of 169 'personally chosen' tracks
over 9 CDs, (and a 20-song video, plus a 136-page book). Nils
just happened to have brought them along with him to permit
the good burghers of St Albans the opportunity of shelling out...
I didn't wait around to find out how much the set was going for.
Not that I wasn't interested, but there were hordes of fans waiting
for him to come amongst them. When I got home I had a look
on Amazon. Cheapest offer, £378.20! There was another £13.61
to pay for delivery. There was, though, a copy offered on Amazon.
com, from a different supplier, for $299.98 plus $3.99 delivery –
which, translated, worked out at £228.77. Hm. Bit of a difference
there.

Then I found a site called fourdogsmusic.co.uk, offering to sell
it for £116 and a few pence, with a 10 per cent discount if one
signed up to their site. I was soon thinking that a couple of quid
over a ton wouldn't be the worst value in the world, and I filled
in the relevant sections for making a purchase. I found there were
'extras' added, including some kind of tax, which produced a final
cost of £141.76, still market-place competitive, but not really giving
me confidence in a company I hadn't heard of before to splash out
such serious dosh.

So I sent them an email:

'I was interested in your Nils Lofgren' *Face the Music* box set. Whilst
browsing the site a pop-up offered me a 10 per cent discount if I
filled in my details. The set was quoted at £116.73 + free delivery.
But I could find nowhere to enter the 10 per cent discount code
I'd been given and when some mysterious 'tax' extra was added
the price was £141.76. Is this right?'

A response arrived six hours later:

'The cost of the CD box set is shown as £139.96, the £116.73 price you were looking at is shown as the price excluding VAT: £139.96 (£116.63 ex. vat). So no mysterious tax then. But very sorry but this fine CD has actually sold out now anyway and is due to be taken off the site. Best wishes, Mike (Newman).'

As ever, one response invites another, so I emailed back to ask whether the box set should still have been offered, as it had already sold out? And, no mention of the offered discount? The subsequent silence was deafening. The next evening, *Face the Music* box set was still for sale at £139.96 with no indication that there were no copies available. Next time I went to check out the fourdogsmusic website, I found this message:

'After 12 years of supplying some of the best music around, (well, in our opinion anyway), Four Dogs Music is taking a break. Time will tell if we will be back gracing the web with our eclectic mish-mash of musical mayhem.'

IN WHICH... I BACK A REAL WINNER

It was Josie's fault. Of that there's no doubt. Within 48 hours of meeting her, I'd abandoned all restraint and done something I'd never expected to do. It had happened so suddenly that I was left feeling a little guilty. But nonetheless thrilled and excited by what she had made me do. I hadn't intended to do it, but I was swept away on a wave of emotion and now felt as though because of her I had a secret I could never share with my wife.

It had started innocently enough at Ascot racecourse on the first Wednesday of May 2018. I was hosting a hospitality box at the races, entertaining 10 people associated with my work on the annual William Hill Sports Book of the Year award which I and bookshop owner John Gaustad, created 30 years previously. Every

MIKE H and I discovered an unexpected vinyl treasure trove in a Seaford gents' outfitters… very much a sentence I never expected to write when beginning this book.

THE 45 which set me on my life's work of record collecting – Duane Eddy's '(Dance With The) Guitar Man'.

CLACTON BUTLINS. Late sixties. Terrible dress sense. Terrible haircut. Life-threatening association with bunch of skinheads. Saved only by inexplicable fact that the two females both fancied me…

ARCADIUM... Deprived through my own financial folly of my much-loved Arcadium LP I consoled myself with this still ravishing reissue version.

MY COLUMN in its vintage heyday – not Shaw how Sandie gatecrashed it for a positive review.

MY TALENTED cousin and 'God-sister', Maxine has never gone right back where she started from, fortunately for her...

BRUCE LANGSMAN had the digital flexibility to rival the Claptons, Greens and Pages, but circumstances intervened, and his potential was never more fulfilled than on this debut LP.

NOW a great friend and racehorse owner, then pal of Steve Marriott, Dusty Springfield, Zoot Money et al, Di Jones was the cutting edge drummer in Peter, Jan & Jon. They were so ahead of their time that in 1965 Record Mirror reported they 'went into hiding on Peter's sister's farm, converting a barn into a studio'. Single, 'Mountain Boy', hit the Radio Caroline chart but Peter foolishly split the band, probably hoping to get back together with a member of his former group, Manish Boys, one David Bowie.

THE GHOST were so keen on my spirited review of their 'When You're Dead' single that they nicked it for a press release.

YOURS TRULY – The signature was still a work in process, as was the career. The haircut was an improvement.

BRIGHTON shop, great supporter of RSD but I don't hold that against them…

OUTSIDE Julian and Helen's great little record shop.

HELEN enjoys a quiet moment in the soft glow of a Second Scene evening… just before I blunder in to ruin the mood.

MATERIALISING in 'Wanted Music' of Beckenham, as if from nowhere, during my 2018 visit, this remarkably turned-out, strikingly stylish dapper gentleman cut the heftiest, nattiest dash I have been privileged to witness during my half century of record shop punter perusals…

JULIAN SMITH's premises may be bijou, but his vinyl knowledge and record collection are immense. Here he takes a sideways look at some of the contents of the latter…

DAVID SUTCH's controversial 'Heavy Friends' LP, featuring Jimmy Page, scraped into the US charts, but this now sought-after follow-up release sadly didn't keep the momentum going.

TERRIFIC promotional leaflet for Kiwi vinyl outlets, including much missed Death Ray Records.

VINEGAR JOE   JSE
27 DRYDEN CHAMBERS
119 OXFORD STREET LONDON W1
01-437 0712   01 734 8823/3984

MELODY MAKER.

BLOWN

MY MIND has been blown!
The date, April 22, the place
Bolton Institute of Tech-
nology, the group, Vinegar
Joe. Their performance was
incredible, their music brilliant.
On behalf of the hundreds of
fortunate people present I
would like to thank Vinegar
Joe and to ask them to return
as soon as possible. — **PETE
BURROWS, BOLTON,
LANCS.**

ELKIE declares her fully reciprocated love for me.

THIS BAG contained the single disc I found to buy in this San Francisco store, a 99 cent Billy Gibbons single.

CONCRETE MOSAIC, my one and only band, short-lived, also featuring pals Martin Wilson and photographer friend Phil.

GAYE ADVERT didn't need to look through Gary Gilmore's Eyes to become an odds-on winner in her career at William Hill where I caught up with her for an interview in the betting shop where she was working.

'HERE WE GO ROUND THE MULBERRY BUSH' written and recorded by Capaldi, Mason, Winwood, Wood, aka Traffic, theme tune to the rite of passage movie which I so loved back in the day.

NOT SURE whether Rock Goddess still boast about this cover version, but I enjoyed interviewing them.

FARX CLUB – here's a signed version of the membership card.

THE DAYS WHEN national newspapers concerned themselves with serious vinyl news, supplied by me…

'HOME TAPING' – The ludicrous slogan employed to bully people into not taping their records.

'LEAPING FOR JOY' – The *Weekly Post* article I enabled to launch Elton John's career.

A GREETINGS card so appropriate that I love receiving it each time from someone different who says 'This is about you'.

AT VANISHING POINT RECORDS of Wellington, NZ, which has since lived up to its name.

ME AT STRAWBERRY FIELD. Forever part of my favourite record title.

winner of the award lands a hefty cash prize, a large free bet – and an invitation to the races. This was that day at the races for the 2017 winner, Andy McGrath, whose excellent book, *Tom Simpson: Bird on the Wire*, about the early, tragic British cycling hero Tom Simpson had captivated the judges, three of whom were present to help Andy celebrate his triumph.

There was a great atmosphere all afternoon. Everyone, including me for once, seemed to have backed at least one winner. Respected broadcaster John Inverdale, there with his wife Jackie, started the ball rolling by backing a horse, whose owners were obviously fans of Debbie Harry, if not Blondie, called Getchagetchagetcha. At 16/1 in a field of four, against a red-hot favourite, the horse seemed unlikely to win. But the bookies' designated 'certainty' blotted his copybook, rearing up as the stalls opened, leaving champion jockey Ryan Moore with all he could do even to stay on the animal's back. Meanwhile, the other three were charging down the track many lengths clear. It was only a sprint, but by the time they reached the final furlong, Moore had urged his favourite back on almost level terms, but in a thrilling, flat-out finish, Getchagetchagetcha held on to win.

By the end of the afternoon most of the guests had departed and just four people, my wife Sheila and I, together with Andy McGrath and his charming partner, Josie, remained in the box. I'd mentioned that a horse called Josie's Orders had won a race a day or two earlier when ridden by my favourite jockey of all time, Nina Carberry – although Josie in the box had known nothing of that. We were chatting, chewing over the fat of a lovely day. An obvious thing to ask people you have only recently met is where they live. When the reply, 'West Norwood' came, I did what I do so often, and immediately asked, 'Are there any good second-hand record shops there?' Josie responded that indeed there was one notable example of the species. A shop called The Book & Record Bar.

Less than 48 hours later I was standing outside this very establishment. The exterior of the shop betrayed its original purpose – as a pub, The Gypsy Queen. Indeed, the building still operates as a social hub and frequently offers live music. I had managed to do a little checking out of the place online and found this assessment on the Brixton Buzz website: 'Owner Johnson knows his black stuff - he built up a collection of over 10,000 vinyl records over the last 40 years, and as a contributor to the yearly *Rare Record Price Guide* you'll be unlikely to find a wildly under-priced bargain here.'

The interior, as I walked in at around midday on a Friday, looked welcoming. Music was playing. A man speaking in a foreign accent - French, probably - who was accompanying a gentleman in a wheelchair, was engrossed in conversation with another man - owner Johnson, I assumed - behind the counter. They looked over briefly as I came in, but continued chatting. My first impression was positive. It was quite neatly laid out. The books were shelved around the edges of the large room and the records, all in plastic covers and in labelled sections - BLUES, JAZZ, etc - looked tidy and in decent condition. I was surprised and very encouraged as I spotted not only a US PSYCH section, but also UK PSYCH and PROGRESSIVE headings. This just could be very much my kind of shop.

I began to flip through the UK PSYCH and adrenalin kicked in as I saw intriguing and desirable records one after the other. I had to stop, look around, check that I hadn't wandered into a parallel universe, and begin calmly to collect up records for potential purchase. Soon there were a dozen or more of them in my little pile. Names I knew but didn't often come across in such shops, like Dando Shaft, Help Yourself, Aynsley Dunbar, Alan Bown, were appearing with every flip. I moved on to US PSYCH, then had a go at 'NEW ARRIVALS'. All the while adding to my heap. I was entertained by some of the little labels attached to records - one advising of a record called 'Sunday All Over the World' that it would cost £10 and that it came 'with Robert Fripp (good) and Mrs Fripp (bad)'. This told me far more than a subsequent review I would read which declared that it 'is an arty, ambitious project that attempts to push the boundaries of pop music'. I slotted the record back and moved on. Aardvark, Illinois Speed Press - still they kept on coming. The Parlour Band. The Smubbs. I felt like I was in one of those daydreams which all too soon reveal themselves to be just that.

I reverted to consciousness with a bump when I totted up the total cost of the albums I'd gathered together. This was a three-figure sum, the like of which I'd never before handed over in one record shop transaction. One which would result in stern looks and long periods of silence should word ever get back to Mrs Sharpe. What to do? Put some back, spend a realistic, modest amount and come back in the future, said the sensible voice in my head. I ignored it. What if I came back and all of these great records had gone to other, bolder customers? I remembered the training I'd been putting in for just such a situation. Long hours spent watching and absorbing the lessons from experts on programmes such as *Antiques Road Trip* and *Bargain Hunt*. Here was an unprecedented opportunity to demonstrate that I could be as ruthless a bargaineer as them.

Fortunately, Michael Johnson, the proprietor of Book & Record Bar, is a genuine gent. He reckoned up a total value, offered a discount and was generous enough when my training kicked in and I boldly demanded, 'Er, do you suppose we could perhaps, er, maybe agree on a fiver less, don't worry if we can't, I'll still pay the going rate.' He gave his instant, good-natured agreement.

Michael always felt he was going to end up as a record shop owner, which he finally managed in 2013, even back in the day in a different working life, spent travelling around the country. 'I would make a point of visiting the local record shop. It was a time when there were piles of now valuable albums being sold for clearance purposes for literally just a few pence, so I bought them up.' He references, as an example, the group Black Cat Bones, whose album *Barbed Wire Sandwich* now has a £500 RRPG quote: 'They couldn't give it away, then, and there were many more similar examples. But I was buying for a purpose, looking ahead to the time when I'd eventually be in a position to open a second-hand record shop.'

I responded that I remembered grabbing a Skip Bifferty album from a pile of them, stickered at just 59p in a local Debenhams 40 years or more ago. I wished now that I'd splashed out on four or five copies, as they can now command some £200. Michael's foresight paid off, but he clearly is not just a businessman. He is someone who genuinely loves the vinyl he buys and sells, and no doubt has an enviable personal collection. Just listening to him discussing records with the customers who came in to trade showed his knowledge.

'Yes, you'll love "Sock It To 'Em J B",' he told one man, who was previously unaware of the single by Rex Garvin and the Mighty Cravers - part of the soundtrack of my disco life in the 1960s.

The man had come in hoping to sell some records for 'X' amount, and had been gently talked down to accept 'V' amount for them and, in another example, 'U'!

I leave, completely uplifted by my morning's work, in the sure and certain knowledge that this is a shop I will return to again and, quite possibly, again.

I head back up the road to nearby West Norwood station, thinking: 'Thanks, Josie - visiting that shop proved a very worthwhile gamble. Rather like my early career change...

IN WHICH... I BET ON MY FUTURE CAREER

Initially, I expected that by launching a new career with William Hill, after my short stint in the building world, my interest in records would have to take a back seat, as I would probably now stop receiving the review copies which had helped so much. I wasn't expecting to remain a bookie for long, so I wasn't over-concerned. Oddly enough, while it can be difficult enough to get on to a press mailing list for all kinds of products, it is often even more difficult to get *off* it. Particularly if you don't try too hard to do so. I'd already managed to persuade some of the record companies to send review copies and information to my home address for fear that other interested parties might start intercepting them before they reached my desk at the *Post*. Which meant that, having somehow forgotten to let them know that I was no longer churning out the Record Rendezvous column, I continued receiving press releases and review request forms which I may have sent back occasionally. I did my best to continue to publicise the records I received – the Hatch End FC Newsletter may seem an offbeat publication to feature record reviews, but footballers buy records too!

Within a couple of years, I had moved through the boardman-counter hand-bet settler-assistant manager chain of betting shop command, and when a colleague from the branch around the corner decided to move on, taking the contents of the safe with him, I was promoted to manager. It was a great job, which I really enjoyed. There weren't then most of the restrictions that there are today and not so much of the frowning disapproval from people who have never gambled on anything in their lives and believe deep down that others should not be allowed such a legal outlet for their interest.

As I began to realise that, if I were to have any chance of returning to journalism, I'd probably need to leave William Hill I spotted an advertisement in the *Sporting Life*, the best read national horse- and greyhound-racing daily newspaper. It had been placed by William Hill, who were looking for someone to work in their Advertising Department, as it was described in the days before Public Relations, Press Offices and Marketing Departments became de rigueur for large companies. The company's managing director, Sam Burns, was, for some reason, conducting the job interview. Noticing that my CV showed I was already an employee of the company, he frowned at me from over his glasses and said grumpily, 'Suppose that means I should offer you the job...'

My delight was tempered when my boss-to-be, Mike, walked in, and asked, 'Is this him?' When told that it was, he directed his next question to me: 'Has he told you...?' He was interrupted by the MD who tried to push him out of the room, but before he left, Mike called over his shoulder, '...you'll have to work weekends, Bank Holidays and evenings without any extra pay?' Just like being back at the *Weekly Post*, I thought, indicating that wouldn't be a problem and wondering whether William Hill had a football team. (It did. I later played for it and when sent off, thus risking a ban for my real club, I gave the name of the then MD, Len Cowburn.)

Once settled into the job, I realised that my success depended on persuading the national press to write about bookmaking in general and William Hill in particular as frequently as possible. I wondered whether there might be a way of incorporating records within that brief, and came up with the idea that the company should start taking bets on records making the charts.

One of the more noteworthy bets of this nature occurred in 1979 when I was approached by Island Records. They had signed a group called U S of A, whose new single was called '2/1 I Bet Ya'. Island said that to support the record they wanted to place a £5000 bet that it would make the Top 10. We accepted the bet at odds of 10/1, and Island decided that they would also design the cover of the record to look like a betting slip, which, uniquely, they did. None of this managed to help the record to become any sort of hit. I also devised a long-term 'Christmas Number One' betting market, which rapidly became one of our, and other 'copy-cat bookies', most popular 'set-piece' bets of the year, with speculation about the next year's festive chart-topper beginning virtually the moment this year's was revealed. Some shrewd, well informed punters would target the Xmas chart market and we often found ourselves facing a hefty pay-out.

It wasn't only genuine punters placing bets. The PR team behind an absolute dirge of a record by a well-known actor plunged hundreds of quid on it at what even at 500/1 were hardly generous odds. Bookies invariably shorten odds when enough cash is staked, so down came the price to 100/1. The plugging team went in again and again... and again, eventually causing a media stir, with my help, as the feeble 45 at one point became 5/2 favourite. Once people actually got to hear the caterwauling, I think it ended up selling about a dozen copies and reaching around Number 578 in the official charts, but the pluggers had achieved their aim of creating a buzz, in the process generating publicity for William Hill.

Christmas 1989 definitely produced an orchestrated, and this time successful, gamble on Band Aid's charity single, 'Do They Know It's Christmas?' taking the festive honours for the second time – but those in the know overplayed their hand by trying to get a ten grand (£10,000) wager on, which instantly sounded the alarm bells. We turned that bet down and quickly slashed the odds to foil the attempted coup, which would have had more chance of producing a bigger pay-out had they drip-fed smaller, less noticeable bets into the market. I had no qualms at turning those involved away once it became obvious what was happening – after all, they were hardly likely to be placing the bets in order to donate their winnings to the charity...

In 1993, Take That were confidently expected to land the Xmas Number One spot – only to fall foul of Noel Edmonds' pink and yellow pal, Mr Blobby! Noel showed support for his spotted sidekick by betting £2000 that his record would win the honour – which he did, embarrassing Gary, Robbie and, er, the other Take That blokes in the process. Serious pop punters had been convinced Take That were absolute certainties with their 'Babe' and bet on them accordingly, forcing their odds to shorten drastically. However, they were spectacularly undone by what would subsequently be often voted the worst song of all time. Mr Blobby communicated only by saying the word 'blobby' in an electronically altered 'voice', yet the single reached No 1 on 11 December. A week later, 'Babe' demoted Mr Blobby from top spot for one week. Once again Take That's odds collapsed as punters bet on them as though defeat were out of the question. I genuinely believed that the 'Mr Blobby' track was going to be one of those novelty Christmas presents with which all parents love to help pad out the sackful of goodies to give their kids. Thus it proved... 'Mr Blobby' made a surprise return to the Number 1 spot on Christmas Day. I did buy a copy of the single for my then very young son, Paul. He has now finally forgiven me.

The Blobby coup inspired other bizarre bids for Xmas glory over the years, adding some seldom-played discs to my collection. For example, in 1999 the BBC News website reported: 'A bunch of all-singing, all-dancing hamsters are threatening to top the charts. The hamster-dance recording using sampling from a cult website is being tipped as this year's Christmas Number One.' A year later, there was another unlikely figure atop the Xmas chart, as the theme song from the kids' show *Bob the Builder* took the top spot.

For a few years, *The X Factor* almost killed off Xmas No 1 betting, as the show ensured that its winner would have a single rushed out to storm the festive chart. But a reaction against this virtual 'rigging' of the outcome saw an organised campaign to defeat *The X Factor* by outlier US rock group Rage Against The Machine, which was reckoned so unlikely to succeed that three-figure odds were offered against it happening – yet it ultimately did.

The spin-off from the Xmas No 1 market was that we began to receive requests for bets to hit No 1 at any time of the year. Just how difficult it was to protect ourselves against 'inside information' became evident when, in January 1991, I was approached by a Mr Parsons, asking for odds that The Clash would top the singles' rankings before the end of the year. Having checked out their previous singles – 'London Calling' had been their biggest, making No 11 in 1979 – I figured 50/1 was a safe price to quote about a group I then regarded as punk has-beens, whose heyday was several years earlier. A few more bets on the same eventuality encouraged me to do additional research, and I was very concerned to discover that the band's 1982 track, 'Should I Stay or Should I Go' (no question mark) had been chosen to launch a multi-million pound advertising campaign to promote Levi jeans. Still, when originally released it only managed to reach No 17, so I didn't panic. But I wasn't feeling like a jeanius when the record charged to No 1 in March 1991, costing the company an arm and possibly two legs. Even less so, when Mr Parsons confessed that he'd had 'an inkling' that the record might be used in the ad campaign. A lesson learned.

Unexpectedly, my job at William Hill enabled me to begin using my journalistic skills once more when I was asked to edit the company's staff newspaper *Showboard*. When I introduced a feature into the paper involving pop celebrities with an interest in horse racing and/or betting, it also enabled me to interview a few of the people whose records I had been collecting over the years. One of them I shared initials with, and Gordon Sumner, aka, of course, 'Sting', was someone whom, as he was roughly the same age as I am, I had watched and listened to with interest. I still own copies of all the Police albums and one or two of his solo albums – happily playing the former from time to time, but frequently taking evasive action to avoid going anywhere near the latter!

When I interviewed Sting he told me how he had stumbled into the world of racehorse ownership: 'I had six Irish builders in my house and we got talking. "Sting," they said, "what you need is a string of racehorses." One of them owned a horse called Sweetcal, so he and I went into partnership. They hadn't told me Sweetcal also pulled a proverbial milk-cart! She wasn't very good...' 'I always back my horses,' he told me. 'It's in good faith to do so. I always bet to win, but I don't bet outside of racing.' Nor was he ever likely to give up recording to become a jockey. 'The first time I ever rode a horse was in Egypt, when we rode round the Pyramids on Arabian stallions – it was like riding a motorbike without handles, but an unforgettable experience.'

Let's be fair to him, though. Whatever your opinion of Sting, surely you have to hand him an accolade for writing one of *the* great lyrics about teenage love. 'Can't Stand Losing You', from the *Outlandos d'Amour* album, was released in 1978 and made a minor impression on the Top 50, but was re-released during 1979 and was a massive hit. For me and, I suspect, other collectors, the lines, 'I see you've sent my letters back/And my LP records and they're all scratched' really sum up those early relationships in which I was forever sending records to girls to symbolise my love for them. I think it was a boy thing. I don't recall (m)any such gifts coming in the other direction. But, faced with Sting's situation, would I have been more miffed at losing the girl, or at the records being scratched? The latter, doubtless.

At that age it wasn't financially easy to chalk it up to experience and just buy another copy or, indeed, to go out and find another girlfriend! This was the final blow for any fledgling relationship. Could you really love someone who could mistreat and abuse defenceless vinyl in this manner? Surely, had you gone the whole hog and married her such unreasonable behaviour would later be irrefutable grounds for divorce. Most of the records I sent, or gave to the girlfriend who ultimately became – and remains – my wife, did, though, get scratched, usually at parties, but at least she never sent them back.

Steve Harley enjoys a bet, too, but told me of the occasion when he totally forgot he'd backed a 28/1 winner. Steve was a great fan of the kidnapped racehorse, Shergar, and was very upset as he saw the great runaway Derby winner beaten into fourth place during the St Leger: 'I'd had a couple of hundred pounds on Shergar long before the Leger, but on the day itself something told me to have a fiver each-way on outsider Cut Above. I watched the race, and was so sad for Shergar being beaten that I was sitting there feeling depressed for some time before I even found out that Cut Above had actually won the race, so I'd backed a 28/1 winner.' Steve and I met again in slightly bizarre circumstances one night when I was acting as a steward for his show with Cockney Rebel at Wembley Arena. I was walking along in an area behind the stage with a friend as Steve was walking towards us. As he came up to us we stopped to say hello to him and my mate, Bill Nicholls, thrust his fist towards Steve and told him, 'I've got nothing else to sign, so would you sign your name on my hand, please?' Steve obliged.

A few years later I was tipped off that a well-known figure from the early punk days was working for William Hill. I investigated and discovered that I was indeed now a colleague of the wonderful Gaye Advert, bassist and focal point of punk band, The Adverts. Music writer Dave Thompson declared that Gaye, with her 'panda-eye make-up and omnipresent leather jacket defined the face of female punkdom until well into the next decade'. I'd been a fan of the band's breakthrough Top 20 single, 'Gary Gilmore's Eyes', and was delighted to be able to interview her in one of the company's London shops, finding her to be a modest, friendly person. She even signed my copy of their album, *Crossing the Red Sea* which came out in 1977 if you believe the record label, or 1978 if you believe its cover! Gaye, who reverted to her real surname of Black, is now a fine ceramic artist, exhibiting her work around the world.

Another way in which I was able to link my job and company to music appeared when the Mercury Music Prize – as it was originally known – was introduced in 1992. I approached the organisers and offered to help them promote the Prize by opening up a betting book on the outcome. They were happy to accept and William Hill enjoyed an exclusive relationship with them for several years. The Prize was won by Primal Scream in its inaugural year, followed by Suede and M People. This proved an admirable source of free music – albeit usually CDs rather than LPs – but beggars and choosers and all that! I also prompted the company to take bets on the Eurovision Song Contest, which went well enough until 2006 when Finland's heavy rock entry, the band Lordi, brought the house down with their 'Hard Rock Hallelujah' only for our odds compilers to decide they still couldn't win, and continue to offer Lordicrously long odds about that happening, until it did...

One of my final William Hill-related record incidents occurred on Grand National day, 2014. It was the 'done thing' for Head Office-based bods to lend a helping hand in a betting shop on this, the busiest day of the year. I volunteered to do so at a branch in Northwood Hills, Middlesex where, unbeknown to me, the manager was a real Beatle buff, from taste in music to his winklepicker boots and Beatle haircut. Top man and very well disposed to me when I arrived and asked him what role he'd like me to play in his shop.

'Could you just welcome punters in and help out the ones who clearly aren't quite sure what they should be doing?' he asked.

No problem, we had a supply of sweets, keyrings, pens and such giveaways and I was well used to dealing with novice punters. The day went well and we had a steady stream of customers coming through. Then a middle-aged guy with a couple of heavy bags, one around his shoulder, the other in his hands, wandered in, looking a little unsure. The shop manager recognised him but didn't know his name. We wondered what was in the bags. I engaged him in conversation and asked him. He was quite happy to show me – he had a stash of perhaps 30 or so LPs in the bags, and some of them were obviously of a type that most record shop patrons I knew would be very keen to get a look at and quite possibly pay significant sums to own.

'What are you looking to do with them?' I asked, hoping he might say, 'Give them to you for a fiver the lot.' Instead, he vaguely suggested he might look for a record shop where he could sell them. I told him that I knew a local guy he could definitely trust to offer him a fair price, and told him how to get to Julian's Second Scene shop, before ringing him to forewarn him. Against my expectations, the chap did go to the shop, but ended up leaving Julian very frustrated as he agreed to sell several of his lesser lights but prevaricated about the really desirable ones – both Blossom Toes' LPs and several others on a par in the rarity stakes. 'I had to give up on him in the end,' said Julian later. 'He kept threatening to sell all of them to me, then argued with himself about whether he'd get more elsewhere. I know full well he wouldn't have done, but I eventually had to tell him to make his mind up, or stop wasting mine and his own time. Perhaps I'll eventually hear from, or see, him again... but I seriously doubt it.'

Neither of us has ever seen the man since.

IN WHICH... MUSIC IS MY FIRST LOVE

In the late 1970s to mid-1980s, I was writing features and interviews for the weekly rock paper, *Music*, after meeting up with the editor, John Shotton. 'House' style was perhaps summed up by the intro to an article I wrote about the Thompson Twins, which was shown on the page by reproduction of the editor's memo to me: 'Provide me with 1000 words about the Thompson Twins – and make it snappy.'

My response was: 'About this Thompson Twins piece, I've got a bit of a problem with the introduction – do we assume that all our readers are aware that the Thompson Twins aren't twins and that there are three of them, that they aren't called Thompson, that they are named after the Detectives in the Tin Tin cartoon strip? Or do we have to go through the rigmarole of explaining all that?'

Memo from editor to GS:

'Provide me with 1000 words about the Thompson Twins – and make it snappy!'

So I did.
It ended with another memo to the editor:

'Please find attached 1000 words about Thompson Twins – I'm a bit stuck for an ending – how about doing something contrived like rounding the piece off with a memo from me to you asking how to round it off?'

And that's how it appeared.
Sometimes we did conventional interviews and actually managed to give readers a little informative insight. Paul Weller, during his Style Council era, revealed to me, 'To be quite honest you can't keep me away from my axe, it's an extension of me – it's the smell of the crowd and the roar of our agent that flips me!' While Bruce Foxton confided he'd written a song called 'Freak', having 'tried to put myself into the Elephant Man's shoes.' Steve Harley surprised me when he admitted of one of his best-known songs, 'Sebastian', 'I don't really understand what the song is about. I thought I did when I wrote it, in my naivety, but really I've been performing it under false pretences for some while now.' Rat Scabies of The Damned claimed in 1984, when they were struggling to be heard and release new product, 'If what we believe in has to suffer then I'd rather do without commercial success. One of our problems with getting a record deal is that many people won't touch us because of our name – how did we get a reputation like that? We've never gone around raping women or molesting children, have we?' I took it that was a rhetorical question. I concluded that the band 'are worthy of note because of what they are, rather than what other people think they should be.'

Articles were commissioned and written about many other groups and individual artists. Guitarist John Sykes, of Whitesnake, told me of his failed audition for Ozzie Osbourne's band: 'He turned up one and a half hours late, well oiled, and fell in the door, so nothing came of it.' I also asked him about Whitesnake's sexist reputation as a result of album titles such as the then most recent, *Slide It In*, (there would be others such as *Slip of the Tongue* and *Come An' Get It*) and a penchant for blatantly sexual record covers. 'I think it's all basically tongue in cheek,' he responded in what I hoped was not intended to conjure up a literal image in the mind of readers.

I enjoyed meeting one of the few all-girl heavy metal bands out there, Rock Goddess. Reading my piece back, I think I just may have fancied one (all?) of them a little, but I didn't allow that to influence my feature – oh, yes, other than saying 'they're bloody lovely, I'm captivated' – and I think I drew a nice comment from guitarist, vocalist and songwriter Jody Turner when I asked her who was the driving force of the band. 'There's no leader in my band!' she insisted.

Rick Wakeman's new LP '1984' was issued in 1981 with a press function held bizarrely enough in a tube train parked in an underground station. I asked him why but never got a plausible answer. I only recently parted with the 1984 t-shirt I was given. Hell-raising drummer Cozy Powell unexpectedly revealed that he had recently moved to one of horse racing's longest established strongholds, Lambourn, where he'd 'become friends with Johnny Francome, champion jump jockey, who is into his music as well'. Powell also owned a racehorse called Drummer Jess, which 'did nothing until we sold him, then proceeded to win twice'. He also spoke of his love of scuba diving and motor racing – both as a participant. He was modest about his career: 'I make solo albums for the Japanese market. The last two have gone gold over there... and cardboard over here!' Cozy died tragically early in a shocking 1998 car accident.

I learned from Robert Palmer, also now departed, how he came up with the title track for his album, 'Pride', when he told me: 'The ambience of the song was created by singing phonetically – to sing appropriate vowels to a series of spontaneous melodies. I then discovered a strange harmony, listened to the results on a tiny distorted speaker and imagined what the words might be.' I'm not sure I followed him then, let alone now.

We record collectors would imagine that members of bands we like are well aware of their recorded output, but an interview with Simon Kirke, drummer of Free and Bad Company, saw me surprise him when he was explaining how he'd first teamed up with doomed guitarist of genius Paul Kossoff in the mid-1960s outfit Black Cat Bones. He had seen them play at the Nag's Head in Battersea: 'I was very impressed with Paul's playing and plucked up courage to speak to him, and said, "Your drummer's not up to much." This cheeky approach worked. Koss told me they were auditioning for a new drummer and invited me along. There was one snag. I had no drum kit! I ended up playing on the outgoing drummer's kit and getting his job.' Black Cat Bones split, apparently without ever telling Simon that they had released an album earlier in their existence. He was amazed when I told him.

Simon and Paul heard Paul Rodgers singing in a band called Brown Sugar and brought him into the fold. Then Alexis Korner recommended bassist Andy Fraser and also suggested the name Free. Simon remembered Paul (Koss) being 'a fantastic driver – he used to drive the band everywhere, he'd drive all night – trips of two or three hundred miles. He could have been a professional driver.' He and Simon both had their flaws. 'I hit the bottle – but Koss hit the pills – and worse.' Simon cleaned up his act; Koss couldn't, and it did for him, firstly affecting his playing, then leading to his tragic death in 1976. Simon climbed back to success along with Paul Rodgers in Bad Company despite revealing that he fancied an alternative career as a travel journalist. 'I'd love to have Alan Whicker's job.'

I interviewed the late Errol Brown for a Hot Chocolate feature to mark the fact that 28 of their 34 singles had been chart hits, most of which he had at least a hand in writing. The one he was there to plug in 1983, 'Tears on the Telephone', just about kept the run going by reaching Number 37. Errol told me about an unusual collaboration between him as a pop-soul artist, and Adrian Gurvitz, lead guitarist in hard rock trio Gun, along with brother Paul, whose biggest hit, 'Race with the Devil' was written by him. Errol and Adrian were recording for the same label and 'kept passing each other in the corridor and mentioning that we enjoyed stuff the other had done. Eventually I rang Adrian, said I was a little bit short of material and would he consider helping me out?' The result was Hot Chocolate's next single, the Brown-Gurvitz track 'I'm Sorry'. It is probably fair to say this gamble by keen poker player Errol ('I'm good') wasn't a huge success – reaching Number 89 in the UK and 57 in Germany.

As a postscript to this story, I was at Second Scene and noticed Julian had put an original copy of the first album by the Gurvitz brothers' band, Gun, on his wall of fame. I wondered whether it was the British release, as I'd bought one on a trip to Amsterdam (no pun intended) in the early 1970s. 'Yes, a British release,' confirmed Julian. 'But you'd never guess what happened recently. A lady came in – very attractive – and introduced herself as Adrian Gurvitz's wife. She was absolutely astonished when I told her how much the Gun albums were worth. She seemed genuinely shocked that they are worth serious money, at least three figures. She also said that her son is a budding musician – but wouldn't tell me his name or that of his band, as she wants to see him make it through his own efforts.'

To do that it would help to have the kind of charisma effortlessly displayed by a gentleman I saw in a Beckenham record shop...

IN WHICH... I SNAP – AMEN TO THAT!

If I hadn't sneaked a photograph of him I'd have wondered whether he was real. I'd just spotted perhaps the single most individual-looking person I've ever seen in a record shop. I was able to grab a snap of this impeccably, if eccentrically dressed, dapper, late middle-aged gentleman who had entered the shop just a couple of minutes earlier and was now clutching a Lou Reed video tightly in his left hand, while his right was holding a rolled, furled umbrella, and two large black plastic bags. On his head was a Panama hat, with a dark ribbon around it. The cuffs of his white shirt poked well clear of the end of the sleeves of his dark overcoat, protruding in fact almost to the knuckles of his Reed-holding digits. The collar of his shirt was lifted proud and high of the red tie, complete with tie-pin, looping around his neck and far down the front of his shirt, some inches past the belt-line of his stylishly narrow, but oddly long dark trousers, which lapped around and over the tops of his black, patent leather, slip-on shoes. On the lapel of his coat he sported a large, circular white badge; on the right sleeve, just above the elbow, he also wore a black armband decorated with a red image.

He looked gloriously out of place, but no one else in the shop I was in, Beckenham's Wanted, gave him a second glance. I had just reached the point in Paul Morley's interesting, if somewhat pretentious, 2016 *Bowie* biography, when the still little-known superstar-to-be 'moves to Beckenham... to stay with Mary Finnigan, a journalist a few years older.' Perhaps the striking customer I'd just seen was something of an homage to that local boy, then 'Davy Jones', in whose honour a plaque was unveiled in 2001 at a Beckenham hostelry, The Rat & Parrot.

I'd arrived outside of Wanted long after its advertised 10am Monday opening time, to find several people milling about outside in the drizzle, unable to gain entry. A note on the door suggested that they would be opening at noon. It was 12.20pm. Being a highly-trained, investigative journalist I was able to see the shop's phone number writ large on a sign above the door. Using all my hard-won experience I rang that number. A recorded message told me there was no one there to answer my query. However, during the time I'd been phoning, the door had been opened and the eager shoppers allowed in. I followed them in to a huge interior area, packed with records, CDs, and DVDs, and an impressive number of genre-identifying tags. Wanted, almost 20 years old, claims to be 'the largest record shop in Greater London' and 'surely the most well stocked'.

'Abbey Road' was playing over the powerful sound system. Trying to find my bearings and discover where the material most

likely to appeal to me could be found, I was impressed by the range
of valuable original copies displayed around the walls. I decided
to start at the 'New In' box, stopping briefly at a 'mint original'
Amen Corner LP, with a £15 tag on it. I am still seeking an answer
to one of rock music's unanswered questions. The B-side to Amen
Corner's hit, 'Bend Me Shape Me' is called 'Satisnek, the Job's
Worth' and was written by the group. What was that title all about?
The only clue to be had was that if you wrote 'Satisnek' backwards
you got 'Kensitas' which even we non-smoking baby-boomers
are aware, was the name of a then-popular brand of cigarettes.
I decided to not trade up to this mint copy, reasonably priced
though it was, because the poor condition, signed one belonging
to my wife, once a huge fan of the band, means something to her.
We really don't need two copies.

I carried on flicking, discovering a *Psychedelic Unknowns*
compilation LP, also priced at £15, which I had never seen before.
This looked interesting. I removed the disc from the cover. It didn't
look too bad at first glance, although I could see a few divoty-type
marks which looked as though they could probably be tracked
by a stylus. I decided to hold on to this one. I finally located the
UK Psychedelic section, and promptly prostrated myself on the
floor – not in honour of the quality of vinyl therein, but because
they were stored literally at floor level. In the process, I nearly
knocked over a small child accompanying her father around the
shop. There were several used Tenth Planet reissue albums in this
area, some interesting titles, but generally around the £20-22 rate
which struck me as a little hefty.

The US section was much smaller and nothing in it attracted
my interest. I looked a little more closely at the *Psychedelic Unknowns*
and, under the rather stronger lighting in this part of the shop, saw
it was in rather more iffy condition than had seemed the case. It
also had a minor, but peeling, bump on the top right hand of the
otherwise protected-by-cellophane cover. Not in the mood to point
these faults out in return for perhaps a fiver reduction I plonked the
record back in its rack, looked at the now torrential rain outside and
cut my losses by trudging back to the station for the hour and a half
journey home with no fresh finds to drool over.

Because of the monsoon I had abandoned my initial plan of also visiting the nearby Rollin Records in West Wickham, which, as it transpired, was just as well. It only opens on Thursdays, Fridays and Saturdays. I came back a few days later to have a look-see. I've seen the shop name shown as 'Rolling' and 'Rollin'' on websites. According to its fascia, it is 'Rollin''. It took a while to get my bearings in the neatly laid out shop, in which all of the records are smartly displayed in plastic covers, and in alphabetical order.

There is a lady out front and a chap who is in and out from the room at the back of the building. Not sure whether they are a couple, but when an obviously regular customer wanders in they all share a joke at the expense of a mutual acquaintance:

'He rang the other day and said: "I'll be in soon, it'll only take 10 minutes as I know exactly what I want." He came in at around 2 pm, and was here until about 10 minutes before we closed. Trouble is he just never shuts up.'

I was initially distracted by the excellent selection of difficult-to-find 1960s treasures to be seen on the wall display – *The Who Sell Out*, Czar, The Gods, Jade Warrior, Pacific Drift, Dulcimer, Trees, H P Lovecraft, Tomorrow, and many more – but, inexplicably, no prices revealed on the name and condition cards attached to the covers. However, all of the shelved record covers in the shop had prices on them, and discs inside them – and by and large they were perfectly fair prices to my eyes. Nothing much looked like an absolute giveaway bargain, but also nothing made me recoil in shock.

The first section I checked out was an excellent rack of what were advertised as psych compilations – there were a great many of those, although I'd say maybe half were actually 'garage rock' rather than psych. Many were on very unusual labels, but I took a chance and decided to buy one which did not appear to be on any label whatsoever. *Dreamtime Downunder* was the title on the clearly DIY cover, offering a dozen titles 'from the Land of Oz & New Zealand', by such little known (completely unknown to me) groups like Lotus, King Fox, Town Criers, Zoot and – my favourite

– Leather Sandwich. Worth taking a chance on at a mere eight quid, I thought. The disc looked pretty unblemished –the plain, light brown centre label was entirely unmarked, with no words whatsoever on either side. I have since played it many times and, although the recording is hardly hi-fi, the psych sound is exciting.

I set off on the mammoth task of going from A-Z through the hundreds of 'Sixties Pop, Rock and Folk', then repeating the procedure for, yes, 'Seventies Pop, Rock and Folk.' Good selection but nothing to grab my attention... until I saw an LP by Mint Tattoo on the Dot label. The gatefold cover caught my eye – on the front, in washed out shades of brown, a healthy-looking, smiling guy with an unthreatening demeanour and a grown-out Beatle haircut posed in front of a fence, overlooked by a number of wholesome-looking young children. However, in the middle of the front cover was a square cut-out, allowing a view through to a red and light blue-coloured tattoo of 'Mint Tattoo' on a skin-coloured background. On the rear, two more, slightly less reputable-looking band members and more local neighbourhood kids – if they weren't so obviously cutesy American, one might have thought of them as 'scallies'. I took it out of its protective plastic to note that when opened out, the gatefold revealed that the tattoo, evident through the front cover, was actually inked on the upper chest of an otherwise naked female torso. On the left-hand side of the fold-out, track details and encouragingly rock-like shots of the three group members down one side and on the other, song details, with the opening track entitled 'Vampire Symphony' which is in four movements, one of which goes by the name 'Leper's Epitaph'. What's not to love about that!? I had to have it for £20. Later perusal revealed that there is a connection between a couple of members of Mint Tattoo and the rather better known, very loud Blue Cheer, via guitarist Bruce Stephens, and keyboards player Ralph Burns Kellogg.

This is why record collecting is so fascinating, if you are of a certain mindset. Having discovered that Bruce Stephens was in both Mint Tattoo and Blue Cheer, I then checked him out some more. I found that he had then joined a band called Pilot – no, not the 'Magic' one! In his version of Pilot, he played alongside Leigh Stephens, who had been in Blue Cheer as well and guitarist Martin

Quittenton, from the excellent English band Steamhammer. Quittenton's other claim to fame is, of course, that he was the co-writer of Rod Stewart's solo hits, 'Maggie May' and 'You Wear It Well'. Drummer Micky Waller also played on 'Maggie May' and, guess what, he was also in Pilot who had formed as a consequence of a meeting between Waller and Bruce Stephens. They turned up on holiday at the same venue and discussed forming a group with mutual acquaintances Stephens and Quittenton.

Having uncovered this backstory to Mint Tattoo, I went online to try to find a copy of their 'Pilot' album. For once there was no question of having to choose between paying more for the vinyl version with fewer tracks, or less for the CD with more. It appears there has never been a Pilot CD. I found a couple of reasonably priced copies on Discogs, both with relatively expensive postage charges, so decided to try the 'make an offer' facility offered by some sellers on there, which I hadn't used before. You make your best bid for the record and the potential vendor has five days to decide whether to accept. I felt a bit of a cheapskate putting in an offer a mere £1.25 below the asking price, but, figuring that there wasn't about to be a rush of people looking to buy the record, I thought by doing so I was only delaying my gratification by a few days at most. That's what happened. My offer was ignored and I was invited to stump up the original asking price whilst feeling a little shamefaced. 'Get over it,' I told myself, 'and just buy the blooming thing.' So I did.

Back at Rollin', I took the Mint Tattoo and Psych compilation records to the friendly lady behind the counter who calculated that £20 + £8 should equal £28, as I'd expected, but then generously said 'Call it £25'.

Not only is Rollin' Records a shop, it also has an online presence – and its own record label. Explains its website: 'Rollin' Records is a non-profit making label dedicated to releasing recordings from artists involved in the R&B, Rock N Roll and Rockabilly genres. All song publishing is retained by the artists, as if they've written it, then they should get the money!'

I vow to come back to Rollin' at some stage, but now I leg it to the station.

Later in the day I emailed the shop to ask why they do not choose to tell customers how much the records whose covers were emblazoned on the wall, would actually cost them if they fancied a purchase. 'Kim' told me: 'You are right, we don't display the prices on the wall! The reason is just because we don't want them stolen. The records would be unsellable if the covers are missing.' Fair enough, if rather depressing in terms of this record shop's opinion or experience of the honesty or otherwise of its clientele. You might also think, though, that any stolen covers would be 'unsellable' without the records inside them.

Having said that, I do own a smart red vinyl disc of the valuable (if pretty unlistenable) *Hapshash and the Coloured Coat Featuring the Heavenly Host and Heavy Metal Kids* LP from 1967, but somehow I have mislaid the sleeve at some unspecified time in the past. So if I were to see the cover displayed on the wall at Rollin' Records I do wonder whether I would be able to resist the temptation of waiting until the backs of the staff members were turned before somehow elevating myself by several feet, unsheathing the cover from its plastic prison on the wall, coming back down without injury, concealing the cover cunningly about my person and sidling in an entirely unguilty manner out of the door? Thinking about it, I doubt it – although such a thing *has* happened in the past, as my friend, Martin Wilson confessed: 'I once stole the cover of a Lightnin' Hopkins LP from the wall of a record shop in Coventry while on a school trip. My mates dared me to do it, so I did. When I pulled it off the wall I realised it had no record in it, but it was too late to stop by then as other customers had started pointing and shouting at me. We all legged it. I've still got the cover, but have never managed to find the record to go with it...'

IN WHICH... I REVEAL VINYL SUICIDE TECHNIQUES

Sellers of second-hand records rely on the goodwill of their customers, who are difficult enough to attract, let alone retain, so I'm not sure that one Portsmouth-based establishment trying to entice people to sell their unwanted vinyl took quite the right tone in its online 'invitation' to do so: 'We don't provide free valuations or recommend other shops. We do not have the time to reply if not interested in buying your records. Therefore, if you don't hear from us within 48 hours we are not interested.' That abrupt attitude is hardly likely to convince potential customers of a warm welcome, is it?

A fellow member of a vinyl-based Facebook group caught my attention when he wrote: 'Visited a record shop that was absolutely packed to the nines with literally thousands of records today and sadly left almost empty handed, I'm sure the guy didn't actually want to sell me anything really. I had money to burn but he had next to nothing priced up and when asked about prices of any records, he just threw out a crazy number. I asked him if he planned to be buried with his stock like an Egyptian King! Maybe he's turning into a hoarder now, not a vendor. I guess he can't bear to part from his children.' Other than that the shop was in England, the writer, Chris, didn't identify a location (although I did later discover it is in Staffordshire). Someone else on the site named a shop with the same odd strategy, in Washington – so maybe this is a worldwide phenomenon! My similar Kiwi experience is outlined elsewhere.

But I then came across an eye-catching example of what is, fortunately, a rare species of business technique, the online suicide note. Scott Halstad, of the website scottsmusicshak.com definitely wasn't in the best of moods in May 2018 when I found his site:

'This blog post may come across the wrong way, but I feel I need to write it. I've sold music on a number of platforms in various online "shops" or "stores". A couple have been successful. But this website – I'm being vulnerably honest here – has not been overly successful. I've tried to figure out why. I don't have the largest inventory because I'm a one-person shop, and don't have the capital the wholesalers and distributors have. I try to make up for that with excellent customer service, very rare items & collectibles & more. I engage with people, try to spend time at social media marketing, do SEO (search engine optimisation), offer promotions & discounts, do free custom searches for potential customers. But I'm not getting any significant ROI (Return on investment). This isn't worth my time & effort.

'I try to add to the inventory regularly; to add diversity (and) what people want. This site tracks searches, so I know what people are searching for. My wife and I have been continually shocked by the search results on this site, what people are searching for. And not finding. And, therefore, not buying. People are searching for stuff we've NEVER heard of, as in most of the search terms are meaningless to us. And between us, we own thousands of albums, and have heard of, seen, or sold thousands more! We're familiar to varying degrees with most groups, most movements & genres from the present, back to the 1960s. We THOUGHT we were familiar with most. We were wrong. You folks are searching for truly bizarre stuff! When people are searching for items I can get, I've tried to get items in. But even when I do that, no one is buying them. Examples include multiple searches for Duran Duran. So I got three DD albums in. Have they sold? No.

'There were searches for Alice Cooper, Pearl Jam, James Taylor, Suspiria, Nirvana, Iggy Pop, Iron Maiden, Linkin Park, Hip Hop, John Coletrain (sic). I now carry something by all of those musicians. None of them have sold. Why? I've gotten new, mint copies, I've gotten used original copies. I've gotten imports & promos. Why aren't people buying them?

'Here's where it gets weird. I'm going to list some of the most recent searches. Some make sense. Some I can carry. Many I've never heard of & don't know who they're referring to.

In no particular order:

- sigrid
- my chemical romance
- brian protheroe
- rolling stones (I carry 2 items by the Stones currently)
- daniel johnston
- teddy huffman and the gems
- morbid angel
- penny henry
- apple bite xtc
- hed kandi
- hot heat
- heavy bones
- bts cd
- yung bleu
- cinematic
- dance gavin dance happiness
- rex nelon singers
- spafford
- chris ledoux
- april wine
- thea gilmore
- mungos hifi
- annihilator
- microwave
- greta van fleet
- thea gimore

'SERIOUSLY???!!! Do any of you even KNOW half of these groups??? I know some of these. And I've shown a willingness to obtain items by groups from past searches. But since NONE of them have resulted in sales, I'm not going to invest any more money on searches for obscure groups. I'll take custom orders, if interested, but even the people asking me to do free custom searches -- in some cases for stuff that DOESN'T EVEN EXIST!!! -- won't pay for the items when I come up with what they're looking for, even when I produce items THAT DON'T OFFICIALLY EXIST!!! Don't ask for rare, impossible to find items or for collector's items or for items that don't exist and then expect to pay $10 for it. It doesn't work that way.

'I collect many rare items for my personal collection. I had to pay triple digits for a rare Gary Numan import recently. That's what you DO when you're ordering a rare import. You have to PAY MONEY for it! They're not damn well free! If you want me to get an impossible-to-find unreleased Czech import of your favourite group, it's going to cost ME hundreds to get, so I have every right to tack on a small finder's fee. But when people aren't even willing to spend $50 on a decades-out-of-print cassette from a small European publisher when there are only 2 copies for sale in the world, you have unrealistic expectations, my friends.

'If I can produce something you claim to want that has never been made before, & I can get it for you for under $100, be freaking glad & pay up! I'm not making a huge profit off this & I just wasted 10 hours of my time searching the globe. Forgive me if I sound ungrateful, but I've poured my heart & soul, and a lot of money, into this site. Sorry for the harsh attitude, but it's beyond ridiculous! If you want free music, please return to Spotify. If you want quality tactile/analog music, I can provide it. But not for free. As of now, I'll ask for a search fee. $10 for a custom search. $20 for a tremendously rare, hard-to-find item. If I find it, I expect it to be purchased. That's only reasonable, considering the hundreds of hours I've devoted to this. Stop wasting my time. Please. Now, have a nice day.'

Definitely the closest I have ever come across to a business-suicide note.

When I next checked Scott's site in late November 2018, this is what I found:

'Sorry, this shop is currently unavailable.'

Clearly, poor Scott had been having a nightmare day/week/month/year/life when he wrote that rant. Here's a nightmare of my own I inadvertently rekindled...

IN WHICH... I ENJOY A PIERLESS EXPERIENCE

The yawning gap haunted me for years. Gave me nightmares. Every time I was told as a child, that we were going on holiday to Southend I began to dream that I would fall into the gap between the Fenchurch Street Station platform and the train we were boarding. And that would be it. No more me. Every summer between the mid-1950s and early 1960s I suffered this mental meltdown, which recurred almost as soon as we got back off the steaming locomotive on the way home.

Now, nearly 60 years later, I was facing the nightmare again. It was a very hot Monday in July 2018, and I was going with my friend, Mike H, whom I first met on a horse racing trip to France some years ago, and whom I think I can claim as a vinyl disciple, to check out the record shops in Southend and Leigh-on-Sea. Mike bought into the serious record collecting ethos and is now as keen as I am – he loves, amongst others, 10cc and its component parts, Joe Jackson, Wishbone Ash, Spencer Davis Group, together with quirky local folk singers and bands.

The train we were about to catch was bound for my old holiday destination, the home of Uncle Charlie, Aunty Bet and my cousins, Vivienne, Jill and Janice. The three girls who would invariably introduce me to new music whenever we shared their home for those couple of holiday weeks. I owe my knowledge of Brenda 'Miss Dynamite' Lee, Chris Montez, and many others to them. They lived in Shoeburyness. A couple of miles down the coast from Southend-on-Sea. We were quite a musical family, all things considered. My cousin, Maxine Nightingale, about the same age as me, would go on to record two Top 10 UK and USA hits – 'Right Back Where We Started From', Number 8, UK, and Number 2, USA, in 1975; and 'Love Hit Me', Number

11, UK, and Number 5, USA in 1977. Maxine's brother, Glenn, was a top-quality session musician for many artists, created his own solo material, and joined the Gap Band. Another cousin, Steve, married a lady whose brother was involved in Dire Straits' management. Still another, my late cousin Dave astonished and disturbed most of the mourners, but delighted me with his choice of funeral music – Chris Rea's 'Road To Hell'.

All these memories came flooding back again at Fenchurch Street. This time, though, I finally banished the demons and hopped on board confidently. Mike and I exited the train at Southend Central. Now was not the time to enjoy the pier, the Kursaal, the amusements, the street illuminations or to go cockling, all those pleasures I'd so much enjoyed. We were here for the serious business of record shop investigating. A short walk up through the slightly down-at-heel shopping centre brought us to the Queen's Road doorway of South Record Shop. This is how it describes itself on its website: 'We sell new and vintage vinyl and new CDs. We stock everything from indie, punk, disco, new wave, psychedelia, electronic, garage rock, soul, rock & roll, hip hop, metal and everything in between. If we don't have it in stock, drop us an email, or pop in, if it's in print we can usually get it within a few days, if it's more obscure, that's exactly what we love to look for!'

From a wide range of vinyl and CD, I selected a 1976 Todd Rundgren LP, *Faithful*, interested to hear how the pro-Brit American tackled some psych standards like 'Happenings Ten Years Time Ago', 'Rain', 'If Six Was Nine' and 'Strawberry Fields Forever', as well as his own Side 2 compositions. At £6 I didn't haggle. Mike was a little busier, finding several albums to buy. The friendly lady behind the counter was a Lou Reed fan, playing a somewhat quirky sounding RCA album of his that I didn't recognise.

We'd found another shop named online – around the corner in Princes Street. Only, at the address given there was a shuttered shop. Next door, there was indeed another record shop. This one, Twelve Tens, opened only on Saturdays, or 'by special arrangement' on other days, but, as 'Dance & Electronic Music Specialists', it probably offered little to tempt us non-dancing oldies. Southend's other shop, The Record Museum in Southchurch Road may or may not exist. According to one website, it didn't open on a Monday, and its telephone number produced a 'number has not been recognised' message. We gave it a miss and decided that Leigh-on-Sea, where we were confident there were two extant shops, was the better bet.

Strolling towards Leigh's main drag from the station, slowed down by the heat and attracted by a welcoming hostelry perched next to the water, we adjourned for a short lunch break before walking up to Fives Record Shop in Broadway, there since 1977. It has a dark brown frontage with, on this day, large sections given over to Florence & The Machine and Ben Howard. It looked promising, but we were disappointed – others may be quite happy – to find that the shop stocks only new vinyl, and what we felt was a rather run-of-the mill selection of new CDs, together with either used, or reduced-price ones.

We set off to find 35-year-old Leigh Record Exchange, a 10-to-15-minute walk, at no great pace, in London Road, which proved to be the hit of the day for us. Mike filled his boots with some Wishbone Ash and Spencer Davis Group amongst his £77 of purchases which produced a very fair and appreciated 10 per cent discount. The shop had excellent rock and, particularly to my taste, prog/psych/sixties sections and I ended up finding precisely what I often tell people I want when they ask what sort of stuff I look for: 'something I didn't know I wanted when I walked in to the shop'. A private pressing on the Audio Archives label (number 078 of 500) on 180-gram vinyl of a 'mega rare 1970s prog album' released in a tiny quantity in 1971, on the SRT label, by Dagenham six-piece band, Collusion, featuring twin guitars – an invitation I usually find irresistible – was my first choice. This exciting item was backed up by a still sealed 'super rare collectable 1972 prog/psych' reissue of the group Bodkin's stab at fame, on Acme Records. This album was recorded in Falkirk – not something you read on the back of many record covers. These two cost me 30 quid, less another generous discount by the knowledgeable shop proprietor.

We headed back to Leigh-on-Sea station, chugging back to Fenchurch Street, entertained all the way by conversations on which we didn't eavesdrop, but which were loudly broadcast to the entire carriage. The first involved a group of schoolgirls speculating on 'Lady Di's death' which they unanimously agreed was 'murder, just like Marilyn Monroe'; the second, two foul-mouthed late teens, one of whom was pregnant but yet to introduce the lucky father-to-be to her family who, she felt, 'are gonna f***in' 'ate 'im, 'e's Greek.' Didn't quite get that – one of my own not very guilty pleasures is listening to Demis Roussos.

Then, on the train from Euston to Hatch End, my home town, I was one of some 30-plus people in the carriage forced to listen to a well-coiffed 50-plus woman on her phone to a friend who had probably hung up some hours ago. She was telling her in huge detail how 'bloody lucky' she had been the day before to attend an Earth Wind & Fire concert at which she was apparently 'touched', by Maurice White. 'He's so marvellous, and he's 70,' she shrieked. Well, actually 78ish – or he would be if he hadn't died in February 2016. She probably meant Verdine White, his still-breathing brother.

Once home, a closer look at the two albums I'd bought from Leigh Record Exchange showed that subconsciously I can't have been over-optimistic about the outcome of an imminent appointment with my GP. They featured Collusion's 'Might As Well Be Dead' and 'Saturday Morning (Down the Dead Highway)', while Bodkin offered just two tracks on side one of their *Three Days After Death* album – Parts One and Two of 'Three Days After Death'. Fortunately, despite my apparent presentiment, I did survive, so I celebrated with an overdue visit to catch up with Julian at Second Scene...

IN WHICH... I'M LOVE-ING IT!

Literally crate-digging, as he thrust his hands into the plastic containers, the middle-aged customer in Second Scene was piling up the records he wanted from the several crates in front of him, in a rapidly growing heap. Julian, the owner, was popping in and out from the back room, bringing in ever more records and the odd cup of coffee for his prolific customer.

'Here's another Love,' called Julian, possibly the fourth or fifth time I'd heard him say that since I'd come in. I was a little surprised because I wasn't aware that singles by that particular band were that commonly available. Or that Julian was given to addressing his male customers in such affectionate terms. He's never said that to me. I noticed, too, that he was also handing over large numbers of Beatles' singles – and the customer didn't seem to be worried about what condition they were in.

'What's twenty-eight times three?' Julian asked me as he jotted down how many 45s he was getting rid of, impressed that I was able to tell him 84 almost instantly, courtesy of my working lifetime in bookmaking. That was just the cost of the number of £3 singles his customer was buying, but there were other, more expensive ones, one at £73. I was becoming a little bemused at the whole situation. 'I don't think I can manage any more crates after this one,' said the customer. 'There's only so many you can go through without beginning to feel the pressure.'

Julian spoke of another customer, who 'comes in regularly and invariably goes through those crates, even though he's done it many times before, which may actually be *why* he does it. I suspect he may be autistic, and I'm not sure what he'll do now you've decimated the titles he'll be expecting to see!'

'I think all record collectors must be slightly autistic,' suggested the customer.

Neither Julian nor I could disagree with him. It seemed to me that this customer's buying habits were exceedingly unusual, as was the fact he'd already mentioned to us that he used to be the son-in-law of Monty Norman, famous for writing the music to the first James Bond movie, *Dr No*, including the 'James Bond Theme', the signature theme of the 007 franchise, and thus receiving royalties since 1962. I asked him why he needed so many singles by Love, and it turned out that he didn't. He was just buying up songs with the word 'Love' in their titles and they, together with all The Beatles, Prince and other groups and singers whose records he was gathering up would mostly be used in his work and not for listening purposes, although he is also a collector himself – hence, I assumed, the £73 item.

Keith Haynes, for it was he, is an artist who uses vinyl records and their covers to help create his works which, when I checked out his website, art-partnership.co.uk looked impressive – and if I had any wall-space left at home I'd certainly be in the market. His online biography explains: 'Born in 1963, Keith's work is noteworthy for his choice of materials, creating works from the "clutter" of pop culture – button badges, CDs or, more uniquely, vinyl records. Whether it's a graphically iconic portrait or a meaningful song lyric, each piece is created from original vinyl records.' Keith's not the only vinyl-minded artist. In 2014, Roger Miles created a pop-up record store as part of a final degree from Chelsea College of Arts. I met Roger on a visit to the record shop he had just begun to run across the road from London's famous Olympic Studios, and he confided to me that his first album was 'Hot Rats by Frank Zappa – and I still own it.'

Olympic Studios, an early twentieth-century building close to the Thames in leafy Barnes, where swans were sunning themselves on a patch of grass next to a busy road when I visited, ceased to be a music studio in 2009, but after four years of closure, reopened in 2013 as the home of the Olympic Studios cinema. In their heyday, the Olympic Studios were amongst the most important such venues in pop and rock history. I was there to see the recently launched record shop almost opposite, which Roger opened up for me in late August 2018.

Bands such as the Stones, Beatles, Hendrix, Procol Harum, Small Faces, The Who, Zeppelin and U2 recorded there between 1966 and 2009, and although no longer used for that purpose, there are nostalgic reminders of its past throughout the building including original Ronnie Wood artworks and nostalgic black and white photographs of the likes of Brian Jones, Scott Walker and Marianne Faithfull. I was there with a friend, Times journalist Alyson Rudd. Although not remotely interested in vinyl records, she is a local resident and she had contacted the proprietor so that I could get a look at the new premises.

Roger, recently Artist-In-Residence at the Olympic Studios, created a collage of hundreds of the albums recorded there, before becoming the front man in the shop, Olympic Studios Records, funded by the owners of the Studios. He explained that one of the unique aspects of the new outlet would be stocking records recorded and mixed in the Olympic Studios – of which he estimated there were some 900. He handed me a list of those titles, with the ones he had already acquired for the shop marked in yellow. Not surprisingly, there was still a significant number of non-yellow titles to track down. The records range alphabetically from A Band Called O's 1976 album *Within Reach*, which they had when I was there, to Zucchero's 1989 *Orro Incenso & Birra*, which they didn't. 'The most popular and in-demand record of those recorded at Olympic has so far been the 1970 album of the show, *Jesus Christ Superstar*,' said Roger.

I was able to look through their stock and although Roger did admit 'there may be a little Barnes-weighting to the prices' I thought they were not outrageous. They clean all of the records with a very high-tech piece of kit whose inner workings remain an absolute mystery to me but appear to achieve their stated objective. I compromised between new and second-hand original, by purchasing a pre-owned copy of the 2017 reissue on silver vinyl of Marianne Faithfull's 1985 LP, *Rich Kid Blues* for £15. I listened to the Marianne record that evening – she originally recorded it in 1971 when at a pretty low ebb in her life. It shows!

Shortly after these encounters, I heard about still another artist working within a vinyl milieu. Entirely by chance, I had an appointment in London's Piccadilly, when a friend told me about an exhibition taking place nearby by an artist who specialised in reproducing classic rock records as artworks. He was talking about Morgan Howell. I duly made a short detour, to Masons Yard, where the famous Scotch of St James club, which attracted high rollers of the rock industry like The Beatles, Hendrix and the Stones during their and its heyday, was and still is located, albeit there was a 20-year hiatus after the glory days had dwindled away. The Scotch is at Number 13 Masons Yard – but Number 4 was playing host to Morgan and his artworks, and, just as used to happen in many films and TV programmes of the 1960s, precisely as I arrived outside, a car zoomed into the kerbside, disgorging a man clutching a variety of items, including the keys to the door.

'Are you about to open up?' I asked him. 'Sure, come in,' he said. Inside, as he turned up the heating and bustled about making tea, asking me if I wanted one, he began to talk about the artworks lining the walls, ranging from life-size examples of his reproductions of singles up to the giant, supersized versions in which he also specialises. One of the most stunning of these is of the Stones' 'Satisfaction', the original of which, he tells me, was sold to Andrew Lloyd Webber for an astonishing £21,500. This immediately made me think his work would be comfortably out of my price range. We chatted away and he said he got into this style of work when he was searching for a type of art which would be original and offer him a unique artistic identity.

Morgan, born in 1965, was introduced to the music of the 1950s and 1960s through his older sister's record collection. The record reproductions are absolutely fascinating. Framed and displayed like this they really brought home what miniature works of art the originals were, from their usually simple but striking designs, to the information collated on the labels. The examples hung around the small gallery area included rock and roll classics. Morgan told me gleefully about the original lyrics of Little Richard's 'Tutti Frutti', written by Dorothy LaBostrie, credited as the song's co-writer on release in 1955. 'In its original form it was absolutely filthy,' he laughed. He's done Chuck Berry records, too. There are examples of Beatles and Stones discs as well as the Kinks, with whom he recently worked on a version of their minor hit 'Wonderboy', which we both agreed is one of Ray Davies' most under-rated songs. Oddly, Morgan said Ray wouldn't sign the finished article (although he did later) – brother Dave did.

We both enthused over some of the sleeve designs and were in agreement that the Island design was a mini masterpiece, as was Immediate's. One of Immediate's singles Morgan had done was 'Tin Soldier', by the Small Faces. 'Tin Soldier' is one of my wife Sheila's very favourite discs. She bought a copy when it came out, and claims it originally had a picture cover, which mysteriously disappeared at some stage. I'd been thinking I should buy her a replacement copy for Christmas. When I showed her photographs of various releases of the single and the picture covers they came in she immediately identified the one she'd had – bizarrely enough, a Dutch release. Now, I nervously asked Morgan how much a copy of his 'Tin Soldier' print would cost me. There was – just – change from 200 quid. OK, not 'cheap' but as one of only 75 copies in existence, not exactly ragingly expensive if you consider the cost of diamond rings.

Morgan is obviously a fan of this 1967 release and was first drawn to the song when he was in a band himself: 'We covered it (badly) in our band when we were kids. That intro is still the greatest in my mind, and the stop... before the power chords and wailing vocal... magical. I always just loved the 'Immediate' bag with its Mod arrow and simple black and white aesthetic.' The easy-going, mod-style-dressed Morgan was great company, and a fund of anecdotes and memories as we swapped stories about some of the artists and their tracks hanging around us. I had to depart all too soon, but I left with the solution to the always difficult problem of what to get the other half for Xmas unexpectedly solved.

I also came up with a way of enhancing the present by seeking out a copy of the Netherlands' pic sleeve single and framing it and the Morgan print together. Thus, for the first time since 1973 when Sheila and I visited an amazing record shop in Amsterdam, we'd truly be going Dutch! I gave it to her for Christmas, and she seemed to really like it. Then she caught a sickness bug, and whilst running a temperature and feeling unwell she 'accidentally', she assures me, threw up all over the framed 'Tin Soldier'. These things happen...

IN WHICH... I STAND JULIAN UP

I hadn't had any chance to speak at any length with Julian to apologise for having told him I'd be in, a couple of days earlier, when he had thoughtfully kept the shop open after his usual 5pm closing time, and I hadn't shown up. He'd sent me a poignant text: 'I've waited 35 mins after I closed, mate. Can I go home?' Which, of course, meant that I owed him and should therefore make a purchase by way of an apology now that I had eventually turned up. I found a couple of likely LPs – an 'official bootleg' by Nils Lofgren, and a Noel Redding Band LP featuring the Hendrix sideman with guitarist Eric Bell, best known for his time in Thin Lizzy.

I'd also brought with me a bag of obscure 1970s singles which I'd been struggling to sell via eBay and figured Julian might take off my hands, particularly as he'd just bought an even more obscure one from me by The Big Spenders (me neither) called 'Cum Ba Ye' (no, not that one) but on the collectable Gemini label. Our arrangement works well – I show him the records and accept whatever he reckons they're worth, or accept them back equally graciously if he has no need for them.

The nearest record shop to Julian's had recently closed its doors for good, and his radius of opportunity had widened. There was still the vinyl cafe in nearby Watford, but other than that, his competition was the sporadically open Chris (Music Archaeology) in South Harrow; Sounds of the Suburbs in Ruislip Manor, only open on two days of the week; Nightfly Records in Uxbridge, which lasted over three years, but disappeared in June 2019; plus the Northwood jewellery-cum-vinyl-selling shop, Estamira, where necklaces, bracelets and earrings battle to divert your attention from the boxes full of vinyl on your left as you walk through the buzz-in door.

A recent visit to the latter elicited the confession that the owner finds Julian's shop a little too claustrophobic and accurately priced and that he has no plans to change his current haphazard system of seemingly chucking records into boxes, on to shelves and down in his basement in an entirely random fashion. 'People like crate digging' he claimed. Yes, but maybe not having Mantovani next to Metallica or Edgar Broughton alongside readings from Edgar Allan Poe. Ninety-nine per cent of his records are not in plastic covers. Even those on sale for £25 to £50 plus. That has to be wrong.

When I was last there he had a Quicksilver Messenger Service gatefold LP featuring Gary Duncan, who had just died, exposed to the elements and only likely to be found by pure chance. 'Your marketing techniques need rethinking,' I scolded him. He didn't seem concerned and laconically said, 'And your name is..?' I think he only sells from his own collection and doesn't look to buy in. He wasn't best pleased, he said, that on a recent visit to a record shop in Chelmsford he was charged £2 for a Troggs' LP with the cover torn in half.

Like the jeweller, Julian also has the advantage of being on a busy road, with often slow-moving traffic, which means that literally thousands of people per day get to see the outside of his shop and his signs explaining the business. He gets a great many people coming in to sell him stuff. While I was there this time a chap came in, who had 'found some records in my old gran's gramophone player' and wondered whether he'd be interested. Julian told him he would need to check them for condition and value, but the man then tossed a small grenade into the conversation by claiming that he had a Beatles' album signed by all four of the group, with strong provenance from a photograph showing the family member (who'd been in the record business and knew the group) with them. This cover could well have been worth four figures if it was as described.

Julian did, though, have a signed Depeche Mode LP for sale. I later found out that he got £200 for it, and that the signed Beatles' album guy never returned. 'I knew he wouldn't, he seemed like a time-waster.' He didn't actually say 'time-waster' but the chap with (or without if Julian is right) the megabucks album might just read this...

One of the few significant autographs I have is one of my treasures: 'To Graham. Love Elkie Brooks. XX'. The signature is on a glossy black and white photograph of Elkie, who captured my attention and affection when she was fronting Vinegar Joe – still the best live act I've seen – as the female foil to Robert Palmer. The band never quite managed to transfer their electric performances to studio recordings and despite three very good albums went their separate ways. In her live pomp she was more

than a match for Tina Turner, both vocally and visually, but didn't
find hit records until going solo, with the likes of 'Pearl's a Singer'
and 'Lilac Wine'.

The reason I had stood Julian up was that I had instead
found myself, accompanied by old pal Martin Wilson, sitting
outside an impressive church in the village of Buckden, near St
Neots, Cambridgeshire, on the steps leading into the graveyard.
We were having our photograph taken by a gentleman who had
been walking past as we were taking a shot of each other. After
he filled us in with some local details – his elderly mother lived
there – we asked him whether he knew where the Vinyl Revival
Store (proud and accurate website boast – 'the only record shop in
Huntingdonshire') we had come to visit might be.

'You're heading in the wrong direction, boys,' he told us and
walked us a few yards back up the road, pointing to what looked
like someone's garden, but which had a small sign attached to the
gate-cum-fence. 'It's in there. I've never actually been in before.' We
invited him to accompany us, and wandered into what appeared
to be a back garden, where what looked like a gardener's shed sat
in a corner. Nudging the door open we saw racks of records and a
couple of young lads sitting on the floor, eagerly flipping through
12" dance singles, one of which was beating away on the shop
turntable.

Our arrival seemed to have alerted the owner to the fact that
he suddenly had five potential customers in his bijou shop space,
and the personable Ian came in to ensure that the half dozen of us
virtually filled the place to overflowing. It was a hot afternoon, and
the dance boys had arrived on bikes after quite a lengthy journey,
which added a certain, shall we say, fragrance to the atmosphere
in there. Our guide, whose name we never did catch, was telling
Ian, in a phrase increasingly familiar to me, that, 'I do have a
record player, but it doesn't work, so I haven't been in a record
shop for years.' Ian pointed to various pieces of both new and
vintage record-playing kit displayed around the shelves and when
he learned that the defunct item was a Bang & Olufsen player,
offered to take a look to see whether he could restore it to active
duty, an offer our new friend vowed to take him up on.

Martin, more of a CD man than vinyl these days, sat outside in the sun, complaining of the lack of CDs, while I delved through the varied selection of brand new and second-hand albums, together with quite a large number of Record Store Day offerings, some with quite hefty reductions. I identified a couple of potential purchases, only to have to opt out of the reissued Bevis Frond record I'd found at what I thought was a reasonable £12, on the grounds that I was becoming more convinced I already had it. So I was looking at a Nils Lofgren and Grin album from 1979 on CBS, for a mere fiver. I had, mind you, definitely seen a copy of Ian's Gordon Jackson sealed reissue LP, here on display for an unlikely £27. I'd recently bought it for £12 at Spitalfields, which really does demonstrate the advisability of not rushing to buy the first copy of any new product you come across, without checking out prices elsewhere.

We'd had a pleasant afternoon chatting to Ian and hearing stories about other record shops and dealers in this area, one of whom, we were told, had recently spent an unlikely sounding four-figure sum buying a northern soul single from another dealer. 'He can afford it, though, he's a multi-millionaire,' he said, which had us assuming he must mean Black Barn Records owner Adrian Bayford who won £148 million on the lottery. We were almost ready to leave when Martin told Ian, 'It's a pity you don't sell CDs as I'm not really into vinyl anymore.'

Ian just pointed, well, pointedly at a large cabinet containing hundreds of CDs, then went and brought in a whole tray full of what might best be described as unconventional live recordings of some big-name groups which he'd picked up at a sale. Martin was in CD nirvana – none of either version of that name's music there, mind you – as he flipped through all sorts of obscure blues and rock, and blues-rock CDs, eventually finding ten he fancied, including live sets by Johnny Winter, Mick Taylor, Walter Trout, assorted elderly blues-men, and very interestingly, Blind Faith. 'How much are these?' he asked Ian, who was a little vague. 'I don't know really, I didn't think anyone would want to buy them.' Martin doesn't have the reticence I often suffer from when it comes to bargaining on price. 'Well, what were you thinking, 10 or 20 pence each?' Admittedly, they were pretty dusty and most of them had photocopied covers and dubious provenance, but I'd been reckoning on having to pay a couple of quid each. 'That's a bit too cheap,' pondered Ian, before agreeing: 'You can have them for 50p a throw.'

Vinyl Revival Store was the second shop of the day for me. On the way up to collect Martin, I'd called in on the Stylus coffee/record shop – another of these increasingly popular hybrids – in Baldock. As ever, once I'd managed to park, I set off in the wrong direction to try to find the shop, pausing briefly en route, once I did realise which direction I should be taking, to consider the multi-meaning sign outside of the Chinese medicine establishment: 'Free Foot Assessments Here.' I carried on perambulating.

This was the kind of record outlet which I am pleased to see as it brings the delights of vinyl to a different kind of audience, but is clearly not aimed at quenching my own vinyl appetite. To be fair, when I checked their Facebook page, of the 59 'reviews', all were five-star positive. The vast majority of the stock I saw in the well-fitted-out, stylish room at the rear of the coffee and cake area consisted of very new LPs by mostly new bands – although Noel Gallagher seemed over-represented.

There was a notice on the wall: 'We buy second-hand records. Must be in good condition. All genres from 1970s onwards.' The notice hadn't been over effective. I could see no evidence of any such animals being sold on the premises, mainly frequented by what struck me, perhaps unfairly, as members of Baldock's 'hipster community', clearly happy to be there in the very acceptable surroundings, but not really focused on record buying. While I was there only three people joined me in that area. Two of them were clearly looking for a table and left immediately; the other one flicked half-heartedly through a rack of records but, like me, found nothing to buy.

Now Martin and I were sitting in a hostelry mainly concerned with alcoholic drinks, supping respectively a rum and a shandy. I had prompted Martin to tell me his 'first record' tale, which involved a holiday with an uncle, who was employed by the camp where they stayed, as an entertainer of the younger residents.

Uncle's forte was devising cartoons. He invited a member of his audience to come up and begin proceedings by just putting a small initial image down on the paper with the marker pen provided. They'd draw a ball, perhaps, or a basic cat, and whilst spouting his pre-prepared patter, he'd turn it into a grand building with flamboyant features or a circus elephant. One day he told Martin he would call him up on stage and wanted him to start things off by just marking a large 'X' on the paper – which, he said, would draw laughs from the audience, but he knew how he'd then turn it into an impressive elaborate illustration.

Martin was soon up there with Uncle, taking the applause, as the drawing act came to an end and the band struck up, as dancing girls appeared on stage. Dazzled by the showbiz glamour and strangely excited by the appearance of the dancing girls, but not knowing quite why, Martin was then overcome by the thrilling music accompanying the new act. When this transformative experience was over, he asked his uncle what the music they'd been playing was. He was told it was Sandy Nelson's recording of 'Let There Be Drums', dating this awakening of his senses and sexuality to, probably, 1961, when the record first entered the charts.

Martin, who'd have been around ten, then made it his business to acquire the single, promptly bought for him by his grateful uncle, and which still occupies a place in his now somewhat larger collection which, he once rang me in a state of high excitement to reveal, included 'a Blackfoot Sue single I've just found in the loft.' I can be as patient as the next person, although not always. On this occasion I contented myself with asking, 'And why do I need to know that?' I was already aware that it was because he was planning his entry into the world of eBay single selling, and had been sporadically calling to tell me about the copy of 'Psychotic Reaction' by Count Five he'd found in the loft, and others by John Walker, Cilla Black, Cymbaline and now Blackfoot Sue.

I recalled the band's name from their 'I'm Standing in the Road' hit from 1972 but had to tell Martin that although their couple of albums might fetch a few quid, their singles were not particularly sought after. 'That's not the point,' he expostulated, 'I sold my car to a guy from Blackfoot Sue in the early 1970s – what a coincidence!'

'Not a coincidence at all, Martin, just a talking point. How did that come about?'

'I'd advertised my MGBGT for sale and this chap turned up at my place and said he was the drummer in Blackfoot Sue and he was interested in the car.'

Quickly googling the group, I discovered that the band's line-up included twins – one of whom, Dave Farmer, was the drummer. It must have been him.

'How much did he pay for the car?'

'I don't remember, but he paid in cash – although the deal nearly failed over one of his demands.'

'Which was?'

'That I included the Afghan coat I'd left lying in the driver's seat in the deal at no extra cost.'

As we drove back from Buckden, Martin told me of a much more recent transformative experience, a couple of days earlier, when he had finally realised his ambition to have a tattoo – proudly flaunting at me from the inside of his lower arm, the image of a skull sitting on a book. 'It cost me 60 quid,' he revealed. 'For another fiver I nearly had "f**k and kill" added underneath.' I was unimpressed. 'You could have bought 120 CDs from Ian for that...'

IN WHICH... I ASK: COULD CDs BECOME THE 'NEW' VINYL?

Megan Page, who speaks on behalf of Record Store Day, agreed with me that CDs seem to be becoming an almost forgotten aspect of hard-copy music collecting. 'Despite the vinyl revival, new CDs still outsell new records by five to one,' she said, as we agreed they are an economic entry point to collecting for those who might ultimately aspire to the vinyl versions, but whose budgets may not yet reflect their preference. Yet, it appears to have become the accepted wisdom amongst many that CDs are virtually worthless in terms of collectability.

John Peel doesn't appear to have been a huge fan, once recalling that: 'Somebody was trying to tell me that CDs are better than vinyl because they don't have any surface noise. I said, "Listen mate, *life* has surface noise." I guess Supergrass's Gaz Coombes would agree with Peel. He once observed: 'My CDs are in boxes in the basement and they've all got scratches on them and cracked cases, and it's almost like we've never cared about CDs. But vinyl has the inbuilt need to look after it, and even with the odd scratch it will still play. And records are full of memories.'

I walked into a local charity shop recently and spotted a solo album on CD by Graham Coxon, the Blur front man, which I had never heard of. It looked intriguing and the reviews I called up on my phone suggested it might be worth a listen. The shop was selling CDs at '99p for 1, £1 for 2'. This is a much more subtle sales technique than it appears at first glance. I would definitely have bought the Coxon CD on its own for 50p, but even at the less than expensive 99p I'd have thought twice – but once I realised I could chuck in a copy of Blur's second album to make up the quid it was a no-brainer, and I made the purchase of music I just would never have even considered buying on vinyl.

You will struggle these days to pay more than £1.50 for a CD in charity shops. Another of my local haunts is now happy to offer '3 for 99p'. One or two may charge an outrageous £1.99. And, yes, many of them will be the CD equivalent of the LPs we are all familiar with that have to be flipped past before getting into the serious buying propositions. But whereas it is the case that it is difficult to find vinyl worth buying in charity shops, this is absolutely not true about CDs. Many charity shops now employ 'experts' to go through the vinyl they are gifted. These 'experts' probably own a copy of the *Rare Record Price Guide* – a publication whose CD equivalent is long overdue – which they flip through when the donations arrive, and price accordingly, very often, it seems to me from long experience, grading every disc they look at as if it were virtually mint in condition. So what occasional gems there may be on offer are usually overpriced. That's if they manage to get through the checking system to be displayed in the shop!

Yet CDs are almost invariably lumped together and priced up as though they are all worth exactly the same. This is a little like the situation which all of us of a certain age recall a couple of decades or longer ago, when records were being regarded as imminently redundant, and shops were desperately marking down the prices of all the stock they had left on the premises in an effort to clear the shelves to bring in CDs, which were regarded as 'the future'. It can't be right, can it? Quite clearly some CDs are more equal and more desirable than others.

CDs are one of the few products which are often more expensive to buy online, because of the blanket postal charges which are levied on them, making them even better value from charity shops where they can be priced at less than their postal cost. At the moment few CDs have very high sell-on values, but that will come in time as the desirable ones, produced in relatively small batches, become scarcer and therefore more collectable.

I recently found a copy of a CD by lower division 1960s psych group The Attack in a Twickenham shop for £4. Even if I was desperate for a vinyl version of this album it could only be a 'new reissue' version as, actually, there never was an original vinyl one, so here it is the music that's important, not the format. The cheapest copy of the only two available from Amazon was priced at over £70. Discogs had more copies but only from overseas sellers and, with postage, the least expensive worked out at £22.76. Of course, I recognise that the higher Amazon price was probably a try-on and would be difficult to achieve, but anyone interested in late 1960s psych and wanting this scarce CD would probably be prepared to hand over up to 20 quid for it. If I chose to offer my £4 copy online, I am very confident I'd get rid of it quickly at a very handsome profit of at least 300 per cent.

A post on a Facebook group to which I belong was singing the praises of a record of which I had no memory or knowledge. *Sinister Morning* was by an artist called Denny Gerrard on the Deram label, from 1970. More importantly, I was reading that the backing band on the record was High Tide, one of my favourite 1960s outfits – and I'd never even heard of this album. A quick check on YouTube to see whether I could find the record, and I was soon listening to, enjoying it, and thinking it was right up my street. A dash over to Amazon where the cheapest CD version available was 17 quid, followed by an online sprint to Discogs where I found a CD 'very good' copy for sale at a mere £5.99 and promptly ordered it. When it arrived two days later it was clearly a mint copy and was still sealed. The original LP was being offered by two or three sellers for amounts varying from £101 to £528 and in various conditions. Is this the sort of money anyone is prepared to risk without actually looking at and touching the item before handing over the dosh? Time from discovering the record to ordering the CD? About 11 minutes.

Once I stopped working full-time and suddenly had time to devote to my record collection that hadn't been available to me since its very early days, I soon realised that I was of an age at which, if I wanted ever to own something, now was the time to achieve it. There would be different ways of acquiring it. I would very much enjoy the time-consuming but rewarding method of visiting record shops to buy things which as I walked through the door, I was entirely unaware at that moment even existed – like the Denny Gerrard album. But once aware I then had the option of paying as little as possible to own it on CD or to search out an original copy which might cost a three-figure sum. Other posters to the Facebook group had already noticed that the cheapest vinyl copy of the Gerrard record available on eBay would set them back £350. Another member of the group assured me that he had a copy of the record up on the wall in his record shop. I didn't even ask him how much he wanted for it.

I'd already made the personal mental stipulation that this was not a route I would be going down. Yes, I owned records worth that amount. Yes, I had profited by selling a few records worth that amount and more. Yes, at a pinch I could afford to buy one or two at that price if I desperately wanted to. But, if I was brutally honest with myself I didn't much see the point. In a 'blind' challenge I wouldn't bet a fortune on my ability to differentiate between a record and a CD of the same album being played to me. The urge to own the much more attractive cover of the LP is an incentive to shell out, but increasingly that desire can be satisfied by purchasing a reissue version at a more modest price. There are plenty of vinyl enthusiasts who seem to regard it as a mortal sin to accumulate CDs. I am not one of them.

Former band-mate and long-standing chum Martin Wilson will not bother himself to sort through records but will spend hours visiting market stalls and charity shops hunting for folk and blues CDs to remind him of visits to Les Cousins club and Cambridge's Strawberry Fair,

He took some 50 CDs to sell to a local shop offering to buy them – only to be offered under 9p each for them. He flounced out, affronted.

CDs are difficult to damage, unlike vinyl, and although the format's biggest disadvantage for collectors remains its size and consequently less attractive packaging, that disadvantage is, to many who are only interested in hearing the music, a positive plus point, particularly when it comes to storage and display. Taking everything into account, I am confident that future collectors will be able to command increasingly attractively profitable prices for collectable CDs.

However, a post on a Facebook group to which I belong, reopened the controversy in November 2018 with a 'No way! Only vinyl' jibe at CDs. It did provoke a reaction. Andre declared, 'I enjoy listening to vinyl, but I never liked this attitude about CDs (when) growing up, don't now.' Ralf agreed: 'Living with both options is definitely possible – don't panic.' One poster declared CDs were responsible for 'a lot of money thrown at poor quality physical product' but more reasonable contributors pointed out: 'Vinyl will always be #1, but I can't play it in the car so CDs can't be ignored.' The overall opinion seemed to be that vinyl is ultimately superior but that there is every reason to benefit from the areas in which CD has the edge, price and size. Then Ed K offered: 'I record my records on to CD. I still have that unique sound of vinyl when I drive, and it helps to preserve my records.'

A few years ago I bought myself a TEAC LP-R500 'CD recorder

with turntable/cassette player' which enabled me both to record vinyl directly on to CD - and even to do likewise with cassettes. Perhaps the only drawback was that this had to be done in real time. This was a brilliant way of getting the best of both worlds, except that, to be brutally honest, the turntable and sound quality were not the highest. Yet, after a year or so of happy recording and listening, when I began to look around to upgrade to a better standard of turntable and recording ability, there was none to be had. I lost count of the hi-fi general and specialist dealers I contacted. All of them could suggest I bought the type of model I already had, but not one of them could give me any information as to how I might upgrade. So, instead, I upgraded my own vinyl system to upgrade my home vinyl listening, but the collateral damage meant the CD recorder with turntable had to be relegated to the shed as I ran out of space.

I'm surprised at the number of second-hand records shops which snub CDs. Even Julian's Second Scene does so. Better Daze record shop in Northallerton, N Yorkshire is *definitely* a vinyl-only outlet, to the extent that they operate the 'Betterdaze Format policy': 'We are a traditional vinyl-only Record Shop and we believe that, after live performance, the only way to hear good music is on vinyl. Therefore, any customer heard uttering the two letters found between "B" and "E" in the alphabet will be subject to a 50p fine. This will not be given to charity but will be spent on biscuits for the staff.'

If I think CDs have a future, I'm not convinced that cassettes will make a serious comeback. I've been thinking about the hundred or so cassettes I still have, despite having chucked away a good number I was pretty confident I'd never get round to playing again. Having nothing on which to play the remaining ones which I can't bring myself to discard, I figured I needed to buy myself a new cassette player, if only to discover whether they even play properly so that I can endeavour to sell them on. More in hope than expectation I walked into the local Sony shop where both staff members were busying themselves displaying to best advantage, several vast television sets selling for two or three thousand pounds.

'Don't suppose you have anything so retro as a cassette player?'
I asked, already doubting a positive response.

'Er, I think we have... one,' I was told, and was taken across
the room and shown it. It was marked up at £75. On the positive
side and probably odds-on given the name of the shop, it was a
Sony.

'Can you play a cassette on it for me to hear?'

'Yes, if you'd like to bring one in...' Hm. He didn't look old
enough even to know what a cassette actually is. Or was.

'Okay, I'll think about it,' I said, heading off on the three or
four paces to the door.

I'd managed two when my arm was grabbed.

'You can have it for £60.'

Reader, I bought it then and there. Two or three hours later, I
was proudly demonstrating the wonders of the new cassette player
to younger son, Paul, who promptly took me into the kitchen and
showed me that his mother's radio/CD player also plays cassettes.

If the CD/cassette discussion hasn't been thought-provoking
enough for you, I'll now tackle another controversial matter...

IN WHICH... I POSE A QUESTION OF MORAL JUDGEMENT

'Johnny Day' only reached Number 44 in the UK Top 50 in
February 1963, but it was one of my favourite singles of the 1960s.
It introduced me to sounds I hadn't heard on a record before and
made me want to check out how they were made and where they
came from. Today I suspect a record such as that would result in
accusations of cultural misappropriation, and would be withdrawn
by the record company almost as soon as it hit the streets. I
wouldn't agree with such accusations or actions. Although having
to accept that others do, I don't see why that should prevent me
from listening to the record.

However, some of you will already be aware that there is another problem associated with the record which was a follow-up to the earlier, more successful, late 1962, Number 3 hit 'Sun Arise'. Both were recorded and, I believe, written by Rolf Harris. All of whose records and paintings are now deemed unplayable and unviewable by virtually every media outlet. If you don't know what the 'other problem' referred to might be I suggest you go online and google his name.

You are also extremely unlikely ever to hear a Gary Glitter record coming over the airwaves. Sid Vicious recordings are differently problematic - as are those by Phil Spector - even more so as they include the original *Let It Be* Beatles' album. You probably won't have to wait that long for a Jerry Lee Lewis record, or even a gig - yet there are those who consider him beyond the pale following the controversy over the age of his wife back in 1958, when he was 22 years old. She was, it was said, nine years younger than him. The resulting furore resulted in the cancellation of his British tour after only a handful of shows.

Other pop and rock stars whose records you may own and who own criminal records of their own include Chuck Berry, Ian Brown, James Brown, Pete Doherty, Jim Gordon, Jonathan King, Wilson Pickett, Ike Turner, and Peter Yarrow. There are others, such as Ian Watkins, formerly of the Lostprophets, jailed for many years in 2013 for sexual offences against children. Have you ever slung a record out of your collection because the artist was a jailbird?

Sadly, I do have some connection to a number of these names. I appeared on Jimmy Savile's *Jim'll Fix It*, typecast as a bookie who took bets from Freddie Starr on the outcome of a pantomime horse race; I have spent some time in 'green rooms' on various TV programmes, discussing the odds for Christmas Number 1 with Gary Glitter, who was there plugging his latest single; I also had numerous chats with Jonathan King over the years, usually about how well an upcoming record of his would do. Mention of King poses a question. As he was the man credited with discovering Genesis, and who produced their 1969 debut album *From Genesis to Revelation*, is it acceptable to play and listen to that record? It is

actually my own favourite Genesis LP, and I speak as no real fan
of their work.

The website Discogs, which doesn't appear to permit the sale
of 'bootlegs' or illegal recordings via the site, seems to have no
such compunction about allowing people to buy examples of the
song-writing and singing talents of Charles Manson, some at very
fancy prices. You'll also be able to find plenty of Harris, Spector,
King and Glitter material without having to look too hard. When
I went on the site, there were 194 copies of King's best known
hit, 'Everyone's Gone to the Moon'. Maybe the company believes
they should not be censoring their users' ability to listen to and
purchase whatever music they wish to – unless it is bootlegged?
And is the company happy to profit from Manson's notoriety, one
wonders? If so, why does it choose to block the bootlegs? Surely
they are, at worst, no more illegal and unacceptable than work by
a serial killer.

The question raised by these and other such examples is
whether an individual's behaviour should influence opinions
about the work they do in whatever happens to be their chosen
profession. Some might say that if a musician's transgressions
result in jail time then boycotting their recorded output is not
only justified but essential. Each individual will have an opinion
of what, if any, censorship there should be when it comes to the
recorded output of those who subsequently fall foul of the legal or
moral conventions prevailing at any given time. So, in my opinion,
it should be left entirely to the individual to decide whether they
wish to listen to or to purchase records by or devoted to the works
of morally dubious artist(e)s.

My own conscience was tested in this regard recently. Where
I live there are several charity shops close by, so when I am called
upon to 'go supermarket shopping' with my better half, I will leave
her to career around the aisles while I have a recce round the
charity shops. In one, I recently picked up an intriguing-looking
CD, entitled *He's Able*, by People's Temple Choir. First thoughts
were, this'll be some sort of happy-clappy, gospel style material. I
looked a little more closely at the cover illustration on the People's
Temple Choir CD later, and it appeared to be a photograph of

heaps of dead bodies. A set-up shot showing actors or models, no doubt. There was a sticker: 'Limited reissue of rare album by Pastor Jim Jones's Church'... Hm. That seemed to toll a bell deep in my memory... 'Plus the Last Sermon and Mass Suicide'. Things clicked into place. This was about the man responsible in 1978 for the dreadful 'Jonestown' massacre. Part of the CD information was a *Daily Telegraph* story from 9 December 1978 – 'The death ceremony was among hundreds of tapes recovered from the Jonestown site.' Jones had ordered a 'revolutionary suicide' amongst his following in Guyana, resulting 'in more than 900 deaths'. The CD sells – well, is offered – for upwards of 40 pounds online. Which is where I promptly put my newly acquired copy. Without ever playing it.

Not only are some artists being forced off the airwaves, but, just as some now wish to see memorials to people whose achievements they deem to have stemmed from actions now perceived as 'unacceptable' removed and/or destroyed, so there seems to be a movement to examine lyrics from decades long gone, with today's perspectives being applied to them.

Might 'Young Girl' by Gary Puckett and the Union Gap, a huge UK Number 1 hit from 1968 which also reached Number 6 in 1974, now be regarded as having somewhat suspect lyrics, for example? Whether you agree or disagree, I'd also invite you to find R Dean Taylor's 'Shadow' from 1972 on YouTube and ask yourself what you think of it. I suspect that one of my great favourites, from 1977, John Dowie's *satirical* masterpiece, 'British Tourist', with its catchy chorus line, 'Most of all, most of all, I hate the Dutch', from his debut EP *Another Close Shave*, of which I still own a much-played copy, would not now be released.

During the 1970s, when Ugandan President Idi Amin was at the height of his infamy, another satirist, John Bird, starred on a popular LP recording which I also own – *The Collected Broadcasts of Idi Amin*, based on Alan Coren's anti-Idi columns in *Punch* magazine, delivered in the style of that all-powerful leader. Again, I am sceptical that in the current climate this could ever be broadcast now.

I was, though, somewhat surprised to read a review of a Rolling

Stones' London concert in 2018 in which John Mulvey of *Mojo* magazine declared that 'the sentiments of "Under My Thumb"... sound viler than ever.' This despite the fact that the song had been 'chosen by audience vote, distressingly.'

Just as well they didn't ask who wanted to hear 'Stupid Girl', I suppose, or even 'Brown Sugar' with its original lyrics. Or ask why the title of one of the band's biggest hits appeared on original 1966 Decca releases as 'Paint It, Black'.

Maybe this is part of the reason that writer Polly Vernon sounded so annoyed with the Stones when interviewing Ronnie Wood for *The Times Magazine* in October 2018 and felt that she needed to tell readers, 'I'm no Rolling Stones' fan. The po-faced feminist in me finds them – their music, the culture they inspired and perpetuate, their ability to go on and on and on while female musicians 10, 20, 30 years younger are written off as haggard has-beens – oh, it's all so impenetrably MALE.'

And let's not even enter the Michael Jackson debate, shall we?

Instead we'll check out the type of record at the foundation of many collections...

IN WHICH... I COMPLIMENT COMPILATIONS

Several of the good folk I mentioned this project to and who were enthusiastic about it – for which many thanks – told me: 'Whatever you do, you must mention K-Tel Records – they were the only LPs I could afford when I first became interested in music, and but for them I may have spent my money elsewhere and never got into vinyl.' Former bank manager, John Gloak, was adamant: 'I hope your vinyl book is going to mention K-Tel, a great name from the past.' So here we are – K-Tel well and truly mentioned. And I'm pretty sure that will also please Dave Grohl who, in 2013, gave the keynote speech at the South by Southwest Music Festival in

Texas. He praised K-Tel for exposing him to music early in his life, specifically, 'Frankenstein' by The Edgar Winter Group: Grohl told the crowd earnestly that the song's inclusion on a 1975 K-Tel Records *Blockbuster* compilation – the first album he ever owned – was 'the record that changed my life'. But, neither Gloak nor Grohl asked me to mention the label almost equally responsible for helping hard-up 1970s teenagers to keep their collection of big hits up to date – Arcade Records.

Arcade's first release was *20 Fantastic Hits*, released in 1972. It rapidly rose to the top of the UK LP chart, replacing the already up and running *20 Dynamic Hits*, K-Tel's first Number 1 album. In the UK, Arcade had three other Number 1 albums:

- *40 Golden Greats* – Jim Reeves (1975)
- *The Best of Roy Orbison* – Roy Orbison (1976)
- *40 Greatest Hits* – Elvis Presley (1977)

K-Tel was founded by a Canadian, Philip Kives, who, in 1962, used his own money and fast-talking demonstration style to create a new kind of TV advertisement. His first product was a Teflon-coated frying pan. In 1966, Kives released the company's first compilation album, *25 Country Hits*. Every copy was sold. The company released compilation albums combining material from a number of popular artists on to a single-theme album, using the tag line '20 Original Hits! 20 Original Stars!' They negotiated directly with artists and labels for the rights to reproduce original recordings.

Eventually, the 'big boys' of the record world, including Richard Branson's Virgin, decided to stop licensing their hits and began putting them out under their own branding – which is about the same time that the ongoing *Now That's What I Call Music...* brand appeared in 1983. This survived to celebrate its 35th birthday in 2018, receiving an accolade from Saint Etienne group member Bob Stanley, whose own group had a track on *Now... 33*, their 1996 hit 'He's on the Phone': 'K-Tel was the only label that could give me and my limited pocket money any hope of keeping up with the kids at school whose dads bought them a hit single or two every Saturday.' Motown launched 'Motown Chartbusters' line-ups, which ran to at least seven editions between 1967 and 72, including hits alongside less well-known cuts.

Let's not forget, though, how some of us had already identified and dealt with the problem of making our own compilations, even before the likes of K-Tel and Arcade. We all had portable cassette tape recorders, and would just record the records we liked off the radio (usually but sometimes the TV) adding our own DJ commentaries, before and after, often specifically for current girl- and boyfriends. You could also create your own pirate radio shows by the simple expedient of playing your own records and adding your own chat before and after spinning the discs. I do remember going round to friend Les Wilkinson's house, where we'd play cards and record our latest programmes before playing them to each other. Hours of innocent fun!

The compilation idea took on a slightly different guise – becoming 'samplers' – when labels wanted to get rock music, whose big names did not always court chart action, heard by a wider market. They lumped together big names with up and coming ones and sold the resulting collections at very attractive prices – 1969's *You Can All Join In* from the Island label cost a mere 14/6d and featured tracks by Art, Free, Jethro Tull, Spooky Tooth, Traffic, Tramline and more. A lack of females, though. A year earlier CBS offered for, I think, 14/11d, *The Rock Machine Turns You On* which did so courtesy of The Byrds, Leonard Cohen, Dylan, Moby Grape, Simon & Garfunkel, Spirit et al. Not many women represented on that album, either!

Liberty's 1969 *Gutbucket* and *Son of Gutbucket* featured Bonzo Dog Band, Captain Beefheart, Creedence Clearwater Revival, Groundhogs, High Tide, Idle Race, Johnny Winter, etc. Well, at least Jo-Ann Kelly got on the latter, alongside Tony McPhee. In 1970, it was the turn of *The Vertigo Annual*, which boasted Black Sabbath, Colosseum, Dr Strangely Strange, Juicy Lucy, May Blitz, and Rod Stewart. Affinity were on this and they included Linda Hoyle in their ranks. Rock was certainly very much a male preserve – at least, according to the compilation compilers.

Soul music got in on the act via the excellent 1968 Atlantic compilation, *This Is Soul*, introducing us to the likes of Aretha Franklin, Wilson Pickett, Percy Sledge, and Carla Thomas. Trojan's *Hot Shots of Reggae* from 1970 featured Ken Boothe, The Gaylads, Maytals, Melodians, Pioneers. The front cover image was a lady holding two six guns, photographed from what today might have been considered an 'upskirting' angle, albeit she was wearing jeans. Perhaps looking back at these compilations does unexpectedly divulge quite a lot about the times in which they appeared...

Another label also achieved notoriety amongst impecunious collectors. Nine-year-old Sean Magee, later to become a good friend as a racing writer, eagerly anticipated the tenth-birthday present he'd been longing for, a copy of the first pop song ever to make an impression on the young man. This was 'Seven Little Girls Sitting in the Back Seat', the Columbia label hit record from November 1959, by The Avons. The record had stormed the charts and Sean, having heard it regularly on the radio, was overjoyed when he received his copy. He ripped the present from its wrapping, and the record from its yellow sleeve, and rushed to the record player to play the disc, anticipating the tuneful delights to come as he put the needle down, only to be dumbfounded to hear the right words, but sung in the wrong way. 'It just wasn't what I had expected. The words sounded the same, but the way they were being sung was just different from the radio version I had lodged in my brain. I was devastated.'

Even now, Sean is still haunted by the memories of this let-down. It wasn't until 1968 when he heard a song called 'Postcard' by a trendy psychedelic group, and realised that this had now become one of his favourite tracks, that he was able to banish the traumas of the 'Seven Little Girls' disappointment to the deep recesses of his mind, which is where they stayed for almost 50 years, until the day he rang me: 'Have you ever heard of a song called "Postcard"? I only heard it once and I loved it, but I can't remember who sang it. I thought you'd be sure to know.' I did, and promptly not only sang it to him over the phone, but rushed to my laptop and called it up on YouTube for him to listen to, whilst putting him out of his misery by telling him the group was called Blossom Toes.

Slowly, as I told him about how I was writing this book and cajoled him into revealing what had been the first record he'd ever owned, the deep hurt, buried and covered up for years began to edge back towards the surface of his mind. What could have happened? He has convinced himself that his parents had bought him an alternative version of the big hit – recorded by one of the many copyist groups of session musicians who in those days were called in at short notice by cunning record companies jealous of rival successes, who would rush out their own versions of these songs, selling them at a price which undercut the real thing. In 1954, Woolworths' stores began to stock versions of hit records on their own (yellow) Embassy label, selling at 4/6d (22.5p), while the genuine hits cost 6/8d (33.5p).

Opinion was strongly divided. Some people loved them and some people absolutely hated them. The decision to record really good cover versions of songs on the hit parade, and get them on the shelves at a much lower price, was controversial. Occasionally the Woolworth song outsold – and was considered better – than the real thing. A few Woolworth artistes switched sides and became stars in their own right.

Was this why Sean had been so disappointed? Had his parents inadvertently bought him the Woolies' 'Seven Little Girls' instead of The Avons' hit? They may well have done but there may be an alternative explanation. Because, as The Avons swanned around in the Top 10, eventually reaching Number 3, down in the lower reaches, scraping its way to Number 25, was the same song, sung by someone called Paul Evans, and released on the London label. Another impostor? Not really – he was the guy who wrote the song, so he was probably entitled to feel pretty miffed himself that some Limey guys had stolen his thunder by scoring a bigger hit version of the song in the UK... even though his own original spent eleven weeks in the US charts, reaching Number 9, while The Avons failed to crack the US chart at all.

There is a cheering PS to Sean's story, as he told me in May 2019: 'I have recently found my father's state-of-the-art Hacker record player, which amazingly, after being dormant for around 60 years, started first time, and played "Seven Little Girls Sitting in the Back Seat" without hesitation.'

IN WHICH... I CHANNEL THE HUNT FOR RECORD SHOPS

Gilbert O'Sullivan greeted me as I walked into Jersey airport after the short flight from Southampton in mid-July 2018. There he was, clad in scarf, overcoat, skinny jeans and dark shoes. Striding purposefully along in front of one of the island's sea walls, heading for who knows where. Possibly his home, and his Frobisher Drive recording studio just a mile or two away from where we had recently landed. He was on the greatly enlarged front cover of his about-to-be-released new LP, his 19th studio album, featuring the evocatively titled track 'Dansette Dream and 45s'.

I started to wonder just how many copies of the new record Gilbert could seriously expect to sell. Would it even be enough to cover the costs of recording it in his own studios and paying the supporting musicians? Seriously, I can't believe that it would sell into six figures, although it appears he is, or has been, 'big in Japan'. A new 'greatest hits' collection would probably pick up some Radio 2 plays and 'oldie' station exposure, maybe an interview on *BBC Breakfast* or the like. But a new Gilbert record? My best guess would be maybe 10,000 copies worldwide. I hope I'm miles out and it goes silver or gold or even platinum. Mind you, I have no idea what that actually means these days.

If I'm honest, I was not going to buy one until I found a cheap new CD copy (which I did on Amazon in March 2019 for £3.10!), and I say that as someone with a soft spot for the man, who first appeared to the music buying public as some kind of 1950s throwback-looking kid in short trousers... wearing a flat cap, showing off a short back and sides, and inventing 'Peaky Blinders' chic 40-odd years before it became trendy.

I had been in Jersey for only an hour or two when I passed 'Lovejoy', the St Aubin antique(ish) shop which had been there for almost as long as I've been visiting the island (the shop closed in 2019) – a mere 30 plus years. There had seldom been anything vinyl in Lovejoy to attract my interest and, indeed, this visit was no different. I looked unenthusiastically through a large quantity of records which all, as predicted by Lovejoy himself, contained music of a brass or military band variety. At the very back of the premises, I spotted a suitcase full of CDs, only one of which I could reach without toppling the piles of what was, to me, junk surrounding it. The one was *Liege and Lief* by Fairport Convention, and, said Lovejoy, it could be mine for just one English pound coin, or Jersey pound note.

I proffered the former, and asked whether brass or military band was the only vinyl variety he stocked. 'At the moment, yes. I acquired a large quantity recently.' He was likely to retain a large quantity of it for some while, I suggested, asking whether he knew where I might find a more rock-related sample of same. 'As it happens, I do,' I was told. 'This guy buys and sells vinyl.' And he handed me a scruffy sliver of paper bearing the name 'Mel' and a mobile phone number.

Later, lazing in my hotel room, I texted a message to 'Mel': 'Hello, Mel. I am on holiday on the island and was in Lovejoy's this morning. He told me you were the man here to ask about pop/rock vinyl, so that's what I'm doing. Do you sell vinyl, or know who else on the island may, I wonder?'

One of my regular Jersey haunts is the racecourse. Off we went for a Sunday afternoon there trying to find a winner or two. If you're a racing fan writing a book about vinyl and the big race of the day, the Jersey Derby, features a horse called Black Night, whose racing colours as sported by the jockey are significantly purple, what are you going to do? That's right, foolishly back something else – which loses! After the racing exploits I received a short text message from 'Mel':

‘Here's my web site: www.discogs.com/seller/whitelabelrecords.’

But I could check out a website at home. I was really more interested in checking the vinyl out where I could see it while on holiday. When I googled Whitelabel Records it declared there was a record shop of that name in Jersey, based in a location called Eagle House, so I responded:

‘Do you have an actual shop in Jersey, or are you purely online?’

Back came the reply:

‘I do have a shop but I'm on a break at the mo. I can drop records round to you if need be.’

No details of the shop location, I noted. Odd. So I ask:

‘When does the shop reopen, I'd like to have a browse. Is it actually in Eagle House?’

Meanwhile, I knew where there were two record shops dealing in second-hand vinyl in Jersey's main town and capital, St Helier. Taking advantage of excellent weather conditions I set off to walk the three miles to visit the pair of them. R&L Collectibles, and Music Scene.

After striding out along the beach in heatwave conditions with no protective shade I was sun-blasted and a little tired when I arrived outside R&L, to find a notice on the door: ‘Back in five minutes’. No indication as to when that notice had been placed there. With possibly four minutes and 59 seconds to kill I thought I'd check out the nearby charity shops. There were five of them, but they yielded nothing in the way of essential purchases, and 15 or 20 minutes later I was back in front of R&L reading the same ‘Back in five minutes’ message. I thought I'd go and ‘do’ Music Scene whilst waiting for the few hours of what clearly passes for five minutes in Jersey to elapse. This shop is tucked away down a side street near the old cinema.

I stood outside the closed shop, reading the message on the window: 'Closed. Reopen 21th Saturday. See you all then.' Yes, '21th'. So I visited the third St Helier vinyl outlet, Seedeejohns. This sells only new vinyl which, as you will no doubt have noticed, can vary quite wildly in price. I was not in the market to pay the best part of 30 quid for a new vinyl issue by any contemporary artists, and baffled as to why reissues of classic Led Zep, Free, Beatles, Stones material should vary in price by several pounds. But, determined to come away with something from my so far thwarted shop visits, I decided to invest a tenner in a brand new, still sealed, reissue copy of the 1983 Thin Lizzy album, *Thunder and Lightning*, probably the cheapest product in the rack.

There is a further communication from 'Mel':

'I'm not based at Eagle House any more, I have a unit out of town.'

But, again, no clue as to where. I ask:

'Are you shut for a long while, only I'm here for another week or so...?'

'Back on Monday' comes the slightly abrupt response. 'Can visit on Tuesday if you are open,' I text back.

'Mel' texts again:

'Tuesday after 2 would be fine. If you let me know what you want (from my Discogs' list) I can take them off the site.'

Tuesday after 2. Okaaaaay... but where? Now I decide on a different tack, and list a number of 'titles which have caught my eye' from 'Mel's online lists, including stuff by Tom Petty, The End, Gilbert O'Sullivan, Nils Lofgren, Nick Heyward, then ask:

'Where would I need to come to be able to see them, and do you have other rock/psych stuff at the shop?'

The answer contains a slight surprise, revealing that 'Mel' is actually 'Mal' and that 'I'll un-list these (records you've named) and send you directions later today.'

Great. Perhaps I will at last find out where this mysterious shop is.

Meanwhile, I have been intrigued by the posters around the village of St Aubin, advertising a forthcoming 'Silent Auction' which is to be supported by a variety of 'exciting stalls'. Wandering into the parish hall the first glance around does not really 'excite'. I take a look at the Silent Auction offerings. The deal is that you can write down a purchase offer, provided it exceeds any offer already submitted, and then at an allotted time the auction closes and the highest bid wins. There isn't anything I am tempted to make a bid for, although the fact that a watch has attracted an initial bid of £2, followed by a next one of £45 – a significant jump – strongly suggests that whoever made it is either a complete time-waster or, more likely, well aware that this particular item has a substantial sell-on value.

I begin a circuit of the 'exciting stalls' and come across one hosted by a charming, elderly lady, amongst whose goods there is a quantity of CDs. They appear at first glance to be in good order. Closer inspection shows them to be in 'like new' condition. There are several Leonard Cohen titles, a few Waterboys, some Donovan, Elbow (why did I go for that?) and, a great find, Frankie Miller.

'Excuse me,' I say, 'Could you please tell me how much you are asking for these CDs?'

'Yes, dear, of course. They're 50p each.'

Now I'm excited. I buy ten, amongst them one I don't really need but which a friend staying at a nearby hotel would love, a 'Best Of' double CD by Frankie Valli and the Four Seasons which, like others I've seen, mysteriously fails to include one of my particular favourites, 'Silver Star'. He'll think I've spent at least a fiver on it and will, I trust, feel obliged to buy me a large drink to celebrate such ostentatious generosity... despite the fact that he'll be thinking, 'I've got nothing to play that on, but it would be churlish to refuse it.' I'd like to think that he will eventually read this confession!

No word from Mal, 24 hours after he has promised to send me details of his shop's location. Nor is there any word after 48... but after 52 comes a lengthy missive via the technological miracle of text:

'Head along St Clements coast road in the direction of gorey (sic), go past the ambassador (sic) hotel, which will be on your left, carry on along the road, past the new development on your left. Carry along the road for about 300 meters (sic)...' By this time, I'm thinking, come on, just give me the address, I am capable of reading a map or using my phone to find the place. '...there is a turning on your left called rue de pontlietaut (sic). If you see Le Hocq pub you've gone too far... Head up the lane and I'm the big house opposite the first street lamp. It has a small drive and a double white garage. It's called ivy (yes, I know, can't be bothered to point it out any more) cottage. If you get lost call me on this number and I'll direct you in...'

Well, now we're getting somewhere, but perhaps he is planning to take me to his shop once I get to his house.

As today is 'the 21th', the date on which Music Scene's proprietor indicated he would be reopening, I decide to risk another jaunt to the premises, and indeed the message was accurate, if somewhat ungrammatical. Danny, the sun-tanned guy who has been running the place for several years recognised me from previous visits and told me he'd been away for a few days in Vienna. 'Means nothing to me,' I replied, only to hear a rush of wind as my favourite record-related joke whooshed straight over his head.

Danny has always had a decent range of less familiar CDs in the prog or psych area amongst his racks, albeit they are usually ones I've seen there before, but this time round I spotted Thin Lizzy's 1971 eponymous debut album – padded out with the tracks from their 'New Day' 33 rpm EP. My vinyl copy of that pretty scarce waxing (up to £300) suffered from being played as we gambolled by the sea in Salou, Spain when I went on holiday with it and several of my pals, shortly after its release. The predictable

result is that it is a little marred by sand scratches. Life can be a
beach, can't it?

Vinyl-wise, Danny has a large section from the fifties, sixties,
seventies and other 'ies' worthy of perusal. I picked out a
compilation from the reissue label Tenth Planet, featuring three
Bill Fay tracks, some other very obscure early psychish bands and,
bizarrely enough, one by Barry Fantoni, the 1940-born author,
cartoonist and jazz musician of Italian and Jewish descent. The LP
was in decent-looking condition, but unsealed and priced at £20,
which, I told Danny, was a little more than I felt it warranted. 'The
record came out a few years ago, I bought five copies. I recently
sold the last sealed one for £30 and thought this one warranted a
£20 selling price.'

'Has it been played?' I asked.

'Only in the shop,' came the far from comforting reply.

'I'd go to 15...'

'No, I'm trying to turn the locals on to psych, I'm sure I'll get
20.'

Not from me, though.

I went back to R & L as well, where the guy in charge had at last
returned from his 'five minute' absence. The owner was chatting
to a friend who had come in and they were now comparing notes
about the holidays, vehicles, records, hi-fis, etc which they either
owned or took, each desperately trying to outdo the other. If one
was planning a £2000+ Barbados holiday, the other was about to
spend £5000 on an Algarve luxury trip. If one's speakers were like
listening to the band in the same room, the other could hear notes
that weren't actually even being played... He showed his mate an
original 1960s Small Faces' LP: 'I've had this for sale in the shop
for £120 for ages. No interest. Just put it on eBay – bidding's
already up to £135...'

His CDs were fairly enough priced but he was telling his mate
that he had just acquired a collection of a thousand CDs – 'mainly
prog'. Some of them were clearly already there in the racks, being
sold for around five or six pounds each. Earlier that week I had
visited a local car boot sale on the island, where an early-middle-
aged man was selling off hundreds of very desirable, excellent

condition rock CDs, for £1 each, of which I had bought ten, only for him to chuck in a free one by Jeff Beck. Another customer handed seven CDs to the seller for pricing. He looked through them: 'Mastodon, Mastodon, Mastodon, Mastodon, Mastodon, Mastodon, Mastodon... seven quid, please.'

I'd asked him whose collection this had been and why he was selling it off at such give-away prices. 'I'm having to downsize. I had hundreds of them and besides I can download them now.' I was suspecting now that he might have been the one who'd sold the CDs to Mr R & L who probably got them for under a quid each and was now banging them out for at least 400 or 500 per cent profit each.

A slight embarrassment had occurred at the boot sale when I realised I had forgotten to bring my wallet with me, so I asked him to look after the CDs while I chased after my wife to get some money – only for her not to have brought her purse. Which meant I had to walk back to our hotel in blazing hot sunshine, get my wallet, walk back in blazing hot sunshine to pay for the CDs, then walk back again in blazing sunshine to stash them safely in a hotel room cupboard – and whack on huge quantities of after-sun cream. This was probably the first time I'd been to a car boot sale and actually almost enjoyed the experience, even though I now had sunstroke.

I'd occasionally stumbled across them in Jersey before, and once or twice come up with decent booty – 'Rejected', a single of which I had previously been totally unaware, by Bern Elliott's former backing group, The Fenmen, was the excellent dividend I received here a couple of years earlier. It cost me two quid, and is not only an excellent psych outing for the former beat group boys which I have no intention of selling, but also gets a £25 rating in the 'good book', aka RRPG. That definitely hadn't made me a real fan of such record-buying opportunities, though, which tend to be overrun with hordes of people with no interest in vinyl, but who are happy to spend hours getting in the way of those of us who have!

One Sunday morning in July 2018, with nothing better to do after listening to *The Archers'* omnibus edition, I had noticed in the local paper that there was a car boot going on a couple of miles away, so decided to take a spin down there to have a look. It was like a ghastly vision of some dystopian future in which an eternal stream of people is forced to wait for many hours in their identikit cars to enter a field, often having to pay for the doubtful privilege, before exiting to wander without purpose around a line-up of hundreds of table top displays or car frontage heaps of household detritus which would struggle to be accepted for most local charity shops, paying a few pennies here and there for something for which they will have no long-term use and definitely no such need.

Having pretended to enjoy the time they have clearly just completely squandered, they return to their vehicle to queue for many minutes before departing the depressing scene, for which relief they will at least this time not be charged.

Many record shop owners to whom I have spoken seem to have tales of the feeding frenzies which they have seen when they have been to boot sales, usually very early in the morning and when anyone seen to be packing plastic is immediately surrounded by vinyl vultures desperate to separate them from it for a matter of pence, and pestering them even while they are trying to lay it out for viewing.

'It isn't an attractive sight or experience,' one told me. 'I don't now tend to go anywhere near them – and for specialist sellers they are practically useless as no one wants to spend any more than the absolute minimum. Yes, you might get lucky and stumble over a treasure or two, but you'll almost certainly invest more in time and tribulation than you could ever make from selling stuff on.'

I have, though, oddly, managed to put together almost a complete collection of Melissa Etheridge CDs for no more than £20 in total via car boots. For some reason people just clearing out a few CDs and DVDs seem to have scant loyalty to La Etheridge, whose music I have enjoyed ever since my wife bought me one of her early LPs as a birthday present. I also really admire the way in which she has the knack of writing songs which offer no obvious clue to the identity or sex of the person at or about whom she is singing them.

A message from Mal finally arrived, asking what time I'd be able to visit him. 'Around 4 would be perfect,' he said. For Mal, maybe, but not for me, and I requested an earlier appointment.

'I'm back home now this morning. I'll be here till 2 if that's any good. Let me know when your (sic) on the bus and I'll meet you at the bus stop at Le Hocq.'

It was ideal. A bus to the Liberty bus station from St Aubin, then the Number 1 out to Le Hocq. As I exited the bus I spotted a middle-aged chap with a large forest of beard, wearing a white t-shirt bearing a quirky 'Moomin'-like design.

Yes, this was Mal. 'I'm 53, I've lived in Jersey in this parish all my life.' Mal led the way off of the main road, down a side road or two and up to a large house with a big double garage outside. But whither the record shop? With a theatrical flourish – appropriately enough, as he is involved with the Jersey Opera House, the leading thespian venue on the island – Mal whipped up one of the garage doors. And, reader, there revealed in all its glory was what could only be described as a record shop, with records racked all around the sides and vinyl LPs neatly attached to the ceiling! 'It's open to visitors who I am happy to invite along. I did run a conventional shop in town but eventually got fed up with having to sit waiting for people to come in,' explained Mal.

I got down to the business of flipping through the racks, from whence I pulled out a John Mayall *Bare Wires* LP (later reissue of 1968 version, non-gatefold but with insert), and Graham Nash's *Earth and Sky* solo album from 1980. Both fairly priced at a fiver each. Then there was the double Record Store Day reissue of The End's *Introspection/Retrospection* (Mal said he had taken some stick from various sources for being able to offer RSD releases and was likely to be 'struck off' in future); Volume 6 of the *Diggin' For Gold* 16-track vinyl compilation of 'demented 60s R&B/Punk & Mesmerizing 60s Pop', also sealed. I also came away with a Stephen Stills' solo record, 'Right by You'; Ry Cooder's *Paradise and Lunch*; an excellent eight 7″ vinyl singles' pack of The Turtles' 'greatest hits', mint in a sealed pack; and, recalling my arrival on the island, Gilbert O'Sullivan's *Off Centre*. Mal generously 'threw in' 12″ singles by likes of Nick Heyward, Tom Petty and Nils Lofgren.

We parted as new best friends with the declaration that I would return to see him and his shop/garages (the other one contained several thousand dance albums and 12"s).

Appropriately, Mal signed off with a text message: 'Hopefully catch u next time you're over.'

I brought home 27 CDs and 11 vinyl LPs (only one double) plus the 8 vinyl single pack, from Jersey. Every morning at 8.12am while I was there I'd meet fellow holidaymaker Duncan Pearce outside my hotel and we would set off on a regular half hour morning walk, putting the world to rights en route. Duncan's passions in life – after lovely wife, Pauline, of course – are classic cars and racing bikes, of which he owns more and knows more about, than any one person should. We agreed that these are his equivalent of my CDs and LPs. During one of our morning perambulations, Duncan asked me what was my ultimate record collecting ambition.

I told him: 'My aim is to own every piece of music I know I like – and every piece of music I don't yet know I like, but feel I might do.'

IN WHICH... I'M LISTING TO ONE SIDE

One of the great, now endangered, pleasures of record collecting is receiving in the post a list of records offered for sale by a collector or dealer. Unlike the insistent, difficult-to-ignore demand of an email to be opened at once, a letter allows one the luxury of deciding just when to end the anticipation as to what is inside by inserting the increasingly under-used letter-opener someone gave you as a birthday present many years ago, into the top of the envelope flap and prising an opening along the top in order to allow access to the contents. Having done so, the waiting letter, still in its now defiled envelope, can be left on the table, or by the armchair, waiting for the moment when the mood is just right. When, after a satisfying meal, with a glass of wine at your side, you feel now is the time to contemplate which particular desirable, temptingly priced piece of vinyl to tick as a possible purchase, and which to run through with a red pen slash as unworthy of consideration, already owned, or overpriced. Sadly, this ritual is becoming increasingly difficult to play out, as fewer sellers offer it as an option.

One who still does is Colin Wilkinson of Aberlour, whose latest missive was alongside me as I wrote these words. I have to send Colin sufficient stamps to cover the cost of sending out the list of vinyl reissue albums which he sells, but I consider that to be a very worthwhile use of petty cash. His 'reissues catalogue' list has some 300 albums listed, described over some 20 foolscap pages, which I pore over keenly, perhaps putting asterisks, ticks and circles next to and/or around titles as I go through. Once I have completed the page-studying, I consider how to narrow down the titles I have nominated to as many as possible for the money I am prepared to invest.

The printed slip of paper stapled to the list by Colin (no better proof of personal involvement) features two rows of images of four black vinyl records at the top left and bottom right, underneath the top one of which is the offer: 'Need help with your collection? Let me know. I may be able to help.' Colin also advertises titles in *Record Collector*, but the lists carry many more alluring prospects. Colin's old-school methods are evident in his ad, listing his non-mobile phone number, with the warning: 'After 6pm, answer machine before'. Then his mobile, but with the instruction, in capital letters: 'NO TEXTS. Leave your CONTACT DETAILS with messages'.

Years ago these types of postal lists were commonplace. I'd receive two or three every month. In the current *Record Collector*, as I wrote this piece, there were few people other than Colin offering any similar service, although a 'Golden Oldies' Huge set sale list 1955-75' could be requested from Dave Sanders of Hampshire. I also receive a regular email list of records for sale from Somerset-based Jon Groocock, who explains:

'I've had two spells of sending out regular mailing lists, as Noiseplate Records from 1990, then as White Spring Records since 2014. I have never seriously considered a shop, I have a real business that would preclude that! But I do like to produce an old-school analog mailing list (I send 32 paper ones out, 450 go by email!!). I have been collecting records since I was 13, the first LP I bought was the Island sampler, *Nice Enough to Eat*, mainly because I couldn't afford *In the Court of the Crimson King*, and, yes, I still have that copy (and a better one!). The first proper LPs I bought were Ten Years After's *Cricklewood Green* and The Who *Live at Leeds*. 14th Birthday money... yes I still have those too.'

When I look back at a 2004 edition of *Record Collector* for comparison to today, I am amused to see one Birmingham-based seller including in his ad a plea: 'Would Mr Angus Prine please send me his address so that I can send him the record he has already paid for, it's Tab Hunter, "Young Love".' A Lancashire seller advises: 'Free catalogue'. 'I have lots more – ask!' invites another from a PO Box; 'Free full lists' are available from Essex. There is even a Japanese dealer offering a list. Those were the days!

Indeed, but these *are* the days, and there is one enjoyable variation on the lists' theme, to which I now subscribe – and which actually comes with free music. Manchester-based Beatin' Rhythm deals mainly in collectable northern soul, and modern, funk-style records, and regularly sends out a list of a couple of dozen such titles available for purchase – including in the envelope a CD containing samples of all the tracks.

I had never purchased a record via twitter, until someone I knew a little, named Paul Jones, posted a tweet in which he wrote: 'Not got my singles collection out of the attic for at least 20 years. So having myself a night of nostalgia. Made sure to pick out some of the least embarrassing ones for this pic.' The accompanying photos showed some Bowie, Prince, Housemartins, Guns N' Roses, B A Robertson and more. He then posted a photo of his first record – a second-hand copy of The Tourists' 'I Only Want to Be with You'. This made me recall thinking that The Tourists, whom I saw many years ago, being excellent at Hammersmith

Odeon as support to Roxy Music, were a more interesting band than The Eurythmics they turned into.

Paul had got the records out to play as his wife had bought him a portable record player. His next tweet declared, 'So old they didn't even have covers', and showed a few sad-looking naked discs. When I looked closely, one of them was the Kinks' 'You Really Got Me' – an advance copy with a label – light lilac in colour, I'd say – no writing credits under the track names, the words ADVANCE PROMOTION COPY with a large A printed on it, and a different colour label to the traditional red Pye. I contacted Paul and asked, would he be willing to sell me the Kinks' record and what condition was it in? Back came the answer: 'A little scratchy maybe, hard to tell on this tin-pot record player. Doesn't jump.' After a little negotiatwitteration we agreed on a mutually acceptable price. The single arrived a couple of days later. I took it out, looked at it closely, tried to clean it up and played it.

Then I wrote to Paul: 'If it was an animal I'd now be putting it out of its misery! I've seldom seen a record in worse condition. I took it straight into vinyl theatre and administered as much medical assistance as I could. You're right that it plays through, but with overwhelming surface defects, and the B-side has a repetitive click for the last third of playing time. That'll teach me not to buy records via twitter...' To his undying credit, Paul offered to reimburse me half of the cost and I settled gratefully for a third – no one had made me make the offer to buy. I doubt I'll ever play it again, but it is an intriguing talking point, and I can now boast that I've purchased a record via twitter. I suspect it is also only a matter of time before I do likewise via Facebook.

I've mentioned the Show Me Your Record Label group to which I belong, but it can't be long before I fall victim to the lure of groups such as the Vinyl Matters Record Company, and what I assume to be its offshoot, Vinyl Matters Record Trader. Then there is Vinyl Hoarders United with a shade under 10,000 members, inviting you to share pictures and information about vinyl collections and 'ones you want to hunt down'. On a similar theme: Funny, Bizarre And Terrible Album Covers with 1601 followers. Perhaps the best chance of purchasing through

Facebook will be via groups such as Vinyl Record Exchange, The Secondhand Vinyl Market and The Record Trader. They have up to five-figure numbers of followers and, although it is tempting to spend time looking through their content, this does seem to pall more quickly than being able to see, touch and read the covers and check out their conditions in a record shop. I do like what I've seen of the Tribute To Very Worst Album Covers group – as do 26,579 others – and I must admit I am rather taken by the design and title of Freddie Gage's LP, *All My Friends Are Dead*, which shows him crouching reverently alongside a gravestone, presumably that of one of his friends.

Let's investigate other methods of buying and selling records…

IN WHICH… I WONDER HOW TO MAKE MONEY BY SELLING VINYL

On 13 June 2018 my postman delivered an LP I'd bought online from a Discogs seller just two days earlier. The speed with which it arrived was impressive. But the package was almost undone already, and also had a worrying-looking crease towards the bottom. I'd bought it on the understanding that the condition of the record was 'VG+' and of the cover 'VG'. Even the quickest of glances indicated that the rating for the cover was over-generous by definitely one, probably two, maybe even three grades. With a split along the top seam of the cover, a potential risk regularly associated with receiving records through the post, and two separately written names scrawled on the back, along with a few more ravages of time since its 1972 release, it definitely didn't qualify as Very Good in my book. Not even Good-plus, really. If I'd seen it at a car boot sale I'd have offered maybe three quid for it, at a record fair, maximum a fiver, which is what it had been valued at by the person I'd bought it from. But of course, to get it, I'd had to pay postage and packing which came out at £4.50.

I knew full well there is always an inherent risk in buying online and you should always expect a slightly less overwhelming item than described. But I was underwhelmed at best.

I wrote a personal message of explanation to the vinyl vendor explaining my thoughts whilst awarding him 'neutral' feedback as I don't believe he was actively looking to short change me and I do know from experience how difficult it can sometimes be to grade an item without leaving room for dispute. He came back offering a £2 refund, while not actually admitting he'd been wrong. I wondered why he hadn't priced it accurately from the start – particularly as before buying it I'd utilised the 'make an offer' facility on Discogs, but he hadn't accepted it. I sent him a note: 'I'm not looking for a refund, although the offer is appreciated. I would have paid the amount requested in any case, but just felt I should say that I honestly thought the cover grading wasn't adequately explained. I'm sure you didn't intentionally mean to mislead.'

The record itself was in decent enough condition, so at least I wasn't upset about that. He isn't the only one. I've frequently seen this happen on eBay, but there you do at least usually get to look at the cover yourself via a photograph, before deciding whether to buy. My own philosophy when selling on eBay is to be as accurate and fair as possible and if in doubt to underestimate fractionally. Here was a microcosm of the always possible disappointing experience and feeling you can get when buying online.

I think many collectors believe they are frequently hard done by when they buy second-hand records – but obviously retain the ultimate weapon of just not buying. But what happens when they decide to sell off some of their own surplus vinyl? How should they go about it without overvaluing their product, thus limiting severely their chances of ever selling the records, or, in contrast, feeling that they have to sell things dirt cheap in order to get any buyer response? Where is the middle ground?

Faced with the 'time to downsize' demand from my better half, I had decided that the only way I could buy into this concept seriously, would be to agree reluctantly to part with records when there was a financial incentive to do so. It is easy enough to get rid of some of the suspect items which every collector accrues over the years through buying stuff which was so cheap it was silly not to, or through buying when under the influence of different substances, or through having a future father-in-law who genuinely appeared to believe that a Bachelors' LP and another by a military band would make appropriate Christmas presents for his hairy, psych-loving would-be son-in-law.

Once these candidates have been dispatched to the local charity shops you're left with the ones which you *haven't* played for many a long year, and, deep down, know that you never will. The Village People, Boney M, The Dooleys, The Nolans, might fit into this category. There are also those who, at first glance, would appear to qualify, but actually definitely do *not*. Class acts like KC & The Sunshine Band, George McCrae, Abba... even some Carpenters' records. The obvious problem here is that those in the 'keeping just in case' class genuinely have virtually no resale value whatsoever. Try finding someone who will actually hand over significant hard cash for Donna Summer, Roger Whitaker or Mud discs. What many 'novice' record sellers fail to grasp is that, by and large, the more successful a record has been, the less its resale value will be, simply because there are so many of them out there now unloved and unwanted.

Let's assume that, armed with a copy of the current *Rare Record Price Guide*, access to Amazon, eBay, Discogs, Popsike and any other publication or online site you feel may help you assess the 'value' of your records, you have identified a few discs which you are confident you could live without and are ready to flog them. Your mates will be either disinterested, or happy to rip you off, thus there is very little possibility of them paying you anywhere near what you feel they are worth. Which means you may decide to throw yourself on the tender mercies of the local record shop(s), should you be fortunate enough a) to live within comparatively easy reach of one, b) to know that it is there, and, c) brave enough to set foot inside!

Before you set off for the shop lugging a heavy bag or case full of unwanted vinyl, be aware that the record shop owner, although sure to be pleasant to you, is likely to have developed via years of practice a convincing technique which ensures that he or she is able to look at a record, admit that it is a desirable copy, yet somehow find a reason why it will be 'the devil of a job' to sell it on, because 'their records were fetching huge money just a few months back but all of a sudden the bottom seems to have dropped out of that market'.

You may also have just read a story in the paper about the 'thousands of pounds worth of records you could have sitting on your attic'. This will convince you your scratched old Beatles, Stones and Ken Dodd records are worth megabucks. Like a headline story in the *Daily Mail* in March 2019: 'Given to charity shop, rare Beatles record worth £20k!' You're wrong. They're almost certainly not. Not to you, anyway.

But you may still have a trump card or two to play with that carefully tended limited release edition, the unusually shaped, coloured vinyl obscurity, the quickly withdrawn commemorative disc, and that autographed Hendrix double album. These will swing it for you, you inwardly smirk. Sure enough, there's an interest: 'Now that one, the limited edition, I've known that go for plenty - but the market was recently flooded when a dozen of them turned up at a car boot sale - not so limited after all! That cut the value by over 50 per cent.'

The coloured vinyl - that *must* be a winner. Who can resist a turquoise-spattered A-side with contrasting velvet-feel vinyl on the B-side? Sadly, it appears, most people: 'Coloured vinyl's all well and good, but that means they've sacrificed the quality of reproduction - and what's the point of coloured vinyl if no one can see it - unless you frame it and hang it on the wall, the colour is irrelevant, and if you *do* hang it on the blooming wall you can't play it, can you?'

What about the one with the dead rock star's signature on it? That your best friend who once went out with him gave you all those years ago when she emigrated. The one he'd handed her with the message, 'Thanks for the hot date, love Jimi' written on it? 'Great, yeah. But can you *prove* you didn't write that yourself? And, well, "Jimi" - Jimi who? Yes, it's written on a Jimi Hendrix record and you might well say it was Jimi Hendrix who wrote it, but why should I take the risk that it might turn out to be a copy owned by Jimi Bloggs, who just signed it himself to impress his mates. Besides, it says "Test Pressing" on it and it doesn't have the cover with the naked girls on it, and that all means it wasn't a proper, released copy, so can't be worth as much as one made once they'd got the pressing right.'

Finally, you may be made an offer. It will be at best a third of what you were anticipating and will be accompanied by much sighing and 'you're lucky I'm in a good mood' remarks, as well as the occasional, 'I could do you a bit better if you wanted to exchange for other records' or 'If only you hadn't played them so much I could have offered twice as much'. By now, you will be feeling ground down and stressed, so distraught at the thought of dragging the records all the way back home again, that you'll say, 'If you make it another tenner you can have them' – and before you've even finished the word 'tenner', you'll feel the money pressed into your palm, and see the records disappearing behind the counter without having been able to discern the lightning movements of the owner, who is no longer acknowledging your presence.

You walk home, head down, carrying an empty bag and a few quid, trying to convince yourself you're a consummate bargainer who has just screwed that tight-fisted dealer out of much more than (s)he was meaning to hand over, particularly when you insisted on at least 50 quid for the Hendrix signature album, which you'd never quite believed was real in any case.

You're wrong. Again.

A week or so later, at the shops or in the pub, someone who knows you well, will say, 'Oh, I was in a record shop the other day. You used to like Hendrix didn't you? I saw a copy of his *Electric Ladyland* double album – yes, you know, the one which normally has all those naked women on the cover. This one apparently had his actual, authentic signature on it, but the records were in a plain white sleeve. You'd have to think that would knock the value down, wouldn't you? It was displayed on the wall, but some old bloke asked to look at it, and noticed not only that the tracks weren't printed on the record labels, but they just had "Test Pressing" marked on them. What's more it was a mono copy. What good is that? Anyway, for some bizarre reason, it was marked up at

£1250, which was obviously laughable. Yet this bloke haggled a bit and then agreed to buy it for a grand. I reckon you should go and check your copy out just in case – blimey if they sell for £1000 you ought to be able to get at least £500 for your copy...'

By the way, that '20 grand' Beatles record. Yes, it was valuable but it went for under half the predicted amount – £9400. And that was before the auction house's deductions.

A record shop owner on a Facebook group I belong to recently commented on where best to sell vinyl:

'What people forget is the chore of selling a record collection: either going from record fair to record fair while only selling the best out of the collection; selling on eBay (not getting top prices perhaps if you don't have a name as a seller already); selling on Discogs/Facebook (only a small per cent of the records you have will sell unless you are selling them cheap). Remember, when selling online you also have to factor the time to grade/ list/research prices/communication with buyers/getting packing material/packing/paypal fees/go to the post office. Also, we as a shop pay half of our selling price for more in-demand records, and maybe a third for stuff that's not so in demand but still sellable. And remember record shops have to pay tax/rent etc.'

One potential stumbling block when posting sold records is the packaging of same. I recently saw a rant from highly respected rock author and collector Richard Morton Jack, absolutely laying into the seller of an LP, who had not removed the disc from the cover and packed them alongside each other to avoid the earlier-mentioned phenomenon of split-sleeve-seam on arrival, where the disc moves during transit and cuts into one side of the cover. I empathise with RMJ but wonder what his advice is for people packing and sending sealed records?

If you don't have a record shop nearby you may well be able to sell your records via the local newspaper – should you be fortunate enough to have one of those. I recently saw an ad on the 'community' board in a local supermarket: 'RECORDS; Marc 07876 ******. Collector wants to buy LPs & 45s from 1950s, 60s, 70s: Pop, Rock, Soul, Jazz, Folk, Classical.' I texted him asking how he would go about it. Would he visit? Would the seller visit him? Would he make an offer there and then? How would the seller know they weren't being ripped off? Was he a dealer as well as a collector?

Optima magazine comes through our door every couple of weeks. In an April 2018 edition was an advert, under the heading 'Articles Wanted': Record & CD collections Bought For Cash; LPs/45s/CDs. Call Robin on 0208 *** ****. 07976 ******.' I sent him a text with the same sort of questions.

The *Harrow Times* newspaper carried a similar appeal, again under an 'Articles Wanted' heading: 'OLD VINYL RECORDS WANTED: Private collector looking for 60s/70s Singles & LPs. Beatles, Stones, etc. Prog/Psych especially. Also Rock CDs. 07969 *** ***'

Marc the supermarket man replied within two minutes of receiving my text: 'I sort the records and books for a couple of charities so hope I'm up to date on prices. I only collect records and am trying to build up my collection again after I lost the last one in my divorce. I only make an offer once I've seen the records.' I replied, asking him what my 'very good' condition Elton John *Captain Fantastic* LP may be worth – and a Dire Straits album signed by all the band members in an effort to tease out some idea of how realistic/honest he would be. Again, a very speedy response: 'I have the *Captain Fantastic* LP. It's a great record but sold over a million copies and has only a low value today. The Dire Straits should be auctioned on the internet. I'd guess £50+ just because of the autographs.'

I felt this was a fair response and didn't immediately suggest a conman at work, so I sent him a list of records that I would be happy to part with at the right price, including the likes of Camel, Alice Cooper, The Truth, Rick Wakeman, Frank Zappa, Jimmy Pursey, Siouxsie & The Banshees, from 1976-84. Back came the answer: 'Thanks for the list, but a little late for me.'

'Robin' did not hang about, either, when contacted. 'Let's talk tomorrow,' he responded within a few minutes. Not sure whether this meant he'd call me, or vice versa. He did call. And kept on calling at times when I was at a gig, at a record fair, watching the Champions League final. We finally spoke. Well, he spoke, I listened.

'I'm 50 per cent collector, 50 per cent dealer' he told me. 'There are only two kinds of music – good music and average music. My collection includes everyone from Abba to Zappa, Clapton to Sun Ra. There are two kinds of people collecting now, either kids getting into it, or people with huge collections who are upgrading what they already have. I usually pay a quarter to a half of the Discogs.' That did not sound like a particularly generous price going to the seller – especially as he emphasised that price was all important and that what he was really looking for was 'as close to mint condition as possible'.

I was already suspecting that there was little chance of any of my 'surplus to requirement' records heading in his direction, but he asked what type of material I would be looking to part with. I threw him a string of 1960s/1970s band names, including Camel, the only one that provoked an admission of interest: 'Let me check my list... there's one Camel album I'm interested in, *Stationary Traveller* – I'd be prepared to pay five to ten pounds for a mint copy.' I checked on Discogs and found the cheapest copy of this 1984 Decca album in near mint condition for both record and sleeve was £20. Buying one for a fiver would leave plenty of room for a sell-on profit. He asked if he could visit to 'see for myself what you've got' but I'd detected a lack of empathy between us and thought such a visit would be unlikely to end well, so I shut down the conversation by suggesting I'd write a list of potential sales and their conditions and send them to him. I didn't.

A week after I sent him an email the man who advertised in the *Harrow Times* responded: 'I'm really looking for records for my collection. If you have any you want to sell please let me know.' I asked for his favoured types. '1960s/early 1970s rock' was the response.

I know this was not a huge sample but I was already getting the impression that, by and large, these were people just wanting to cherry-pick records for their own collections at the cheapest price they could get away with. Nothing wrong with that in principle, but initially giving the impression that you have a wide range of interest and that you'll probably buy across it is somewhat misleading. I also wasn't keen to ask strangers into my home where, for all I knew, they might well be prepared to use high-pressure tactics to acquire the few valuable records in any collection at knock-down prices. But they could be useful for someone who had inherited a vinyl collection from a recently deceased relative and had no idea what to do with it or how much, if anything, it might be worth. Could be, but I doubt it. These ads are appearing in local papers and shops all over the country. My advice – be careful if you decide to respond.

My wife Sheila knows exactly what to do when I peg it. She has Julian's number and contact details, and will almost certainly use them before remembering to contact a funeral director.

There are other options which allow you to retain the ultimate sanction of having a big say in how much you get for your records, while allowing you to keep hold of them if you aren't offered that Holy Grail amount. They're called eBay, Amazon and Discogs. They too have their drawbacks for the unwary or inexperienced.

With eBay, you can list items for a length of time decided by you, for a price decided by you – either the starting price for an auction lasting as long as you choose, or a 'buy now' price. On Amazon you can list your 'for sale' items at the price you choose and leave them there until they sell, or you forget you ever put them there. If the latter, you'll probably be surprised eight months down the line when someone buys a record you now realise you took to the charity shop a while back. If this should happen (it did to me only recently) you'll either have to come clean and risk abuse and a bad review from the would-be purchaser, or buy a copy yourself elsewhere, almost certainly for more than you are charging for your own copy (this is what I did), and swallow the loss to avoid the adverse fall-out.

So, you work out all the rules and offer your 'no longer wanted' titles for sale to the world at large. Not always easy to decide how much to charge for them. I recently decided I was unlikely to play a 1998 CD I owned by highly rated guitarist, the late Mike Bloomfield. A quick look on Amazon suggested it could be really valuable. Just one 'new' copy available for sale – and that at a price of £80.98 (+£1.26 p/p). I must admit I was sceptical about that price – after all, if there is only one copy on a site the seller might try it on by offering a massive price just to check whether anyone out there will fall for it. OK, I'll have a little look at what it might cost me on the Discogs site – and discover that here, too, there is just a single copy for sale – and this one will cost almost twice as much in post & packing when sold – £2.50 in all. But if you want the CD, this is where you'd buy it, as the asking price for a 'mint' copy, is just a fiver. How about eBay? Three copies available here, the most expensive £8.77 + 6.14 p/p. My analysis – no one is likely to pay 80 quid, so forget that. But the other prices are low enough to make it well worthwhile sticking the CD back on the shelf!

You may though hit the odd jackpot or two after doing your homework. Who would have guessed I'd get 90 quid for a Paul Nicholas 1970 single Polydor B-side? Few would have realised that this obscure B-side, 'Run Shaker Lee' (A-side 'Freedom City') would have been so highly prized by collectors that they'd offer almost £100 to own my copy. That's nice money for records which originally cost under a quid, but, again, there is a catch. Firstly you have to know that the record might appeal to collectors. Once you've done that, and found a buyer prepared to shell out unexpectedly attractive amounts of money, you have to pay the costs of putting it in front of them to buy, and then packing and sending it.

A member of a Facebook group, Show Me Your Record, posted a note to members, noting that a copy of an LP by the group Can appeared to have gone recently for an incredible 8,198 euros, despite the *Rare Record Price Guide* rating it a respectable but hardly stratospheric £150 in top condition. Another member quickly posted an explanation: 'I think there are some "ghost-bidders". After a "false" purchase, a complaint will be done to get back the eBay fees.' So, beware of fraudsters who are seeking to give the impression that some records are worth far more than they genuinely are to sucker gullible buyers into paying through the nose. This is easily done, when you consider that there can be multiple original issues and very similar-looking reissues of certain records over a period of years. Some have genuine three-figure values whereas others are worth a fraction of that, yet cunning wording and misleadingly cropped photographs can give the impression that a goose-like record is worth a swan-like small fortune.

Even as I was writing this piece a friend informed me of a signed album by The Who – all four of their signatures on the record, up for sale at over $1000 on an auction site. He was impressed, particularly as the long-dead drummer Keith Moon had apparently signed a record which came out two years after he passed away. Caveat emptor. And that, as far as I'm aware, isn't the name of a prog-rock band.

23 November 2017 was not only my 67th birthday, but also the first time I had endeavoured to sell some records via an auction. I had earlier attended a music auction at SAS Auctions, near Newbury. I had seen their catalogue, and I'd taken a fancy to a couple of items so I decided to spend a day doing something I'd never done before. It was a fascinating event and I ended up purchasing around 40 LPs and 12″ singles by P J Proby, someone whose records I had previously shown almost no interest in acquiring. This wasn't, though, just a pile of his 'greatest hits' in various formats, but a whole box full of his output – singles, LPs, even a framed CD with an artwork showing the singer with some nubile friends. Many were on obscure labels which just looked different and which I figured I might be able to move on for a profit if I acquired them for the right price.

It was quite a nerve-wracking moment when I decided to join the bidding, having earlier taken the precaution of equipping myself with a bidding number just in case. The opening price for the Proby selection was, I think, £20. I just slung an arm up occasionally, mindful that I wasn't looking to pay over 50 quid, and ended up buying the job lot for 40. There was a few extra pounds added to that for the auction's commission. I should say at this point that I still own much of the material I bought – but I have sold a few of the records and at least retrieved what I paid.

This positive auction experience persuaded me that I should try selling, too, so I took a stern look at some of my vinyl-related possessions and dug out some lesser known Beatle-related LPs, singles, cassettes, picture discs I'd acquired, to create one lot; removed a heap of Beatles books from my private library, and packed up a few dozen press releases and publicity photographs of bands from the record reviewing days, chucked it all into the car and drove down to the auction house. The in-house expert took a quick look through the stuff, told me he thought most of it would be saleable and that he'd give some thought to how best to make it up into appealing lots. In the end he made 14 separate lots out of the material, all but four of which sold at the initial 'birthday' auction, the rest of which were re-offered at the next auction, when they too found buyers.

I can recommend the whole auction experience as being a positive one. Perhaps my view is coloured by the fact that I had some decent items to put up for sale and all I had to do ultimately after delivering them to the auction house was sit back and wait for the cheque to arrive. I didn't even attend the sale in person, but it was easy to follow progress online.

I spotted a timely warning in an unlikely location, cautioning that a decision to sell off your vinyl in any way and for any reason might come back to haunt you. A full-page advertisement appeared in *The Times* on Friday 27 October 2017, alongside the illustration of a heap of records piled up, with an unsleeved one on top, that was clearly aimed directly at anyone with a record collection who was pondering a sell-off.

See whether you can guess what kind of business placed it?

'You're absolutely right.
Selling your record collection will create more space.
But it will also create something else.
A void.
Part of your essence will disappear.
Forever.
The party where you heard that amazing track.
Met that amazing girl.
Then...
The album you and your best mate bonded over.
The song that reminds you of mum.
It's so much more than a record collection.
It's the soundtrack to your life.

And you're going to give it up to a complete stranger. Really?'

This clever and subtle ad was placed by the Yorkshire Building Society.

I think I've discussed all of the viable selling methods in this chapter – if you don't fancy experimenting with any of them, though, don't worry, you could always just package them up and send them off to me... If you did that, you'd be adding to an already bloated collection to which I can never resist adding another member. How might I feel if, for whatever reason, the collection suddenly vanished?

IN WHICH... I CONTEMPLATE DEVASTATING LOSS

Writer Ed Vulliamy, who was moving from the UK to Arizona in January 2011, shipped his 1600-strong record collection out to the States. Then 56 years old, he'd been collecting since he was 12, and had stayed loyal to vinyl. 'I've always listened to vinyl, never threw any away. I dislike the metallic edge on digital sound and couldn't download my way out of a paper bag even if I wanted to.' As a result of a mix-up over the shipping arrangements, the US Customs ended up destroying his records. All of them. 'The right paperwork did not reach the right people. My books and records had been "released to carrier for destruction" by US Customs in Phoenix.' Ed was, like the collection, shattered. I think all record collectors will empathise with his comment that: 'I felt as though the physical evidence for most of my life had vanished.'

But, drawing strength from some deep-hidden source, he set about re-collecting the entire collection after a friend gave him six of the albums he'd previously had – by Neil Young, Sly Stone, The Beatles, Electric Flag, Stoneground and Poco. He has

gradually managed to gather copies of the majority of his former
records together, having done so by enlisting help from friends,
acquaintances, and John Stapleton of Bristol's Wanted Records,
as he set about the task, which must have initially been soul-
destroying to contemplate, and ultimately rather more costly than
when he had originally acquired them.

I just hope an insurance pay-out is covering the cost. Mind
you, I've found it very difficult even to explain to insurance
companies just what a record collection is. I have virtually the same
conversation every year when renewing my contents insurance and
we come to the matter of valuables or individual works of art worth
a certain amount. I begin to endeavour to explain the concept to
someone who seems never to have even heard of or come across
vinyl records before, or just refuses point blank to believe that,
even if they do exist, they could have any value whatsoever, let
alone a four-figure one.

'Are you talking about a proper work of art, a painting?'

No, a single vinyl LP record I own which I could sell for £1000
at least, so I need to know it will be covered if stolen.

'I should think so.'

That's not a definitive answer, is it?

'You're covered for works of art worth up to...'

Oh, forget it...

I did once suffer a radiator malfunction in a room in which
some records were stored on the flooded floor and, to be fair
to the insurance company involved, they did pay out without
complaint even though the records had not been 'individually
itemised in advance' as they would have preferred. I can just
imagine what they'd have said, had I actually sent them a list of
a couple of thousand singles and LPs and asked for confirmation
that each one was individually covered against fire, flood, theft,
and accidental damage.

I've often wondered, just what does my own record collection
really mean to me and why do I have it? I can only conclude that
it comes down largely to ego. Why do I love the collection so
much, and continue contributing to its enlargement? For sure I
love talking about, looking at, and listening to it. I have no reason

to believe (sorry!) that it will ever be otherwise. But would I be suicidal if I were somehow - through theft, fire or some other disaster - to lose the whole thing? Logically, no, I would not. I may feel bereft. But I might also think that it was a great excuse to start collecting all over again from scratch. As Ed V probably will do in time.

Would a replaced collection end up looking exactly the same as before, or be significantly different? Somehow, I suspect the former. It would not be as large, for sure. Because I wouldn't bother replacing the records which I now know I will never listen to again... despite the fact that I can barely persuade myself to part with those same records and they form a hefty part of the collection. Obviously, as some of the records I now own are pretty valuable, and many others came to me free of charge in the first place, it would cost rather more to reassemble the entire collection now than it did originally. No change from the best part of 50 grand, I'd estimate.

There's little doubt that I do enjoy being able to boast that 'I have' some of the LPs which have lived in the collection for many a long year. But that's just bigging myself up to myself, really. Because who else is remotely impressed? Julian, maybe, occasionally. And that's because he seems to have convinced himself I have records that I really don't. But no one else. Why shouldn't we collect to impress ourselves, though? Others aren't impressed. Often they just think you're a bit of a tosser who got lucky and don't actually *care* that you've got records they'd like to have.

Why else do vastly expensive works of art, valuable classic motors, original printings of rare books vanish into private collections, never to be seen by the hoi polloi again? So that those with the private collections can not only look down their noses at everyone else, but also so that they can be the only ones able to drive, look at or read a particular desirable object, and listen to the originals of similarly rare records. But to spend years creating a personal treasure trove of items important, if not essential, to the conduct of one's life is to pour so much of oneself into that process, that to lose it for some totally unexpected reason could result in a potentially life-damaging impact. As some have discovered, to their cost.

There's a very catchy, rocky track called 'She Stole It' on *Best of British*, the 1999 LP by former Small Face Ian 'Mac' McLagan and the Bump Band. And what is 'it'? Well, McLagan's lyrics explain that 'I've been collecting records since 1962', but then reveal that his 'little girl' has left him a note, telling him that 'she stole my record collection', explaining that 'I turned my back for a minute, she left and took 'em all'. Then he reveals what was in the collection: in one verse; 'Hank Williams, & Muddy Waters, Aretha & Otis Blue' – a great selection. But there's more – 'Stones, Beatles, & Buddy Holly, Chuck Berry and Booker T' ... and more still: 'Elvis, Gladys, Curtis, Mavis, Sly & The Family Stone'. The song sounds amazingly autobiographical so maybe this tragic tale actually happened to the much-missed keyboard ace Face.

Unless we are extraordinarily well organised, we've all surely misplaced records. 'I know it is here somewhere, but I just can't put my finger on where it is'. Less frequently, but even more frustrating when it happens, we may have completely lost records, never to be found again. There are many ways in which to lose one's valued vinyl. Like the one which happened to Meno Fernandez, who posted a tragic-sounding yarn to a Facebook group to which I belong in October 2018 that: 'I kept them in the attic of my shop in a milk crate. When I came across a turntable I thought, what a great excuse to play my old albums. When I climbed up to get them, the milk crate was gone. My wife said something to the effect of "I thought you said they were all junk". I think they're all gone. That milk crate had the first album I bought – over 50 years ago.'

If Gordon Green's experience is anything to go by, though, Meno will eventually recover from the blow: 'The records I lost were 78s with artists like Jelly Roll Morton and his Red Hot Peppers, Bessie Smith with her amazing voice and early Louis Armstrong records.' Gordon is the former proprietor of the Neuadd Arms Hotel in Llanwrtyd Wells, Mid Wales, who suffered a personal disaster when he moved from there: 'When I left the Neuadd I was looking for my traditional jazz collection, when I noticed the children sniggering. They had taken them down to the playing field and played frisbees with them.'

Writer and broadcaster Danny Baker has always been a keen vinyl man and his twitter feed (@prodnose) regularly features photographs of him posing with different LP covers in the background.

In November 2018 he revealed a deep-seated regret: 'Every now and then I think about all those LPs I saw in the skip at the council tip that time. Beyond reach, they were. It haunts me...'

Novelist Tim Lott weirdly decided of his own free will to lose his collection, revealing in *The Guardian* in 2004 that: 'I remember one day staring at my collection of several hundred vinyl LPs – scratched, withered covers, records played half to death, some of them with me for nearly 30 years – and thinking, "Enough". These things are ghosts, memories, clutter; hardly played, barely loved anymore. The reactions from some of my friends – mostly men – were horrified. How could I do it? It was like withdrawing support from your favourite football team (which I had also done) or leaving your wife.' Well, I'm with his mates!

1960s DJ and TV personality Simon Dee split up with wife Bunny in the early 1970s, by which time he'd amassed a huge record collection – 'practically every single and album by a major artist from 1964 to 1970, plus preview discs and acetates. I had an acetate of Sgt Pepper months before it was released,' he told biographer Richard Wiseman. But having moved out of his home during the domestic split he 'discovered Bunny had been so hard up... she'd sold the whole damn lot for 50 quid!' Dee then spent 15 years rebuilding his collection only for burglars to steal 'thousands' and, bizarrely, 'hundreds of others were slashed to pieces'.

Elton John also lost his massive record collection – but in a very worthy cause. It consisted of 70,000 singles, albums, cassettes, CDs and studio tapes which 'right before I got sober' he decided to sell to fund the AIDS Foundation he was setting up at the end of the 1980s. Amazingly, it took Stephen MH Braitman, accredited senior appraiser affiliated with the American Society of Appraisers, 20 years to value and prepare it for auction. The collection was sold at auction for £166,600 to someone from St Louis, Missouri. In February 2011, though, Elton showed that he had the heart of a true record collector when he said, of selling the collection: 'I really regret it now.'

Always remember, your collection could disappear overnight for a variety of reasons...

IN WHICH... A LOSS IS DEALT WITH, BY GEORGE!

London photographer Julian Ward's record collection disappeared in an unexpected manner in 2012, outdoing all of the stories in the previous chapter. He explained: 'My entire record collection, an over 30-year obsession with The Who, vinyl, and 12″ 1990s indie classics, had been mistakenly passed on to a charity shop by someone while in storage.' Julian was left in 'a desperate and frantic state'. Determined to replace them, Julian began scouring record shops in Brighton, where one of the shops he visited was The Record Album. This is a record-breaking shop in its own right, having opened in 1948, and been run by George Ginn since 1962, shortly after he'd bought himself out of the RAF. When Julian visited George's shop, the proprietor was a still-youthful 82. The shop had a well-deserved reputation for specialising in film scores and soundtracks and Julian was so impressed by George himself that he ended up photographing and making a short film about the octogenarian which can be found online.

In 2018 George finally decided the time had come to retire from the shop and, 'driving a hard bargain', he sold it to two former *Times* journalists, Keith Blackmore and David Chappell, both of whom I'd come into contact with during my life in the betting world. When a mutual friend told me about their new venture, I knew I needed to go and see for myself how they were making the transition from Fleet Street to Terminus Road, Brighton.

I remembered visiting the shop on a couple of occasions when George had been in residence, even buying a couple of LPs from him. I particularly recalled, with some amusement, discussing with this elderly gent the work of 1960s acid rock band, Quicksilver Messenger Service. Misremembering that the shop was to the left of Brighton Station as the traveller exits the concourse, I turned in the wrong direction, but soon corrected myself and arrived in Terminus Road, where the corner shop with its blue frontage is in a prominent position, albeit only if you're heading out of town away from the seafront.

'George was very much old school,' said David. 'He had an ancient, 60-year-old, pound, shillings and pence till, which I must emphasise has now been decimalised, and he only accepted cash payments. He cleaned records in the shop's sink with soap, warm water and loving care, and would have nothing to do with CDs – mind you, we're not into CDs either and don't sell them.' George would also sometimes lose sales by telling buyers who only had credit cards with which to pay, that they'd have to go and draw some money out from a cash machine. David and Keith quickly introduced payments by card when they took over, telling me: 'The place had really been preserved in aspic and needed something of an update without, though, losing its appeal and atmosphere. Fortunately, George's long-term customers seem to be happy with what we're doing and have not only told us so, but demonstrated their confidence in us by continuing to come in.'

Another easy-to-implement way of freshening up the appearance and appeal of the shop's stock has been to ensure that all of their records are now smartly dressed: 'A decent plastic sleeve not only protects the record covers from progressive adverse thumbing damage, but also transforms the overall look of the album instantly. There is a small cost involved, but since introducing it we have had to order in more plastic sleeves as people have begun asking to buy them from us.'

George's declining mobility had influenced his decision to retire. A little surprisingly the deal done was to buy all of the stock – he didn't want to take any of the records with him. 'I think his wife didn't want him cluttering the place up – and he was only allowed one record at home. Besides, he didn't own a record player!' While we were talking in the shop, George rang, asking whether he'd left his 'Japanese Walkman' (was there any other type!?) there. Despite a rummage through drawers, cupboards and shelves, there was no sign of one.

Keith and David had been looking for a suitable career change and were both enthusiastic about the record shop idea, despite having no experience of that side of the counter. 'It was like becoming cub reporters again,' smiled David, and Keith added, 'I was already an interested amateur, so just had to add experience.' Continued David: 'We knew the deal would put us into a shop with a solid reputation and a unique niche market which we felt we could enhance and expand, even though it would mean a steep learning curve for both of us. George knew his trade inside out, but there are always different ways of approaching a business. For example, there is a great deal of stock here which has been in the shop for years without selling, so we'll look at ways of moving it on. We also want to maintain his reputation for selling records in excellent condition with all the various inserts and extras they may come with. Building an online presence is an intrinsic part of our business plan and will really widen our prospective reach – but we won't just dump everything online, we want to enhance the experience of coming in to a real record shop. We know we also have to increase awareness of our location, which is a double-edged sword – close to the station but not en route to the seafront, although we do pick up plenty of business from people coming down to the town from the other direction, walking or seeing us from cars.'

Even at this early stage they were already welcoming in a wider audience of buyers and sellers, both in age and music genres – 'Six weeks ago someone brought in a collection of Led Zeppelin original label LPs all in excellent condition, which we quickly put for sale at appropriate prices, and we also acquired a brilliant condition copy of one of my great favourites, Van Morrison's 'Astral Weeks'. Keith told me, 'We want people to be able to buy records from us that can be regarded as valuable artefacts.

'Younger customers are also turning up now – it probably helps that we also often have younger people behind the counter in the shop, and they are buying classic rock records as well as material by newer bands – there's definitely an upsurge of interest in LPs from the 1990s, for example, which was a time when vinyl was in a downward spiral as CDs were enjoying their heyday. Members of the generation which grew up then are looking to add vinyl copies of their favourites from that decade to their collections.'

I will be making a point of visiting the shop regularly in future to check out their progress and wares – and I made a start on supporting them practically by purchasing an Earth & Fire LP I spotted in their 1970s rack. It also helps that during our conversation David and I discovered that we were both already supporting something of mutual interest – Luton Town FC!

From the Brighton seaside I headed for another watery vinyl opportunity...

IN WHICH… I'M FLOATING AN IDEA…

Do you remember that 1977 hit 'Float On' by The Floaters? It made Number 1 in the charts, although Number 2 may have been more apposite, and caused the more scatological amongst my circle of friends much hilarity. It came floating back into my mind when I received an email from a friend: 'Just back from a nice day out. Started at Regents Canal floating market in Mile End – basically 6 barges. However one of the barges was selling vinyl (ended up with 2 albums to carry round all day!).' Really? A floating record shop on a barge? Crikey, I have to catch up with that.

Which I did on 23 August 2018 when Luke, skipper of the barge, occasional performer in small venues and owner of the records, parked his vessel in the posh Thames-side town of Marlow. We found him easily enough and I was soon rifling through a varied, decently priced selection of records, as well as a few CDs – one of which was a double Seeds set which I bought for a fiver. Luke has a wide selection of obscure folk LPs – and that, I think, is his own personal preference, but he is knowledgeable across most of the genres. He's been doing this since 2014. 'I started it with my own collection, I had a boat already and a job that I wanted to leave, my only real asset was my addiction to records.' Luke's vinyl activities are seasonal. 'I spend winters mostly in London and then once the festivals and events start I travel to as many as I can. I'm based at Springfield on the River Lea. Generally, I'll only stay somewhere for a weekend. I travel as far up country as Birmingham.'

I found an LP of very early Jefferson Airplane material which I snapped up, along with a two quid obscurity by Limey, a four quid *Robin's Reign* by Robin Gibb, one of my not-so-guilty pleasures, and a Marble Arch label psychsploitation album by Hell's Preachers, *Supreme Psychedelic Underground*. Some have claimed that this is a freelance outing by Messrs Blackmore, Lord and Paice on a Purple day off, although it probably isn't. But it is nice to have a disc which, reckons website psychedelicbabymag.com: 'leads the listener to wonder what dimension these performers were operating in'. My most expensive purchase was the eponymous String Driven Thing LP, in a most acceptable condition, for 15 quid. I enjoy their work and am gradually picking up their entire oeuvre.

Luke Guilford was engagingly chatty, happy to pose for a photo; the location was attractively scenic, my good lady was very happy for once to accompany me on the hunt and pleased to be able to enjoy a leisurely elevenses in a pleasant local cafe in which we were served by a startlingly Ian Wright-lookalike barista. Early in 2019 Luke announced: 'This weekend is the last upon my current boat, the good ship *Tashtar*! She's been a fine base for many years but it's time to search for a slightly larger, but mostly taller home...' Whilst talking to and reading about Luke, I discovered where he goes to refresh his own collection – a place I'd never come across before – a stall within Wood Street Market in Walthamstow, called Vinyl Vanguard, and run by 'Mike'. So, within a couple of days of my jaunt to the floating shop, I was being brought back to terra firma by the delights of Walthamstow Central!

I arrived at the town's over- and underground train and bus hub, entirely baffled as to which direction I needed to point myself in, and a little concerned that if I asked anyone for the way to the one landmark I knew of 'Hoe Street', I ran the risk of being misconstrued. It was around 11am but Walthamstow, including Hoe Street, which I had now managed to locate courtesy of a street map appeared unnervingly underpopulated. Had some national disaster occurred whilst I was sitting on the tube train? There seemed to be no one around. From Hoe Street, I took Forest Road, which then joined Wood Street – where the market lives, so in I went to this atmospheric warren of little units, each with its own speciality.

I soon found the record unit – or so I thought. It was only after I'd spent a good few minutes looking at the vinyl, which was sharing space with football memorabilia, that I realised that it wasn't run by Mike at all. In fact, it was run by guitarist and artist, Jeff, and was called Nobby Lawton's Olde Footy Shop. Whatever the name, I bought a record I'd never heard of before. I'd been trying to sell a single, 'Spare the Children', by a group called Studd Pump on eBay. It was on the little-known Penny Farthing label and dated from 1971, but didn't attract a single bid. I'd tried to find out details of the group, and it transpired that it had links to psych favourites (Les) Fleur de Lys and that one of the members was called Graham Maitland

When I picked up one of Jeff's LPs by a group called Glencoe, released in 1972, I noticed that one of the members was called Graham Maitland On keyboards and vocals. Not only that, one of the others was bass guitarist Norman Watt-Roy, the Blockhead-cum-Wilko-Johnson sidekick. I bought it for a tenner and on hearing it later, loved it. 'Hippie-rock' one of the publications I consulted, called it, which I thought was rather damning with faint praise. Then – as seems to be the way of things record collecting – it turned out that Mr Maitland was also briefly involved in another group that I have enjoyed. Hopscotch produced two singles: 'Look at the Lights Go Up' (co-written by Mr M, although he didn't co-write the B-side, boasting the inspired title, 'Same Old Fat Man') in 1968 on United Artists, worth £140 says RRPG; and a year later, 'Long Black Veil', (a tenner) which has Maitland's co-written 'Easy to Find' on the difficult to find B-side. Before this he was also a member of the group The Scots Of St James, who banged out a couple of 1966/67 singles which appear on various compilations.

Delving deeper, here was Graham M again, this time as part of Five Day Rain, a psych-cum-prog outfit whose one LP appeared in 1970 in very limited quantities. I found yet another reference to him on a recently issued record attributed to One Way Ticket, and called 'Return Journey'. This actually consists mostly of Brian Carroll, whose name appears as co-producer of the Five Day Rain release, along with the other One Way Ticket man, Damon Lyon-Shaw.

How could anyone ever have accessed this type of fascinating trivia by downloading or streaming, I wonder?

Back in Wood Street Market, I was now wondering where the 'Mike' I was looking for was. The unit called Mike's Records seemed to offer a clue, so I wandered in. I engaged in a very interesting chat with said Mike, who has run the unit since 2002. He no longer has a personal collection, he told me, but the unit doubles up as such, which doesn't apparently inhibit him from selling the stuff he likes himself. Mike's had a sign above the unit, indicating that he sells 'Record's, CD's, DVD's and Video's'. Apostrophes thrown in for free, clearly.

But there was no sign of the artworks which were said to adorn the unit run by Mike which Luke from the floating record shop frequented, so I was again in the wrong place. Which meant, unless someone was literally taking the Michael, that there were an impressive and varied three record-selling units in the market, and further investigation duly saw me in the shop concerned, Vinyl Vanguard, admiring the oils by local artist Ruth. This Mike was equally as welcoming as the earlier one, but was also unable to come up with a record I wanted to buy, despite having a wide spread to choose from. You know how it is – you can't always get what you want. Mike has an admirably binary take on music: 'The great jazz musician Duke Ellington was once quizzed about the best kinds of music; his response: "There's only two kinds" – good and bad. That's my take on music too – my tastes are highly eclectic and that's reflected in what I offer for sale.'

Mike has written a book and presented radio programmes about jazz, adding that he has 'spent a lifetime building up my own cherished collection of records'. Having recently read a piece raving about them, I'd bought a Mamas & Papas LP, *Deliver*. When I returned home, I discovered that I already owned it.

But at least they are both *real* copies...

IN WHICH... I COME ACROSS FAKE NEWS

There is always much discussion around the question of whether any copy of a record known to have been produced in small numbers, and to be exceedingly rare, is actually the genuine, real thing. I read a post on the Facebook group, Show Me Your Record Label... Is it the first issue? on which someone had put up photographs of some BBC Transcription Service records. Underneath, another member posted the response: 'Watch out for "boots" of these things.' To which another replied: 'Thankfully, when I purchased these in the mid-1970s they preceded the flood of convincing fakes of more recent years.'

'Convincing fakes' is such a fascinating phrase. If something is so convincing, can it actually be a fake? If it genuinely is a fake, can it be convincing? If you believe a fake to be genuine, then what harm is being done? Unless, of course, you try to sell it as genuine when you know there is some doubt. But isn't the onus always on the prospective purchaser only to buy if he or she is convinced the convincing item is absolutely genuine but is prepared to love it anyway if it isn't! The problem is always that if anyone, for whatever motive, declares something to be 'fake', it is almost impossible to disprove that negative. The art world regularly throws up doubt over the authenticity of paintings. TV series *Fake or Fortune?* is hugely popular. Surely, though, if you genuinely believe, or want to believe, something is genuine, then for you it is.

Also, we shouldn't forget that there are also always plenty of people anxious to 'diss' anyone who has something which they covet but do not actually possess themselves, on the basis that they don't want to acknowledge that anyone could have outdone them. Another correspondent posted that he had seen 'endless copies' of the fake records being discussed, sold at a well-known regular record market 'for a tenner'. Presumably at that price they are making no pretence to being genuine, which may or may not make them a victimless crime, but certainly makes them much more affordable than something which may or may not be the real deal. But then came another riposte: 'seen black and white label "boots", but never seen any "fake" copies – these would be tough to fake.' Now, people were arguing over whether what were clearly being sold as fakes if going for a tenner, really *were* fakes. Perhaps they were fake fakes?

Collecting is a very personal matter, and until and unless items are being bought or sold on the open market, only the individual who has a particular collection can know whether they are satisfied with the bona fides of their own records or even whether the records they are telling everyone else are genuine, actually are. When, though, did it become worthwhile for those of slightly lower honesty than most, to endeavour to deceive collectors of vinyl records by creating 'knock-off' copies to be sold at suspiciously cheap prices by dodgy traders online, at car boots and record fairs? And for more practised rogues to create almost exact facsimiles of rare, sought-after records?

Publications listing values of records appeared in the States in the mid-1970s, thus saddling individual records with a documented price. As an established record collector of my acquaintance put it: 'That's when it became very profitable to create an item with the sole purpose of duping someone for money.' Never forget, though, that record collectors had to put up with many years of abuse from the makers and manufacturers of records and CDs, who accused anyone who ever dared tape a record or radio programme on their cassette recorders of 'killing music'. They achieved this by printing a message and a skull & crossbones style logo on LPs and cassettes, 'Home Taping Is Killing Music', rather than encouraging people to tape what they wanted, so that they would become more familiar with music, which they would probably then go out and buy in a more permanent format. This persecution of innocent music lovers caused me long ago to lose any sense of shame over buying bootlegs, many of which may be poorly recorded, but often represent the only way of hearing music which has – or had – been withheld from the market for some reason.

Nor am I someone who wishes to commit to Hell and eternal damnation folk who make available to purchasers music they can't buy elsewhere without shelling out megabucks to acquire. I'm not so keen on bootleggers who put out fake copies, usually shoddily recorded and packaged, of new material – but for anyone with a little nous these are usually easily identifiable and avoidable.

In December 2018, four men in their 60s were sentenced – two of them to jail for up to ten months – for 'making and selling thousands of fake northern soul records online', reported *The Times*. It was said that police had seized some 55,000 records and that the men's actions had 'cost the industry about £500,000.' I read a fair amount about the case but still couldn't work out where the industry had suffered this hefty loss. It seemed to be mainly 45s being 'faked', but obscure ones which aren't readily available. Had the 'industry' wished to avoid this apparent loss, shouldn't they just have made the records available as re-releases? If the people buying the records did not know they were 'fakes' (and many had spelling mistakes or mismatched covers and other giveaways for the wary) then *they* were the ones who were being conned, surely, and not the 'industry'? I've bought plenty of records on unfamiliar record labels because I know full well I can't find them anywhere else for a reasonable price. I have no idea who profits from the money I'm spending, but if the record I've bought does what it is supposed to, and plays the music I want to hear that I can't get elsewhere, I won't complain. An audience wanting northern soul records is by definition pretty much bound to be a knowledgeable one, so I'd imagine that a good number of them will have been aware they were taking a chance in buying these records. But perhaps I'm missing something. Perhaps at this point, it is right to stress the difference between fakes and bootlegs, as I understand them.

Bootlegs are illegally issued records, usually releasing material which has otherwise not been made available by the bands and record companies themselves, usually for reasons of quality control. Most people buying them are entirely aware of what they are purchasing. The first bootleg I acquired was a Hendrix album, *Wow!* I just double-checked. It appeared in 1970, containing performances recorded at Woodstock and Monterey, and in August 2018 was still around to buy for around £20.

Fakes, though, are designed to resemble the real thing as closely as possible – to be virtual reality made actuality. They are illegal imitations of authenticity, deliberately created to fool collectors and part them from their cash. The only saving grace may be that those being fooled sometimes believe that they are effectively buying something for well under its true worth and are happy to be doing so. They may naively think they are deliberately fooling the person selling them the product, when the exact opposite is happening! Then there are also, of course, 'reissues' which are actually sold as such, but may later be passed off by unscrupulous sellers to poorly informed buyers as genuine originals.

This is a fascinating area of collecting, but could it be construed as being unfair of me to suggest that where forgeries are of obvious poor quality, surely it is incumbent on the prospective purchaser to spot it and buy, or not, on that basis. I am happy to buy new reissue versions of stuff now virtually impossible to obtain as originals for less than the cost of a mortgage, but will also pay fair prices for originals rather than new versions if they come up. But fakes are a part of human life in many areas and our own inbuilt bullsh*t-detecting facility should kick in when we come up against what we suspect to be just that...

IN WHICH... I GET BLADDERED

Forty-eight hours earlier, I'd still had a gallbladder. By the time I began typing this chapter, in late 2018, I no longer had one.

In between, in the pessimistic anticipation that I might not be around in a few days to do so, I decided that now was the time to make a self-promised trip to have a look at the vinyl delights of Reading. Early impressions of the town, which I'd never visited before were a little shrouded by the clouds of vape emanating from a significant percentage of those passing by and around the beggars taking the afternoon sun in the streets surrounding the main station. A small lady in white carrying a large black dog in her lap came by in a wheelchair as I struggled to establish my whereabouts. I couldn't find a street map and never quite know how to find google-map or whatever it is called on my mobile. I located the Harris Arcade where I was aware one of the shops was located by the simple expedient of looking over the road as I left the station behind me, and spotting it sitting there. Having chalked that one up I left it where I could come back to it and went looking for the one I understood to be in Oxford Road.

The passer-by I asked for directions was so nervous that I was about to mug him that he upped his walking pace, causing me to do likewise, as he assured me, 'I've never heard of it, it's miles away. Goodbye.' As I gave up the pursuit I realised I was standing next to a street map, perusal of which revealed that Oxford Road was hiding itself all of about 800 yards away at the end of one of the main shopping streets. When I arrived at the shop, the man in charge was looking over a guitar which two guys had brought in to sell him (musical instruments also a speciality here at Music Man) and which they were confident was 'worth 800 quid according to the internet'. Mr Music Man wasn't so sure.

'It's worth 150 to me.'

'170 – we had to get a cab to bring it.'

'No. 160 – the cab would only have been a tenner.'

'Okay. Done.'

For that guitar they could also have bought 50 of Mr Music Man's healthily priced and wide selection of rock and other genre CDs and still had a tenner for the cab home. Sadly, his records did not impress me in either their conditions or prices, so I opted for Wishbone Ash, Ritchie Blackmore's Rainbow and Leslie West solo CDs. I retraced my steps, with the assistance of a purple number 17 bus, to the shopping precinct and the Harris Arcade. A few yards into this attractive line-up of bijou shops, I came across J.I.M. – 'Just Imagination Memorabilia' ('Ask for Jim' says his leaflet) – 'retro dance vinyl – toys – comics and much more.' So much more that it makes it somewhat difficult to manoeuvre around the limited available space. The guy looking after the premises clearly had stylish jazzy blues tastes and was playing music of this type. CDs were offered at very low prices – an average of two quid – although the records were more highly valued and not that appealing to me. I enjoyed looking, but couldn't persuade myself to buy.

Sound Machine, further into the Arcade, is a rather presentable unit of a record shop. Two chaps behind the counter, two different generations. Behind them a tempting selection of valuable 1960s and 1970s covers. In front of them a nice new cabinet of 'Just In's, and all around any number of additional stock. Mellow atmosphere. I find a nice copy of the Shanghai (Mick Green on guitar, Cliff Bennett vocals) LP that you *don't* often see – *Fallen Heroes* which, at two quid short of a tenner, was a no-brainer.

However, I had little time to listen to Shanghai, before I found myself walking towards the Central Middlesex Hospital with more internal organs in place than I would own by mid-evening. The last time this happened had been in the late 1970s when I was 28, and spent a couple of weeks at the Middlesex Hospital in central London, having a cartilage removed from my right leg. It saved my football career, but I was never the same afterwards. These days a cartilage op probably doesn't involve any sort of stay in hospital and keyhole surgery enables it to be done in minutes. When I came round following the op, I couldn't shift the leg, despite the urgings of the brutal female physio who demanded movement from the moment I opened my eyes. In the bed opposite a fellow in for the same treatment was lifting his leg up and down with no apparent adverse effect. I was worried. My op must have failed. Next morning, I was still marooned motionless in bed while the guy over the way was up and moving around the ward. When the doc who had carried out our ops came round with his gang of trainee medics he reassured me that the procedure had gone well – but the man opposite was now packing his bags and preparing to leave. It transpired they'd opened his knee up, decided there was no damage to the cartilage, stitched him back up - and sent him on his way. Phew!

Lizzie, one of the nurses on the ward was a Boz Scaggs' fan. I'd never heard of him then, but I tracked down some of his records in tribute to Lizzie, who wrote on the 'Get Well Soon' card which I still have: 'What can I say but that BOZ IS KING!! Lotsa love.' I have enjoyed his stuff ever since and often wonder where Lizzie is these days, what she's up to and whether she's still, like me, listening to the Scaggster. Back to the present, and even in such an august institution as the Central Mid ACAD (the first ambulatory care and diagnostic centre in Europe) ward, I might have guessed that music would play a part in the experience.

Over a blood test, I'd met old-school hospital sister, Angela, and we'd not only bonded over a love of early 1960s and onwards music, but also treated the ward to a duet of one of the Bee Gees' finest, 'How Deep Is Your Love?'. Or maybe I was hallucinating in an anaesthetically induced haze? It seemed real at the time. She is of similar vintage to me and sat down for a chat when my departure for theatre was delayed while they hunted for a bed. It soon transpired we had a two-year-old grandchild each, as well as a shared love of Motown, and Lulu's version of 'To Sir with Love'. Angela raised the stakes with Billie Holiday and I countered with Tony Joe White. She outclassed me by revealing she listened to her music on a Bose system.

Now they came to wheel me off to face the knife - after the anaesthetist almost caused a cancellation of the whole thing by ill-advisedly knocking a large lump off of the high-tech bed I was laying on. The docs eventually decided they wouldn't need it. The less said about the surgery the better, but they refused to let me depart the next morning with what they removed as a souvenir. Shame. I wanted to add it to my cartilage which sits in a bottle on the shelf next to my laptop. I spent a few days feeling sore and sorry for myself but decided that I could probably survive the few days in Liverpool we'd booked with friends, albeit at slower than normal pace.

I was surprised by how much I enjoyed doing the Beatle

things when we arrived. Sure, there is something of a theme-park atmosphere about the 'Cavern' area, where the recreated site is over the street from the actual location of the club where the boys learned their trade. As we wandered around there late on our first night it was possible to imagine that this must have been pretty much how it was back in those formative years. Music was pouring out of the bar windows into the street's chilly air – a band hammering away with more gusto and guitar than subtlety and empathy.

One or two offers of illicit substances were made as we walked along. Drunk youngsters enjoying the sights and sounds staggered past, there was a slight edge of potential disturbance in the air. Watchful bouncers leaned against entrances, alert to any possible outbreak of violence. We took photos in front of Cilla's statue and alongside John's image on the actual Cavern site, laughing and reminiscing amongst ourselves. Then, as we walked along, a young man suddenly raced past at full sprint, threw himself into a wall, bounced off it, and crashed to the pavement, curling himself into a human ball (title of great psych LP by my 60s idols, The McCoys) and whimpering. Friends or acquaintances of his took their time to come and check on his condition, one offering me drugs as he strolled past.

Next day we visited The Beatles Story – much more informative about the early, Liverpool-based days than the later hippy-dippy times – and enjoyed a Magical Mystery Tour on a blue and yellow coach, which took us to see all four of the lads' early homes and haunts, including, inevitably, Penny Lane and Strawberry Field. Just the words 'Strawberry' and 'Fields' retain the power to provoke nostalgia in me, even though this was the first time I'd been anywhere near their source. But to think that these two words and a street name had inspired a pair of the finest songs ever committed to vinyl was enough to plunge me into memories of my own earlier years and to remind myself yet again of The Beatles' extraordinary musical abilities.

The trip gave me the opportunity to explore the record buying and selling scene in the city. Half a dozen shops sit within relatively close proximity, along Liverpool's Bold, Slater, and Renshaw Streets, with Seel Street, School Lane and Smithdown

Road also boasting record-buying opportunities. First port of call was the well-stocked, attractively fronted Probe Records, but it was disappointing to find no pre-loved/owned vinyl on offer, even though the depth of their new and reissue selections was impressive. In the Jacaranda Records Phase One in Slater Street, we found again a majority of new vinyl with a relatively small stash of second-hand records. Interesting features here were the bar, and the chintzy garden-shed listening booths equipped with little record players on which you could listen to prospective buys.

Also in Slater Street is dance music specialist record shop, 3 Beat.

A little more appealing to our tastes was Renshaw Street's Eighty One which is situated at – well, work it out for yourself – and boasts on its sign: 'Cafe – Venue – Record Store'. Reaching the vinyl involves a climb up a slightly rickety, steep set of stairs, but the journey is worthwhile as you emerge into a nicely bulging room of records of all types. Slightly pricey records, I'd say, although Mike delved deep and found an excellent £17.50 copy of an early Spencer Davis Group LP. He brought it over to show me and we gazed at the surface of the vinyl which was not exactly pristine but which did not seem to be suffering from severe scratches. A request to the youngish fellow running the place resulted in him giving us an on-the-spot demonstration of the cleaning capability of the expensive-looking machine there for just that purpose. Impressively, it turned the badly marked surface of the disc into a sparkling, reflective, mirror-like clean thing, which played very well when he then slapped it on to the Planar turntable. He slightly reduced the effect when he launched into great detail about why the record might be subject to the odd jump because he couldn't ensure that the turntable was completely level, due, he claimed, to the inaccuracy of the chippie responsible for installing the surface on which it was sitting. Like so many things in the record collecting world – someone else's fault, guv.

Hairy Records was apparently one of the longest established record shops in Liverpool, when it moved to a new address in Bold Street in 2012. It then appeared to become The Music Consortium, but we failed to find it under either of those names and scrutinising the internet suggests it has become an online rather than physical presence. However, Bold Street does contain an Oxfam outlet from which I purchased a double Doves CD, before we sought out Dig Vinyl. And you do need to seek it out because only a very small notice outside and a tiny wall-mounted sign at the side of the Soho vintage clothing shop it shares, are there to identify its whereabouts down in the basement it has called home since 2014.

But it would take the accolade as the best Liverpool record shop we found, in the eyes, ears and wallets of Mike and me. And (well, well, well) it was also certainly the *only* shop we found here, or indeed anywhere else, with its own brick-built water well bang in the middle of the records. The chap behind the counter did not appear to be positive that it was a working well. 'Why would you have windows in a working water well?' he asked. Why indeed? But there seems to be no doubt that there is water at the bottom of the well. And some excellent records and CDs at the top of it. I snapped up albums by Dennis Wilson, Spooky Tooth, The Honeys and a great psych compilation CD from Past & Present. Very competitive prices here, a cafe in which to rest and gloat over finds, and a boutiquey style shop to walk through en route to discovering this excellent venue.

When I arrived home from Liverpool, I discovered that my car required a new cambelt (whatever one of those may be). While this was being done, the Audi showroom gave me one of their newer models with which to escort Mrs S on her weekly Sainsbury's outing, although at 38 grand, it's unlikely to be my next permanent conveyance. When I returned to collect my own refurbished vehicle, the service chap rushed through the details of what had been done to it, before asking me excitedly, 'What was the great music on the CD in your car?' It transpired he'd been listening to a CD by Creation, which I'd recently bought and had left in the player. When I told him the track was probably 'Makin' Time' he immediately looked it up on his mobile, logging on to something called Shazam to identify the track and save or download it.

Then he asked me had I heard of Jefferson Airplane or Big Brother & The Holding Company and could I recommend any similar music that he may be able to source. I suggested Quicksilver Messenger Service and he quickly found 'Pride of Man'. From there we jumped to Fleur de Lys, by which time he was agreeing to buy a copy of this book when it was published. At this point he mentioned another of his favourites, Brian Protheroe, who had a hit with 'Pinball' in 1974. When I later told Julian at Second Scene about this, he too declared an unexpected fondness for the Protheroe single.

Julian's shop was packed with heaps of boxes full of unpriced records yet to be sorted and graded.

'We decided to try sending out flyers – and it worked. We've had loads of local people bringing their records in. Some of them have no idea what they've got and say they were about to give or throw them away – they're grateful for any offer of money and despite knowing that they would almost certainly accept very low offers I do feel obliged to offer them a fair price. But then there are the others who have a ridiculously inflated price in mind and think I'm trying to rip them off if my offer doesn't measure up.' The new approach was paying dividends and Julian told me he'd brought in a good selection of unusual records as a result: 'Have a look through, I'm sure you'll find something.' I did – a McKendree Spring LP, and the brilliant 1973 self-titled Byrds' album which for some reason I omitted to buy at the time – for 20 quid the pair.

Now that I was back from the home of The Beatles, I once again found myself faced with a decision to make between them and their eternal rivals...

IN WHICH... I'M BEATLING ALONG

Once again it seemed to come down to a choice between Beatles or Stones. Both of my football teams were playing away, giving me a 'free' day to concentrate on record collecting. But where to go? Perhaps The Christ The Saviour Parish Church in

Ealing, advertising itself as: Record & CD Fair & Beatles Day, Christ Saviour Church Hall, New Broadway, Ealing W5 2XA – beatlesdays.com. Or, maybe the latest Twickenham Record Fair, being held at St Mary's Church Hall, just a minute away from the Eel Pie Records' shop down Church Street, Twickenham, and very close to Eel Pie Island, where, in June 1963, the fledgling Rolling Stones took to the stage, beginning a five-month residency at the Eel Pie Island Hotel.

The Stones' residency that summer coincided with the release of their debut single 'Come On' – a rallying cry that proved presciently irresistible to a significant section of the teenage audience, including myself. Not only that, the promotional photograph showing the previous record fair at the venue included a shot of the back of yours truly's head, snapped during crate-digging activities there. I decided not to press for an image rights' payment. But, as I hadn't experienced a 'Beatles Day' I headed for Ealing.

Arriving there I could spot the spire of the church hosting the record fair, piercing the cloudy sky above the town. Approaching the venue there were several posters and notices pointing the way in, and a large yellow Beatles-decorated van was sitting in the grounds. The arrows on the posters sent me all the way round the church without identifying a way in. On my second circuit I spotted a youngish chap looking equally baffled.

'Any idea how we get in?' I asked him.

'All the doors seem to be locked,' he replied.

'Not the best business plan for encouraging visitors,' I responded. He agreed.

'Are you a Beatles fan?' I asked.

'No, I love visiting churches.'

Eventually I located the very modern hall nestled alongside the ancient-looking church and, after another false start trying to identify a door that actually opened, I was finally inside. The advertising blurb was accurate. There was Beatle bootie galore on display. However, in the interests of accuracy, most of the music being played while I was there was 1960s psych and the majority of buying interest did seem to be in the general stock of the sellers present. I felt the vinyl on offer – new and original – was generally overpriced. The exceptions unfortunately were not titles I wanted. Once again, though, there were very reasonably priced CDs, of which I nabbed four: an Andy Fairweather-Low, a Boz Scaggs, a Franz Ferdinand and a Wishbone Ash. All four for... any guesses? A tenner.

The Beatles' memorabilia didn't really appeal to me. I have all the Fab 4 LPs I need or want, along with a decent collection of Beatle-related books and mags, all acquired a good few years ago. There was a relaxed atmosphere in the hall, the sellers seemed well acquainted with each other and quite happy chatting, no one worrying that there weren't hordes of buyers. The impression was that these were people happy to be sharing a day with like-minded folk, listening to music they enjoy, possibly making a few quid, but probably covering the relatively modest costs of hiring out a church hall. More of a hobby than a business. I could see the attraction, and if I wasn't tied to football or horse racing on Saturdays, then I'd probably consider joining their amiable congregation.

A day or two later I was in the Notting Hill Gate area's Music & Video Exchange shop, resisting the temptation to buy what I felt was a very reasonably priced (£9 reduced from £14), original copy of the Mystic Number National Bank LP on the Probe label. It looked in decent nick, but I was turned against it by very poor reviews when I looked on online. ('Some of the least impressive soloing you've ever heard on a major label – rating one star'; 'absolutely nothing going on here'; 'this track sounds like something they might have played at a local Marriott Hotel'; 'boring beyond tolerance. Bloody awful, I would suggest true psychedelia fans ignore it'.) I did listen to it on YouTube later in the day and it *is* a bit 'heavy rock by numbers', with somewhat unoriginal, uninspiring guitar licks, and almost comedy vocals. The 'Blues So Bad' track is one of the most appropriately named tracks I've ever come across. I was so alarmed by the bad reviews, though, that I found an £8 CD of Antipodean 1960s band, Larry's Rebels, and bought that instead. It's terrific.

I walked the mile or so to Rough Trade West in Talbot Road.

I think it must be me, but I've never really bought into the Rough Trade philosophy. Their shops always seem a little predictable and pricey, if I'm honest – and I rarely spot my idea of value for money records. Canadian band Rough Trade (whose 1982 LP, *Shaking the Foundations*, I own) adopted their name in 1974, two years before that name appeared over a shop frontage. RT shops are usually in areas frequented by plenty of passing trade and/or tourists, so they probably believe rightly that the clientele they attract can afford, and is happy to pay, prices calculated to help support hefty running costs. The first shop opened in 1976 and they now have five – in Bristol, Nottingham, two in London, and in Brooklyn, USA. As their website boasts: 'Fundamentally, our stores provide creative, independent minds, a shared place of discovery and congregation'.

Of course they do. But are they making – or do they want to make – friends? People who will walk away very happy with what they've bought, and who will rush to return again and again. Not people who feel that perhaps they've been overcharged. I don't quite get that vibe. I may be mistaken and may just find myself in a bad mood every time I enter one of their shops.

This one had all the new vinyl and CDs upstairs with, in the corner, a steep stairway with a notice: 'DOWNSTAIRS FOR VINTAGE VINYL'. It was accurate enough, but the only reason I kept flipping through the ranks of pretty run-of-the-mill rock at prices I'd rate some 25 per cent higher on average than they could be found for elsewhere, was to listen to the mellow-voiced 'longhair' sitting behind the counter who was conducting a conversation about the shop's stock, saying that he'd recently asked his boss whether sales of vinyl were still increasing as rapidly as they had been. The answer he'd had was that they weren't. But he felt this was probably because when they had been rising they had done so from an extremely low level, and now had to be compared with recent much higher levels of sales. He was also critical that so many saleable items were being left 'in the back, gathering dust, rather than being put out for sale'.

As I left, empty-handed, having found absolutely nothing whatsoever to tempt me, I was thinking: 'That's really pissed me off'.

At precisely that time I saw in the playground over the road, a man kicking a football towards his son to head into an imaginary goal, only for the ball to flash too high, over his head, rolling towards a small, dirt area:

'Damn. Straight into the dog toilet.'
'Know how you feel, mate,' I thought and walked on...

IN WHICH... AN ANOREXIC MANNEQUIN IS PROUDLY REGARDED

'Good morning, Graham,' said Duncan, as we met for our regular early morning stroll. My immediate response was to begin singing: 'Good morning, Starshine...' The lyrics had sprung into my head as soon as Duncan had spoken. I automatically sang the chorus and saw in my mind a green and black record label with a slight tear in it. Duncan chuckled. 'I don't know how you do that', he said, 'but you do it all the time. Singing a lyric from a record to match almost every occasion. Where do you keep them all stored in your brain?' I had to tell Duncan I was aware of the phenomenon, but had no idea where it had come from and how it started. It is almost as bad as my near involuntary propensity to whistle whatever tune comes into my head, almost certainly untunefully and to the irritation of anyone and everyone within hearing distance. I can only blame my Dad, who was another frequent whistler – but usually only of songs by his favourite, Judy Garland. Duncan was right, though. Whatever the occasion I seem to be able immediately to call up a suitably titled track and sing a fragment of it.

By the way, should you not be familiar with the lyrics of 'Good Morning Starshine', the Top 10 hit for Oliver in 1969, here is a sample: 'Glibby gloop gloopy, Nibby Nabby Noopy, La La La Lo Lo/ Sabba Sibby Sabba, Nooby abba Nabba Le Le Lo Lo/Tooby ooby walla, nooby abba nabba, Early mornin' singin' song.' My memory of the green and black label is accurate. I checked, and it was on the Crewe label, which came in those colours. And those last four words, immediately prompt me to start mentally singing: 'Woh, woh, woh, woh, my love she comes in colours, you can tell her from the clothes she wears...' That, of course, is from Love's wonderful, 'She Comes in Colours', a single in 1966 which also includes the great line: 'Expressions tell everything, I see one on you...'

Everyone has favourite lyrics. Two of my particular favourites come from the heyday of Roxy Music's eccentric genius. I've always delighted in hearing Ferry sing, 'Rhodedendron is a nice flower' in 'Do the Strand', while 'Lumber up, limbo down' gets me every time in 'Love Is the Drug'. Also from the pen of Mr Ferry – in 'In Every Dream Home a Heartache', he writes of a sex doll: 'I blew up your body/ But you blew my mind'. Probably my favourite lyric of all, and I have to admit that this can change from time to time, is by one of many forgotten-by-most 1960s acts who flared briefly and were soon gone. Back in the great days of pirate radio the Major Minor label used to promote its records via Radio Caroline, playing snippets of the tracks they wanted you to hear and rush out to buy. The tactic worked, and from the moment I first heard, 'A tenement, a dirty street/Walked and worn by shoeless feet', I was hooked. I just had to own a copy of 1967's brilliant 'Days of Pearly Spencer' by David McWilliams. Staggeringly, it failed to chart in the UK, although it sold over a million copies in all and was a huge hit in France and Holland. The song was about a homeless man McWilliams, from Northern Ireland, had encountered, and featured a sweeping orchestral arrangement by Mike Leander and a chorus sung as if through a megaphone – this low-tech effect was achieved by recording the vocals from a phone box near the studio.

Incomprehensible examples also have their place in the pantheon of great lyrics. I'm not sure I quite understood him then, let alone now. But when I interviewed the late Robert Palmer about the title track of his LP, 'Pride', of which he was one of three songwriters, he did add the memorable quote: 'My favourite line is "Anorexia Nervosa mannequin".' And why, of course, wouldn't it be?

Just as my favourite record shop is Second Scene...

IN WHICH... I DATE JULIAN

I suppose it was inevitable. I was now actually making a date to see my local record shop owner. I'd been in to see Julian at Second Scene one Tuesday afternoon, but had barely had time to put in an order for a cup of tea when offered and cast but a cursory glance over a couple of covers, when I noticed a missed call on my phone which turned out to be a message to ring my wife asap. We were having the rendering on our house changed to some super-duper, upmarket substance which they use on the outside of space exploration rockets – or some such high-tech wonder-material. To put the new stuff on they had to take the old stuff off – in the process of which exercise they had also removed most of what held one of our bigger windows in place. The result was that you could now see through the gaps exposed to the outside world from the bathroom in which it was situated. Mrs Sharpe was pretty certain it was only a matter of time before the window fell and the walls came down. Like a reporter making his excuses and leaving the scene of an interview before getting to the crux of the story, I had to leg it before my house toppled to the ground. I sent an anxious text to the head chap in charge of the rendering work, demanding that he drop everything and immediately rush round to save my home. Eventually this situation was resolved but I felt the need to complete the visit to Second Scene which I'd begun. I sent Julian a note the next day asking him if he'd be in the shop that afternoon.

'I am, but I'm sorting job lots upstairs, so won't be very sociable. You about on Friday?'

'Will the afternoon be okay?' I responded.

'Yes, that's better for me'

'It's a date, then...'

Having stood him up once before, I had to be on time.

I was just a little late, but Julian was busy outside the shop when I arrived shortly before 3pm:

'You remembered our date, then?'

After we'd congratulated each other on our powers of recall, I asked him what he was doing, shuffling about several lines of £1 records on what looked like a large shelf extending from the bottom of the shop window.

'I've put this in to take the cheap records. Looks good, doesn't it?'

'Yes, but why don't you add some kind of cover to go over the records and keep them a little more secure?' I asked. Then I answered my own question. 'Although, I suppose that would be pointless. After all, it isn't as if someone is going to come along and nick a load of Cliff Richard, various artists and middle-of-the-road crooners, is it?'

'Really? The other day when I came back from lunch, someone came in and offered to sell me a bunch of records which I soon recognised as my own, which they had helped themselves to outside!'

'How much did you offer them?'

I told Julian again that his shop window needed an eye-catching design to attract the attention of passing drivers and walkers. What had happened to the proposed psychedelic makeover I'd heard one of his customers offering to create for him?

'He only dashed off a couple of ideas, but we never got any further with it.'

I told Julian a recent tale of woe over two John Pantry LPs I'd decided to buy. He is an obscure psych figure who produced a large number of excellent songs recorded by an equally impressive number of bands who may well have been created just for that purpose, back in the late 1960s and early 1970s, before, it would appear, discovering God with a very capital 'G', and reportedly becoming a vicar. I'd decided that after years of searching for much of his stuff unsuccessfully, I'd bite the bullet and buy the records from Discogs' sellers. One of them was his final 'pop'-orientated LP, the other a compilation of tracks written, and in some instances also recorded, by him, entitled *The Upside Down World of John Pantry*. This latter record was a Tenth Planet reissue of tracks recorded between 1967 and 1969. Together with postage from Greece, this would cost me 30 quid, but was described as 'mint' for record and cover, and contained an insert. The seller boasted a very high percentage rate of customer satisfaction. I was, though, a little miffed, when he sent a note to say the record was on the way, but could I reimburse an additional 2.80 euro cost charged by his local post office? Er... no!

When the record arrived it was perhaps the best, most securely wrapped item I've ever purchased. It took me the best part of half an hour to get it out of the box, in the process inflicting a nasty little jagged cut to a finger whilst bringing bread knives, scissors and teeth to the task. When the contents were revealed, there was an excellent cover. No problems with its description. Likewise, the insert. It had obviously been 'fingered' once or twice, but then who hasn't? Otherwise pristine. So, hopes high for the record. Hopes soon dashed. The record could not be described as anything other than a passable VG in my opinion. It was dirty, dusty and very scuffed from, I think, the heavy inner sleeve in which it came, which also had a seam-slit down one side. I wrote to the seller, in very measured and restrained terms. I was going to keep the record anyway, but I wanted an explanation. My ten-line email received this response: 'It is an UNPLAYED copy, so I can't understand about scuffs etc. If you don't want to send the additional postage, never mind.' Breathing a hefty sigh, I just wrote back pointing out that 'unplayed' does not equate to 'mint'.

Annoyingly, I had a similar problem with the solo Pantry LP which was advertised as 'Near mint' which I thought was quite a creative use of the word 'Near', clearly used in the same manner in which I might describe New Zealand as 'Near' Australia, despite the fact that it is a few hours away by plane.

The Near Mint record was at best VG+ in both cover and disc condition.

Challenged on this, the seller offered:

'I really thought it was a lovely copy. It's a tough LP to find and I'm usually pretty tough on conditions. Sorry it wasn't up to standard.'

Maybe I was just doubly unlucky, but buyer beware.

Julian took the story as another very good reason to buy from a shop, where you can check the condition personally and not have to pay postage, adding:

'I've never heard of John Pant... what was his name?'

Helen was now playing a record through to check its grading. Julian asked her what she planned to charge for it. 'Well, it's filthy and has a good few marks.'

It was playing remarkably well and sounding excellent, with a strong blues vocal, accompanied by driving guitar and wailing harmonica. Julian looked over at what I could now see was a double album with the gatefold spread out on top of some other albums. 'Nice record' he said, probably to encourage what I did next.

I looked at him. 'I think I'll have it.'

An instant illustration of the difference between direct and remote selling. If I had received this record having bought it online, I'd have been shocked by its appearance. Having heard it played through and decided to buy despite the condition, I was perfectly happy. Helen offered to clean it on the shop's in-house equipment and we agreed on an £18 price for what I now knew was *Fathers & Sons*, on the Chess label, LPS 127, and featuring Muddy Waters, Otis Spann, Michael Bloomfield (guitar), Paul Butterfield (mouth harp), Donald 'Duck' Dunn, and Buddy Miles. A very impressive line-up over the 16 tracks, all recorded in April 1969, six of which were 'recorded live at Super Cosmic Joy-Scout Jamboree'. The SCJSJ, explains the cover is (or more likely was) 'an Academy of open enquiry designed to explore all cultural concepts, with the idea of creating new approaches to ethics, religion, philosophy, art and science'. I later checked the record out on the Discogs website and could find only one copy available from a UK seller. It was a 'near mint' copy going for £40 plus £3.50 postage. I was very happy with what I'd got.

After our in-shop date had finished, and we had agreed to see each other again to continue the relationship, albeit without any guaranteed long-term commitment to each other, I took the train back. As I disembarked I couldn't help overhear the conversation going on between two fellow commuter travellers: 'Well, that's the trouble with tortoises... they can't tell you when they're ill.'

A bit odd – but not as odd as mates can be...

IN WHICH... A FRIEND'S PLEAS DON'T PLEASE ME

It was a plea from the heart on behalf of a journalistic pal – how could I resist? My friend Chris has ensured his permanent place in my affections for the wonderful and completely true story he once told me of the days when he was a jobbing magician at children's parties to raise the odd bob or two. He was flashing his wand at an upmarket function being held at a prominent Brighton venue which more usually hosts sell-out big-name band concerts. Chris was entertaining his young audience by plucking coins from their ears, turning water into Pepsi, making the awkward ones disappear, etc, when the whole event was thrown into disarray as loud rock music boomed out from the empty arena behind them. Tonight's band was staging a run-through prior to the show. Chris was having none of it. Putting his glamorous assistant in charge of the rowdy kids he strode off to 'have a word'.

Marching up to the stage where the group was riffing away, he shouted up, 'Oy, mate, we need to have a chat...' One by one the musicians stopped in their tracks. When they were all silent, Chris explained his predicament and asked whether the group would please desist for the next hour so that he could finish off his stint. Listening patiently, the vocalist/guitarist politely apologised and assured Chris he would be able to conclude his show without interruption. Chris returned to the kids, happy that Bryan Adams meant what he had said... and he did!

Fast forward a while and I had received a plea from Chris's usually charming wife, Sandra. The plea was hidden in an email invitation to pop round to their house for the evening: 'Chris got a vintage record player for his birthday. He's asked if you can bring a vinyl please!!! He's got some but they're in the attic!! Thank you. X' I'd been vacillating about whether actually to attend this combined anniversary-cum-birthday event for our friends from not far down the road. Now, to be honest, I felt slightly miffed. What, Chris *does* have some records, but he can't be arsed to retrieve them to play at his own party? So, let's give Graham a call, he's got loads so he'll just drop everything, get a few together and bring them over.

And what is this use of the term 'a vinyl' by Sandra in her email? What's wrong with calling a spade a record? I know she's a few years younger me, but I think she really should be aware of the proper terminology. I suppose I'll have to go along with it, though. My wife wouldn't want me to get stroppy with friends. We haven't got that many local ones these days! So I send back an email: 'Who/what does he like?'

'Anything 1960s! 45s apparently!'

What rubbish! 'Anything 1960s'? Doesn't she *know* how many styles of music that encompasses? They've been married 25 years yet she doesn't know what type of music he likes! Being the nice fellow I am, I drop everything and whip through my 1960s singles. I select some Beatles, Stones, Searchers, Otis Redding, Stevie Wonder, Kinks, Troggs, Supremes – and Twinkle's 'Terry'. I figure I know his musical leanings better than his wife – and I'm proved right when, after we arrive, he flips through the discs and seizes upon...

'Twinkle! "Terry" – I loved that single. That wasn't her real name, was it?'

There follows an interlude during which Chris endeavours to work out the technicalities of switching on the controls to activate the mechanism inside the tasteful blue box in which the record player is encased. Switching to '45' and lifting the arm to place it on the edge of each, er, vinyl, and then working out that in order to actually hear the resulting music it is necessary to turn up the volume control, we finally hear Ms Ripley's sombre, dulcet tones... to the incredulity of the younger members of the assembled partygoers.

After three or four songs the novelty clearly begins to wear off. Chris wanders away to circulate amongst the guests, newcomers who know us come over to look delightedly at the record player, but soon clear off again, complaining that it is too loud. I begin to remember how I always used to feel at the gatherings of yore. Jona Lewie's perceptive lyrics return to my brain: 'You'll always find me in the kitchen at parties'. Or, in my case, in the corner with the record player, acting as the DJ, spinning the singles to create an atmosphere and getting everyone up to shake, as we used to say, a tail-feather.

Sandra makes no effort either to congratulate me on my choice of records to play or to listen to any of them, and eventually takes the executive decision that it should be turned off and replaced by some form of automatic music technology of which I have no understanding. As soon as I can, and once we've enjoyed some of Chris's white wine, some very nice salady, smoked salmony, ricey grub, some cake, some of Chris's champers, I gather up the records, some of which inevitably have come out of their sleeves, pack them into a carrier bag, make our excuses, and leave, not quite in a huff, but...

As we exit, Chris tells me, 'I've got loads of records in the attic, I must get them out... in the future.'

'Yeah, let me know when, and I'll come and value them for you,' I lie. Haven't been round there since...

Part of my motive in writing this book has been to step up my campaign to encourage friends and lapsed vinyl lovers to rediscover that formerly important emotion. Two messages I received on Monday 25 September 2018 convinced me that my persistence was finally paying dividends. Les, a long-term mate, was in Glasgow with his wife, Aydee, a native Scot, but took time out to send me via WhatsApp, a photograph of him on the threshold of a record shop he had just visited – Missing in Glasgow. I'm getting through to Les, I thought – a contemporary who used to love and buy records and who still attends gigs.

But if this was an unexpected indication that vinyl could be on the verge of a return to Les's life, the next message, a text, was a bombshell. My best friend, Graham Brown who was deep into his music as a teenager and who gathered around him an enviable collection of vinyl and catalogue of gigs – including Hendrix live – had been resisting all of my entreaties to revisit this period and return to the community of vinylists. But now here he was, sending me a text asking: 'Best of Keef Hartley LP. £25. Worth it?'

I knew he was on a short city break holiday in Newcastle with wife Anita. I knew he was once a Keef Hartley Band fan who owned at least one of their original LPs from the era. But I was also aware he hadn't bought any vinyl for many a long year. Now he was considering reacquainting himself with the experience. Before I could call him, my mobile rang and there he was, enthusing that his trip to the 30-year-old RPM Records in Old George Yard, Newcastle, had resulted in one purchase already and the strong possibility of another.

'I've bought an old MFP record with Jeff Beck and Terry Reid on it for three quid already. I was considering buying a double LP by The Band which looked very reasonably priced until the bloke behind the counter pointed out that it only contained one of the two records! That made me think that here was an honest man and I then spotted this Keef Hartley Band album and wondered whether it was fairly priced, so decided to ask you.'

I told him that as compilations don't tend to attract big money it wouldn't be worth buying as a long-term investment, but a quick look online confirmed that, if it was in decent condition, that price seemed fair enough. I was confident that he would be buying it to listen to, and that it would contain plenty of music he'd like and didn't already possess. I had to resist the temptation to shout 'Yeessss!' whilst speaking to him as he'd shown no previous inclination to get back on the vinyl horse from which he'd dismounted many years back, despite my other attempts to persuade him to let me look through his collection to value it for him. Obviously my accumulated efforts had finally ground him down.

Just about a week later I found myself looking at a double LP of Keef Hartley Band live performances at the BBC. In apparently new condition, it was in a very attractive replica Deram gatefold cover and on sale for £25. Perusing the credits I noticed that there was a great deal of Miller Anderson input and decided to buy it even though Keef Hartley's jazzier side had never appealed to me that much. I thought I'd let Graham know about this coincidence, so sent him a text. Almost immediately he was on the phone: 'I'm on a train to Reading. Yes, I'll have the Hartley album.'

Ah. He'd either misread my text or deliberately misconstrued it. Regardless, he was clearly well on the way to becoming an enthusiastic, revitalised fan of vinyl – at least when Keef Hartley was on it. I decided to let him have the record and look for another, or a CD copy for myself. Feeling like an evangelist who has just converted a lost soul back to the path of righteousness, I even negotiated a 10 per cent discount on the cost for him...

Being able to add Graham and Les to the likes of other friends (the two Mikes, Colin, Roger, and one or two more) meant that although I couldn't yet claim as many disciples as that other fisher of men, and no females whatsoever, my efforts were certainly chiming with a few lapsed LP folk. I must admit, though, that I was less successful in my efforts to inveigle Mrs Sharpe back into the fold! Despite my cunning plan to utilise my wonderful Brennan machine to impress her with a stream of her old favourite records.

If you don't know what a Brennan is, I think you should do, as to me it is the 'old school' equivalent to Spotify, downloading and streaming. It is a small machine, no larger than a compact DVD player, on which you can 'record' CDs in a couple of minutes and then be at liberty to play them back in any order you wish, or entirely randomly. Even a techy dunderhead like me was able to join it up to a couple of speakers and, although I know it is tempting fate to say so, it has given me no problems over the several years I have owned it. It now contains all of my CDs, so has some 25,000+ tracks to choose from.

Advert over and I can assure you I have no connection with

the company and had no inducement or incentive offered to write about the machine, while I need none at all to tuck into a particular delicacy...

IN WHICH... I REALISE – I'M 'RECORD GUY'

For decades I have been in search of the perfect club sandwich. I have kept records of where and when I ate a contender for the honour. The front runner for many years had been the one purchased from the hotel around the corner from Prague's Wenceslas Square. It fought off opposition from various contenders all over the world, largely, but not entirely because it was consumed in a lounge area frequented by many of the most beautiful ladies of the Czech capital. I am sure that their presence was entirely unconnected to the fact that the hotel brochure contained large advertisements for escort services.

Attending London's Spitalfields Market record fair in October 2018, I had purchased for £30 an original Wild Turkey LP, one of the short-lived Jethro Tull spin-off group's albums, but I wasn't expecting that the decision to break for a glass of wine and a snack would result in a new leader in the 'club sandwich competition'. But, out of nowhere, Spitalfields' The Grocer, describing itself as a 'Market Tavern', leapfrogged the Prague leader with an absolutely delicious combination of sourdough bread and succulent chicken with the requisite accompanying fillings.

My fellow crate-digger Mike H had alerted me to the fact that a friend of his was desperate to acquire a copy of Peter Frampton's fourth album. 'It has a photo of him with some sort of mark or mask on his face.' I had a look around to see whether I could find a copy, but none appeared.

On the way home from this otherwise satisfactory journey – both from a foodie and vinylie point of view – I caught the bus.

A couple of stops away from my alighting point I saw 'Book Man' in the bus shelter. For years this gent in, I'd guess, late middle age has been appearing, come rain or shine, at a variety of stops along various routes I use. Always standing, always clutching and apparently reading a thick book. Not always the same one. Never speaking to anyone. And certainly never getting on a bus. My sons and I dubbed him 'Book Man' and report sightings of him to each other. He was looking relaxed today, a warm one, respectably turned out in trendy shirt and what I believe are known as 'slacks'. Neither troubling, nor engaging with anyone. A small enigma. I suddenly had an alarming thought. Did he ever reflect on 'Record Guy', the elderly, unshaven, often scruffily dressed fellow he'd frequently see on the H14 or H12s stopping at the bus shelters where he reads? Always clutching a bag containing what could only be an old-fashioned LP, never getting off the bus, neither talking to, nor engaging with, anyone. Looking, well, like some kind of out-of-time weirdo.

A couple of days later, having taken my car in for its MOT, I realised I was close enough to pay a visit to Revolution Records shop in Stevenage's 'Old Town', to which I had never been. I was drawn to it after reading two almost directly contradictory opinions expressed on the shop's Facebook page. One visitor declared: 'Cold coffee served by lovely lady. Not even a token apologie (sic) after mentioning it.' This was followed by another viewpoint: 'Chilled coffee shop – browse, buy or just listen to great vinyl. Lovely place.'

While I was there no one availed themselves of the coffee option. When I walked in, it was to hear a couple of gents of mature years discussing with the counter guy various Who-related matters. One was telling the others that Roger Daltrey had been unable to find anyone whose drum-playing ability would enable them to play the role of Keith Moon in a film – to, I would imagine, absolutely no one's surprise.

I liked the way the floor of the record section is covered underfoot in vinyl records. Another chap came in looking for any record at all from 1988 which would be appropriate for a friend's celebration – birthday, wedding anniversary, I didn't quite

catch which. He looked at every record in the place then with a
sunny 'cheerio', departed, recordless. A different customer made
a purchase, then spent several minutes deciding whether to take
a receipt for the record he'd bought. Then there were just myself
and the counter guy in there. He was playing a Tom Petty track,
and ventured: 'He'll certainly be missed'.

I agreed and mentioned the recently announced death of
Jefferson Airplane main man, Marty Balin. Then he chucked in
the name of Charles Aznavour, also just departed. I said I thought
he may have been slightly under-rated because of his nationality,
but he pointed out that he had sold countless millions of records.
We then discussed how death did not seem to diminish the appeal
of the groups in which some of the now departed had built their
reputations. He observed that 'The Troggs seem to be touring
with no original members at all', to which I noted that the same
is true of Dr Feelgood. Whether Dave will ever reappear since the
sad death of partner Chas in 2018, I doubt.

I complimented his selection of records on offer. Very varied,
some seldom seen titles, plenty of different genres and overall
extremely competitively priced.

'We used to operate out of a different site in the town, but
when we moved here, I decided to overhaul the buying policy and
aim for higher quality and being more selective, cutting down on
the type of titles which may make up the bulk of other shops'
stock. I became much more choosey.'

I ended up buying a new reissue LP by the group Fynn McCool,
(£9.99) and went close to adding a Lesley Duncan LP for a tenner.
Others nearly made the cut – Wishbone Ash and Sonny Boy
Williamson, to mention just two – but there was no sign of the
sought-after Peter Frampton LP. With free local parking another
plus, the day had gone well and when I arrived home, it was to
discover another message from my friend Mike H. 'That Peter
Frampton LP – turns out he meant Peter Gabriel – and he's just
told me that he's found it in his collection – so he doesn't need it,
after all!'

Mike was exasperated, but I just felt peeved...

IN WHICH... VINYL PEEVES APPEAR

*Price stickers attached to the actual record covers, and, even worse, those informative stickers attached to the outside coverings of sealed records, which thus have to be discarded when opened or carefully removed without tearing, then attached to new plastic covers.

*Displays of records in racks for sale not placed in plastic covers.

*Inappropriate music being played in record shops when you are the only person in there and clearly unlikely to be interested in that style.

*Shop staff blatantly ignoring you and making no effort to acknowledge your presence when you are the only person in the shop.

*Arriving at a record shop whose website says it is open, when it isn't.

*Record shops with no second-hand stock.

*Records listed for sale on a record shop website which become unavailable when you ask in the shop.

The peeves above are mine. I do, of course, have many more, but here is one suggested by a contributor to an American website, Dangerous Minds, possibly hiding their true identity behind the name, 'Emma Peel' and looking to avenge themselves: '"Vinyls" is a GARGANTUAN peeve of mine.'

To which the response of one 'Locode' was: 'The plural of vinyl is vinyl.'

Which was promptly rubbished by another poster to the site, calling him or herself A Shelf of Bossks (no idea!): 'No, it isn't. Mass nouns don't have plurals. The plural of "vinyl" is "I don't understand mass nouns".'

All three contributors appeared to have peeved each other! But they are not the only ones fixated on this issue – there is a whole website dedicated to the controversy, called predictably enough:

thepluralofvinyl.com. On another site, Language Log, Mark Liberman took it on himself to spell things out: 'If you don't hang out with millennial hipsters, you might not have noticed that cool kids are listening to music on turntables playing old-fashioned vinyl records. And you might also have missed a fascinating case of peeve emergence: the "rule" that one of these objects is called a "vinyl", while (say) three of them should be called "three vinyl", never "three vinyls". According to this "rule", instead of "many of these records", I could have written "many of these vinyl", but not "many of these vinyls". This is an issue that some people feel very strongly about.'

Correspondent, Drowned In Sound, added a snobbery element to the debate: 'Just a heads-up, so you can stop saying/typing "vinyls". Cos doing so makes you sound like you buy your music exclusively from Urban Outfitters.' Given this drive to eliminate 'vinyls' I find myself drawn to the opinion of Richard Hershberger, who declares: 'In the event that I find myself in the midst of this crowd, I will be sure to use "vinyls" as frequently as possible.' I doubt he'll be alone. Ray Girvan, for example, will side with him: 'I was born in 1956, and I recall "vinyls" (= "vinyl records") to go back decades (I particularly remember the term from *New Musical Express* in my early teens).'

Google Books confirms early references:

'While a few audio purists might quibble over the fidelity of some of the vintage vinyls ...' – *Time* magazine, Volume 84, 1964

'When the LP development began, Mendelssohn had the albums remade as ten-inch single vinyls' – *The Atlantic*, Volume 205, 1960

On this occasion I am definitely happy to let Mr Liberman make the final statement on what appears to be a case of one group of people endeavouring to compel the rest to go along with their own belief, backed up by little evidence: '"The plural of *vinyl* is 'vinyl'" is an invented "rule", more or less the opposite of the general patterns in the language, which a convinced minority has promoted to the point where people are tarred and feathered for saying "vinyls". This is an unusually pure case of peevological emergence, without either tradition or logic on its side, and also (as far as I can tell) without any single authoritative figure behind the idea.'

BUT on August 7 2019, Amazon invited me to buy 'two vinyl for £30'. Depressing on more than one level.

On a different site, the Steve Hoffman Forum, an American poster named Scarecrow declared: 'Another huge peeve of mine: I'm a firm believer of "don't buy unless you intend to keep". Otherwise leave it for someone who actually values it.' Petroskf offered: 'Record buying peeve: people who cry about the death of brick & mortar record shops, but then brag about the deals they scored on Amazon.' Here's one from a New York chap which will resonate with many and baffle others, who'll say 'Just push 'em back, man!': 'I hate when folks don't push forward facing LPs so they are leaning back in the row they are flipping thru once they are finished.'

Some others: 'People who buy vinyl to just frame it, or just display.' To which someone responded: 'I'm that guy. I buy Rick Griffin covers to frame. Most of the times the music's not very good but Rick Griffin is one h.e.double.hockeystick (sic) of an artist. His covers look awesome on the wall. However, if you could actually listen to the music on some of his albums you're a better man than me.'

This one would certainly aggravate most collectors: 'There is a thrift store near me who write the price ON the jacket in some kind of black crayon like pencil that doesn't come off. I have found a handful of things there that would be EX-NM if not for the writing.'

Here's Brooklyn's Wally Swift with a pet peeve: 'People that think that they can hold up a box of records forever while they take 20 minutes to inspect or Google each record as they proceed through the box rather than pulling everything that interests them, stepping aside and doing all that. At my Flea Market, flippers and collectors alike are united in their disdain for this and anyone that tries it gets communally harassed and driven away.'

My peeve is a sleeve peeve, wrote 'rockledge': 'I hate it when I am in a hurry to look through a bunch of 33s and I take a disc out to look at the condition, put it back in the sleeve, and the damn sleeve won't go back into the jacket.'

From yet another interested party on peeves: 'My peeve is people who claim to be buying the record to listen to but care as much about the condition of the jacket as the record. Who cares about labels and stickers and writing on the cover?'

And Tony ACT in Canberra will resonate with many would-be buyers who are feeling peeved:

'The word "rare" on eBay when there are 50 or more of them up for sale at any time across the globe.'

Enough vinyl vitriol, already... here's someone I'm Di-ing to tell you about.

IN WHICH... 'MOUNTAIN BOY' IS REBORN

One of my mate Mike H's greatest successful record hunts was to track down a copy of the vinyl debut of a much-loved mutual friend. Di Jones also goes under the name of Jan (too complicated to go into!). She was the drummer in the early 1960s pop outfit, Peter, Jan & Jon. Their obscure 1965 HMV single, 'Mountain Boy' (POP 1442) written by Lou Stallman & Sid Jacobson, backed by 'I'm Looking Out' penned by group member Peter Jensen, had always seemed a thing of unlikely legend to her friends, until one finally emerged on eBay, where it was snaffled up by Mike, who was happy to dig deep to shell out for the 75p auction-winning bid. He was able to arrange a hearing for friends, at which we were all appropriately impressed by Di, who had begun beating the skins on a pop single long before the world ever heard the name of the late Honey Lantree, whose tub-thumping graced The Honeycombs' 1964 smash, 'Have I the Right', another single which should have a question mark in the title but doesn't.

I'd first met Di when attending the famous Melbourne Cup

horse race. She and her friend Julie were in the same row of seats as myself and my wife. We raised a glass to each other as we watched one of the 12 scheduled races, prompting Di to inform us: 'We always stop drinking after the sixth race.'

'That was the seventh,' I pointed out.

'Oh, well, might as well keep going, then. Cheers!'

After Peter, Jan & Jon, Di would become part of the girl group, Vicki and The Ladybirds, but chart success eluded her. However, her immersion in the pop world meant that she met many of the movers and shakers of the mid-1960s and beyond. When she told me she had a signed Dusty Springfield LP, I just had to see it, so we travelled down to her seaside pad and Di persuaded Julie to unearth her long-neglected stash of albums from their dusty retirement home on top of a cupboard.

I'd volunteered to look through and value the discs for her. It didn't take that long, really. 'Great record, awful condition' was, I soon realised, the default verdict on some lovely music, including the signed Dusty, which was virtually unplayable. Mind you, Di was unrepentant, with a heartfelt response: 'They were played at some great parties and the memories they represent, unlike the actual music, are irreplaceable and as vivid today as when they happened.'

Her memories include knowing Brian Jones, and Steve Marriott ('a sweet boy'), and having boyfriends including Zoot Money, and the early 1960s hit singer Shane Fenton who would clock up half a dozen Top 50 singles with his group, the Fentones, during 1961 and 1962. His real name was Bernard William Jewry and he would later become even better known as Alvin Stardust. Di insists, 'I dumped *him* not the other way round!'

Although my heart was almost broken to see the disrespectful way in which her records had been stored, Di did provide a little salve for the soul as she generously let me choose one of the records to keep – I opted for one which clearly hadn't appealed to partygoers as much as others because it wasn't in that bad nick – it was Roy Harper's 'Stormcock', which, though, didn't come out until 1971, by which time it is possible Di had realised she should be a little kinder to her vinyl!

There was, as I had suspected, a story behind 'Mountain Boy', as there is behind virtually every single recorded. Few ever get told, most are lost for ever, but patient probing of an initially reluctant Di finally produced details of her trailblazing, very enviable career in pop music:

I'm afraid the memory of three fun years in the 1960s has faded somewhat considering the full and hectic life I have led since then!!! However, here are some details of those years, up to 1966. I learned to play drums from a guy in Putney who advertised lessons in *Melody Maker* and who turned out to be the drummer at the London Palladium (can't remember his name). In 1963, I advertised myself as a 'Girl drummer' in MM and a few groups and a guy named John Richardson got in touch. With his then girlfriend, he was starting an 'All Girl Group' from scratch. After an audition with him (I think I was the only drumming girl around!) I got the job and hence Vicki And The Ladybirds were founded – lead guitar, rhythm guitar, bass guitar and myself. After months and months of practice, we were still not brilliant, but John managed to get us dates up and down the country in working men's clubs, dance halls and theatres.

Although we were a novelty we were really not much good as a group; dates ran dry and it was decided to disband. Vicki went on to marry John and did a few dates as a solo singer in the north; after a year or so John started his own business selling DIY tools, went to America and I am still great mates with him today, often going to stay with him in Vegas. There was only one other significant girl group around in 1962-1965, the Liverbirds, a group of Liverpool girls who, like us, didn't last that long!

Not perturbed I again advertised, this time in *New Musical Express* and met Peter Jansen who himself had formed a group in Maidstone called the Manish Boys (named after a Muddy Waters' track). David Jones (later Bowie) joined the Manish Boys, described a little harshly by Paul Morley in his book, *The Age of Bowie* as 'an unwieldy, scruffy collection of average musicians' – and the rest is history.

Peter and I then met Jon Edwards and, in 1965, the three of

us formed Peter, Jan & Jon. Peter on lead guitar, Jon on bass and me on drums. We toured a lot of the American Air Force bases in France and the UK and it was on one of these dates that we met David Bilk, brother of Acker, who got us to record 'Mountain Boy', an old Springfields' song from their 1963 LP *Folk Songs from the Hills*. Peter wrote the B-side (to get royalties from the A-side – in those days you shared the royalties from both sides by doing so). This resulted in us recording jingles for Radio Caroline, and they in turn played 'Mountain Boy' very often. It got to Number 40 in the Radio City charts. Fame at last!

David Bilk also got us a residency at the 100 Club in Oxford Street which was quite a coup in those days. However, as with many groups, Peter was quite a bully regarding the next recording choice. He and Jon had a massive fall out, so here ended yet another pop group stint for me. I then joined a showband, which was great fun. It was run by a guy called Rory Blackwell who was very much a character of those times and had founded one of the first rock 'n' roll bands in the UK. At one point he had Georgie Fame in his band. In 1968, *Rory Blackwell's 1968 Rock'n'roll Show Live* LP was released. We again toured US bases in the UK but, after some months of being on the road again and thinking there must be more fun than staying in guest houses and B&Bs for the rest of my life, I quit the heady heights of life on the road and my dreams of becoming a girl Beatle, opting to travel abroad with a knapsack on my back, two friends and fifty quid in our pockets.

Shane Fenton I met on a gig with Vicki And The Ladybirds. He was a fun guy and we had a laugh for a few months. Same with Zoot Money, nothing serious, but no one took life seriously in those days. I never met the Honeycombs and Honey Lantree.

But I did meet Ms Lantree – at a Joe Meek-related event when her old friend Screaming Lord Sutch totally failed to recognise her. Amazingly, upon hearing Di's story, I realised that I also knew John Richardson via my career at William Hill. He placed a bet with me, which is still running. All he has to do to collect £500,000 of winnings from his wager of £50 at odds of 10,000/1, is to live to be 100 years old – and then father a child, by what we delicately phrased as 'the conventional method'!

I love visiting Di at her home on the Sussex coast – even more so since she told me about the local men's outfitters which, past the shirts and ties, around the jackets, and through the trousers, boasts a stash of vinyl for sale at the back of the shop. She escorted Mike H and me to the shop, Crosbys Menswear & Hirewear, in Seaford in late June 2019. Owner David Wink invited us to browse the vinyl – 'You're a bit late, we sold a lot over the weekend' – displayed alongside a Royal Ascot-type suit and an ad for Jockey underwear. I pondered a Canned Heat live LP, after looking around at various not-for-sale items from David's own collection, including an *Ogdens' Nut Gone Flake* ('You really need the original metal box to have a proper copy') and plenty of Hendrix ('*Both Sides of the Sky* is recent but it's a great album'). Neither of us eventually made a purchase here. It was, though, marvellous to see discs by the dinner jackets, three-piece suits next to thirty-three and a thirds, vinyl amongst the vests.

Di's story may be of 'nearly, but not quite', but it is ultimately uplifting. Another friend's foray into the world of recorded music ended tragically.

IN WHICH... I REMEMBER BRUCE LANGSMAN

In the small town of Petone, just outside of New Zealand's fine capital, Wellington, I was brought up short when I unexpectedly came face to face with a dead friend. Petone's thoroughfare, Jackson Street, is one of, if not *the* oldest still active shopping streets in the country, while NZ's first organised horse racing took place on the beach here in 1842. Amongst Petone's finest shops, is Lo-Cost Records. I had a huge shock when I first entered the premises – and found myself face to face with Bruce Langsman.

Bruce is probably the finest guitarist you've never heard of. Back home shortly afterwards, I wandered into Rollin' Records in West Wickham, a shop I'd never visited before. Again, I was confronted by my late mate – again staring at me from a wall, again on the front cover of the 1969 Pye label LP, *Little Woman You're So Sweet* by Shakey Vick, the blues outfit for which he was lead guitarist.

Here he was, twice in quick succession, reminding me not to forget him in this book. A 'very good' copy of the Shakey Vick LP will set you back some 50 quid. It is justifiably sought after by blues-rock purists. I took my copy along to 56-year-old Bruce's funeral in 2006.

Thin, moustachioed, extremely tall, Bruce was older brother to Rex, who was closely involved with a local football team I occasionally turned out for and who said of his brother: 'Bruce was always very proud of his six foot six inches height since reaching it as a late teenager!' Every time I saw and heard Bruce play guitar I thought he had as much ability as many of the stellar names of the British blues boom, who were much admired, sometimes deified. I believe Bruce really could have been a contender in the 'Guitar Hero' stakes, although as a non-musician myself I had no way of knowing whether I was just impressed because I knew and drank with him.

Here's what website All Music says about Shakey Vick: 'Formed in 1968 in Birmingham, Shakey Vick was a short-lived blues band fronted by Graham (Shakey) Vickery (vocals, harmonica). Bruce Langman (sic) (guitar), Nigel Tickler (bass) and Ned Balen (drums). Signed by Pye Records in 1969, "Little Woman You're So Sweet" was recorded live at Birmingham's Mothers club, a popular venue on the "underground" circuit. The raw atmosphere enlivened a set comprising largely of tested blues standards.'

Courtesy of mutual friend Dave Carroll, I had acquired a CD copy of a Shakey Vick and the Blueshawks live gig which features Bruce's playing, and was described on Shakey's own website himself as 'a live recording made at the 100 Club'. Bruce's contributions to the 1991 recordings are decent enough, but if you listen to the two tracks here recorded in 1968, you'll notice that his playing on both 'City Life' and very clearly on

'Low Down' is more vibrant and prominent than on much of the rest of the material. I think your own ears will be telling you that Bruce's talent was far more obvious in the late 1960s than by the time the early 1990s came around. All of us are more energetic when we are looking to make an impact on the world and maybe become resistant to risk and less adventurous as we get older. If we are also befuddling our senses with alcohol, the difference is more pronounced.

I asked Bruce's brother, Rex, to supply some memories of his older sibling. They graphically demonstrate the 'Bruce problem':

When Bruce left school, he trained as a TV cameraman. That didn't last long as he went 'professional' with his first group, Blues Transportation, then moved to the Cliff Charles Blues Band with Phil Collins on drums. Needing to work to earn 'proper' money, he became a window dresser with Moss Bros in Leicester Square. That ended when Bruce somehow put his arm through a shop's front window. He moved on to the BBC, working for several years in the Graphics dept, often seen on *Grandstand*, sitting behind David Coleman. He then settled at Thames TV, taking a good redundancy payment at 41, which kept him in pubs for a few years. He never worked again. We arranged a 'Bruce Night' a year after his death and we keep close to the same dates in April each year, varying the venues relating to where the bands played, like a pub near the 100 Club, and the Swiss Cottage, where it all started with Shakey Vick's Big City Blues Band's weekly gig at the Blues Loft.

Now, we've adopted the Metropolitan Wetherspoons pub, near Baker Street station. Stories aplenty are wheeled out:

Dingwalls in Camden Town was a club where guests sat at a table and dined while bands played. Once, a certain drunken band member fell off the stage on to a dining table, knocking all the dinner plates flying while the guests were still eating. The manager immediately threw Bruce out of the club!

At the Crown, Twickenham, the band played on too long so the pub landlord switched off the electrical supply and came onstage to remonstrate with them. Bruce threw his guitar at him, only for word to go round that Bruce had beaten him up.

Bruce took a great interest in Chicago Blues music in his teenage years. The Yardbirds, in particular Eric Clapton, were role models. He bought albums by Muddy Waters and Howlin' Wolf, and started teaching himself guitar. Like Clapton, he used Bert Weedon's book *Play in a Day*. He progressed as a blues guitarist in local bands, eventually joining Shakey Vick, who were on the verge of a record deal with Pye, who wanted Shakey Vick's band to record an album at a live gig, and chose Mothers club in Birmingham. The album is still sold around the world 50 years on, in discerning second-hand shops.

The band went on tour to Denmark, where Bruce lost his virginity, but gained musical experience. They continued with regular UK gigs, but Bruce's drinking was already problematic. He and Shakey had their differences as a result, vocalist Shakey locking the drunken Bruce in the dressing room during a gig in Exeter, feeling the band would be better doing their second set without him. Inevitably, Bruce moved on, splitting with Shakey and forming The Nighthawks blues band.

'Bruce and Rex approached me while I was drumming in an improvised jazz trio,' recalled drummer Mel Wright, 'asking me and band-mate Ron Skinner – vocalist and bass player – to join him in forming a Chicago-style blues group. We needed a blues harp player, and Bruce suggested Stuart Witcher, who was running a blues club at The Crown in Twickenham. We met for our first rehearsal at a pub on Brixton Hill. Individual characteristics began emerging in the band. Ron had immersed himself in the history of black American blues. His strong voice and choice of songs soon made us a reputable band on the London blues scene. Bruce equally had a great passion and empathy for blues guitarists, and his interpretation of the Hubert Sumlin, Albert King, Muddy Waters band styles became the bedrock of The Nighthawks. Our combination of blues influences set us apart from the emerging blues-rock style that was popular at that time.'

The new band landed a weekly residency at Hampstead's Three Horseshoes, attracting Radio One DJs John Peel and 'Whispering' Bob Harris, who mentioned the band on air, resulting in a guest-spot on the popular Mike Raven show. They had other bookings as well, but one evening Bruce's ongoing flaw saw him again drinking before a gig, which upset the others so much that they *all* left the group. Bruce somehow managed to find replacements, and a band called Nighthawk existed for a while.

'I would rate Bruce's guitar work as Premier League in his early 20s and 30s,' Rex said, but with the honesty of siblings, added: 'I'm afraid drink took over. He was very strict as a blues purist. I'm sure he had the talent to play all sorts as a session guitarist, but didn't want to know. In his later years Bruce sold off all his vinyl records – as well as, unbeknown to me at the time, all *my* Beatles LPs, but there were a few blues CDs I inherited from him. Bruce was also into film scores and some classical music, as well as blues.'

Rex, occasional band drummer, produced an unissued LP for The Nighthawks in March 1970 and managed to locate the cover of the record, but was unable to find the vinyl itself. Thanks to Mel Wright, I have a CD combining its ten original tracks, with six more from a March 1971 session.

Rex also unearthed a CD of the band's performance on the prestigious Mike Raven show on Radio 1, which, it shows on the cover, was broadcast on 4 April 1971. Mel Wright recalls, 'We all gathered round to hear the broadcast at Stuart's mum's flat, before playing a gig at The Robert Peel pub in Kingston.'

'The tracks on the Raven show were never released,' said Rex. They are excellent, and would make a great (re)release set. The five tracks were "So Mean to Me", "Sweet Mary", "Mystery Train", "She Turns Me On" and "Play House". That means there are 21 Nighthawks' unreleased tracks out there, from which a terrific tribute set could be compiled. I have also acquired copies of Bruce's session work on LPs by Errol Dixon and Juke Boy Bonner LPs.

Mel recalls working with another blues legend: 'In 1969 at a concert at Conway Hall London, hosted by Alexis Korner and radio presenter, Mike Raven, Nighthawks were reunited with blues-man Champion Jack Dupree with whom we had previously played. Jack was short, of stocky build. He stood on the piano stool to try and match Bruce's height.'

Studio 51, the 100 Club and The Marquee were other clubs where The Nighthawks played, supporting touring blues-men, gaining experience and blues credibility. The band looked to be heading along the type of route taken by Fleetwood Mac, Chicken Shack, Savoy Brown, Ten Years After, perhaps on their way to similar stardom. Mel remembered: 'Ron came up with a solid set of lesser known blues classics for us. Stuart's harp playing and singing were joyful and Bruce's guitar playing was just a magic combination of rhythm and lead, typical of his hero, Lightnin' Slim. Stuart bought a transit van and printed "The Nighthawks" on the side. We responded to an ad in *Melody Maker* to record an album in a day! The studio was in Hitchin, Herts. We were joined on the March 1970 session by excellent blues pianist, John Fairweather who played with us at 100 Club gigs. Rex took over as producer of the ten tracks, and did a fine job. We hawked the album around record companies: RCA, Decca, Vertigo – unsuccessfully.'

This was the crucial moment at which Bruce and the band stood poised on the cusp of the big time.

In October 1970, billed as Nighthawks, they played at Twickenham College of Technology, supporting trendy darlings of the day, Principal Edwards' Magic Theatre, whose records were being released on John Peel's Dandelion label. Bruce and the others were finally moving towards breaking in to the more mainstream rock circuit.

'We had no trouble getting gigs – beginning with our own "blues clubs" at pubs, including The Crown at Twickenham. We had a Sunday afternoon spot at Studio 51, near Cambridge Circus, a basement club run by two portly older women, which had quite a blues history – Cyril Davies, Alexis Korner, the Stones and Downliners Sect played there. The National Blues Federation began offering us gigs and arranged for us to accompany New Orleans-style pianist Errol Dixon. We fell out with Errol after he

booked us for a recording session at a studio and never turned
up. Without telling us, Bruce did a session for him on his album,
That's How You Got Killed Before.'

I have owned this 1970 Transatlantic label LP since its release,
and on it the uncredited Bruce launches some stinging licks and
great all-round playing. I think this album represents Bruce's
finest recording moments and Rex told me that even their father
was astonished to hear the quality of performance: 'I played the
album to our dad, usually a jazz-buff and he was amazed at his
son's guitar playing! I wish Bruce had taken general guitar playing
seriously enough to do more session work.'

Adds Mel: 'We accompanied Champion Jack Dupree, and
played with Arthur "Big Boy" Crudup the day he arrived from
the USA. Bruce even tuned up Arthur's guitar for him, and we
appeared with him on BBC2's *Late Night Line Up*.' Other support
gigs followed with blues legends Howlin' Wolf, Son House and
Lightnin' Slim. 'Later, we played gigs and recorded with Texas-
based Juke Boy Bonner who was making an album in London for
Liberty Records, *Things Ain't Right*, while the band was also busy in
its own right, gigging with the Jackie Lomax Band and Wishbone
Ash.'

Music paper, *Sounds* gave a fine review in June 1971 of their gig
at the 100 Club – 'What a tremendous Chicago-style blues band.
Their boys know how to use their instruments without flamboyant
gestures – just see them wring the notes from their instruments.'

But, as so often happens, on the brink of a breakthrough, a
band falters and begins to break up. Mel pinpoints the moment:
'Stuart left. He was keen to develop his own style as Wolfie
Witcher. It was a blow. I always thought that the spirit of the band
was lost without Stuart; he and Bruce were close drinking buddies,
sharing an inseparable sense of humour.'

Their momentum was lost, even though: 'We found a sax
player, Phil Thomas and started a Sunday night residency at The
Three Horseshoes, Hampstead where we were lauded by *Time
Out* magazine, gaining the attention of John Peel, Bob Harris,
and record producer Peter Eden who booked us into Pye Studios,
where we recorded an unreleased album. I think it was our best

recorded work, showing off the band's most popular gig material: "High School Confidential", "Mama Talk to your Daughter", "My Babe", for example.' Bruce's guitar playing was exemplary – nailing his rhythmic style down. Despite the quality of their performance, Peter was unable to get a deal for the album and Mel was also unsuccessful with his contacts at Decca. I've failed to locate a copy of this session.

Ron left the band in 1972 and although Mel stayed for another year, he 'lost my temper with Bruce one evening at The Three Horseshoes when he turned up drunk. I gave my notice in that evening. Bruce phoned to apologise, and ask me to stay. I stuck to my decision.' The ascent was over. In a sad postscript, Mel and Bruce 'met one lunchtime at a pub in Edgware. He hadn't lost his zest for playing as he pulled out old photos of the band, urging us to get back together for a reunion gig. He was even planning to buy a new guitar. We never did play together again, as Bruce died a short while after. He was a week or so away from his 57th birthday. Although Bruce's behaviour at gigs was unpredictable, his sense of humour was highly entertaining and I am still very moved by his guitar playing.'

Nighthawk Stuart Witcher is also happy to pay an affectionate tribute to Bruce: 'Not many people know that as well as being Nighthawks Blues Band members, we were also members of a band called Dumpy's Dirt Band, a forerunner to the popular Dumpy's Rusty Nuts or DRN. A mass firing occurred in that band. Bruce and I were included. For weeks, during a residency, when the leader was doing a solo with his eyes shut, the rest of the band would all swap instruments, then back again before he opened them (Bruce's idea). The audience loved it and were in on the joke, but one day he opened his eyes too early and caught us, and that was that. During that prank Bruce would play the drums – and very good he was too.

'I lived in Putney. Bruce spent the night of Ronald Reagan's presidential election there, "a presidential" being Bruce's rhyming slang for "an erection", which caused many an innuendo over a few pints. We watched it on the TV, demolishing a bottle of "Old Grandad" bourbon at the same time, resulting in me finding vomit on the high ceiling the next morning. The evidence pointed to the tallest person. Case closed!'

Another sickening Stuart story concerning Bruce emerged: 'One of the Nighthawks' vans had a sliding door, and returning from a gig in Surrey, Bruce began to feel unwell. We were doing about 80 miles per hour down a hill when the door suddenly flew open and Bruce did a projectile vomit out of it! There was puke all down the side of the dark green van. It was raining quite hard and I presumed that would wash it off, but it didn't. The acid content in it turned the paintwork beneath a lighter shade of green and every time I approached it after that day, I was greeted by a perfect pattern of Bruce's chunder.'

I was never in Bruce's bands, but he was there in my social world for many years. A long-standing mutual friend of Bruce, Dave Furlong, recalled an example of his rather anarchic sense of humour:

'He invited me and a couple of friends up to meet him for a drink at the BBC after he'd finished work. We arrived and told the receptionist who we had come to see. Bruce appeared at the Reception desk. He took one look at us, told the receptionist, "I've no idea who these people are" and walked off, leaving us dumbfounded!'

You can imagine the hilarity with which such tales were greeted when they were told at the time amongst Bruce's contemporaries, most of them no strangers to the inside of a beer glass. We would concentrate on the 'fun' element, the 'oh, that's just typical Bruce' aspect of a story which probably contained within it an unheard cry of help from a youngish man whose drinking and consequently his life, was spiralling out of control. I think we all believed it was only a matter of time before Bruce's fretboard talent would stop us fretting about his boozy behaviour. It wasn't, though, an era or environment in which anyone would even think of taking a friend aside and suggesting that their intake of beer was excessive enough to affect their future health and life prospects.

Listening to Bruce's recorded legacy definitely invites thoughts that he was an unfulfilled talent. There are splendid examples of his ability when concentrating on his playing, immersing himself in the music, complementing the musicians around him, and suddenly illuminating proceedings with a short, sharp flurry of perfectly judged, empathetic notes. Yet he was also a troubled individual, whose demons often got the better of him, leading to occasions when even those of us who knew him well might deliberately turn in the other direction if walking up to a bar against which we suddenly spotted Bruce leaning unsteadily.

It would be wonderful to be able to compile an LP and/or CD of Lanky Langsman's greatest recorded moments and get it out for those who weren't around at the time, or who remember with nostalgia, watching and hearing him in action, to enjoy and treasure. I think there'd also be a much wider market to be tapped into.

Well known gig promoter Ron Watts brought many blues legends over to the UK to play at London's 100 Club, Wycombe's Nag's Head and many more venues. In his autobiography, *Hundred Watts*, Ron poignantly wrote of 'two girls from Stokenchurch' who would come to the blues gigs: 'One of them got married to Bruce Langsman, who played guitar for Shakey Vick and the Nighthawks. They made a nice couple and I hope they're still together and happy.'

The book was published in 2006, the year Bruce passed away.

IN WHICH... THERE ARE DEATHS IN THE VINYL FAMILY

It was always unsettling to hear of another departed record shop as I was writing this book. But I soon realised I had to come to terms with such unwanted news. If an outlet was closing there was presumably a good reason, and besides, new shops appeared to be opening relatively regularly to replace them, albeit not necessarily in the same places. In the course of writing this book I visited hundreds of record shops and fairs, but that still leaves plenty of others to get round to in the future, which I fully intend to do.

But during the course of my research I'd become particularly partial to taking the local H12 bus over to South Harrow, the original home of second-hand 'royalty' in the shape of Sellanby. When Sellanby closed down I was convinced that there would never be another shop in that part of the borough in which I have lived virtually all of my life. But a couple of years ago, and in almost the identical location which spawned Sellanby – South Harrow Market, directly under the local tube line, so close that you could feel the place rattle as the trains chugged into and out of the station – a young, part-time DJ, father, and knowledgeable music fanatic and vinyl freak named Chris took on a unit and set up his second-hand record shop, the nicely named Music Archaeology.

When I first heard rumours of its existence I was keen to make his acquaintance and once I did so I would make regular trips over to see Chris every few weeks. He was clearly not getting rich from the amount of money I and his other customers handed over as he kept telling me about his 'other' part-time jobs and roles which helped to keep the wolf from the door. I began to think he was perhaps slightly over-egging the 'struggling to survive' story, but on Tuesday 31 July 2018 I sent him a text, telling him I was planning to come over and see him at the weekend, only to receive the following reply: 'Hi, Graham. Alas. The shop is no more. Emptied last week. I kept some and sold everything else as a job lot. I may open up again, but smaller. But right now I'm not sure.'

A poignant farewell from the man who enabled me to add a good number of scarce items to my collection. Chris is young, enthusiastic and now experienced enough to reopen elsewhere when the right opportunity presents itself. I salute you, Chris, for having the bottle to start at the tough end of a business which needs commitment and courage to enter. Shortly before this book was published I heard from Chris again: 'I will get another place at some stage – but for now in full-time work, still doing record fairs. Been picking up stuff – selling some, keeping loads. Enjoying music as I don't have to sell it.'

A couple of months after Chris closed, I heard that a bigger story seemed to be breaking. Cambridge's Black Barn Records had quickly become a favourite destination when I visited the city. I'd rapidly realised that they stocked much of the material I craved, and had spent accordingly when able to get up there. Now, I was told that the owner of the shop – well, shops, as he had acquired another in Haverhill – was talking about closing them down. In April 2016, the *Daily Mail* reported: 'Adrian Bayford and his then wife Gillian became two of the biggest Euromillions winners (£148m) in history after scooping the huge sum in 2012. The 45-year-old, who was running a second-hand record shop at the time of his win, has now returned to his retail roots by opening Black Barn Records in Cambridge.' Although I never saw him actually in the shop, and there were stories that the shop was not being run in the most secure way possible, it seemed to be a very viable business. But the rumour mill was hinting that closure may be imminent. I searched the internet for clues, but found none. I rang the shops but could never get through to speak to anyone and calls were never returned – another ominous sign. Then on Saturday 10 November 2018, Martin texted me. He'd been to visit the shop in Cambridge: 'It's gone. Shop empty.' All the stock seemed to have been removed, he elaborated, but there was no explanatory message to be seen.

There was still no media confirmation. Nothing on their Twitter or Facebook pages. Little doubt, though, that another great record shop had been and now gone. A Facebook page on which a collector named Scott White had posted that BB was closed when he visited, had produced a response saying that Bayford 'is selling up apparently (sic) and moving to Oz'. But what would be happening to the stock, then? I managed to find someone in the business who had some information on the situation, telling me: 'He was rumoured to be closing a couple of weeks ago in preparation for going to start a new life in Australia. The whole thing was a vanity project anyway, and he must have lost money. He reopened his old shop as a Haverhill branch in the summer, but it has only opened erratically, I think he has a mass of second-hand records – but heaven knows what he is planning to do with them.

Then, on a sunny morning in London, 10 April 2019, I was stunned by shock news from the other side of the world, some 11,704 miles away in New Zealand, which completed a devastating triptych of vinyl tragedy: 'The jewel in Newtown's musical crown, Death Ray Records, have sadly announced they'll be shutting up shop after six years of servicing the community with a kick-ass selection of new and used records from throughout Aotearoa and beyond.' This was terrible news. I'd been there only a couple of months earlier, when there was no such inkling.

Known as 'Apa' or Boss Dude, the Death Ray owner had absolutely understood record collecting/ors: 'People who want to shop cheap are always going to do that. My true customers will pay the extra $5. They walk in and their shoulders drop, and their backs untense, and they're totally in their zone. That's what you get from digging through records, and you don't get that on the internet. I've got lots of customers who come in and will go straight to the rare section. It's better than being on crack, or an alcoholic. I've got guys who had fun times when they were young but have decided to lay off all that business, and have gotten into record collecting really heavily. I know some guys who buy and buy and buy and they're listening to their records, and there are others might listen a couple of times and then it goes into the collection.'

It would be unrealistic to expect that these and other recently deceased shops could magically return to life at some stage. Each one we lose takes with it some of the spirit of record collecting and deprives us of a unique atmosphere, as all record shops are different, and irreplaceable – other than by new, exciting ventures in the same field which will bring with them their own take on this wonderful, ongoing vibrant vinyl world to which we all contribute in our own ways. I still mourn, four or more decades on, Dave's record outlet in Wealdstone, initially operating from the rear of his Dad's greengrocers. Dad was a dead ringer for Old Man Steptoe, long-haired Dave as wannabe trendy as son 'Arold. Fruit & veg outside, exotic vinyl (and other substances) out the back. I bought a Van Der Graaf Generator LP one day. Brought it back, baffled, the next...

No point in getting too maudlin or angry about things...

IN WHICH... I FEAR RECORD SHOP RAGE

Collectors Paradise (no apostrophe) in Chesham is an odd place. Very odd. There are hundreds – thousands, probably – of LPs and CDs, but a considerable cornucopia of other stuff for sale: 'Toys, including Corgi, Dinky & Matchbox; Pokemon cards; Model Railway Trains; Old Silver; Collectible China.' Then there's the boss. 'I've got a lot of vinyl, haven't I?' said Dale, the owner, rhetorically I thought, as I entered his shop for the first time. Clearly he was not expecting a negative answer. In order to avoid an argument or discussion I just replied, 'Yes, but so have I', which this, to me, somewhat Dickensian-looking character pretended not to hear.

The volume of vinyl might not be in question on this Monday in August 2017, but, as he had some good titles in bad covers and worse condition, the quality most certainly was. Despite a lack of plastic protection and a plethora of scratches on surfaces, most of the records were priced as though they were in mint condition. Time and again I picked out an excellent, desirable title, but soon shoved it back, scared off by price and/or condition.

Eventually I'd been through a couple of hundred records without finding anything demanding to be bought except a copy of a 1968 Beacon Street Union LP, *The Clown Died in Marvin Gardens*, a US psych scarcity, probably valued in the high double figure region (their other album gets a £100 rating in the latest RRPG) for a well-preserved copy, and which I did not recall ever seeing in the flesh before. Here, it was dressed in what seemed to be a home-made, or home-adapted cover. For once that morning, I found that the surface of the album appeared acceptable, though. I had only rarely seen this around in vinyl and despite owning it on CD, I was prepared to pay the £20 asked to buy this unique copy.

Now I turned to his CD shelves with more success. Again, a wide selection of decent titles, invariably, though, in rather better nick than the vinyl. I bought three £7 titles – including one by Trees – in order to take advantage of his 'fiver off if you spend £20' offer. I think, though, he'd have been better off pricing everything at a fiver in the first place and offering no reductions. Because had he done so I reckon I'd have bought four rather than three and he'd have been £4 better off.

As I paid for my purchases, I looked a little more closely at Dale, about my age, who seemed to be obsessed with telling his rather younger, bored-looking female assistant absolutely every single thing he'd done at the weekend. She eventually stood up and told him she had to nip out 'for five or ten minutes to the bank. They've closed my account, you know. It just disappeared online.' 'Have you,' he asked her, 'paid off that 50 quid overdraft?' 'Well, no, but it's outrageous.'

A unique combination of vinyl and boxing memorabilia is the unique selling point of Heroes, which, some months later, decided to open next door to Collectors Paradise. When I first walked into the shop, it was to see a 50-something chap seated behind the counter. We exchanged 'good morning' greetings with each other. The shop was otherwise empty, a little chilly, over-crowded stock-wise and it had a sterile feel to it. Records were competing with the boxing memorabilia for floor-, wall- and shelf-space.

Imagine my surprise, when the in-house sound system almost immediately selected some kind of DJ-style, trance-style floor-filler for an age-group far younger than mine, likely to appreciate such a 'banging' (assuming this is an appropriate term to use) tune. The volume was of heavy metal velocity, and my browsing of a Lesley Duncan LP, of a far more gentle disposition, was genuinely curtailed by being compelled to listen to it. I tried looking towards the counter to see whether I could indicate that I wasn't enjoying the music. But I failed to make eye contact. So I tried huffing and puffing. No reaction. Finally, I threw my hands up in the air, enunciated carefully, and audibly: 'F'fucksake', before flouncing out. Much though I felt I'd enjoy Ms Duncan's album, which was fairly priced at a fiver, I wasn't now going to give him the satisfaction of receiving any of my moolah.

Instead, I walked straight into Collectors Paradise where an elderly gent was regaling Dale with tales of his army days in Libya, and even competing with the Pat Benatar album being belted out by singing some old army song, to generous but gentle applause from boss and customers. Having noted Dale's somewhat garrulous, eccentric manner before, I wasn't surprised at this, but as I delved into the vinyl, I confirmed that the prices on offer were again too rich for my constitution.

I made a beeline for the CD shelves packed with reasonably priced fare, and a pretty wide range of genres. Some sealed Led Zeps, including bonus tracks from Jimmy Page's remasterings were only seven quid each, but I passed them over, remembering how infrequently I feel the mood come on to play their records these days. Instead I wheedled out a Joanne Shaw Taylor at £6, a Meic Stephens at £4, Skid Row (the original Gary Moore version) for just a fiver, and an unusual psych-prog Mixed Up Minds compilation at £6 – a total of £16, after Dale's discount was taken off.

Dale was complimentary about my choices and told me about an Eastern European female blues singer called, I think, Popovich, when he spotted the Shaw Taylor. He also laughed that he'd had to tell a couple of other would-be buyers that the Skid Row CD was not by the US hard rock band of the same name. I paid his young female assistant.

Leather-Jacket had now been joined by another record hunter. The two obviously knew each other and Dale told Leather-Jacket: 'Look at this watch, it's antique, I researched it and priced it at 200 quid, but the only offer I've had was from a chap who offered half that. I came down to £140 but he hasn't budged.'

'Is he your only watch-buying customer?'

'At the moment.'

'Well, he's clearly interested, and if he won't pay more you're going to have to accept the only offer you've had, aren't you?'

'Suppose so.'

Leather-Jacket paid for his records and said he was going to pop next door, but he was soon back:

'There's no one there.'

Having paid for my CDs, I spoke to Dale about next door's shop, telling him of my experience.

'Well, I had a woman in here recently who told me she'd passed a comment about his prices being a little on the steep side, and he promptly told her to clear off, in rather more colourful terms than that.'

'That's good customer relations, isn't it?' I commented.

'He took on those premises recently, and I think he only has taken a year or so initially. He came in and told me he intended to put me out of business,' claimed Dale, 'But I've been here for twenty-one and a half years. He said he was bringing 10,000 records in to sell, along with sporting memorabilia.'

'Surely he'd be better off liaising with you so that you could complement each other and then bring in more business, as I'm sure more people would make a trip here if they knew there were two shops together,' I suggested.

Clearly there was a rare case of close proximity record-rage going on and these two didn't seem to be hitting it off with each other. So I asked neighbour Michael Lagdon at Heroes for his thoughts on operating next to Dale:

'I have collected vinyl for over 30 years and, having been a DJ around the world, have also amassed a lot of vinyl needed to keep up with the latest genres. I play music at some of the big boxing shows and have been a boxing fan for a similar length of time and that is why most of the memorabilia in the shop at present is boxing related. It was coincidental that the adjoining shop sells vinyl. He has been in Chesham for over 10 years with vinyl on sale, but that is not his main trade. It does help me a little bit being next door as people who used to come to him are now spilling over into my shop and boosting my trade – as a collector it's good to find two shops so close.'

Back in Chesham some months later, it was a Monday morning. Dale and a (different) young female assistant were shelving boxes full of model cars, Bob Marley was playing on the in-shop system and customers were popping in to pass the time of day with Dale. Business seemed brisk. I'd tried to go in to Heroes initially – the shop was shut with a handwritten telephone number on the door the only indication it was still trading. In the window, displayed LP covers were fading from exposure to the sun. Dale seemed to have the upper hand in their rivalry. 'I wouldn't run a business like that,' chortled Dale when I asked him about next door, and when I checked the Heroes' website there was little, if any, reference to vinyl.

Later, discussing these two rivals in Second Scene, Julian agreed that Dale's records could be better kept and his prices were usually far too high. 'I think he prices them directly from a guide, but doesn't bother checking condition – but you can often find something underpriced, though.' Julian was spot on. I went through Dale's vinyl, finding a sealed copy of G T Moore & The Reggae Guitars' scarce, 8-track 2017 LP, *The Harry J Sessions*, for a very fair £12. The other several hundred I went through were either in my opinion too expensive or in poor condition. I also helped myself to his 'fiver off if you spend £20 on CDs' offer, picking up albums by Justine, Human Beast, Chantel McGregor and Micki Free.

I departed, wondering how Dale's Heroic battle would ultimately play out, only to receive an explanation from Mike at Heroes for his Monday absence: 'Have just got back from holiday so the Monday being closed was a one-off.' Mike also explained why his website was not at its best: 'New website is currently being built and should be launched next week.' But I must admit he then surprised me by explaining why 'I am not expecting to list much vinyl on the site, only special items.'

I didn't quite understand this until he revealed: 'It's not worth the hassle with awkward buyers of vinyl challenging grading, etc, or even swapping their old scratched vinyl for my better copies.'

I was shocked to think fellow record collectors could stoop to such a dishonest act.

IN WHICH... I WONDER WAT'S GOING ON

In Watford I unexpectedly discovered a surprisingly listenable, previously unknown-to-me psych record in the LP Cafe. I'd noticed that this Bump album, priced at £15, was not wearing an inner sleeve, prompting a '10% off' reduction offer from the boss, which I rejected, demanding, and getting, it for a tenner. This was recompense for having to put up with the lack of vinyl manners by the bloke who had parked himself at a table, with boxes full of records which he was working his way through, at the same time cutting off access to several of the racks, and only shifting slightly and not exactly willingly to let me pass, when nudged to do so. Perhaps it is a Watford thing.

It is early February 2018 and I am in the subsequently closed down Sounds Retro in Watford. There is only one other customer in the shop, and we have ended up next to each other. This youngish chap in mod-style gear is flipping through a rack, next to the one I have just begun to examine, but his arm is impinging on my section. A non-verbal battle of wills, subtle nudges, sighs and meaningful grimaces ensues. Finally, he reaches the end of his section and, without ever having surrendered any space, moves away. If record shop owners don't always see eye-to-eye the same is true of record collectors.

For example, I risked the wrath of psych-ologists in May 2018 when, during a Facebook group discussion about which records contributors have found to be disappointing once they've acquired them, I ended up in a row with punk musician Lenny Helsing. I had watched as people put forward LPs by psych groups such as Open Mind, Fire, Human Beast, then decided to weigh in with an opinion of my own: 'As for overrated, how about 13th Floor Elevators? One song wonders to me, I'm afraid.'

Lenny, vocalist, guitarist, songwriter for bands including Belsen Horrors, November Crime(s), The Green Telescope(s) and Thanes, as well as a writer for *Ugly Things* magazine, was outraged:

'Graham Sharpe: ehhh are you joking man the Elevators are one of the key groups in the whole of the 1960s psychedelic music spectra. Not only that but they reside right up at the top end of this realm with all three of their studio albums containing many, many great songs and electrifying performances, to say nothing of the screeds of truly far out lyrical poetry... and all the other bewitching sounds they possessed!'

We agreed to disagree, as I pointed out that I hadn't actually said I disliked the 13th Floor Elevators and do own most of their work.

The Harpenden Record Fair was quite crowded, pretty warm, and there was a considerable aroma of mustiness in the air. Who can say why? There were a significant number of dealers flogging new reissues, some of them from Japan, for reasonable pricebands of £10 and £15. These took up much of the display benches. They were doing pretty good business and I heard a guy, who was apparently buying for the Aussie market, and having his purchases sent over there, chatting with one or two of them, although he mentioned that the UK was now no longer his major source of vinyl to sell at home.

I was tempted by a live Free CD of two gigs in Japan, then wondered why. Presumably, they weren't singing 'Alright Now' in Japanese, and I already own that song about nine times on different Free records, so I put it back even though it was only £8 and the buyer had a sign saying he welcomed 'reasonable offers'. I didn't think 50p would count as reasonable. A man was telling his friend, 'I was sure I'd find a copy of Hendrix's "Electric Landlady" here.' I wasn't sure whether he'd mistaken the great but no longer with us Jimi for the equally worthy but also no longer with us Kirsty MacColl.

A little annoyed that I had forgotten to bring my phone with me, as the publisher of this book, whose offices are in Harpenden, had promised to buy me lunch if I called him while at the record fair, I thought I'd cut my losses and leave vinyl-less and lunch-less. I decided to make one more quick circuit of the hall before heading off. A dealer at one of the stalls told me, 'I'll take an offer for anything', then I heard a possible customer telling him: 'I love Grand Funk Railroad. I'll buy anything you've got by them.'

'I've only got the one you're holding.'

'I don't want this one, I'll buy any other one. I love Grand Funk Railroad, but this is the only LP of theirs I've got.'

'I haven't got any others.'

'But I'll buy anything by them. I really like them.'

I pondered telling him I have a GFR oddity – a 33 rpm single which plays the same track on each side despite the label claiming different songs. But I couldn't be bothered, and again set off to take my leave, pausing briefly to flip through a box of records I hadn't yet seen. In it was a copy of *Stretching Out* by Alan Bown. This record has a memorable gatefold cover, depicting in black and white a close-up view of someone, it looks like a man, deliberately pinching and painfully pulling the skin on his left arm farther outwards than it seems to want to go. I recognised it, but thought I didn't own it. I looked at the surface of the record which, in the dingy, dim light of the hall looked OK. The price was reduced from £12 to £10 which seemed pretty generous. After a little more thought, I reckoned probably I *did* own it. But at a tenner, it was still a safe bet that I could flog it in the event that I did, so I thought I'd buy it.

Then I turned up another gatefold record, Buzzy Linhart's *The Time To Live Is Now*. I have one of his already and remembered it being decent, so a four quid price tag was appealing, as was the Grease Band one – okay, it was not an original, but a Charly label reissue but, still, that's a quality label and they were a quality band. Then there was the £4 *Fanny Hill* album by early 1970s US female rockers, Fanny, the one of theirs which I didn't have. It came with an original lyric sleeve, and hand-decorated inner sleeve boasting a previous owner's illustration which spelled out 'Fanny

Hilly' but advised 'ignore the last "y", it just looks good'. And, oh, karma – here was a Lesley Duncan LP, *Everything Changes*, the one I'd recently been planning to buy in Chesham's Heroes, before I'd been driven out of the shop by the banging club dance music!

By now, I was chatting away to the very personable man selling the records, who had been telling me about the despicable behaviour of some people claiming to be dealers who had been rude to him and mishandled some of his records earlier on. Not so despicable as the behaviour of the two men who, according to Andy Hibberd of 101 Collector Records in Farnham, were guilty in early 2019 of stealing thousands of pounds worth of records from various vinyl outlets. He posted photos on twitter and described the perpetrators as 'scum'. I hoped he didn't mean me and my friend Jon, who had been in his shop the day before.

But back to Harpenden, where the records I'd sorted out totted up to £27. After a little bartering we agreed on £22. Surely saving a fiver by bargaining didn't amount to industrial level stealing.

IN WHICH... I SIGN OFF

I had recently returned from a trip to New Zealand with my wife, to visit family living there in general, and infant grand-daughter, Georgia in particular. Whilst in the record shop, Lo-Cost, in Petone, I'd helped a middle-aged lady who was wondering which of several records to buy her husband. I pointed her towards an early Jethro Tull LP as the best investment – and she told me how she still rages at her sister for getting rid of her record collection while she was off travelling for an extended period. 'I wouldn't have minded so much, but I had a signed Beatles' album and a Lennon book of my Dad's – he'd worked for, or with, them at one stage.' They would have more than paid our fares to Kiwi-land, but I've never managed to find Beatle autographs.

On the flights over and back I killed time by watching a few films – and found three recent ones of which I'd been unaware, all featuring records, record shops and record collectors, and which I'd recommend to readers yet to see them. On Chesil Beach features a scene crucial to the plot set in a record shop where the 'hero' is working; Juliet, Naked, written by Nick Hornby, includes a record collecting obsessive fan of an obscure singer-songwriter and demonstrates an unsettling number of my own shortcomings; and Hearts Beat Loud opens with a scene in Red Hook Records in which a customer rebukes the unimpressed owner, Frank, by telling him: 'You can't smoke inside.' He receives the deadpan reply: 'Buy something and I'll put it out.'

My wife and I were still suffering from the effects of jet-lag from the flight home when we decided to breathe some fresh air into our lungs by walking to the paper shop, one Sunday in early 2019. Before leaving we caught up with events in Ambridge by listening to the omnibus edition of The Archers and I was delighted to discover that Kenton Archer had introduced record decks and vinyl records to the entertainment offered at the local pub, The Bull. He launched the Ambridge vinyl revival by playing Jeff Wayne's War of the Worlds LP.

On our walk, I began to tell Sheila that I thought Second Scene's Julian had finally discovered his Holy Grail. I'd been in to see him the day before, buying a copy of an LP by Colin Hare, formerly of Honeybus, and an original 1967 Cat Stevens' album. Julian had been elsewhere in the building when I arrived, and I greeted his wife, Helen. Her phone rang, and she told me, 'A chap is coming to collect 1200 records he's bought from us.' She explained that, like all record shops, they acquired many almost unsaleable records. Julian had initially solved this problem by giving them away to local charity shops – until they began to tell him they had quite enough old movie soundtracks, Jim Reeves records, Black & White Minstrel LPs, m-o-r classics, and the like and could no longer take them. 'They used to welcome and thank us for them, now they turn us away.'

Without any great hopes that it would produce any sales,

Julian had begun lumping large numbers of these currently unwanted, unloved discs together and listing them for sale online as collections. This would be the second such collection which had actually sold, and now the gentleman who had bought them had turned up. He'd arrived without boxes to put them in, or help to get them in his car. Julian obliged, then came in to the shop where the three of us speculated on why the man may have been prepared to pay a three-figure sum to acquire them.

We were joined by the man himself, who reminded me a little of an ageing Neil from the TV series, *The Young Ones* and was, according to Helen, just as pungent as one might imagine Neil to have been. But he showed an understanding of music – discussing early ELO LPs, for example – which suggested that he was well aware of what he was purchasing, so it remained a mystery what he would be doing with them. He seemed in no hurry to enlighten us. Julian was so delighted to have shifted them out for money, that almost before the man had departed, he listed another tranche of unsellables online for opening offers of £470 or more. And, as he told me later, he soon flogged off another chunk to a lady who used them instead of tiles to decorate the walls of her loft extension. On a later visit he was out, having sold two four-figure job lots of otherwise unwanted records to Polish sources. No, NOT to make Polish sauces!

I noticed a framed photograph on the wall, which hadn't been there last time I'd come in. Closer observation revealed it to be of The Beatles in their early days. There was also a typed letter in the frame, explaining how the writer had been in Plymouth in November 1963, where the group had been playing, around the time that they had just stolen the show at the Royal Variety performance. These two items were accompanied by a piece of paper with four biro-penned signatures, at the top of which was one by Paul McCartney who had helpfully appended under it, lest anyone be unsure of his identity, the word 'Beatles'. The three other members had clearly expected their identities to be perfectly well known by anyone seeing them and had not included the group name alongside the hand-written names. The signatures had been authenticated by a leading auction house, explained

Julian, and had turned up for sale recently at a regular local auction, to which he and Helen had repaired, interested to know how much the autographs might sell for. Julian was surprised that only he and one other bidder present, along with a single internet bidder, showed any desire to own this great item, and, although he didn't tell me how much it had cost him, he came out on top of what must have been a competitive bidding war. I was later able to discover that the final bid at the auction was £2300. (It was listed on the auction house's website.) However, Julian's investment was now, in his opinion, worth 'about 5,000' sovs.

It was probably just as well I hadn't known the auction was happening. I might well have found myself bidding against Julian, and a beautiful and vanishingly rare friendship between Watford and Luton fans could have come to a difficult end. As I was recounting this story to Sheila, she commented: 'Yes, it was a pity I lost my Beatle autographs.'

I stopped dead in my tracks as Sheila continued power-walking along. I was thunderstruck:

'You had The Beatles' autographs and lost them?'

'Yes, my brother's friend worked at Elstree film studios when The Beatles were filming there. He got a set of their signatures which he gave to his wife who offered them to me. Don't forget no one dreamed they'd ever become valuable back then.'

'So you accepted them?'

'Yes – but they got lost when we got married and moved into our first home in Fairfield Drive.'

This was the maisonette in which I had nearly come to blows with neighbours when I marked the announcement of Elvis Presley's passing with a late-night playing session of the great man's best-known vinyl works. At some volume.

'Did I know this at the time?'

'Yes, you seemed a little annoyed when I told you...'

The rest of the walk home was conducted in silence.

...AND VINYLY

I've had a wonderful time visiting record shops, talking to collectors, and collecting my own thoughts about what is a long-lasting obsession for so many. One of the most bizarre stories I came across during the writing of the book appeared in *The Times* in November 2018. It was illustrated with a photograph of a man leaning his ear on a maturing cheese while listening to an LP playing on a turntable. The caption read: 'Beat Wampfler, a Swiss cheesemaker is experimenting with maturing his product by playing it a variety of sounds through small speakers below the cheese – including songs by Led Zeppelin and A Tribe Called Quest.'

Along the way, there were many unexpected moments. I thought it would be good to round off with a few which may make you smile...

I am in nearby Northwood, telling a young lady: 'Of course, I'll move out of the way so that you can see the earrings.' I was quite happy to shift over. She had asked politely and she naturally wanted to see in the mirror how the gold earrings she was contemplating buying looked on her. I was blocking her view. So I'd budged, and temporarily stopped rifling through the shelves groaning under the weight of records fighting for customer attention in what may well be a unique establishment – a jeweller-cum-second-hand-vinyl shop, most recently calling itself Basement Vinyl. Probably, I suppose, because Records In A Damp Cellar Reached Via A Smelly River Of Effluent From The Nearby Takeaway wasn't quite as eye-catching a name. We both left happy. She bought the earrings, and I departed with several LPs.

I visited Rough Trade at Dray Walk, Old Truman Brewery, 91 Brick Lane, London E1 6QL on Friday 13 October 2017, but bought nothing as they had no second-hand items as far as I could see. It was, though, a huge shop, and did boast a record shop first for me. It had a 'central casting' bouncer on the door. Whether to stop people sneaking out with nicked records or to 'persuade' passers-by to come in was unclear.

'His wife's died. I suppose that'll mean I'll lose one of my best customers.' This was the odd reaction by a South London record shop owner when, in my presence, he took a call from one of his customers telling him of the death of his wife. I'd have thought he'd now be likely to see *more* of the sadly bereaved man...

The proprietor of the excellent Viva Vinyl record-shop-cum-cafe in Hove was explaining that her husband's huge record collection became the basis of the shop's stock: 'When we realised it would cost the same to put the collection into storage as it would to rent premises for a shop, that's the option we decided on.' Then she revealed the type of customer service necessary not to lose business: 'Shortly after we opened, a customer wanted to buy four records with a credit card. I realised I hadn't arranged for a credit card facility. So I drove him to the nearest cashpoint. Now I do have a credit card machine.'

Fellow Wealdstone FC supporter, Roger Slater, now living in the West Country, was telling me about his claim to be perhaps the youngest person ever to attend a 1960s Rolling Stones' live concert: 'Probably because of my sister, 12 years older than me, I was taken to my first Stones' concert in 1964 (I was five at the time) at Greenford Granada, because her then boyfriend and, later, husband rose through the stage playing the Compton Theatre Organ during the interval...'

'When I got it home, I looked at it, thought of what it had cost me, and was promptly physically sick.' This was Martin, owner of Sounds That Swing in Camden, telling me how he paid well over what he could really afford to get an obscure Elvis Presley record.

Not everyone *gets* record collectors and record shops, but that is part of the terrible fascination of this whole micro-world, to those of us who do. Those who don't can rail against us. The character 'Uncle Geoff', played by Geoff McGivern, was told in the opening episode of David Mitchell and Robert Webb's late

2017 Channel 4 'comedy' series *Back*, that 'vinyl is making a comeback'.

'Yeah, for c***s,' he responded.

But, do we care? I, for one, certainly do not.

EPILOGUE

IN WHICH MY FAVOURITE RECORD DEALER, JULIAN SMITH SIGNS OFF WITH A CAUTIONARY TALE FOR BOTH SIDES OF THE COUNTER...

BEATLES-MAN brings in a shabby, self-made, extremely well-thumbed, photocopied booklet. It's laid out before me with the expectation that I will share this gentleman's excitement at finding the 29th label variation of 'She Loves You'. Initially, I thought it my duty to assist in the quest of studying multiple black and white pictures of Beatles' record labels on which 'Northern Songs publishing' was written over two lines instead of three, or the typeset gap was larger, the font different. I could go on. Twenty-nine times in fact.

At some point I realised that when I did find one of these elusive variations, I was making £4. Consider the time I spent: buying, sorting, then calling in the collector, who will now drink a cup of coffee in my shop, and discuss with me all the other label anomalies he's found recently – for the next hour.

My point being, at some point you have to realise you're running a business and deal with this, and similar other countless customers in a certain way. As a fellow record collector I can understand to a point where this chap is coming from, but from a bank manager's point of view, the man's a record short of a complete box set.

Perhaps this is where record shop dealers get the 'grumpy owner' tag from!

JULIAN LEIGH-SMITH, proprietor of Second Scene Records, Bushey, Hertfordshire.
March 2019

BIBLIOGRAPHY

Araujo, Bento, *Lindho Sonho Delirante: 100 psychedelic records from Brazil 1968-1975*, London: Poeira Press, 2016

Ashforth, David, *Fifty Shades of Hay*, London: Racing Post, 2018

Atkins, Caroline, *What a Hazard a Letter Is: The Strange Destiny of the Unsent Letter*, London: Safe Haven Books, 2018

Barnes, Marcus, *Around the World in 80 Record Stores: A guide to the best vinyl emporiums on the planet*, London: Dog 'n' Bone, 2018

Begley, Sharon, *Just Can't Stop: An Investigation of Compulsion*, London: Simon & Schuster, 2017

Blake, Mark, *Stone Me: The Wit and Wisdom of Keith Richards*, London: Aurum Press, 2008

Bruno, Frank, *Let Me Be Frank*, London: Mirror Books, 2017

Calamar, Gary & Gallo, Phil, *Record Store Days: From Vinyl to Digital and Back Again*, New York: Sterling Publishing, 2009

Chapman, Rob, *Psychedelia and Other Colours*, London: Faber & Faber, 2015

Crafton, Adam, *From Guernica to Guardiola*, London: Simon & Schuster, 2018

Crompton, Richmal (both Rick Wakeman's, and my, favourite author!), *William and the Pop Singers*, London: Macmillan Children's Books, 1965

Findlay, Harry & Harman, Neil, *Gambling For Life*, London: Trinity Mirror Sport Media, 2017

Gray, Daniel, *Black Boots & Football Pinks: 50 Lost Wonders of the Beautiful Game*, London: Bloomsbury Sport, 2018

Gregory, Tom, *A Boy in the Water*, London: Particular Books, 2018

Hepworth, David, *Nothing Is Real*, London: Bantam Press, 2018

Hornby, Nick, *Fever Pitch*, London: Gollancz, 1992

Jones, Graham, *Last Shop Standing*, Kent: Proper Music Publishing Limited, 2009

Jones, Graham, *The Vinyl Revival and the Shops That Made It*

Happen, London: Proper Music Publishing Limited, 2018

Joynson, Vernon, *The Tapestry of Delights: The Ultimate Guide to UK Rock and Pop of the Beat, Psychedelic & Progressive Eras*, Boise: Borderline Publishing, 2014

Knight, Henrietta, *The Jumping Game: How Trainers Work and What Makes Them Tick*, London: Head of Zeus, 2018

Lewis, Michael, *The Fifth Risk: Undoing Democracy*, London: Allen Lane, 2018

Litt, Toby, *Wrestliana*, Norwich: Galley Beggar Press, 2018

Moist, Kevin M & Banash, David, *Contemporary Collecting: Objects, Practices and the Fate of Things*, Maryland: Scarecrow Press, 2013

Morley, Paul, *The Age of Bowie*, London: Simon & Schuster, 2016

Nash, Graham, *Wild Tales*, London: Penguin, 2013

Newey, Adrian, *How to Build a Car: The Autobiography of the World's Greatest Formula 1 Designer*, London: HarperCollins Publishers, 2017

Ochs, Michael, *1000 Record Covers (Bibliotheca Universalis)*, London: Taschen Books, 1966

Plenderleith, Ian, *The Quiet Fan*, London: Unbound Digital, 2018

Spence, Simon, *Immediate Records: Labels Unlimited*, London: Black Dog Publishing, 2008

Thompson, Dave, *Alternative Rock (Third Ear)*, Maryland: Backbeat Books, 2000

Vulliamy, Ed, *When Words Fail: A Life with Music, War and Peace*, London: Granta Books, 2018

Watts, Ron, *Hundred Watts: A Life in Music*, Morecambe: Heroes Publishing, 2006

Wells, David, *Record Collector 100 Greatest Psychedelic Records (High Times and Strange Tales From Rock's Most Mind-Blowing Era)*, London: Diamond Publishing, 2005

Wiseman, Richard, *Whatever Happened to Simon Dee?*, London: Aurum Press, 2006